Business-to-Business Marketing

STRATEGIES AND IMPLEMENTATION

**Daniel Michel, Peter Naudé,
Robert Salle and Jean-Paul Valla**

palgrave
macmillan

First published 1996 by Economica, France
Second edition 2000 by Economica, France

This edition published 2003 by
PALGRAVE MACMILLAN
Houndmills, Basingstoke, Hampshire RG21 6XS and
175 Fifth Avenue, New York, N.Y. 10010
Companies and representatives throughout the world

PALGRAVE MACMILLAN is the global academic imprint of the Palgrave Macmillan division of St. Martin's Press, LLC and of Palgrave Macmillan Ltd. Macmillan® is a registered trademark in the United States, United Kingdom and other countries. Palgrave is a registered trademark in the European Union and other countries.

ISBN 0-333-92194-1 hardcover
ISBN 0-333-92195-X paperback

This book is printed on paper suitable for recycling and made from fully managed and sustained forest sources.

A catalogue record for this book is available from the British Library.

Library of Congress Cataloging-in-Publication Data

Business-to-business marketing : strategies and implementation / Daniel Michel . . . [et al.].
        p. cm. – (Profitable marketing relationships series)
    This book is an adaptation of a successful French text.
    Includes bibliographical references and index.
    ISBN 0–333–92194–1 (cloth)
    1. Industrial marketing.   2. Industrial marketing – Management.
3. Marketing – Planning.   I. Michel, Daniel.   II. Profitable marketing relationships.
HF5415.1263 .B873 2002
658.8'04 – dc21   2002073547

10   9   8   7   6   5   4   3   2   1
12   11   10   09   08   07   06   05   04   03

Printed and bound in Great Britain by
J.W. Arrowsmith Ltd, Bristol

Business-to-Business Marketing

Contents

List of Figures

List of Tables

List of Examples

Acknowledgements

The theoretical basis of business-to-business marketing is something that is largely due to the work of researchers grouped into an informal body called the International Marketing and Purchasing (IMP) Group, and to this group of colleagues and friends we gratefully acknowledge the input that they have had in the development of our own ideas.

Within that broad group, researchers and professors at EM Lyon contributed to a precise formalisation of the theoretical ideas expanded upon in this book, and their contribution is also gratefully acknowledged. An early version of their ideas formed the basis of earlier editions of this book, published by Economica in French (*Marketing Industriel*, 1996, 2000). We started from a first translation, undertaken by Chris Flower, who spent many hours on our behalf, as did Dorothee Capelazzi in preparing the final manuscript and perfecting the numerous figures. Ronald Palmer brought his textile expertise in providing us with the technical terms in Chapter 2.

Our thanks go to the five anonymous reviewers and the comments that they made on earlier drafts of the text. Finally, Peter Turnbull at Birmingham University kindly supported the project from scratch, and to him we owe our thanks for including the book in his series on Profitable Marketing Relationships.

Every effort has been made to contact all the copyright-holders for material used in this book, but if any have been inadvertently omitted the publishers will be pleased to make the necessary arrangement at the earliest opportunity.

Introduction

The focus of this book, as suggested by the title, is on business-to-business (B2B) marketing. We are not concerned here with the more normally accepted view of marketing, of how to get consumers to buy yet more of some fast moving consumer good (fmcg) or similar product, with some optimal tweaking of the traditional 4Ps. This must mean therefore that this book is not aimed at the traditional undergraduate market segment doing a first course in marketing. We had in mind as we wrote this book a different segment altogether. In fact, by excluding that segment, we believe that we have been able to focus on our attention on three other segments, which tend to have largely overlapping needs. These are the senior undergraduate in his/her third or fourth year of study, the MA/MBA student, and the practising manager who finds sudden exposure to the different requirements involved in getting to grips with how business markets operate.

Throughout this book, therefore, we have assumed a basic knowledge of marketing. This might be based upon experience in the case of the practising manager and/or MBA student, and upon earlier courses in (usually consumer oriented) marketing in the case of the undergraduate student. But, having made this assumption, it frees us up to take a slightly different approach to that which is most commonly found in many undergraduate textbooks. We have attempted throughout this book to be hopefully more integrative in our approach than is the norm in many textbooks. Rather than use individual case studies to illustrate single points, we have tried to use a few examples, based on our own experience, throughout the book. A particular example might be used to stress points surrounding the design of an offer at one stage, and then be referred to again later to illustrate a point about segmentation or about strategic implementation. In this way, by returning to the same examples in different chapters, we hope that we have managed to illustrate the very integrative nature of what good business-to-business marketing is all about.

A second point of departure is to stress that business-to-business marketing is not a single, standalone topic. Too often we see books on consumer marketing, services marketing and business-to-business marketing as if they can all be neatly compartmentalised and understood separately. This is definitely not the case. On the one hand we have companies selling many thousands of variants of say, pumps, industrial paints, or drill bits. On the other, we find a firm selling the one-off manufacture of a turn-key factory, a tunnel, or a motorway. There is no way in which we can reasonably argue that their marketing task is similar: the former have some clear differences and yet overlaps with consumer marketing, the latter almost none. And yet both are clearly involved in business-to-business marketing. So there is a high degree of variation to be found within the nature of just what constitutes 'business-to-business', and we hope that we have captured this diversity in our different chapters. As will become clear to readers, the focus of this book is on B2B marketing. Exchanges between firms imply both goods and services. Selling goods does include a lot of services that need to be rendered by the supplier to the buyer. Our intention is not to deal with pure services marketing (even if we dedicate Chapter 11 to this area), but to stress the importance of service in all B2B environments.

The structure of the book is represented in Figure I.1 (see p. xix). Chapter 1 sets the scene, making the link between increasing globalisation and the need for companies to focus on managing productivity. We introduce here the differences between what we term *simulated interaction* or *direct interaction* marketing (for which read, roughly, business-to-consumer or business-to-business marketing), and also explore that different kinds of business-to-business marketing that we will cover in more detail later. Chapter 2, still part of our broad introduction to the subject, then examines business-to-business marketing in more detail, introducing the important notion of relationships and the interaction model, and looks at how these might vary across different business-to-business environments. As argued above, there are different kinds of business-to-business marketing, what we identify in Figure I.1 as generic B2B offers (which form the substance of most books, or chapters within books, on business-to-business marketing), and also offers based upon technological innovation, pure services and major projects. The point here is not only that these different kinds of business-to-business marketing environments exist, but also that they might well have to co-exist in the same firm. We find examples of a firm used to offering a 'normal' product to the marketplace suddenly finding itself under pressure to launch an offering based upon technological innovation, services, or major projects. Examples of how to deal with this diversity are to be found throughout the book.

The next four chapters (Part I) are then concerned with examining the *strategic foundations* that underpin business-to-business marketing. Chapter 3, which seeks to develop our understanding of business-to-business purchasing is based on the very simple notion that purchasing is the flip side of marketing, and therefore lies at the very heart of understanding how to implement good marketing strategies. In order to understand better just how buyers buy, we offer the use of the Risk Approach Model, which we have helped to implement in many different environments. However, the implementation of good marketing strategies involves having good knowledge, and the basics of marketing information systems and business-to-business marketing research form the content of Chapter 4. This is followed by Chapter 5 that looks at how a supplier's marketing strategy will need to vary dependent upon both their own internal resources and the needs of the external marketplace, and as such will form a natural overlap with many MBA courses in strategic management. Chapter 6 then develops these ideas in more detail by discussing the role of segmentation, and also introduces the Markstrat Model, which lies at the heart of our approach to dealing with how to link segmentation, resources, offers, and customer management.

The next six chapters (Part II) are more concerned with the *implementation of strategy*. Chapter 7 examines the vital issues surrounding the design and management of the offer, whether this is based upon a product, service, or combination of the two. While we include pricing here, the issue is clearly broader than just setting the price, and must include the notion of relative perceived product quality. Having designed the offer, Chapter 8 examines ways of which to deliver it to the marketplace – the traditional role of distribution, and the obvious question of whether to go direct via your own sales force, or to make use of distributor of some kind. Issues surrounding communications and advertising are examined in Chapter 9. In Chapter 10 we look at one of the issues that is more particular to business-to-business marketing, dealing with how to market offers that are based on technological innovation, and how to manage the integration of the R&D function into the marketing plan. Chapter 11 then looks specifically at the marketing of services within a business-to-business environment, and Chapter 12 at the marketing of major projects.

Finally Chapters 13–15 (Part III) move on to discussing issues surrounding the *design of business-to-business marketing strategies*. Chapter 13 explores the role and organisation of marketing, looking at different kinds of marketing dependent upon the level of interaction required, and also at different structures of the marketing function possible within the organisation. The objective of Chapter 14 is then to look at how strategic implementation is handled within the company, and also at the role that scenario planning plays within this. Finally, Chapter 15 raises some issues of relevance to those that will be involved in international marketing, trying to ensure that the offer design and delivery are suitable to the increasing level of complexity that we all see around us. This requires us to re-examine some previous issues (segmentation, for example), within a broader geographic environment.

Finally, we offer an Appendix to the book that examines some issues surrounding the WWW and e-commerce. Although we have looked at these issues in earlier chapters (Does the WWW offer the firm strategic advantages in terms of implementing transaction-based or relationship-based strategies? What are the implications for distribution, advertising?) we attempt here to do the impossible, to take a snapshot of a phenomenon that is moving so fast, and to offer some tentative managerial insights.

Figure I.1   The structure of the book

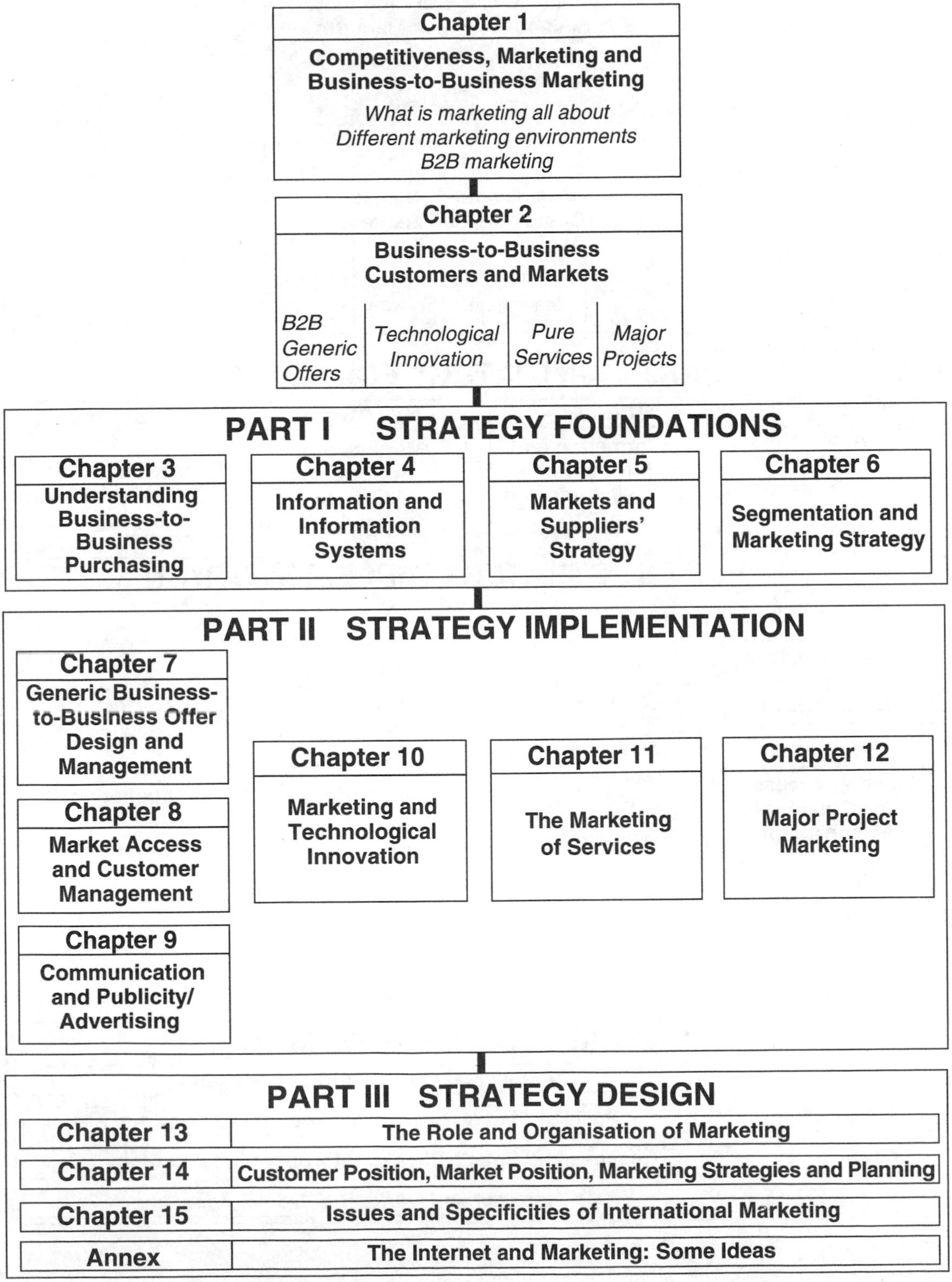

Chapter 1
Competitiveness, Marketing and Business-to-Business Marketing
What is marketing all about *Different marketing environments* *B2B marketing*

Chapter 2
Business-to-Business Customers and Markets

B2B Generic Offers	*Technological Innovation*	*Pure Services*	*Major Projects*

PART I   STRATEGY FOUNDATIONS

Chapter 3	Chapter 4	Chapter 5	Chapter 6
Understanding Business-to-Business Purchasing	**Information and Information Systems**	**Markets and Suppliers' Strategy**	**Segmentation and Marketing Strategy**

PART II   STRATEGY IMPLEMENTATION

Chapter 7
Generic Business-to-Business Offer Design and Management

Chapter 8
Market Access and Customer Management

Chapter 9
Communication and Publicity/ Advertising

Chapter 10	Chapter 11	Chapter 12
Marketing and Technological Innovation	**The Marketing of Services**	**Major Project Marketing**

PART III   STRATEGY DESIGN

Chapter 13	The Role and Organisation of Marketing
Chapter 14	**Customer Position, Market Position, Marketing Strategies and Planning**
Chapter 15	**Issues and Specificities of International Marketing**
Annex	**The Internet and Marketing: Some Ideas**

Chapter 1

Competitiveness, Marketing and Business-to-Business Marketing

What is marketing all about
Different marketing environments
B2B marketing

Chapter 2

Business-to-Business Customers and Markets

B2B Generic Offers	Technological Innovation	Pure Services	Major Projects

PART I   STRATEGY FOUNDATIONS

Chapter 3	Chapter 4	Chapter 5	Chapter 6
Understanding Business-to-Business Purchasing	**Information and Information Systems**	**Markets and Suppliers' Strategy**	**Segmentation and Marketing Strategy**

PART II   STRATEGY IMPLEMENTATION

Chapter 7			
Generic Business-to-Business Offer Design and Management			

Chapter 8	Chapter 10	Chapter 11	Chapter 12
Market Access and Customer Management	**Marketing and Technological Innovation**	**The Marketing of Services**	**Major Project Marketing**

Chapter 9
Communication and Publicity/ Advertising

PART III   STRATEGY DESIGN

Chapter 13	**The Role and Organisation of Marketing**
Chapter 14	**Customer Position, Market Position, Marketing Strategies and Planning**
Chapter 15	**Issues and Specificities of International Marketing**
Annex	**The Internet and Marketing: Some Ideas**

1 Competitiveness, Marketing and Business-to-Business Marketing

Just how important is it for firms to be marketing driven? The debate continues: it is probably more generally accepted that firms dedicated to producing consumer goods (aimed at private consumption) have to be marketing oriented, but it is possibly more questionable for firms dealing with other firms (i.e. in business-to-business situations). In the consumer environment, marketing has a long history, having set up procedures such as advertising and brand management that have been much studied, developed and professionalised. Marketing executives are appointed; every one knows their responsibilities and how they fit into the particular organisation. However, within business-to-business environments there is a lot more uncertainty. Many large firms, often with thousands of employees, do not have a 'Marketing Director' and express doubts and reticence about the discipline; and yet are nevertheless successful in managing their activities and do so to their customers' satisfaction. And yet we find other large firms in the business-to-business arena with a formalised marketing approach, well integrated into their overall business operations.

In this debate about the usefulness of marketing, several viewpoints are possible. One is to argue that consumer-based marketing methods and tools are applicable in business-to-business environments, with only minor adaptations. Alternatively, we can stress the differences between consumer and business-to-business marketing, focusing more on the importance of managing the direct relationships that firms tend to have with their business customers. This is a very different approach, arguing that we need to personalise the design of marketing strategies in all cases, whatever the type and number of customers to be served. Obviously, this becomes highly problematic for those firms serving millions of business or professional customers all over the world. In this book we propose adopting a third approach. For very definitive reasons that this book will illustrate, we believe that it is necessary to think of several 'types' of markets. Each type of market has its own particularities, requiring that managers adjust their ways of designing and implementing marketing strategies.

We believe that it is useful to base our position within the context of international competition, in order to examine the question of the contribution of marketing to a firm's competitiveness. This we do below, and we shall then establish why and how the manager's marketing approach must be adapted to different situations.

Competitiveness, Productivity and the Firm's Strategy

International Competition and Competitiveness

The structural transformation of the world economy since 1980 has profoundly affected competition, and hence the strategic actions of firms. These changes have their roots in the postwar period (such as the Bretton Woods Agreements, General Agreement on Tariffs and Trade (GATT), and the World Trade Organisation (WTO)).

Two phenomena are particularly significant. The first is the growing degree of *globalisation*: exchanges between countries are increasing faster than production. Consequently, national firms are losing market share within their traditional national territory to foreign competitors. Therefore companies are increasingly forced to survive by increasing their market shares in foreign countries. Competition is getting tougher and tougher as global exchanges increase. Firms are being forced to expand their activities on a worldwide basis – or at least on a larger front than just their original country.

In parallel, and this is the second phenomenon, the *nature of competition* has changed. Increasingly, we have seen firms based in developing countries (Asia, South America, or Eastern Europe) appearing in markets such as textiles, consumer electronics, electrical equipment, cars, etc. These countries benefit from lower cost structures than their competitors in developed countries because of significantly lower labour costs. Although such emerging competitors might not adopt the best manufacturing techniques, might lag somewhat in their innovativeness and perhaps have slightly lower labour productivity, we still see that their lower wage structures bring them real advantages in some markets. These advantages are often being reinforced through technology transfer to local partners by firms eager to gain a foothold in these territories.

Added to these two phenomena is the relentless increase in the demand for *improving profitability*. The American pension funds set very demanding standards for the return on their capital investments, first at home and then in the those countries into which they have diversified their investments. These standards then tend to become worldwide standards. A firm aiming to raise money to sustain its development must show an attractive level of profitability to win investors. For those firms still manufacturing in developed countries, and we shall adopt this point of view from now on, tremendous challenges exist (Porter, 1990). They have to maintain their competitiveness while dealing with their relatively high labour costs and demands on their return on capital.

Competitiveness and Productivity

Competitiveness, as Porter stresses, is a vague and uncertain concept. It can be more usefully examined through another concept: *productivity*. Productivity is an

Figure 1.1   Definition of productivity

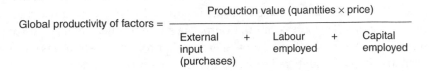

economic term that relates the output of an organisation to the means (or factors) employed to obtain it. Several definitions of productivity are in common use. It can be expressed in *physical units* (the number of manufactured items, number of hours worked, etc.) or in *value terms* (production value, cost of the labour used, etc.). Productivity can be, and is, often examined for a specific factor of production: for capital or for labour, for example. For our purposes, we shall use a general definition, the 'global productivity of factors' which is the ratio between the value of an output and the value of the factors (total costs) that made the production possible (Figure 1.1). These values are expressed in constant terms to eliminate inflation effects.

This definition has two advantages. First, it allows us to relate output (production value) to the combination of factors that made it possible. Secondly, it allows useful comparisons to be made: between two competing firms or two national industries manufacturing the same goods (cars, for example) or two nations on a global basis. This is an important definition, and some of the major issues surrounding the management of firms are clarified within it.

The value of the output achieved relates the *quantity manufactured* (i.e. the obtained market share), and the *price* (i.e. the capacity to get such a price level from the customers). These two items (market share and price paid) are the result of the customers' evaluation of what the firm is offering *vis-à-vis* the competitors' offers. They establish a kind of 'market value' of the firm's offering. An increase in this value, all else being equal, implies improved productivity. Increasingly, the marketing task is all about managing the delivery of this value (Gale, 1994).

A dynamic combination of the factors of production allows managers to improve productivity. An increase in the capital employed (for example, a new and more efficient machine) advantageously replaces costly labour. An innovation in the manufacturing process (another form of capital expenditure) may reduce the quantities or the value of the input materials used, thereby improving productivity. This result can also be obtained by incorporating innovations or productivity increases from suppliers. It is important to note that the productivity of a company is in turn affected by the productivity of its suppliers (see Mory–Ancel in Example 5). We shall return to this concept many times, particularly when dealing with the concept of the value chain and supply chain management.

This first level of our analysis of productivity highlights some interesting points. But we can take it further. Two factors seem to be decisive in understanding how continuously to improve productivity. One is innovation. The other is what lies under the term 'purchases' or outside inputs.

As Porter (1990) stresses, *innovation* is the driving force behind the growth of firms within developed countries. Some innovations play on the numerator as well as on the denominator of the ratio in Figure 1.1. They can allow management to reduce labour (an increase in the output per hour), intermediary consumption (by improving material efficiency or using more productive suppliers) and the capital used (perhaps through redesign of the manufacturing process). One of the most impressive examples of this approach was the replacement of the 'classical' steel manufacturing process by the 'electrical' process. In addition to enabling manufacturers to decrease their prices, the electrical process resulted in both a better quality product and improved manufacturing flexibility, thereby helping the suppliers better to meet their customers' demands.

The innovative firm needs to maintain its competitive edge for as long as possible. This advantage allows them simultaneously to gain market share while also maintaining prices and improving production costs. Competitiveness and productivity are interrelated, in the sense that the former depends largely on the latter. Success stems from the ability of the firm to manage innovation by making the right choices and investments, especially concerning ways to gain a reduction in labour costs, or utilising more efficient business processes. In micro terms, firms in developed countries can maintain manufacturing activity through a relative reduction in labour, basing their strategies on cost reduction and cost competitiveness as well as on maintaining price levels. On a macro scale, any such substitution of capital for labour in a stagnating or contracting market inevitably leads to an increase in unemployment. Any country facing such globalisation threats can find full employment only through the development of its industries' innovative capacity, so investing in 'new' activities that less innovative countries, industries, or firms find harder to replicate.

At this stage we should not neglect the fact that innovation does not stem only from the discovery and implementation of new technical principles. It also results from the ways a social body – a nation, or a firm – generates and sustains *innovating perspectives*. However, this whole debate lies outside the scope of this book and we shall mention it only in passing. Education, motivation, eagerness to progress, reasoned risk taking, confidence in one's own potential support what we shall say on this subject. Relying on this way to progress does not automatically mean that its negative consequences have to be ignored. To sum them up briefly we can say that they tend to reinforce the advantages of the most powerful countries and/or firms. Public authorities, with a broadened remit, have to regulate working environments and set the macroeconomic conditions. And to do this while not to destroying its positive aspects.

The other aspect is the impact of *outside inputs* (or *purchases*). This may be even more difficult to understand than innovation. It encompasses the direct supply to the firm of raw materials, semi-finished products, capital goods, energy, various services and so on. In this way, a customer is integrally related to and affected by its supplier's productivity. Given this perspective, it raises the possibility of transferring tasks to suppliers able to undertake them in a more productive way ('make or buy' decisions). But this approach also includes 'indirect supplies', if this expression may be used. These elements are not as obvious as direct purchases and they do not appear in the formula in Figure 1.1. They are nevertheless important and need to be taken into account.

Several schools of thought underline the impact of these indirect supplies to understanding the firm's competitiveness. If they differ in their formulation, they all stress the fact that a firm may improve its productivity both through its internal operations and through its ability to make use of changes in the external environment. The first approach says that the productivity of a firm depends on the productivity of the *whole set of industrial operations* leading to a finished product, a piece of furniture, a cloth. The efficiency (the conditions of forest exploitation, the ways trees are felled, the quality of the sawmills, etc.) explains the productivity of a furniture manufacturer as much as its own strategy or its distribution network. This idea of the set of industrial operations is very similar to that of Porter's *value chain* (1985) that brings a complementary interest in allowing a detailed analysis of the performance of the activities of a firm in relation to its suppliers and its customers. Various authors (see Håkansson and Snehota, 1995; Ford *et al.*, 1998) have also stressed the importance of the *networks* in which a firm is acting. Networks are made of a variety of possible stakeholders: suppliers, universities, public or industry research centres, industry organisations, customers, specialised or general consultants, national or international authorities and so on. They make up for the firm a natural source of information, of scientific progress, of relationships with other key players of an industry, or of supply of goods and services. The intrinsic quality of these networks counts as much as the way in which a firm uses and exploits them. The fourth approach considers the notion of *cluster* (Porter, 1990, 1998). This concept stresses the fact that often one nation or even one area inside a nation generates a group of competitive firms in the same industry, for example printing presses in Germany, ceramic tiles in Italy, plants and cut flowers in the Netherlands, hifi systems in Japan and so on. Within an industry, several clusters may enter into competition through the firms involved – or, inversely, firms and economies enter into competition through their clusters. This concept of clusters has implications both for the management of national economies (i.e. role of public authorities) and for a particular firm's management.

We shall come back on several occasions in this book to the interrelationships between the individual and the collective games that a firm has to play. This constant duality (do I look after myself or my supply chain/network/cluster?) has important implications for the design and implementation of any firm's global and marketing strategies.

The Firm's Strategy and Competitiveness

As Porter (1985) argues, firms have to choose between two generic strategies: whether to focus on increasing *production value* (value competitiveness, or differentiation strategies) or on *cost reduction* (cost competitiveness or cost leadership strategies).

Value competitiveness is possible only if customers are willing to purchase an offer at a price higher than that charged by the competition. To do this, there must be some recognition that it offers greater value. The origin of this greater value varies, and can be based on any of a number of possible attributes. It might be superior quality, brand image, on time in full delivery (e.g. innovation time, or continuous upgrading of the offer), the capability to offer a variety of complementary offers, efficiency of international networks and co-operation, etc.

The recognition of this additional and valued attribute by customers potentially creates what the economists would call a *monopoly situation*. It results from the fact that customers value a particular attribute of a specific offer. They no longer think that all competing offers are identical (or substitutable, in economists' terms), believing instead that one particular supplier offers material advantages. Even if limited in time and scope, these differentiated offers are usually highly profitable for those firms that are able to build and manage them.

Another recognised way to increase non-cost competitiveness is for firms to increase the variety of what they offer, often called *structural competitiveness*. Any company eager to develop such a strategy needs to adopt a structure that enables it to sustain this strategy in the long run. For example, the English textile industry has seen many of its companies disappear in the face of fierce international competition from lower-waged countries. Those companies that have survived have tended to organise themselves to react faster to changing fashions and market trends. This corresponds to broadening of the variety of what they can offer. Making these choices profoundly altered the strategic behaviour, operations, and structure of the firms. They now show a far deeper understanding of what represents *value* in the eyes of their customers. In Italy, Benetton's strategy was clearly based on a similar philosophy. One point to be made here is that we must recognise that these non-cost or differentiation strategies *do involve costs* (e.g. in innovation, quality, or variety). These have to be closely controlled in order not to lose the price advantage and so to degrade profitability (see Figure 1.4, p. 9).

Cost competitiveness concerns cases in which companies' offers are largely substitutable for each other. These cases correspond to those market segments in which price plays a major role in the customer's purchasing decision. In this case, winners develop strong competencies in managing their internal costs.

The overall extent to which a firm is competitive can be defined as its ability to be productive within its competitive arena which, as we argued above, is increasingly global. As we said before, competitiveness and productivity are interrelated. There are many potential sources of both: labour costs, personnel quality and training, access to scientific knowledge, conditions favouring innovation, the value of the company's offer (intrinsic quality, image, services, delivery time, etc.), access to highly productive suppliers, availability and cost of the necessary capital, etc. are all potential routes. The numerous possible combinations of these various levers require the firm to optimise the relationship between its external market position

Figure 1.2   Competitiveness and firm strategy

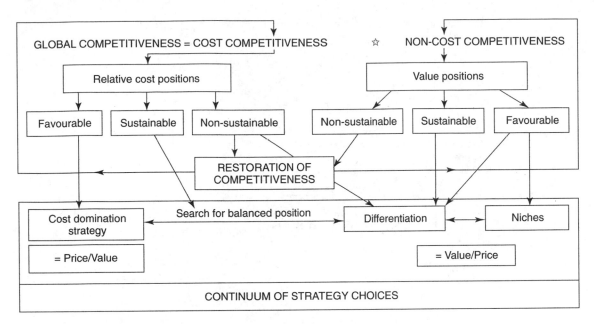

and its internal organisation. Two fundamental conditions have to be met to do this. First, management needs excellent *information* covering the requirements and operating conditions of its customers, its competition and on the productivity levers available in the environment. The second is the quality of *management* itself: their capacity to understand how their markets evolve and then to adapt the organisation, to motivate the staff and to position it according to their strategic choices.

We find here the classical definition of firm strategies (Porter, 1985): domination through either *cost* or *differentiation*. Among the latter, 'niche' strategies represent a particular choice. These choices are expanded upon in Figure 1.2. The process begins with the identification by managers of the conditions favouring either a cost-based or differentiation-based strategy, and also of the competitors' positions. An evaluation of these internal capabilities, of the constraints within the environment, of the strengths and weaknesses of the competitors, and of the demands of potential customers, then allows management to choose a position and to design the corresponding strategy. This is usually a time-limited equilibrium position, some combination of cost competitiveness and yet also elements of differentiation. However, this position tends to become unbalanced over time by the evolution of the very factors that contributed to its original definition, and hence has to be continuously monitored.

On the bottom left-hand side of the continuum of choices, the Price/Value position means that the offer is founded on competitive prices based on a favourable relative cost position. On the right-hand side the Value/Price position indicates that the customers, or at least some market segments, value some aspects of quality for which they are ready to pay more. It is important to stress that this is not a static

Figure 1.3 Management of strategic evolution

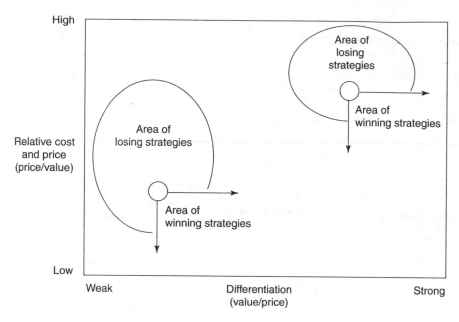

Reproduced from Lindon Brown and Malcolm H. McDonald, *Competitive Marketing Strategy for Europe*, 1994, with the permission of Palgrave Macmillan.

picture, and positions are hardly ever definitely acquired or held over the long term. The offer to the marketplace has to be upgraded continuously through efforts that have to be directed in the right direction (Figure 1.3).

A price/value position can be made ever more competitive through cost reductions that allow the firm to offer the same quality for a lower price. Alternatively, competitiveness can be improved by increasing customer value without any related cost, and therefore price, increase. To achieve a radical repositioning of the company on the cost/differentiation map (i.e. a move to the upper right-hand corner) is a far higher-risk strategy. This is because offering an increase in value that is achieved by increasing basic costs and hence selling price, runs the risk of possibly reducing *perceived value*. Similarly, any cost reduction that will also lead to a perceived decrease in value might be dangerous. A differentiated position can be upgraded or improved by increasing the level of differentiation without incurring cost increases.

Figure 1.3 graphically illustrates this reality: winning areas are narrow but there are many losing strategies. It also indicates the interdependence of choices. It is always relatively easy to think of product or service attributes that will bring recognised value to customers. However, it is much more difficult to achieve this without any concomitant increase in cost and in price, which usually corresponds to what the customers want. To achieve this means diligent management of the *design to cost* process. This involves recognition of the fact that true competitiveness is based

Figure 1.4   Sequential development and integrated development

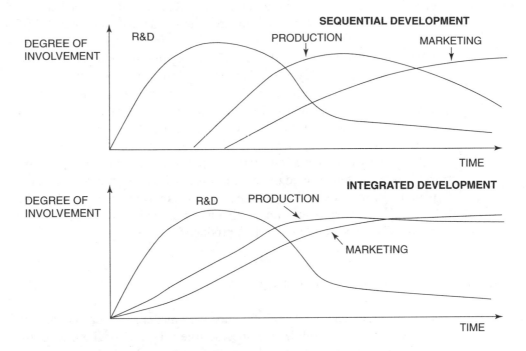

on three interrelated approaches: knowing what represents *real value* to your customers (commercial and marketing innovation); the ability to design an offer that
integrates these value elements (research and development (R&D), design innovation); and the ability to *control costs* (manufacturing, process innovation). One of
the major issues in management is therefore to organise the various functional
processes so that they follow a well-integrated path, rather than a sequential one
(Figure 1.4). Historically industrial firms used to let the Research and Development
Department go their own way, initiate development work and advance on new products' definition. Further on manufacturing and marketing (or maybe just sales?)
would be allowed to come in on the process. Therefore inadequacies with customers' requirements or with production capabilities would be discovered and
solved under urgency and at high cost. Recent research on the factors of success
of new products (Cooper, 1988; Balbontin *et al.*, 1999) confirms former results
(Booz-Allen and Hamilton, 1982): (1) driving the initial steps of development is
critical for the success of new products, (2) successful products are fed with significantly higher expenses in the initial steps, (3) a large part of these expenses is
dedicated to market research and assessment and requires marketing expertise. The
assignment of *multifunctional teams* to the development of new products is increasingly often the path to success.

So the competitiveness of a firm in its international markets is its ability to
acquire and keep customers through the *continuous development of a sustainable
competitive advantage*, based on an ongoing appreciation of what constitutes value

for customers, as well as of the social, technical and economic factors that influence both production and market development. The degree or variety of choice is related to how the market is structured, as we described above. All of the factors are linked, and nothing is ever secure. Evolution within the environment, of customers, competitors and of factors influencing internal company efficiency, requires managers to constantly re-evaluate their competitive position. It is particularly important to be cautious about the myths concerning technical innovation. While we would stress that innovation is an absolute necessity, it does not provide any advantages *per se*. Advantages accrue only if there is a *perceived relative increase in value* from the customers' viewpoint. Any deficiency on some point may unbalance the whole operation. For example, it is generally accepted that Philips' V 2000 video system offered remarkable quality in performance. But that did not compensate for the lack of pre-recorded cassettes on offer in the market, the lack of the commercial coverage and a price that was relatively high compared to JVC's competing VHS, and so the (superior) product failed.

Competitiveness and Marketing

We have argued above that all functional elements are interrelated, with each function within the firm fulfilling a specific role. The role of the marketing function is to collect, formalise and circulate data on customer value. It is to these topics that we now turn.

The Marketing of Value

The rationale of this approach is based on the fundamentals surrounding the competitive efficiency of the firm: to acquire and to keep customers requires that they perceive at least a partial superiority of the firm's offer, and recognise its advantages. *Perceived customer value* is the outcome of a commercial offer that gives the customer operating, social and/or economic advantages. There are numerous possible ways to achieve this, owing to the diversity of clients and the variety of technologically feasible answers. For companies operating internationally, this variety increases considerably, and makes even more crucial the accurate evaluation of the choices open. The role of the marketing function is to identify this diversity – i.e. to understand what constitutes value for all potential final and intermediary customers, to manage this knowledge base and to make it available and understandable to the rest of the company. This is the price that needs to be paid in order to put the company in a position to generate the offers that bring success in the marketplace (Figure 1.5).

The concept of value that we are introducing here is similar to that of quality, or rather to relative perceived quality, that we shall examine later: the customer's evaluation of the firm's offer relative to that of its competitors, at the proposed

Figure 1.5   The marketing of value

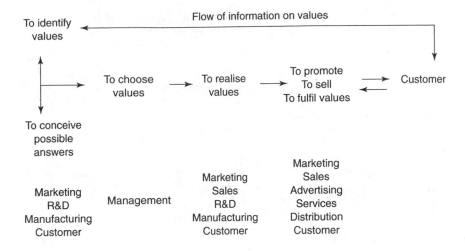

prices. The role of marketing is to ensure the quality of the offer, and to communicate this value to the marketplace. This might mean attention to *quality defaults*, since the offer is likely to be unsuccessful and the firm's image damaged if the quality of the offer is poor. But attention must also be paid to *quality excess*, where customers are not willing to pay for those advantages where the costs outweigh the added value. An overqualified offer may fail (if the market is not substantial enough) or can lead to unprofitability (where the price obtained is not high enough to cover the costs incurred).

The Marketing Approach and the Interaction Concept

The role allotted to the marketing function must lead us to examine the process of exchange between a vendor and a buyer. It is insufficient to perceive it as a transaction, an exchange of a product or service for money, which is the classical point of view of the economists. Rather, we have to expand on this view, and take into account the myriad of often invisible and intangible processes that surround the formal exchange process. The market economy is founded on a 'free' process of adjustment and alignment between what is on offer and what is demanded. We know that quantities and prices are determined in the market through complex adjustment mechanisms. These mechanisms serve to give any firm positive or negative feedback from the marketplace. But this process of ratification does not tell us anything about the efforts and choices that led the firm to propose the offer originally. Any company varies its offer according to its own internal resources, the characteristics of the potential markets and its position relative to its competitors. This analysis leads the company to propose a particular offer, and to implement a way of dealing with, or relating to, the target customers. It is this wider task for

Figure 1.6   The marketing approach for the design of an offer

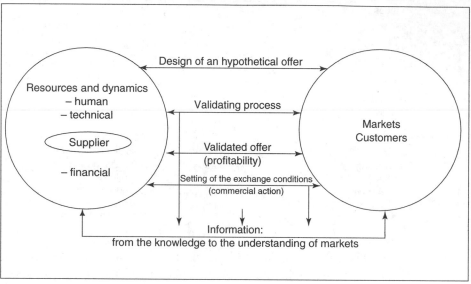

Competition in a segmented market

which the marketing function has responsibility, and one that we will now examine in more detail.

As Bartels (1968) stated, 'the marketing process is a process of interaction among the participants, during which the respective expectations may or may not be satisfied'. This identifies the importance of marketing as a *process of interaction*, one that aims to deliver value, but where failure is always possible. In addition, the process is *time-dependent*. What is at stake is not only the decisive moment at which a potential customer makes a positive or negative decision. Rather, this decision is influenced by the success of two earlier phases within the interaction process: defining the offer and setting the exchange conditions. The definition of the offer results from a sequence of interactions between the vendor and its markets that leads to the definition of an offer supposedly acceptable by the market and profitable for the vendor. The setting of the exchange conditions (i.e. availability in time and place, practicality, functionality, associated services, etc.) is the second set of decisions that contribute to the final outcome. We shall see later how the sequential or simultaneous timing of these two phases contributes to the definition of different marketing environments. For the time being, we shall simply describe the marketing approach for the design of an offer, whatever the environment.

Our approach to marketing is outlined in Figure 1.6. We believe that it offers a logical and structured viewpoint that is both simple and yet also highly practical. The manager's first task is to understand the broader conditions within which the exchange will ultimately take place. The state of the economy and social conditions influence the overall demand for products and services. This is commonly referred to as a *PEST* analysis (assessing the influence that Political/legal change, the Economy, Social trends and Technology have on demand). To design an acceptable offer is a kind of alchemy, combining the firm's overall internal resources and the external needs of the market. From this alchemy (and in this book we intend to describe all the elements of the recipe, among the first of which is segmentation) stems a *hypothetical offer*. This is a kind of initial draft, whose final characteristics will be determined after a sequence of *validation* between buyer and supplier. The management of this validation phase is one of the most active periods of *interaction* between the vendor and its markets. The vendor is not guaranteed success and, with as much thoroughness as is possible, needs to try and ensure that its hypotheses about the market's needs are valid. The company needs to listen carefully to the market's reaction. This listening involves a range of methodologies that make up the discipline of market research. The process leads to modifications of the initial hypothetical offer, to end with a *validated offer*. This has to be both what the market wants, and capable of being delivered profitably. This offer must then be delivered, based on a range of interrelated commercial actions, which we will describe in more detail as we proceed.

We will now examine how this general approach takes particular forms, dependent upon how the exchange situations vary. Our intention here is to characterise these different situations that we shall from now on refer to as '*marketing environments*'. This process will help us to define the overall domain of business-to-business marketing, and will also help us appreciate its internal diversity.

The Various Marketing Environments

We have already expressed our position that if marketing is one of the disciplines of management science, and that means that it relies on a unique approach, then it offers a variety of different environments, each of which requires the utilisation of slightly but significantly different analytical tools.

There is a range of important academic literature dedicated to this debate. We shall refer only to some major contributions. Some authors (Fern and Brown, 1984) come to the conclusion that marketing consists of a single unique approach, whatever the environment concerned. Others firmly favour the idea that different kinds of markets exist, each of which needs to be treated differently: industrial marketing (Corey, 1962; Håkansson and Östberg, 1975; Håkansson and IMP Group, 1982; Bonoma and Johnston, 1978; Webster, 1992) or service marketing (Blois, 1974; Shostack, 1977; Grönroos, 1990), for example. To simplify matters, and avoiding a theoretical debate that we recognise exists but which does not fit within the objectives of this book, this divergence can be explained by taking a variety of perspectives.

Some Perspectives on Marketing and its Diversity

One approach to understand diversity within marketing is to take a historical approach. Marketing as a management discipline emerged from practice towards the end of the 1930s. This happened in the United States of America, and within a particular setting: managers within Procter and Gamble trying to study how optimally to market their range of different and competing brands. They did this by using a range of newly developed methods (consumer attitude studies, market tests, etc.). These developments were closely followed by emergence of marketing as an academic discipline in the 1940s, with the formulation of the well-known '*marketing mix*'. These practical and academic developments were in fact rooted in a particular economic environment. The growth of the US economy in the postwar years saw a rising standard of living, which resulted in a rapid growth of private domestic consumption of branded consumer goods. The successful exploitation of this environment by a number of firms (Procter and Gamble, Coca-Cola, Gillette, Colgate, and others) and the dominance of American universities in management science at the time, both contributed to reinforce the developing theoretical approach, and also to spreading the message beyond the USA. The temptation to apply the same consumer-based approach to other environments (in particular, to services and to business-to-business markets) came from the success of the original approach. However, as we shall see, this did not always work, and inadequacies surfaced.

Over time, greater attempts were made, both within firms and on a theoretical level, to try to understand how marketing might work in environments radically different from the traditional one based on consumer goods. These attempts followed two different paths. The first one focuses analysis on the actual exchange, or more precisely, on the *commercial exchanges within competitive systems*. The approach seeks to better our understanding of the ways in which exchanges are practically worked out (Bagozzi, 1975; Williamson, 1975). This approach gives equal importance to both vendors and buyers, as well as to other stakeholders in the exchange (government and intermediaries, for example). This view leads to our first definition of the discipline of marketing: *marketing is a scientific discipline applied to a specific domain of management science, that is to the understanding of commercial exchanges within competitive situations*. This perspective has in turn influenced many in the area, and this in turn has led to the introduction of the second viewpoint.

This second view is more practical, and places the debate at a different level, that of the perspective of the supplier-buyer dyad. From this stance, *marketing as a management task is a group of methodologies and techniques aimed to guide the exchanges between buyers and sellers in such a way as to optimally manage lasting and profitable relationships within competitive environments*. This is the viewpoint that we shall adopt. We shall develop the 'techniques' throughout the subsequent chapters in order to show how we can use these tools in the optimal management of buyer–seller exchanges.

A Tentative Explanation of the Diversity of Marketing Environments

Can the relationship between the Coca-Cola Company and Kevin Smith, a regular 5-cans-a-day man living in Manchester, be described in the same way as the ongoing relationship between PPG, an American paint manufacturer with plants throughout Europe, and one of their largest Italian customers, Fiat? Logic tells us that there are very different things driving these two relationships. However, it is nevertheless not easy to define a general explanatory framework within which all possible exchange environments can be classified in a rational and meaningful way.

Within what we might call a 'guide to managing exchanges' for the supplier, we have already identified two different phases: one concerns the *design of the offer*; the other the *setting of the exchange conditions*. Marketing success is the result of a combination of both of these processes, which develop differently according to the type of environment encountered.

The Interaction Perspective

The design of Coca-Cola's offer to Kevin Smith encompasses several attributes: the variety of products available (regular or diet variations?), taste and appearance, volume, shape, and pricing, for example. A formalised process in which consumers are requested to give their attitudes and feelings on the various issues determines just what Coca-Cola decides to deliver on these attributes. This first phase sets up the design of the offer. When the validated offer emerges, it will be marketed via the chosen distribution channels: supermarkets, hotels and restaurants, vending machines, etc. This second phase corresponds to what we called the setting of the conditions of the exchange. Both phases are not entirely independent and Coca-Cola will proceed with minor adaptations according to the requests of the different channel members. But the same aluminium 330 ml can is available in each channel throughout England. However, during all these processes Coca-Cola has never actually spoken to Kevin, and the company may well ignore the fact that he is one of their customers. But Kevin is still happy with his daily diet of coke.

For PPG the situation is different. On the one hand, they may supply a wide range of paints to one of Fiat's plants. But in a second plant they supply Fiat with a more advanced technological application that requires the permanent assistance of PPG technicians to run the paint shop within Fiat's factory. And at a third plant, PPG has been the dominant supplier over a number of years, with their technicians often giving advice and assistance to the Fiat designers. When the management at Fiat's plant were considering upgrading their paint shop installations (seeking productivity improvements and also compliance with new environmental regulations), they looked to PPG for information and help on what innovations were possible concerning painting processes and machinery. Important and lengthy exchanges took place between the executives on both sides. Fiat so appreciated the high level of competence of their supplier that its managers decided to entrust PPG with the total

Figure 1.7   Simulated interaction and direct interaction

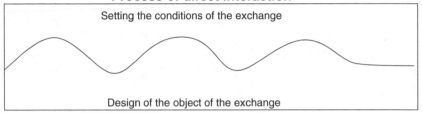

design and then ongoing management of the paint shop inside their manufacturing plant. This evidence of support from Fiat so impressed PPG in turn that they increased their own efforts, gathering a team with all the internal and external resources required to ensure that they would succeed in managing Fiat's paint shop. By working together, the two companies raised and resolved many problems and suggestions, which led through successive adaptations to the final project. Here the processes of designing the offer and determining the exchange conditions develop simultaneously, and are dependent upon the two companies interacting closely, which was not at all the case with in Kevin's marketplace. We summarise these differences in Figure 1.7.

The example of Coca-Cola illustrates what we call a process of *simulated interaction*. The design of the object of the exchange (the offer) is realised through a succession of testing and adjustments: concept tests, formula tests, packing tests, graphics tests, simulated market tests, test marketing, etc. These tests are based on appropriate samples of the population of target customers. There is no direct relationship or interaction with the individual customers as such. The relationship is established, often through an anonymous market research agency, with a selection of customers (a sample) selected so as to be a statistically reliable representation of the segment identified. This is why we use the term 'simulated interaction'. While the extent of satisfaction, and remarks and suggestions from individuals will be taken into account, this is most often under the form of percentages: having 50 per cent 'satisfied' or 'very satisfied' might be considered insufficient to launch a new offer. The initial proposal will therefore be modified according to the insights provided by the sample data, and a new version will be tested again to judge the effects of the modifications. If the company gets a positive response from say 80 per cent or more, it might decide to launch the product. However, the object of the exchange has not yet been 'sold' to anybody in the proper sense of the term. The whole process was a simulation. To sell it, the firm must now set the conditions of the exchange: identifying the means through which consumers will get to know of the existence of the offer and its characteristics, making sure that customers know where they can find it, the price, etc. This sequential process of simulated interaction corresponds largely to market environments where there are numerous and dispersed customers, which is usually the characteristic of mass consumer markets. In our terminology, such simulated interaction corresponds to a weak intensity in the level of supplier–customer interaction.

Direct interaction, based on our PPG example, encompasses the same sequence of adjustments and checking. But these phases are now managed directly and interactively with the identified customers. This usually corresponds to a few important, large customers. The process of designing the offer is intertwined with that of setting the conditions of the exchange. The economic exchange (the sale) is in fact the result of the social exchanges between the actors involved.

These two examples reveal three different levels of the intensity of these social exchanges. These are the nature of *market demand* (concentrated vs fragmented); the *importance* of the particular individual customer to the supplier (from negligible to extremely high); and the *complexity* of the decision making unit (low in the case of individual purchasers like Kevin Smith, high in the case of Fiat). As we will argue later, all relationships can be usefully and meaningfully analysed by assessing how they vary across these three levels.

Within direct interaction environments, we can find a wide variety in the *intensity* of the supplier–customer relationship. This is a choice that managers have to make, and the choice of the appropriate level of interaction must be based on many factors. These include the existing market and customer behaviour, the competitive situation and also on the resources of the firm and the characteristics of the offer that it intends to market. A company can adapt and change the way in which it deals with its customers – the level of intensity can increase or decrease over time. Of course, companies will often manage their different relationships with varying degrees of intensity. The three dimensions according to which relationships can be managed are identified in Table 1.1. Although they will be discussed in more depth later, it is important to realise that each one has implications for how relationships are managed, and hence for how a company uses its resources to manage its specific marketing strategy.

Table 1.1   Characteristics of simulated interaction and direct interaction

	Simulated interaction	**Direct interaction**
Market demand	Dispersed large numbers	Concentrated low to average numbers
Importance of an individual customer to the supplier	Weak	From average to very high
Characteristics of the decision making unit (DMU)	Simple	From complex to highly complex

Figure 1.8   A model of commercial exchange

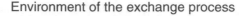

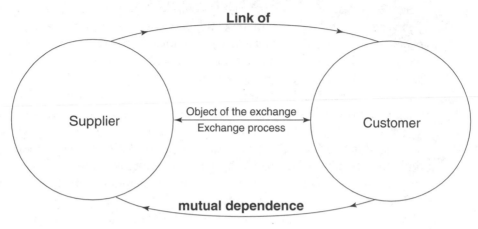

Source: Texier and Valla (1988).

The Perspective of the Conditions of Exchange

The interaction perspective that we have just described throws some initial light on the phenomena we are trying to explain. It can be used to describe in an effective way how relationships are established and maintained between two actors involved in a commercial exchange. If we enlarge our perspective to include the exchange itself, we find another dimension to consider. According to Homan (1961) 'interaction between individuals is an exchange of goods both tangible and intangible'. By extension, it is possible to analyse a social link between two persons according to a framework that identifies the *actors* present, the link of *mutual dependence* between them, the actual *object of the exchange*, the *exchange process* itself, and a *specific environment*. Given that our interest is confined to commercial exchanges, we can now provide a simple model (Figure 1.8) of the different elements of the exchange.

Some definitions will be useful here to explain what these terms all mean. The *actors* can be organisations (any legal entity with public or private status, or even the government) or else individuals acting either professionally (lawyers, consultants) or else as private individuals (households, singles). Some actors can simultaneously be both suppliers and customers (in the case of organisations and professionals), while others are customers only (private persons), constituting what the economists call the final household consumption.

The link of *mutual dependence* between the actors reflects the dynamics of the forces at work during the exchange process. The extent to which the two parties might negotiate directly depends on the relative importance of the actors involved. Kevin Smith just assumes that he is not in a position to negotiate with Coca-Cola, and does not even consider this an option. However, he will discuss in great detail the redecoration of his house in Manchester with the interior decorator that he carefully selected. Similarly, it is understandable and logical that the three different contracts between PPG and Fiat are all the result of lengthy and careful negotiations, given the respective size and importance of both organisations.

The *exchange process* is a more complex area, and it can be analysed in different ways. It might be possible to observe the actual exchange itself, to see evidence of the commercial transaction by examining individual invoices relating to particular exchanges. But this does not tell the full story. We also need to pay attention to the underlying process of *interaction* that precedes the exchange. By adopting this approach, we are able to differentiate between continuous and discontinuous exchanges (Woodward, 1965). *Continuous* exchanges would involve evidence of ongoing, repetitive transactions, such as the purchases of bread, milk, eggs, paper pulp for a paper maker, wheel bearings for a car manufacturer, etc. *Discontinuous* ones, on the other hand, would involve purchases such as a car, a washing machine, a journey to the 2000 Sydney Olympics, a hydraulic press, or a new motorway. The distinction between the two provides us with an objective analysis of the type of transactions, their frequency and the consequences that they can have for the types of relationship between the actors. However, we prefer to study the process of exchange through a different approach that takes into account the *background*, or *unseen*, processes as well. When this is done, it leads us to a better understanding of both the type (simulated or direct) and the intensity (see Chapter 2) of the interaction between the actors before, during and after the transaction.

The *object of the exchange* can fall into one of three categories: pure products, pure services and product/service combinations. These categories are important, because they imply different behaviour patterns between the supplier and the customer. A product can be bought according to its attributes, its performances and its price, elements that can be evaluated in a relatively tangible way. The exchange is characterised by a transfer of ownership of the good from the supplier to the customer. However, a service cannot be analysed in the same way. A service is intangible, a promise to fulfil a future task, made by a supplier to the customer. While it involves the sale of intangible attributes (an airline journey, a hotel night, the concept behind an advertising campaign), the sale is often based on very tangible attributes that remain the property of the service provider (an aeroplane, hotel building, creative or skilled people, etc.). So we can differentiate between a manager purchasing a flight ticket from an airline company in order to attend a business meeting, and the same person buying an aeroplane to fly to the same destination on holiday. A service implies the participation of the customer in the delivery/consumption of the service, and this leads to a more intense supplier–customer interaction than is usually the case in the sale of a product. As services are forming an ever-increasing share of economic activity, it is logical that suppliers need to be ever more diligent in integrating a service element into their delivery. An even more fundamental question relates to whether or not it is still realistic or even meaningful to think about anyone as selling pure products. Given that we can argue that all business-to-business marketing is concerned with solving your customer's problem more efficiently than he or she can, then it can all be said to be service oriented. This question is at the very heart of some recent developments in business-to-business marketing, and we shall deal with it later in a more in-depth manner.

The *environment* reflects a group of constraints and opportunities that influence what customers want and how they will behave, and hence have an impact on the possible actions of any supplier. However this influence is highly specific to the particular industry or profession under scrutiny, and for this reason does not form one of the dimensions that we use to characterise the marketing environments.

A Synthetic View of the Variety of Marketing Environments

Trying to sum up natural complexity with a simple representation or model is not an easy task, and always slightly pretentious. However such a tentative synthesis might help to facilitate our understanding of the different marketing contexts, so we take the risk. Two of the elements that we have just presented seem to us to have more explanatory power than do some of the others. Using them in the matrix in Figure 1.9 allows us to show a simple classification of the various marketing environments that exist.

Figure 1.9   Matrix of the variety of the marketing environments

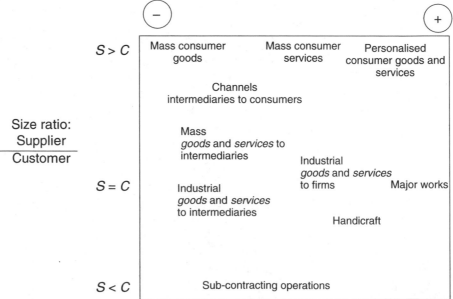

Intensity of supplier–customer interaction

Note: S = Supplier.
        C = Customer.

On the horizontal axis we have the *intensity* of the supplier–customer relationship. This varies from being very low in the case of Kevin Smith, right through to the intense relationship we described between PPG and Fiat. As we shall note many times in the forthcoming pages, this variable has major consequences for the design and implementation of marketing strategies. It has particular consequences for how a company should organise the marketing function, and also for how it defines and executes its daily operations.

The vertical axis attempts to capture the essence of the degree of *mutual dependence* between the respective forces. It does this through the use of very simple criteria: the ratio of the *relative supplier/customer size*. Utilisation of this single variable, relative size, masks a more complex notion of relative importance or power of the two players. However, that is too complex and subjective a criterion to be used here. We felt that the size ratio seems to explain enough of the variety between the different environments to justify its use.

Let us briefly offer some comments on each of the marketing environments that we identify in Figure 1.9:

- *Mass consumer goods marketing* corresponds to the very classical and publicly accepted view of marketing (Kotler, 1967). The managerial alternatives available to the manager in this environment are summarised by the well known 'marketing mix' concept as implemented by the firms we quoted above (Coca-Cola, Procter and Gamble, etc.). As a basis for the design of marketing strategies, the marketing mix is valid in this environment, but has no managerial validity in the other situations that we describe below. We particularly question the term 'industrial marketing mix' which has sometimes been employed. This book aims to demonstrate the practicality of our position. However, the marketing mix concept does raise a fundamental principle: the need for there to be coherence between the *objectives* of a marketing strategy and the approaches open to managers to *implementing* the strategy. In order to seek this coherence between strategy and implementation within the business-to-business environment, we propose the use of the 'Multistrat' model, which we introduce in Chapter 6.

- The field of *mass consumer services* (e.g. retail banking, or life assurance) has historically been the most critical of the triumphalism of the marketing mix (Shostack, 1977). The main difference between this environment and the mass consumer goods markets is that any service offering always requires the establishment of some form of personal relationship between the service provider and the recipient. This is of course missing in the marketing mix framework – it gives managers no indication of how to devise a strategy where personal relationships are involved. In our view, a higher level of supplier–customer interaction has to be considered when designing a service marketing strategy. This is examined further in Chapter 11, which focuses specifically on business-to-business services marketing.

- *Marketing of channel intermediaries to consumers* draws specificity from the fact that these organisations are in daily contact with their customers. Their marketing task consequently utilises some aspects from the marketing of service as well as from mass consumer goods.

■ *Marketing of mass consumer goods to channel intermediaries* is the traditional approach adopted in the fast moving consumer goods area, the strategy that Coca-Cola adopts in its interactions with Sainsbury's, Carrefour or Wal-Mart. This marketing environment has changed radically over the past few decades as retailers have grown in size from a small shop of about $40\,m^2$ (still the norm in many Mediterranean countries), into chains of multiple hypermarkets of up to 10 or $15\,000\,m^2$ more typically found in northern Europe. Within any given country there is a great difference between dealing with 100 000 small independent grocery retailers compared to interacting with a restricted number of large buying units, each representing hundreds of large stores. The relationships that are established between manufacturers of consumer goods and their distributors is a particular variant of business-to-business marketing, and as such many of the approaches developed in this book can be applied in such environments.

■ *Marketing of personalised consumer goods and services* requires a higher degree of interaction between the supplier and its customers than is implied by the marketing mix concept. The supplier needs to modify or readjust completely its whole organisation in order to make the relationship as personalised as possible. For example, Porsche, the well-known car manufacturer, will paint some models according to the wish of individual customers – which means that there are many models being driven indicating the football club colours of the players/owners. Or, for a small extra payment, Nike will personalise your shoe by superimposing your name over the 'swoosh' on the shoe. What is important here is to appreciate what this level of interaction implies for the supplier: all of its activities involving marketing communication, organisation, product design, the manufacturing process, pricing, and control need to be geared towards customer interaction. Obviously, therefore, this environment corresponds predominantly to luxury goods and services.

■ *Marketing of industrial goods and services to firms* lies at the very heart of this book. The same marketing principles are applicable to both manufacturers and distributors, and therefore we group these two categories together. However, these two different actors also establish particular kinds of links between themselves, as explained below.

■ *Marketing of industrial goods and services to intermediaries* belongs to a particular marketing environment that we shall examine in some detail in Chapter 8. A high degree of interaction is often established in order to try and ensure satisfaction to the final user.

■ *Handicraft marketing* is a pretty much ignored in the marketing literature. It is characterised by an extremely high degree of supplier–customer interaction (see Kevin Smith above) that craftsmen have to understand and master in order to succeed.

- *Major works marketing* is a very different, from both buyer and supplier perspectives. It implies a very high level of interaction with very specific characteristics. The practice of formalised project management exerts a strong influence on proper business-to-business marketing. We dedicate a specific chapter to this subject (Chapter 12), and shall often refer to these characteristics throughout the book.

- Finally, *sub-contracting marketing* also exists. This refers to those marketing situations where a supplier, very often smaller than its customer, carries out work that is largely defined by the customer. The fundamentals of business-to-business marketing apply fully in such environments.

Our objective in the section above is to show that the design and implementation of marketing strategies have to be *adapted* to the various different marketing environments. Marketing managers must understand this diversity, and be able to identify the characteristics of the different environments within which they act. The main thrust of this book is dedicated to the environment described above as 'marketing of industrial goods and services to firms'. This is the area on which we focus, even if some characteristics are applicable in other areas (such as organisations, associations or public bodies that are not 'firms' in the commercial sense of the word). In addition to this, we also deal with some particular environments (e.g. services, major works, technological innovation) that serve to enlarge our perspective.

We acknowledge, but do not expand upon in any more depth here, the affect that *e-commerce* is having and will continue to have upon how markets operate. In terms of Figure 1.10, it will decrease the importance of the size ratio as a meaningful analytical tool, while also altering the possible intensity of the supplier–customer interaction. So we can both have closer relationships brought about by highly personalised electronic linkages, or more 'hands-off' relationships via electronic auctions.

Returning to the Notion of a Marketplace

Traditional economical theory defines a market as the place where the seller's offer and the buyer's demand interact, and end with the agreement on a price. The definition of a market requires:

- agreement on the definition of the product, its offer and its demand
- organised contact between sellers and buyers
- visible competition between sellers and buyers
- the definition of a geographical area
- the formalisation of the transaction through an agreement or a contract.

It is then possible to define the world market (or European or Chinese) for cola-based drinks, cars, or whatever. This concept of a market is based on the economists' model of pure and perfect competition, which is also the foundation for the marketing mix concept. However, we have introduced the notion that a variety of marketing environments exist. We described these by looking at the size ratio between suppliers and customers as one dimension, and the intensity of the supplier–customer relationship as the other. But if there are various types of marketing practice, is this not because there are different types of markets? So we would argue that while we do need a definition of a marketplace for both operational purposes (What's the size of this market? What's our market share?) and understanding how it functions (Who are the major players? Just how do we interact with our customers?), that definition cannot be based on the concept of pure and perfect competition.

Economic theory recognises the fact that the pure and perfect model of competition relies on a set of unrealistic assumptions. It consequently introduces complementary theories leading to the definition of markets with imperfect competition (monopolistic competition and oligopolies) or indeed those with an absence of competition (monopolies, oligopsonies or monopsonies). However, these have proved to be insufficient to characterise the functioning of all markets, and so further theories have been formulated. We shall mention just two of them: the theory of *transaction costs* and that of the *social construction* of markets. We provide just a brief summary of these theories below, and the interested reader should consult the references provided.

Transaction cost theory (Williamson, 1975, 1985) starts with the observation that the execution of any exchange (or transaction) carries associated *costs*: costs of acquiring information, costs of accessing the market, costs of negotiations, etc. Markets can therefore be classified according to the level of costs incurred. Managers then try to reduce these costs by establishing more efficient methods of organising their exchanges. One of these methods is the establishment of 'hierarchies' between actors, i.e. the domination of one actor by another (e.g. via vertical integration, supply chain management, etc.). Observation of business-to-business markets shows that many of them display such hierarchical structures (e.g. the integration through capital acquisition of its distributors by a major steel producer) or quasi-hierarchies (long-term, single-source contracts between a supplier and a customer). There is an underlying issue here, that the transaction *cost* of a product is not always equal to its purchase *price*. If a different method of exchange allows a company to reduce its transaction cost, the buying price is only one element of the true global cost. So we find that two actors may be able to find a better level of utility (i.e. value creation for both of them) by going much further than managing the plain transfer of ownership of a good based on price competition. These fundamental issues of supply chain management can all be interpreted using the notion of interaction that we presented earlier.

The notion of the *social construction of markets* (Favereau, 1989; Saglio, 1990) brings more of a sociological perspective to the observation of how markets operate. According to Saglio, 'sociologists observe that real markets are systems of conventions historically built by the interaction of several actors'. There is, he argues, no one basic model as the classical economists alleged, but rather there are a variety of ways in which markets can function. For example, a particular industry might currently apply a range of discounts to its customers. However, going beyond the generally accepted range will end with a price war, and hence no one 'breaks the rules'. We see that there have been co-operation mechanisms between firms from the first days of industrial activity that served to determine dimensional standards, which in turn established compatibility between different products (railway gauge to dimension bogies, wheel and tyre dimensions for cars, etc.) or quality standards to facilitate choice (Woolmark = pure wool). From this perspective, the issue is to build relationships between (often competing) stakeholders that lead to a simplification and regularity of the transactions. This depends largely upon the construction of *mutual trust*, which again is basic to our interaction approach.

To conclude, marketing is vital because it helps firms maximise the chance of relating efficiently to their markets. However, just what is 'efficient' will vary according to the particular marketing environment. In this first chapter we have outlined an approach to help us in identifying the various possible environments. In the rest of the book we examine those in a business-to-business field more closely.

References and Further Reading

Bagozzi, R.P. (1975) 'Marketing as Exchange', *Journal of Marketing*, 39, 32–9.

Balbontin, A. *et al.* (1999) 'New Product Development Success Factors in American and British Firms', *International Journal of Technology Management*, 17:3, 259–80.

Bartels, R. (1968) 'The General Theory of Marketing', *Journal of Marketing*, January, 29–33.

Blois, K. (1974) 'The Marketing of Services: An Approach', *European Journal of Marketing*, 2, 137–45.

Bonoma, T.V. and Johnston, W.J. (1978) 'The Social Psychology of Industrial Buying and Selling', *Industrial Marketing Management*, 7, 213–24.

Booz-Allen & Hamilton (1982) *New Product Management for the 1980s*, New York, Booz-Allen & Hamilton.

Brown, L. and McDonald, M.H. (1994) *Competitive Strategy for Europe: Developing, Maintaining and Defending Competitive Advantage*, London, Palgrave Macmillan.

Cooper, R.G. (1988) 'Predevelopment Activities Determine New Product Success', *Industrial Marketing Management*, 17, 237–47.

Corey, E.R. (1962) *Industrial Marketing, Cases and Concepts*, Englewood Cliffs, Prentice-Hall.

Favereau, O. (1989) 'Marché interne/marché externe', *Revue Française d'Économie*, 40:2, 152–74.

Fern, E.F. and Brown, J.R. (1984) 'The Industrial Consumer Marketing Dichotomy: A Case of Insufficient Justification', *Journal of Marketing*, 12, 68–77.

Ford, D. *et al.* (1998) *Managing Business Relationships*, New York, Wiley.

Gale, B.T. (1994) *Managing Customer Value*, New York, Free Press.

Grönroos, C. (1990) *Service Management and Marketing: Managing the Moments of Truth in Service Competition*, Lexington, Lexington Books.

Håkansson, H. and Österberg, C. (1975) 'Industrial Marketing – An Organisational Problem?', *Industrial Marketing Management*, 4, 113–23.

Håkansson, H. and Snehota, I. (1995) *Developing Relationships in Business Networks*, London, Routledge & Kegan Paul.

Homan, G.G. (1961) *Social Behavior: Its Elementary Forms*, New York, Harcourt Brace.

Kotler, P. (1967) *Marketing Management, Analysis, Planning, Implementation and Control*, Englewood Cliffs, Prentice-Hall.

Porter, M.E. (1985) *Competitive Advantage: Creating and Sustaining Superior Performance*, New York, Free Press.

Porter, M.E. (1990) *The Competitive Advantage of Nations*, London, Palgrave Macmillan.

Porter, M.E. (1998) *On Competition*, Boston, Harvard Business Review Books.

Saglio, J. (1990) 'La construction sociale des marchés', Paris, Rapport GLYSI.

Shostack, L. (1977) 'Breaking Free from Product Marketing', *Journal of Marketing*, 41:2, 73–80.

Texier, E. and Valla, J.-P. (1988) *Epistémologie et marketing industriel: object, paradigme et classification*, Cahiers Lyonnais de Recherche en Gestion.

Webster, F.E. (1992) 'The Changing Role of Marketing in the Corporation', *Journal of Marketing*, 4, 1–17.

Williamson, O.E. (1975) *Markets and Hierarchies*, New York, Free Press.

Williamson. O.E. (1985) *The Economic Institution of Capitalism*, New York, Free Press.

Woodward, J. (1965) *Industrial Organisation: Behaviour and Control*, Oxford, Oxford University Press.

Discussion Questions

1 Why should you study Business-to-Business marketing?

2 Can you name some suppliers in Business-to-Business environments in at least two different industrial sectors? Can you then name some of their customers?

3 Comment on the idea that a marketing strategy model such as the 'marketing mix' model is specific to a very specific marketing environment? And which one?

4 Can you express some arguments supporting the idea that different marketing strategic models have to be designed for different marketing environments?

5 Why is the customer involved in many steps of the process of building a supplier's value chain?

Chapter 1
Competitiveness, Marketing and Business-to-Business Marketing
What is marketing all about
Different marketing environments
B2B marketing

Chapter 2
Business-to-Business Customers and Markets

B2B Generic Offers	Technological Innovation	Pure Services	Major Projects

PART I   STRATEGY FOUNDATIONS

Chapter 3	Chapter 4	Chapter 5	Chapter 6
Understanding Business-to-Business Purchasing	Information and Information Systems	Markets and Suppliers' Strategy	Segmentation and Marketing Strategy

PART II   STRATEGY IMPLEMENTATION

Chapter 7			
Generic Business-to-Business Offer Design and Management			

Chapter 8	Chapter 10	Chapter 11	Chapter 12
Market Access and Customer Management	Marketing and Technological Innovation	The Marketing of Services	Major Project Marketing

Chapter 9
Communication and Publicity/ Advertising

PART III   STRATEGY DESIGN

Chapter 13	The Role and Organisation of Marketing
Chapter 14	Customer Position, Market Position, Marketing Strategies and Planning
Chapter 15	Issues and Specificities of International Marketing
Annex	The Internet and Marketing: Some Ideas

2 Business-to-Business Customers and Markets

In Chapter 1 we defined marketing as the function of the firm in charge of the necessary interaction with markets and customers. Marketing has to understand what constitutes value for customers, to transmit this understanding within the firm, and manage the ways in which value will be created and promoted. We asserted that the level of interaction might vary depending on whether the firm is involved in simulated or direct interaction with its customers. Based on this approach, we argued that there were several different marketing environments, each requiring a particular marketing approach. We also briefly mentioned in the Introduction that the term 'business-to-business' does not correspond to a single approach to marketing, as is often implied. It is time now to be more precise about what constitutes the business-to-business world. Our aim is to define the common characteristics of business-to-business markets, and also to provide the reader with insights for simultaneously understanding their differences.

Four main aspects can be used to identify the different facets of business-to-business market environments. These are described briefly and then discussed in more below:

1. *The question of market definition: the Technologies–Applications dilemma*
Defining the business or the boundaries of the product market in question lies at the very heart of the marketing task. It is absolutely necessary to measure major indicators such as the volume or the value of the overall market or the market share. Within a business-to-business situation this definition is not obvious. For example, a producer of steel sheets may well define its overall market as being 'steel sheets'. But it may then look at various application sectors such as car manufacturing, building industry, shipbuilding or computers. Each of these application sectors calls for a specific, sometimes significant, commitment in terms of the technology involved on the part of any potential supplier if it is to be considered as one of the players in that sector. Both perspectives seem to be complementary at first glance. However, a company has to make *trade-offs*. It can usually not compete in all potential technology–application areas, and so they compete as far as the firm's resources are concerned. As we shall see below, making choices between different product markets lies at the heart of the firm's strategy.

2. *Demand market structures*

Suppliers face different market structures, mainly in terms of buyer concentration. For example, a firm's marketing strategy cannot be undertaken in the same way if it has 15 major customers worldwide, as in the case of with car manufacturers, or with 5 million garages, as in the case of car maintenance.

3. *The supplier–customer interaction and its consequences*

The classical definition of a market and of competitive situations as proposed by the economists is not applicable in the case of exchanges between firms. As noted in Chapter 1, the interaction concept implies *durable links* between any supplier and its customer base. The reality of these links requires us to change our notion of a market, understanding the role that relationships and ongoing adaptation play in business-to-business markets.

4. *The impact of the environment*

The analysis of a firm's environment reveals its position as one of the players in a broader group of industrial operations, value chains or clusters. These affect its competitiveness and its organisation. These notions allow us not only to have a better understanding of the conditions of a supplier's activity but also of its customers. They bring a complementary and insightful understanding through ordering and structuring the world in which the firm is acting. The environment is not a simple group of forces that affects the firm, and to which it has to adapt. It is a field in which the firm is placed, that brings threats but also some possibilities.

Some of the ideas that we are to develop in this chapter have already been mentioned in Chapter 1. We shall define them in a more precise way in order to deepen our understanding of business-to-business markets and their diversity. Firms very often have to act simultaneously in different market environments, and that leads them to adapt their internal organisation in order to be efficient in each of the markets. Marketing managers in business-to-business environments also move from one environment to the other, and must therefore be able to adapt their ways of operating. It is necessary for any marketing manager to grasp the dynamics and functioning of the business-to-business markets as being different from the more typical consumer perspective. What we will deal with here is valid from two perspectives: the supplier's position and activity *and* the customers' dynamics and behaviour. Later on in the book (Chapter 3) we shall align ourselves more closely with the suppliers' perspective.

Market Definition: The Technology–Application Dilemma

One of the most commonly accepted definitions of a market is the mapping of a particular product onto a particular customer group. Selling lawnmowers for amateur gardeners defines a different market from selling lawnmowers for profes-

Figure 2.1 The technologies–applications matrix

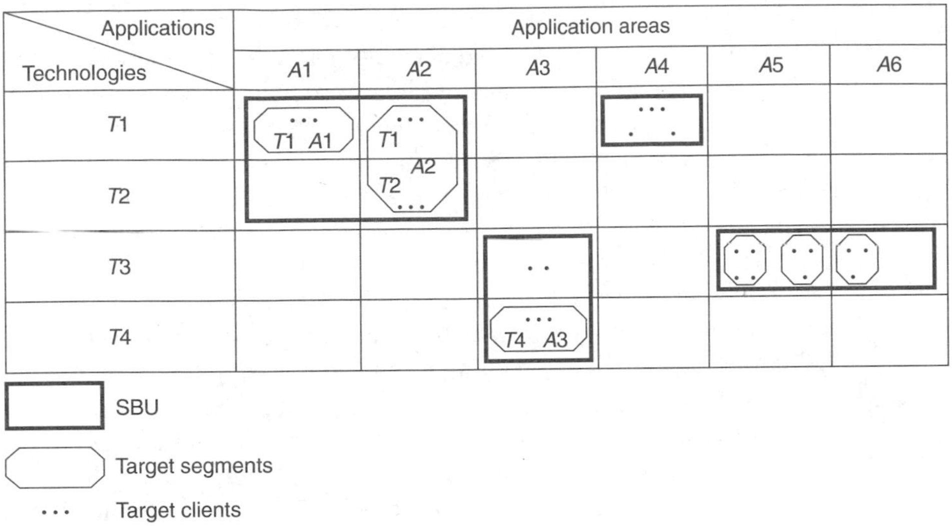

Applications / Technologies	Application areas					
	A1	A2	A3	A4	A5	A6
T1	··· T1 A1	··· T1		··· · ·		
T2		A2 T2 ···				
T3			· ·		·· ·· ··	
T4			··· T4 A3			

☐ SBU

⬡ Target segments

··· Target clients

sionals, and selling seeds to amateur gardeners is another market altogether. Similar or different technologies give birth to different products aimed at various types of customers. Each overlap between customers and products defines a particular *market*. However in the business-to-business environment firms possess and develop technologies, and the word 'technology' implies a much broader view than 'product' and provides access to a great variety of industrial sectors. Thus a steel manufacturer can develop sheets for car bodies, ships, building, aeroplanes, trains, submarines and so on. In each case it would meet different types of customer request and in each case different competitors and different substitute materials as well. A different steel sheet is needed for the making of the doors or of the bonnet of a car. Each of these cases can be defined as an *application* of the technology to a particular use. So it is possible to describe the range of markets accessible by any particular technology as a set of different applications. As a firm usually develops related or complementary or even different technologies, the accessible range can be described as a *technology–applications matrix* (Figure 2.1).

It is therefore possible to define the firm's *accessible market* as the complete set of applications open to the development of its technologies. The intersection between a set of technologies and an application can be described as a market on its own or a *market segment*, meaning that the requests of the corresponding customers are relatively homogeneous. It does happen that some of these intersections present a high degree of similarity, and they can then be grouped within the same definition of a market or a market segment.

Depending on the firm's capabilities, and also on the capabilities of the competitors and/or substitute technologies in each potential application, some of the available applications are not really open to the firm. It then has to choose between the potentially accessible applications. This choice allows us to define the *real market*.

The differences between the accessible and the real market are not set in stone. They depend on the dynamics of the firm's technologies, as well as on those of the competition and also on the evolution of the requests of the customers. At one point a firm can hold a strong position in one 'market' owing to the impact of its technologies. If its technologies are then threatened by substitute ones, whether new or old boosted through new developments or regulation, the firm is likely to lose business. It then faces a major choice. It can either pursue the development of its technologies in order to gain access to other markets or market segments (other technology–application intersection), or it can also acquire substitute technologies with the intention of maintaining its position on an application. In any case it means that the mastering of an application requires important *investments* from a supplier. We find here one of the foundations of strategic choices and of the firm's resources allocation, questions examined in detail in Chapters 5, 6 and 7.

This implies that strategies might be technology or application oriented. This argument is not new in the marketing world (see, for example, Bennet and Cooper, 1979) since the question has often been raised as to whether a firm's strategy should be market or technology oriented. These authors mention differences between consumer and business-to-business markets, arguing that a marketing strategy for consumer goods would normally be market oriented. But they were sceptical about the application of such a definition to business-to-business environments, having in mind the ways technology develops through mostly technically defined paths. While we share their concern, we are not sure that a completely technology-based strategy is the answer either. As one of the executives of the Alcatel Group said to us '*Once we have the customer, we will always develop the necessary technologies to serve and keep them.*' True, this came from a company more oriented to the major works part of the business-to-business world, and one therefore more accustomed to the assembly of partners and technologies to serve a customer. In fact we find here a *market-based strategy*. And this opportunity is not limited to that particular type of marketing environment and is open to any strategic process, as the example of the development of the firm Plastic Omnium shows (Example 1 and Figure 2.2).

Example 1 and Figure 2.2 reveals a new strategic alternative. In the past, suppliers tried to offer their customers alternative technical solutions. For example, a glass manufacturer in England might invest in a plastic packing unit. But they remained two different business units following their own strategies with only some areas of co-ordination. However, the plastic packing unit was later sold to a large plastic packing manufacturer. Plastic Omnium presents an entirely different story. It presents its customers with an offer generated by a *portfolio of technologies* and undertakes all research in order to optimise choices in each case from the customer's perspective. This approach will lead us to question (Chapter 5) some approaches to strategic decision making, and to propose a marketing strategy based upon first analysing the technologies–applications issues. But already we have to modify the

Example 1   Strategic Development of Plastic Omnium

This firm was founded in 1947 to exploit the new possibilities of plastic materials, then still relatively unknown. Starting with one technology (injection of materials such as cellulose products) for one application (technical parts for cars: armrests, for example), it developed either through applying newer technologies, or through investing in new applications. The matrix below gives a simplified representation of this evolution that took place over some 50 years.

We can see that the international and highly diversified Group stemming from the initial firm faced major choices of investment and resource allocation between multiple technologies and applications in which it had to invest in order to maintain its competitive capacity. As the Group's strategic objective was to be a world leader in its activities, its evolution was realised through successive acquisitions of French and foreign firms. The international development also required investments to gain a foothold in many countries. This resulted in a level of debt that the management wanted to reduce.

This series of evolutions and reflections led Plastic Omnium to sell its 'inside car equipment division' to the American Visteon on 30 June 1999. This asset disposal allowed the company to reinforce its leading position in other activities from a sounder financial base. And that is where the approach is interesting. Beginning as a part manufacturer (producing parts on quotations based on customers' design), the firm progressively became a subsystem designer (design of complete systems, such as whole instrument panels). A further step was implemented when Plastic Omnium started to undertake the complete research required for the design of a new model for a car manufacturer. This evolution, whereby they undertook the overall design of the petrol tank circuit, led Plastic Omnium to offer their customer a choice among all the available technologies. At this point, the supplier has little credibility if it remains just a 'plastic transformer' – it must show an equal mastery of all the possible technologies. This requires considerable investment in terms of Research and Development, Manufacturing Technology and Marketing, and also in its capacity to integrate the customer's development team. This movement is possible only through significant internal reorganisation (new competencies and know-how, new allocation of internal and external resources). It also enables the company to develop a new ability to spot and integrate resources belonging to other organisations, through acquisitions or co-operation agreements. So Plastic Omnium followed a strategy based on the mastering of an application for which it developed and assembled the necessary *technologies, competences and resources*. This remarkable move was made possible through a very narrow co-operation with one of its historical customers, Renault. In such a case a simultaneous and parallel redeployment of resources has to take place at both the supplier and at the customer.

Note: In 2001, *Plastic Omnium* covers 5 activities: Automotive External Equipment, Energy Automotive Systems, Services, High-Performance Plastic Materials and Medical. It employs more than 7000 staff worldwide and achieves a turnover of nearly 1200 million Euros in 24 countries <www.plasticomnium.fr/groupe/index.shtml>

perspective of the matrix in Figure 2.1. The Plastic Omnium example shows that the question cannot be fully understood by simply studying the technology–applications overlap. A supplier combining all the competences, know-how and resources necessary to cover continuously all the possible ways to realise an application can cover an application. The question is a fundamental reflection on all the resources–applications overlaps. This leads us to propose an enlarged reflection scheme (Figure 2.3) where the term 'technologies' is replaced by that of *resources*:

Figure 2.2   Plastic Omnium: technologies–applications development

Applications / Technologies	Automotive	Domestic appliances	Household rubbish collection	Playgrounds	General industry	Pharmacutical Industry
T₁ INJECTION ■ Cellulose	Technical parts (1947)	Technical parts (1948)		Modular		Ophthalmology ferrules and stoppers (1946)
■ Polypropylene and others materials	Instrument-board (1967) Fenders (1978)		Dustbins (1964)	Parts for		Vaccination rings (1962)
T₂ BLOWING	Tanks and motor-fuel circuits (1986)			Children's		
T₃ ROTOMOULDING	Petrol tank circuit			Games (1986)		
T₄ FLUOR RESINS TRANSFORMATION					Special parts (1966)	
T₅ TRANSFORMATION OF PLASTICS WITHIN STERILE CONDITIONS						Parts for medical diagnosis (1992)

Figure 2.3   The applications–resources matrix

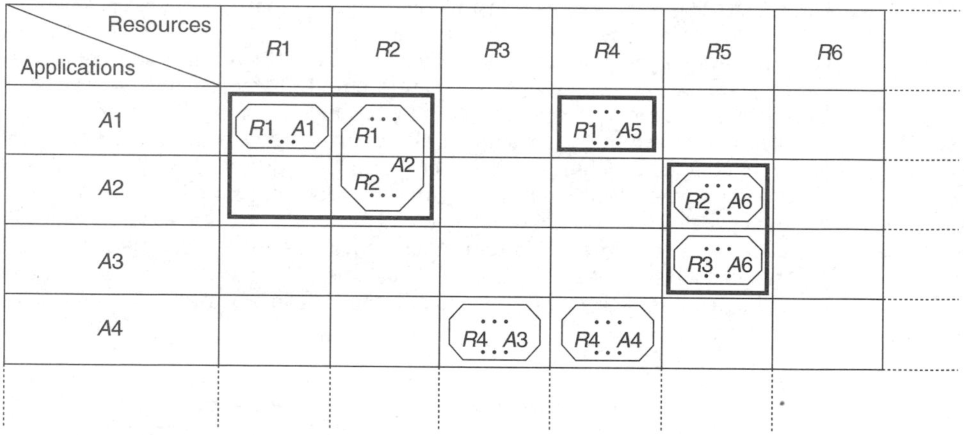

human, technological, competences, financial, know-how and internal organisation and external co-operation and partnership agreements. This scheme also seems suited to other marketing environments, such as the service industry. In these activities, competences are often more important than technology. Mory–Ancel (Example 5) is good illustration of this point.

The applications–resources matrix provides a broader perspective than Figure 2.1. Its purpose is to alter the logic somewhat: if all the initial development steps at Plastic Omnium were explained through the technologies–applications matrix, we would not find any hint of the last development, the petrol tank circuits. The important point is that this development came about through the company undertaking research based on its own resources. It is a case of the supplier undertaking tasks *previously handled by the customer itself*, a phenomenon that is increasingly prevalent in the automobile and other industries.

The conclusion that we want to stress here is that the very basis of developing a marketing strategy in a business-to-business environment lies in reflecting on the interaction between resources and applications. The other elements of strategy depend on this initial approach.

Structures of the Demand Market

In Figure 2.1 we indicated three strategic groups: SBUs, target segments and target customers. That was deliberate. In a business-to-business environment, marketing takes into account the notion of the market as well as that of an individual customer, depending on the level of detail required. The individual size and the number of customers that a supplier is serving are important elements for the definition of a marketing strategy. This is not linked to the broad definition of an industrial sector, such as the car industry for example. Within this industry, part- or sub-assembly manufacturers might have roughly 25 (or fewer) customers worldwide, if we think of a customer[1] as being a large group such as General Motors, Toyota or Volkswagen. But a garage equipment manufacturer may have something like 5 million customers, on the same geographical basis. Who could naively claim that these two types of suppliers can develop the same marketing approach on the ground that they act in the same business-to-business industry?

As Figure 2.4 shows, we have a very broad view of a continuum of business-to-business environments, according to the degree of concentration of the customers.

A *dispersed customer base* leads a firm to utilise a marketing approach that takes some of its characteristics from consumer goods marketing, although with major differences as well. As we shall see with the Multistrat Model (Chapter 6), the marketing approach starts with the technological choices of the firm that open a broadly

Figure 2.4   Continuum of business-to-business marketing environments

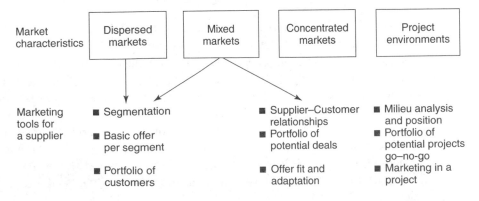

defined market. This market is then *segmented* (see Chapter 5) in order to define a *basic segment offer* that is designed to appeal to the needs of a well-defined segment of the market with a rather standardised solution. Within this segment all the customers do not offer the same degree of attractiveness for the supplier, which means that suppliers need to make choices among their possible customers and to manage their *portfolio of customers*.

A *concentrated customer base* presents a completely different picture. Here, there is very little possibility of the supplier being able to choose between customers, and each one has to be considered as a major potential buyer. Therefore the main task is to establish and maintain *customer–supplier relationships*. But an established relationship gives rise to a variety of deals that are not equally attractive or profitable to the supplier, who then has to manage a *portfolio of deals*. The importance of each customer, and the differences between the deals, lead suppliers to be able to manage an *offer adaptation* in each case, based on the same core technological bases and competences.

Projects or major works present yet another picture. Most often the customer is a one-off assembly involving a one-off application. Each operation is often very large (a dam, a bridge, a large toll system, a turn-key factory, a Millennium Dome, etc.) and both the customer and the implementation will never appear again in exactly the same form. Marketing in such environments consists of three steps. These are permanently *watching the milieu* inside which the relevant actors are preparing further operations; *screening the deals* in order to decide whether the supplier should get involved (the go/no-go decision) and under what form; and finally *marketing within a deal*, working with all the players involved on both the customer and supply side in order to build the final offer and have it chosen by the customer. Chapter 12 will develop in some detail this particular form of marketing.

As we stated earlier, firms often deal with different market structures. These *mixed customer bases* lead to differences in marketing organisations and methods. A good choice can be made only if managers are conscious of all these differences, and establish the degree of variety linked to the specific environment of their firm.

The Interaction Concept and its Consequences

The Alcatel executive quoted on p. 32 used the word 'customer' to describe his strategic orientation, not the terms 'market' or 'market segment'. In doing so, he expressed one of the main characteristics of business-to-business marketing – that is, considering a particular, single customer as a strategic group in itself. But he was just expressing their current business practice. These practices were investigated in some detail by the European IMP Research Group (Håkansson, 1982; Turnbull and Valla, 1986). These investigations led researchers to focus attention on the individual behaviour of the internal actors involved in a relationship, and at the same time on the institutional outcomes of such behaviour. The main theoretical result of this stream of research is the importance given to the concept of cus-

Table 2.1   Characteristics of 139 supplier–customer relationships in Europe

Criteria	Semi-finished products	Components	Capital goods
Average length of the relationship	13.55 years	9.60 years	11.09 years
Average number of adaptations from the customer	4.05	4.17	4.77
Average number of adaptations from the supplier	3.90	4.04	4.98
Customer's human resources investment: average number of individuals concerned	7.18	13.5	14.0
Supplier's human resources investment: average number of individuals concerned	8.7	7.1	5.7

Source: Primary research carried out at EM Lyon.

tomer–supplier relationships. It is during this interaction that relationships are managed, a perspective that lies at the very heart of understanding the dynamics of business-to-business markets.

Supplier–Customer Relationships

The characteristics of these relationships, resulting from observations that we have made over the years (and summarised in Table 2.1), identify several essential features:

■ The first is the *active participation of the two partners*, which can be seen from the way in which both parties adapt to each other's requirements during the relationship. This clearly goes with the definition of direct interaction developed in Chapter 1, with each partner explaining their requirements and being the initiator of new proposals.

■ The second is the notion of *reciprocal investment*. Both parties commit important resources, whether human, technical or financial, to find a solution to the problem in the customer's activity. This notion of reciprocal investment can be empirically linked to simple analytical tools, for example by trying to assess the cost of a relationship, either during its creation (see Figure 2.4, for example), or at any other time during the life of an exchange relationship.

■ These first two characteristics are linked to the fact, already underlined in Chapter 1, that the object of the exchange has to be understood as the *supplier's contribution to its customer's activity*. Here again there is a large variety in the extent of the contribution, but that is always the way in which to analyse a supplier–customer relationship: as a supplier, how can I best contribute to my customer's activity? Even if objects exchanged can be described as banal (or commodities), suppliers never are 'commodities'. As suppliers of efficiency and productivity, they can always differentiate.

■ The number of people involved in the relationship is often high on both sides, which suggests the existence of a *supplier's selling centre* able to meet the demands of a customer's *decision making unit*. The relationships between those involved is an indication of the importance assumed by the social exchanges, required as much for the technical elaboration of solutions as in the construction of reciprocal confidence upon which the efficiency of the exchange process relies.

■ The *stability of relationships* is the outcome of the interdependence between supplier and customer in an inter-company environment as soon as the relationship appears to be profitable for both parties. It is also linked to the fact that a satisfying relationship with a supplier represents an investment for the customer. The customer must check the supplier's reliability, learn to work with them, establish confidence, exchange technical information, and carry out tests together. These tasks cannot easily be done with a number of suppliers at the same time. Once the customer has chosen a supplier, that customer must attempt to capitalise on the investment. Of course, the same goes for the supplier.

The example in Table 2.2 provides some real data from an actual buyer–seller relationship, summarising the set of operations that were conducted to establish a new relationship. It illustrates with precise details the concept of supplier–customer relationships. *P* is a paint manufacturer, targeting the market segment of car wheels (because it possessed a technology well suited to the specific requirements of wheel painting). *D* is an important (6 million wheels a year) British wheel manufacturer that *P* recognised as a potential target customer. Developing detailed efforts to gain *D*'s business was seen as a core part of *P*'s commercial action plan.

In Chapter 3 we will go into more detail in developing our understanding of customers' buying behaviour and also in developing practical tools for a supplier (particularly the risk approach model). But we still have to describe other aspects of business-to-business marketing that need to be taken into account in order to give a broader picture of the different environments encountered by managers. We showed above the results of some research work that indicated average numbers on some important criteria and one example of live interaction. But having described the different elements that make up the interaction phenomenon, we must, however, understand in more detail how and why the degree of direct interaction can vary from one environment to another.

The Interaction Model

The main characteristics of the interaction model are shown in Figure 2.5. It is easy to see that this is an extension of the commercial exchange model presented in Chapter 1 (Figure 1.9).

Table 2.2 Example of the process and the cost of building a new supplier–customer relationship

Dates	P^b	I	D^a	I
1 Jun.	**Initiation** ■ Commercial approach, contacts, visits, meetings, cost analysis, first proposal		■ Change of the managing director ■ 10 persons visit P	
15 Jul.		20 mds^c	CONSIDER P AS A POSSIBLE SUPPLIER	10 mds
15 Jul.	**Preparation of final decision** ■ Selection of right technology, survey of D's plant, trial in pilot tank, laboratory tests and checks, trial programme Painting 1000 wheels, check tests with D's customers		■ Technical meetings, specifications, checks, investments in equipment ■ Trial programmes with customers ■ Draft of specifications document	
30 Nov.		300 mds	APPROVAL SUBJECT TO A MAJOR CUSTOMER'S DECISION FINAL OK	60 mds
30 Nov.	**Preparation of the order process** ■ Contract, pricing ■ Cleaning programme, cleaning and filling main tank ■ Initial trials and laboratory tests		■ Contract, pricing ■ Cleaning and filling ■ Disposals	
2 Jan.	PLANT READY FOR PRODUCTION	30 mds	PLANT READY FOR PRODUCTION	30 mds
2 Jan.	**Starting production**		**Starting production**	
1 Apr.		100 mds		100 mds
	Expenses	100 000	Expenses	55 000
	Total mds	450	Total mds	200

Notes:
a: D (col 4) is a vehicle wheel manufacturer.
b: P (col 2) is a paint supplier.
c: Mds = man-days.

The interaction model consists of four facets, which offer both a conceptual basis that is useful for understanding exchange dynamics, and also a methodological basis, which has given rise to the methods and working tools presented throughout this book:

■ *Participants in the interaction*: both supplier and customer can be analysed individually as a social system by including the individual's personal stakes within their organisation (individual objectives, expectations and experiences). There also has to be acceptance of the fact that these characteristics are also influenced by the particular strategy of the firm and the particular project(s) being undertaken.

Figure 2.5   The interaction model

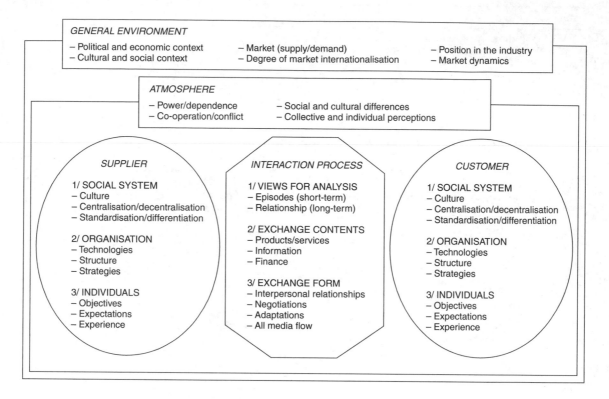

- *The interaction process* itself can be analysed from a short-term perspective (the transaction: episodes, incidents, negotiations, interpersonal contacts, etc.) or using a long-term perspective (the relationship length, stability, allocation of resources, etc.).

- *The atmosphere of the relationship* involves the climate that exists between the two parties. It is based on mutual dependence or a feeling of dependence, co-operation, cultural and social differences, and mutual confidence or lack thereof. It conditions the process of interaction as much as being the result of it;

- *The general environment* indicates that the interaction takes place in a broader context, which partly conditions the way in which it operates. This can be analysed as follows:

  - The *general economic, social and political environment*, whose influence can be clearly identified in a given relationship. For example, interest rate instability and exchange rate fluctuations can affect the way in which a supplier interacts with its customers, by greatly affecting the relative short-term position of suppliers from other countries.

■ The *environment close to the supplier* (the competitors, and the company's position in relation to their own supplier base) can help to explain a supplier's relative competitive position;

■ The *environment close to a customer* (their competitors and customers, the relationship network of which the company is a part) also supplies us with information concerning exchange conditions.

The interaction model is one of the major theoretical foundations of the approach that will be presented in the chapters that follow. It contains the essential concepts for a detailed analysis of relationships in an intercompany environment. But, as we said earlier, it takes various forms according to the types of relationships that are established between suppliers and customers.

The Degrees of Direct Interaction

The identification in Table 2.3 of low and high degrees of interaction characterises the extreme positions in a continuum. Occupying a particular position on this continuum in a given period partly corresponds to the constraints that market conditions and customer demands have on the supplier. But a supplier does have some

Table 2.3 The degrees of direct interaction

Degrees of interaction / Criteria	Low	High
Number of customers	Hundreds, thousands	Some units, tens, hundreds
Degree of interaction in the design of the object of the exchange	Low	High
Mode of determination of the object of the exchange	Mainly set before selling	Jointly built before, while and after selling
Nature of the offering	Not really open, slightly negotiable, adaptable only on secondary elements	Open, flexible Modular Widely negotiable on all its elements
Status of the customer	Named, personalised	Named, personalised
Type of social exchange with the customers	Personalised relationship Low frequency of contacts Use of distribution channels Reduced selling group Predominance of the buying function at the customers	Personalised relationship High frequency of contacts Rare use of distributors Complex selling group Complex buying centre at the customers
Major criteria for the success of the marketing strategy	Market share	Position achieved with each customer and on the market

choice, and can offer customers a range of issues open to negotiation, dependent upon both its competitive position and its global competitiveness. To meet the variety of customer demands, a supplier can adopt one of two strategies. The first is to build a (large? reduced?) range of standard offers. The second is to design an adaptable offer based on a combination of modules rooted in the same technological core and expertise. We shall develop this point further in Chapter 7.

So far we have explored the particularities of the relationships between suppliers and customers in a business-to-business environment. We have already mentioned that decisions in such a situation do not depend only on these relationships but also on 'external' factors rooted in the environment of both players. Looking at these factors will be our next step.

The Impact of the Environment

Different concepts and frameworks have emerged in the economic and business community in order better to understand the issues of the general economy of a country, of an industrial sector, or of a particular firm. These are important, and while Chapter 1 did mention some of the external opportunities and constraints that partly shape the strategy of a firm, we need to discuss them in more detail.

The Value Chain

We concluded Chapter 1 by underlining the role of marketing, together with the other company functions, in the determination, creation and promotion of the distinctive value of the company. Let us now develop this notion by using Michael Porter's ideas of the value chain (Figure 2.6).

The concept of the value chain has two bases. First, company strategy involves the creation of *competitive advantage* which corresponds to a *value* which is recognised by the customers and whose market price is greater than the costs involved, which in turn leads to a profit margin (see Chapter 4). Secondly, Porter's approach implies that all company activities contribute to the creation of this value, and hence to the company's relative competitive position. Thus, it is important to analyse the company in a way that highlights the interdependence of activities and consequently their contribution to the creation of value. The distinction between supporting activities and primary activities clearly emphasises that the process of creating and marketing the offer makes up the strategic backbone of the company.

One example will clarify our interest in the concept. A supplier of rigid plastic packaging designed a new box spray for use in the gardening industry (a box spray is a plastic container filled with some kind of garden insecticide: the box typically has a moveable section that can be pumped in order to release the powder inside). The supplier approached a producer of garden products, and proposed replacing their current plastic box sprays with a plastic model costing 20 per cent less, and

Figure 2.6   The value chain

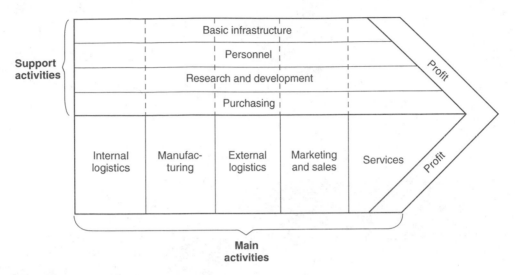

Reprinted with the permission of The Free Press, an imprint of Simon & Schuster Adult Publishing Group, from *Competitive Advantage: Creating and Sustaining Superior Performance* by Michael E. Porter. Copyright © 1985, 1998 by Michael E. Porter.

which also had many other advantages (resistance to humidity, for example). The purchasing and marketing services department accepted the offer and launched the new boxes, much to the satisfaction of the supplier. Unfortunately, due to a problem of internal co-ordination, the production department noticed a difference in size and rigidity of the new model that led to a 50 per cent increase in overall packaging costs. The final cost was 15 per cent higher for an identical sales price. Thus, a fault in the chain of events meant the expected advantage disappeared, and a disappointed supplier. This makes the point that the creation of value is valid only if it considers the *totality of operations* and the *actors* who contribute to the creation of the end value, within a real 'system of value', as shown in Figure 2.7.

The interest of the value chain concept is twofold. First it stresses that all activities inside the supplier organisation participate in the creation of value. It then becomes one of the objectives of management to *optimise the contribution of each internal activity or function* to the production of customer value. Secondly, attention has to be brought to the links between the firm's activities and those of *external players*, including the final customer. And that identifies another goal to be optimised, namely the activities between the players involved.

The Notion of the Industrial Sector

This notion comes from the observation that a product or service goes through a series of intermediary stages before being handed over to the end user. This idea is simple and logical. If we look a little further, we can see that this covers a number of definitions, depending on how the concept is utilised.

Figure 2.7   The system of value

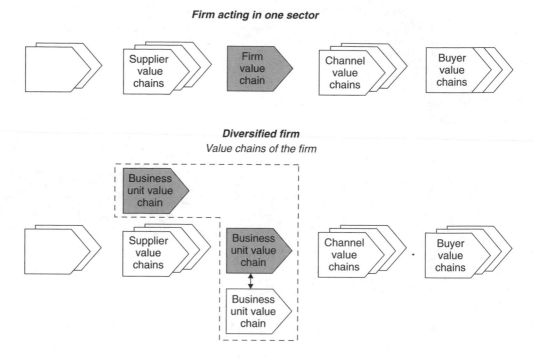

Reprinted with the permission of The Free Press, an imprint of Simon & Schuster Adult Publishing Group, from *Competitive Advantage: Creating and Sustaining Superior Performance* by Michael E. Porter. Copyright © 1985, 1998 by Michael E. Porter.

The first definition is that which coincides with the succession of technical operations that any raw material undergoes before becoming a *usable product*. Thus, wool is washed, carded, woven, dyed, cut and sewn to become a jacket. It is easy to understand that any change in this process can alter or even transform the market position of the company introducing an innovation. Again in the textile industry, the introduction of the Jacquard electronic loom meant that patterned articles could be woven automatically, whereas before this involved a number of different steps. The new system creates greater flexibility in production, which can follow the demand, increase the number of models on offer and reduce the need for large stocks. Part of Benetton's success is due to this method of exploiting available technology.

This shows us that economic actors use technical operations, and that the *supply chain* (or industrial sector) can become a basic analytical tool to understand the industrial operations and strategies. It is within a supply chain that we can best analyse and understand the vertical integration strategies, where objectives are usually to reduce costs, improve the security of supply for one particular stage of the chain, or to reduce dependency on supply chain partners. The Tomei group, for example, designs and manufactures low-to-middle-range hifi equipment. The group has integrated its suppliers of electronic components upstream and its distributors

Figure 2.8   A simplified representation of the textile sector

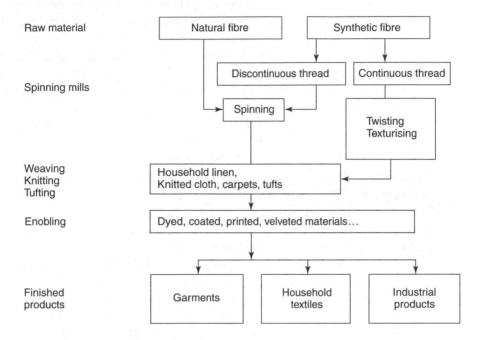

in Europe and the USA downstream. Consequently, certain analysts say that Tomei will become the world leader in these market segments over the next decade.

The term 'supply chain' is also used, and although outside the main theme of this book, we use it to describe and to analyse economic activities in a descriptive way, for example the wood, textile, electronics or other sectors. Structuring economic activity in this way allows us to examine exchanges between industrial sectors using an inputs–outputs matrix. We can also examine the industrial policy of a country by looking at notions such as *leading sectors* (to ensure new techniques are promoted within the industrial sector), *independence* (to improve the balance of exterior exchanges) and *sovereignty* (to guarantee a nation's long-term independence. This link between the framework (a national economy) in which the sector is situated and the supply chain concept still means thinking of it as operating within just one country. However, a 'European sector' is perhaps on the horizon for certain industries. This means that the industrial supply chain is a rich and complex concept that needs to be positioned in a specific context, as we shall do below with the French textile industry.

An initial representation of the industry (Figure 2.8) shows the different operations involved (spinning, weaving, finishing, end product). The use of chemical fibres avoids the spinning process but includes throwing, which gives the yarn physical properties which are adapted to the end uses. The links between the technical activities of the production system from upstream to downstream are obvious. It is true that such an industry uses outside sources (energy, production equipment, computing, various services, etc.), which are not part of the process as such. The self-consumption of the sector represents about 42 per cent of the value of the final product, which explains the economic weight of the raw material transformation processes, and also the importance of the purchases at each stage in the sector. Of course, the different stages are not structurally similar. Those upstream (spinning and weaving for example) are more capital- and technology-intensive than those downstream, (clothing manufacture and retail, for example) which demand considerable labour.

This analysis may explain why the textile sector has such a low degree of vertical integration. Upstream activities combine productivity and flexibility through heavy investments in productivity (the production of 100 kg of yarn dropped from 10 hours in 1980 to 1 hour in 1990) that has subsequently led to an increase in company size. The companies in the clothing industry are not as large. However, if the degree of integration is low, the succession of transformation operations and the economic actors who perform them allow us to understand a certain number of points that are also characteristic features of industrial marketing.

First, it visually illustrates the idea of *derived demand*. It is household clothing consumption that determines the activity of the sector. So activity in the sector is the result of variations in household buying power, decision by households as to how they spend their money (is clothing a priority?), fashion, and competition coming from other areas of expenditure, etc. The industrial actors can react to these variations, but their possibilities are limited. The volume of demand can also be affected – given that we are still in the framework of a national economy – by competition imported from abroad. This means that in business-to-business marketing, competition, traditionally speaking, can also be analysed as competition between national supply chains. Thus, the analysis of a 'national' supply chain can reveal the presence of weak links whose poor performance may penalise all the actors if and/or when international competition is suddenly made possible following the suppression of artificial barriers (rules, standards, quotas). For example, the performance of the Japanese steel industry, which was stronger than the American one in 1970–85, helped the competitiveness of the Japanese car manufacturers when entering the American market.

If imports can reduce the output of a national sector, then often the prices of imported goods are lower than local prices. Thus, problems linked to price will run through the industry, usually from the bottom up. The appearance of substitution products has meant trouble for many industries, and raised the need to modify technologies and look at prices to regain competitiveness. Thus, the steel supply chain for producing flat sheets for the car industry reacted strongly to the threat of new composite materials and ensured considerable improvements on their technology.

Conversely, technological innovation can be introduced by upstream actors and affect later stages in the process, requiring that they have to change their own production methods to make them compatible with the new technology if and when it is advantageous for their own activity. Earlier we mentioned the advantages of the Jacquard loom. In another field, the Placoplâtre company introduced 'placoplâtre'[2] to the market, and significantly changed traditional activities in the building sector: a new profession, 'the platists' emerged and replaced the bricklayers, plasterers and painters. The new material can be put up by much less skilled workers, and it is also easier and quicker to use, and therefore cheaper. However, it took the company many years to have their innovation accepted by their downstream operators, since it involved them changing their traditional approaches. This just illustrates the difficulties and the risks that are linked to innovations and the use of innovations, mainly when resistance comes from downstream links. The identification and understanding of such resistance are key points for the successful introduction of any innovation.

However, this first look at the notion of a supply chain, even though it has allowed us to examine some characteristics of business-to-business marketing, takes into consideration only a small degree of complexity. A more detailed representation of the textile sector offers more scope for reflection, as shown in Figure 2.9.

This allows us to see that the textile sector could be divided into three sub-sectors depending on the nature of the raw materials used: natural (agricultural), artificial (cellulose) and synthetic (oil). In the past the terms 'wool trade,' 'silk trade' and

Figure 2.9   A more complex representation of the textile sector

Textile sector: technical connections

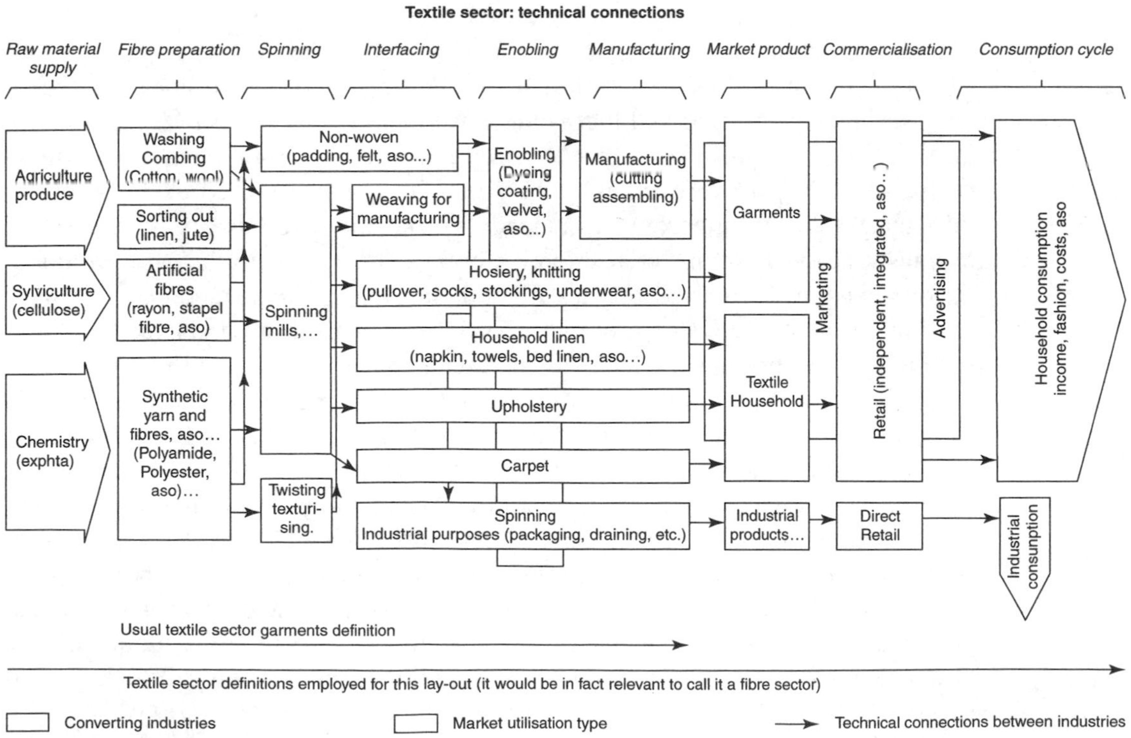

Source: Bellon and Chevallier (1983).

'synthetic trade' were used. However, the increasing flexibility of the production materials (with machines able to handle different yarns simultaneously), and the development of mixed fibres and new textiles (for sportswear, industrial applications, etc.) have led to a combination of industrial operations, with such ramifications that the original sub-sectors are now hardly noticeable. Technical innovations on yarns and their treatment have led to the substitution of materials and processes, and new applications have affected the textile sector and the conditions under which national sectors can fight increasing international competition (international textile trade increased fourfold between 1965 and 1990). The length of the supply chain introduces another type of complexity. The simplified representation did not mention the marketing of the final product. Indeed, this cannot be separated from the rest of the supply chain. We could even distinguish types of outlets that specialise in textiles (clothes shops, shoe shops, etc.) from the supermarkets and hypermarkets. The increasing market share of the supermarkets and hypermarkets in parts of Europe has had important consequences: looking to source cheaper materials abroad has forced prices down, influenced brand policy, defined quality standards, delivery date expectations and responses to fashion trends, etc. Thus, it is important to take the industry as a whole when talking about textiles.

From the Industrial Sector to the Network

The description above of the notion of a supply chain will help us to understand issues important for business-to-business marketing. However, it does not clarify one aspect of the market, and that is the ways *actors make decisions* and the way in which *interrelated actors influence each other*. For example, a German industrialist supplying sub-assemblies to the automotive industry tried to find uses for the metal waste resulting from the company's production processes. One option was to transform the waste material into disk brakes. The company began developing the disks and made some prototypes, carried out tests internally, and made changes resulting in a new series of prototypes that were then sent to a car manufacturer with whom the company already had good technical and sales relationships. Based on common agreement, further tests were made. The tests were positive, and this led to the sales stage, with positive technical and sales perspectives. The supplier's sales department took over and approached the purchasing division. The response from them was that the manufacturer did not in fact buy disc brakes, but bought sub-assemblies including disks from a specialised manufacturer, and in no way could the process be changed. The sales department then approached the manufacturer who said that the disks were part of their added value and also a way to make use of their own metal waste and under no conditions could they bring in supplies from the outside. The result was a research and development project that went to waste.

There are two lessons to be learned from this. First, as we mentioned in Chapter 1, it is vital to start marketing planning at the very beginning of a research project, and to avoid concentrating on the purely technical aspects of the operation. One of the roles of marketing, in the search for information, is to analyse the decision making process of current and potential supply chain partners, and also to understand the range of industrial operations covered by the project. This is even more important when the project is external to the supplies usually marketed by the company, and therefore external to that part of the industrial system of which the firm has experience. Secondly, the risk is even greater when a technical innovation takes a company (without their necessarily knowing it) into a new market about which they have absolutely no commercial position on which to base their marketing strategy.

But the marketing analysis of a supply chain is not sufficient to answer all the questions raised. We also need to examine the decision making processes between all the actors in the channel. These processes are influenced by the state of the industrial system at a given time, in other words, the implicit agreements or the distribution of roles and jobs within the channel. Any modification to a system that is operating smoothly represents a potential strategic threat to the actors in it. To introduce change in such instances requires two tasks. The first is to analyse the *systems of influence* (for more details, see Chapter 3) that people not necessarily part of the main sequence of activities have over other actors or decision makers in the network. An influence can be decisive in a number of situations. The second is the identification of these agreements made between groups of actors within the sector, some of which have a relative degree of autonomy. The identification and understanding of the different ways in which a network might be structured is one of the key strategies for a supplier wanting to penetrate a new sector.

The first element will be simply illustrated by the process of examining the introduction of a veterinary drug (Figure 2.10) in the chicken production supply chain (for meat). The laboratory wanting to introduce the new drug to counter the Marek disease had to identify the various actors and their levels of influence in the sector: the Agriculture Ministry, the Purchasing Co-operative, the veterinary consultant, the poultry sanitary adviser, the slaughterhouse, etc. The egg sector has a different structure, which shows how important it is to clearly define the nature of the relevant supply chain.

Of course, not all actors have the same role, the same skills, or the same influence, over the buyer of the drugs. This detailed work to identify the actors comes from commercial action that we will study in Chapter 3, but it is essential to understand how it is part of the decision process of the supply chain.

One way of examining a sector is to understand the level of *vertical integration*, in other words where one actor takes over a part of, or all of, one several other actors. This integration can involve the partial or total control of the capital of the other actors, but can also cover various exclusive supply agreements or the definition of technical standards. In the previous example, a food chain could decide to integrate the slaughterhouse upstream, or even the three stages of hatching, breeding and slaughtering. Downstream integration is also possible, from breeding to the slaughterhouse. Other actors not presented in Figure 2.10 can also intervene. In this

Figure 2.10 The poultry production sector (for meat), as seen for the adoption of a new veterinary drug

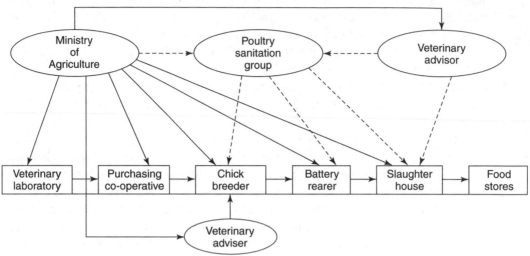

specific type of activity, animal feed suppliers have often integrated the operations performed by their customers.

Other than integration, a number of agreements can occur between actors in one or more stages of the supply chain. These agreements are usually contractual. A chain of food stores can, rather than integrate upstream, choose agreements with a slaughterhouse, a breeder and a hatchery to define the type of chicken, breeding conditions, feed and delivery times to their retail outlets. They can impose veterinary and draconian sanitary conditions for the breeding environment, and even the brand of vaccination to be used against the Marek disease. In such conditions, it is obvious that the veterinary laboratory must adapt to such changes brought about by the creation of new or different relationships between the customer and suppliers. A detailed examination of the supply chain in this industry from a business-to-business marketing perspective reveals systems of agreements linking actors who belong to the different stages (Figure 2.11), and whose knowledge is essential for the definition and the operating of marketing actions.

This new description illustrates the change from a general viewpoint to the perspective of business-to-business marketing. The actors have names. They are legal entities behind which there are people with whom personal relationships are established, which can be professional but also friendly. The two cases presented in Figure 2.11 show two very different types of networks from among the numerous possible combinations. In case 1, Food integrated upstream to control the chain of production of chickens in order to have total control of the quality and regularity of supply. It made an agreement with a Dr Veto to ensure the definition of the standards of breeding, the slaughtering and the control of operations. To become a supplier for one of the companies in the chain required the agreement of the person

Figure 2.11   The networks in a sector

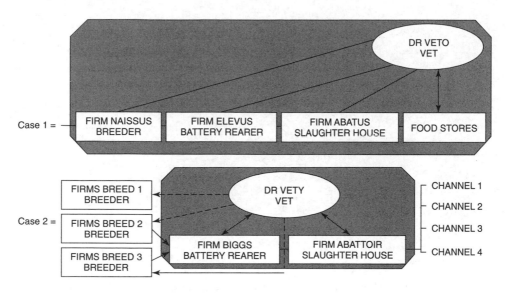

Source: Michel, Salle and Valla (1996).

responsible for Food supplies and that of Dr Veto. In case 2, the company Abattoir signed an exclusive supply agreement with the firm Biggs and, within this agreement, the two companies agreed to work with Dr Vety. However, Biggs reserved the right to obtain supplies from three selected hatcheries. In this second case, the agreements led to a lower centralisation of the decisions and greater flexibility between the different actors. In both cases, the players did so in order to improve the effectiveness and the productivity of their operations. Different players can choose different ways of achieving this, dependent upon a number of different factors: their belief in management philosophy, their culture and risk profile, opportunities, variations in capital or resources available and so on. A supplier should therefore remember this, and analyse its operations to operate in the best possible way. It must always take into account that customers choose a particular type of organisation, believing that in doing so, they can improve their productivity through better operations and relationships.

Our examples have offered some insights into the particularities of the phenomenon related to the notion of networks. We now need to expand on this notion, and point out the consequences for the design and operating of a business-to-business marketing strategy.

The Notion of a Network

The IMP Group (Håkansson, 1982), in carrying out their studies into buyer–supplier relationships, noted the role of *indirect relationships* (i.e. actors from

Figure 2.12   Example of a simple network of actors assigned to an exchange relation

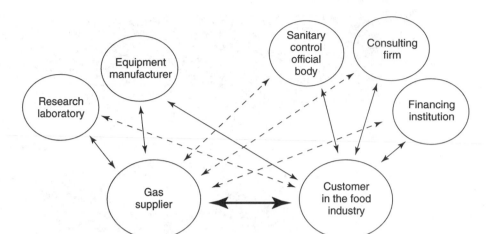

outside the organisations of the two exchange partners), which seemed to be important in the creation or the development of exchange relationships. In fact, the identification of these indirect relationships was an unexpected outcome of the study of these relationships (Håkansson and Snehota, 1995).

The simplified example (Figure 2.12) of a relationship between an English manufacturer of special industrial gas and one of his Italian customers in the food-processing industry can illustrate this phenomenon. The gas manufacturer was contacted by an Italian company that was marketing foodstuffs, concerning the supply of special gases for the conservation of packets of fresh products. The solution to their technical problem involved advanced tests and analysis that the gas manufacturer could develop with one of their usual partners, a public research laboratory. A technical solution was found, but one that involved the production *in situ* of gases in order to increase efficiency and avoid any danger to the end customer. After much technical and financial negotiation, a contract was drawn up, but which involved the participation of many actors outside the direct supplier–customer relationship.

Each of the external actors represented in Figure 2.12 plays a particular role in setting up the exchange relationship. Each actor controls one of the key elements: the public laboratory allowed the finalising of the innovation has part of the know-how of the production start-up process; the equipment manufacturer is an invaluable partner for the operation of a production unit on the premises; the Italian sanitary control organisation has to produce a certificate of compliance to allow the marketing of the finished product; the Italian consultant has to validate the technical quality of the solution *in situ*; and finally the financial institution is the customer's financial partner and lends the money required by the customer. In Figure 2.12 the solid lines represent the essential relationships for the project's success, and the dotted lines the less important links which could always help the supplier in a specific situation. Can a supplier simply ignore these relationships and act, for example, as if relationships with the Italian customer are not their concern?

The answer to this question can be found in the detailed analysis of the operation of the industrial system shown in Figure 2.12, and also in the capacity to anticipate the probable behaviour of the actors, according to their role, their decision power and their individual and collective interests. There is no one simple answer, other than questioning each actor individually just in case. In a simple system such as this, the option of reduced risks is possible. In more complex cases, some having more than 30 actors, choices have to be made so as not to waste human resources.

The network approach developed by the IMP Group allows us to use a conceptual framework to understand what is required. The *network concept* can be seen as a simple extension of the interaction model. From this perspective, the study of one exchange relationship has to be inserted in the framework or structure of the industrial system to which it belongs. We need to determine the external actors (the indirect relationships) that make up the system of influence that partly shapes the particular exchange relationship. Among the indirect relationships identified, some are strategic and linked to central actors of the system. These have to be systematically taken into account for the design and implementation of the marketing action suited to this type of exchange environment.

Generally speaking, if we accept the existence of long-term supply chain relationships, this implies that it is often necessary for many companies to unite their joint efforts to see a project come to life, or to develop a joint market position. In our example of Placoplâtre, success can be attributed to the company whose long-term efforts and determination paid off. However, it is also logical to think that other actors were associated with the company: architects, design offices, contracting companies, building materials traders, etc. They all felt at some time the need to be part of the development of the new process and to adapt their strategy accordingly. Placoplâtre also needed them. Links were made, including the transfer of information, exchanging experiences, suggestions, working together on sites, etc. Most initial links were made between the other actors and Placoplâtre. However strong social links can also exist between some of these actors, and it is easy to imagine these companies creating personal relationships which have absolutely nothing to do with Placoplâtre, but which allow them to work together on other projects.

Networks, as illustrated by this example, result from a series of exchanges between actors who participate in industrial activities. They emerge naturally and develop over time. Any actor can initiate new exchanges in the network and thereby instigate structural change that will have consequences for the strategies of the other network members. However these relationships are often informal and difficult to know about for an external actor, which means that access to information on the networks of a business-to-business system is not always easy.

To make matters worse, while companies need to be aware of the changes that are taking place in the system around them, such information is not always easy to utilise. Indeed, it is often when approaching one of the actors in the system that one is able to discover the ramifications of the network and to identify the actors involved. At this point in the book, we must simply remember the potential importance of all indirect relationships for a real understanding of successful exchanges. This is particularly clear when talking about a foreign country, where the exporter will discover one or more national networks. It is important to understand that these networks can, and often will, oppose the entry of new actors into the market. European and American factory design consultants and sub-contractors in the car industry realised this when contacting Japanese manufacturers: the barriers to entry and strength of the links between the manufacturers and their networks of contractors became visible little by little, and often the only solution was to work directly with one or more of the sub-contractors.

The final characteristic of networks is the large variation in possible configurations. A network is a geographically variable structure, there being no precise borders or limits, and an actor can belong to several networks according to his or her activities, often for the same activity. This obviously raises problems for the field of market research in a business-to-business environment, which calls upon particular techniques based on a *qualitative approach* that will be dealt with later.

There are many reasons for the existence of networks and their importance in business-to-business marketing. The actors carry out or develop economic activities that require the creation of relationships with other actors who control specific resources that are required to fulfil the task. The first strategic benefit represented by the networks is this complementarity and the sharing of resources and the engagement of related activities. But such common interests can also lead to conflict, which can come from an actor wanting to retain the power in a network, or the relative domination of certain actors. If a network is based on certain equilibrium, it can often be upset: a technical innovation brought into the network, the wish to modify one's position (usually in the quest for improved added value), or by the desire to increase one's power out of self-interest. The analysis of a network involves various factors: *composition*, *contribution* and *position* of each of the actors, the relative *weight* of the actors and their contribution, as well as their *evolution*.

The above analysis of networks is based on a series of concepts that needs to be clarified. The notion of the structure of a network, which allows us to better understand both its composition and organisation, is one example of a concept. Also, networks are not stable entities, evolving over time just like any other social system. The identification and understanding of their dynamism is an important element in the analysis, principally concerning the identification of changes in position of the actors in a given network. In addition, the concept of *position* in the network, allowing us to measure both the importance (degree of influence) and the role (function) of a particular actor is equally important in the analysis. This can lead to the identification of central actors who hold key positions, and peripheral actors whose contribution is more indirect and marginal. All of these concepts help to make a meaningful analysis of the systems of influence in a given network, or in the context of a particular supplier–customer relationship. So we see our notion of relationships as being both wider and more useful in the perspective of a supplier's marketing strategy than the classical and simpler notion of the 'decision maker'.

The idea of networks will reappear in other chapters of the book: those covering strategy, market research, and also the chapter devoted to innovation and emerging technologies.

Clusters

The theory of *clusters* (Porter, 1990) bears some similarities with the three preceding approaches, but presents another complementary perspective to those that we have already studied. 'A cluster is a geographically proximate group of interconnected companies and associated institutions in a particular field, linked by communalities and complementarities' (Porter, 1998). The difference with the three other concepts lies mainly with the words 'geographically proximate'. According to Porter, the competitiveness of a firm cannot be explained by looking only at its own resources and strategy. Another major element is the capacity of the firm to make use of a large set of external supports. And unlike the more traditional network approach, these supports are most often provided within the local environment (Figure 2.13). A similar approach may be found in other authors who discuss 'industrial areas' or 'industrial networks' (Piore and Sabel, 1984).

The theory is based on two elements. First, a firm is better able to develop its productivity and competitiveness through its relationship with *outside forces*: university research centres, official authorities, suppliers, related industries, sophisticated local demand, etc. This part corresponds well with the definition and the importance that we gave to the 'inputs' factor in the global productivity ratio. Second, these outside forces are to be found within *geographically constrained areas*. In a given cluster, forces and resources enhance each other to achieve mutual improvement. And this movement does so 'without threatening or distorting competition or limiting the intensity of rivalry' (Porter, 1998). Geographical proximity reinforces trust between players, and reduces transaction costs. Therefore it strengthens the ability of a firm to innovate, to discover new opportunities and be flexible enough to seize them.

An example would be the automotive industry in the Eastern Cape region of South Africa. With the local, and indeed national, market being too small to guarantee sufficient volume for all producers, the local players have had to resort to a cluster-based approach to enhance their competitive environment. Manufacturing companies in the region co-operate by jointly interacting with the local university to develop staff, and they also share initial training costs for all staff between them, before bringing staff back to their own factories for company-specific training. In addition, they have also all been able to lower their overall individual cost bases by co-operating in sourcing overseas components. Sharing the container and

Figure 2.13   A representation of clusters

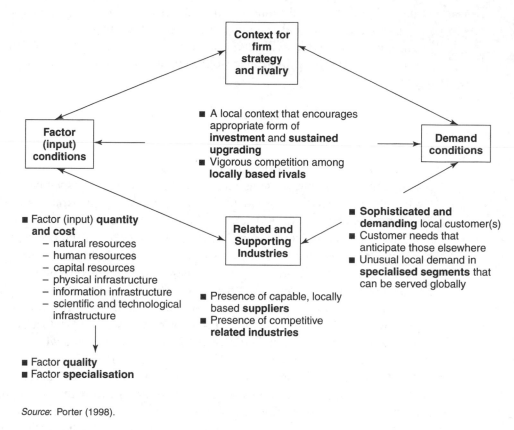

Source: Porter (1998).

transport costs in shipping components from Europe has been to each player's individual advantage. However, they still retain a keen competitive position *vis-à-vis* each other in the local marketplace (we are indebted to Professor Gavin Staude of Rhodes University in South Africa for this example).

Conclusion

We now have a broad view of the industrial system within which a company operates, remembering of course that the company can operate in more than one system. The thorough understanding of a business-to-business customer depends on many sources. The knowledge that the supplier acquires about its customer's internal value chain is a natural starting point. However, it must also be based on the range of technical operations which form the supply chain, the network(s) and cluster(s), and the system of value creation of which the company is a part. These notions will help to understand the following chapter that deals with business-to-business purchasing.

Notes

1. We shall see later (Chapter 6) that this definition is not the only one possible, and that we need to differentiate between a 'marketing customer' and a 'legal customer entity'.
2. The 'Placoplâtre' technology basically consists of panels of dried plaster that are manufactured to be directly assembled and installed to make up partition walls. It is a rapid and effective approach to building internal walls without having either to lay bricks or get involved in plaster casting.

References and Further Reading

Bellon, B. and Chevallier, J.M. (1983) *L'industrie en France*, Paris, Flammarion.

Bennett, R.C. and Cooper, R.G. (1979) 'Beyond the Marketing Concept', *Business Horizons*, June, 76–83.

Håkansson, H. (ed.) (1982) *International Marketing and Purchasing of Industrial Goods: An Interaction Approach*, New York, Wiley.

Håkansson, H. and Snehota, I. (1995) *Developing Relationships in Business Networks*, London, Routledge & Kegan Paul.

Michel, D., Salle, R. and Valla, J.-P. (1996) *Marketing Industriel. Stratégies et mise en oeuvre*, Paris, Economica.

Piore, M. and Sabel, C. (1984) *The Second Industrial Divide*, New York: Basic Books.

Porter, M.E. (1985) *Competitive Advantage: Creating and Sustaining Superior Performance*, New York, Free Press.

Porter, M.E. (1990) *The Competitive Advantage of Nations*, London, Palgrave Macmillan.

Porter, M.E. (1998) *On Competition*, Boston, Harvard Business Review Books.

Turnbull, P.W. and Valla, J.-P. (1986) *Strategies for Industrial Marketing: The Management of Customer Relationships in European Industrial Markets*, London, Croom Helm.

Discussion Questions

1 What are the consequences for a supplier's marketing strategy of the fact that they have to invest considerable resources to order to obtain just one new customer?
2 Why should a customer dedicate important resources in order to change a supplier?
3 How would you describe the applications that can be covered by one technology? Choose one technology and try to name different applications.
4 Referring to a variety of business-to-business relationships, can you determine the reasons that define different degrees of intensity of the supplier–customer interaction?
5 Why are networks important for the design of a marketing strategy in business-to-business environments?

Part I Strategy Foundations

Chapter 1
Competitiveness, Marketing and Business-to-Business Marketing

What is marketing all about
Different marketing environments
B2B marketing

Chapter 2
Business-to-Business Customers and Markets

B2B Generic Offers	Technological Innovation	Pure Services	Major Projects

PART I   STRATEGY FOUNDATIONS

Chapter 3	Chapter 4	Chapter 5	Chapter 6
Understanding Business-to-Business Purchasing	**Information and Information Systems**	**Markets and Suppliers' Strategy**	**Segmentation and Marketing Strategy**

PART II   STRATEGY IMPLEMENTATION

Chapter 7			
Generic Business-to-Business Offer Design and Management			

Chapter 8	Chapter 10	Chapter 11	Chapter 12
Market Access and Customer Management	**Marketing and Technological Innovation**	**The Marketing of Services**	**Major Project Marketing**

Chapter 9
Communication and Publicity/ Advertising

PART III   STRATEGY DESIGN

Chapter 13	**The Role and Organisation of Marketing**
Chapter 14	**Customer Position, Market Position, Marketing Strategies and Planning**
Chapter 15	**Issues and Specificities of International Marketing**
Annex	**The Internet and Marketing: Some Ideas**

3 Understanding Business-to-Business Purchasing

As mentioned in Chapter 2, each company is part of a complex network of actors. Through its relationships, the company gains access to the resources and the skills that it requires in order to develop its offers to the marketplace. The whole process of access to, control of and management of these resources is an essential element of the company's commercial activity. This task is largely the domain of the purchasing function.

Since 1980, the purchasing function has changed in many ways, and continues to evolve. Many explanations exist for this evolution. One of the most important is the impact that the success of Japanese companies, particularly their automobile manufacturers, had on management theories and practices. The European and North American manufacturers believed in the virtues of the traditional, adversarial, competitive environment, based upon multiple suppliers and ongoing negotiations, the aim of which was always to reduce the supplier's prices. Meanwhile, the Japanese proved the efficiency of a system based upon having *stable relationships* between a contractor and a far more limited number of parts manufacturers. Unlike the classical market model, in which the only adjustments are of the price, the Japanese used a different model, based on the creation and development of relationships, in which the co-ordination of activities is based on confidence and co-operation. From the 'law of the market', which is external, and largely beyond the control of the individual company, we have moved to the creation of joint standards and a more local way of operating, set up jointly by both supplier and customer.

This evolution does not mean that price is unimportant in this new configuration, but rather that many other factors that can create value are also recognised. The shock was tremendous, both in terms of economic competition and the impact on managements' ideas concerning what constituted efficient supplier relationships. Principles and practices were challenged, either rapidly or in great detail, according to country and industry. Today, however, most managers speak with at least some knowledge of the ideas behind *kanban*, of just-in-time, flexible workshops, zero stock, and zero faults, to name but a few. And this is accompanied by terms such as 'partnership', 'co-operation', 'mutual confidence', 'long-term relations', 'design to cost', etc. For example, Ford, during the late 1990s, aimed to cut their number of worldwide suppliers from 1650 to just 600, while at the same time giving these selected suppliers 5-year contracts – as long as they delivered 5 per cent real reductions in cost each year. Likewise, Dell is famous for giving single-sourcing contracts to its suppliers – as long as they reside within a maximum of 15 minutes' drive from its factories in Texas, Ireland, or Malaysia (Magretta, 1998).

Company purchasing policies have been affected by the fact that, as the Japanese companies first showed us, internal industrial management systems have either been extended to include suppliers, or have radically changed their relation- ships with them. Many industrialists have claimed (and Ford and Dell have set out to show) that the economies and innovations sought by managers, may be obtained more efficiently with stable and ongoing suppliers through co-operation and the rationalisation of the supply chain, rather than by simply putting pressure on prices. It must be understood that although our understanding of industrial purchasing has changed a lot, and will continue to do so, competitiveness will remain a major factor – as can been seen by the pressure on prices made by industrial buyers on their suppliers. Such changes have an effect on the supplier's behaviour towards the customer. They also affect the whole company operating system, from how it conceives of its market and supply strategy, through to the everyday behaviour of its employees. This clearly shows that an understanding of purchasing within a business-to-business context is the cornerstone upon which a general understanding of business-to-business marketing can be built. After looking at some of the main characteristics of purchasing and the purchasing function, we will briefly look at those factors that affect purchasing decisions, based upon the many works devoted to the subject. We will describe a method to help us understand business-to-business purchasing decisions: the *risk approach*. In this chapter we have not looked at the case where the purchasing centre is split between several organisations, as is the case in project marketing. However, we shall deal with this further in Chapter 12.

Buying and Buyer Characteristics

Approaches to management have been affected by three factors in recent years. First, that part of the industrial network most vulnerable to competition is constantly searching for ways to improve *international competitiveness* (see Chapter 1). And this search for competitiveness is made more acute by the requirements of the financial institutions that become the shareholders of an increasing number of major international firms. Secondly, the increasing number of new production technologies are harder and harder to develop and manage, often requiring exter- nal assistance. Finally, the need for greater flexibility in the production process means changing supply procedures, from separate elements (discs for brakes, pads for brakes, etc.) to complete sub-assemblies (car brake systems, for example).

The consequences of these changes are significant, especially if we look at the percentage of purchases to company turnover. In Europe, this has gone from between 40 and 60 per cent to between 50 and 80 per cent since 1990. For example, LMT, which specialises in radiotelephones, saw its turnover rise from the equivalent of 30 m Euros to 90 m Euros between 1980 and 1990, and yet at the same time purchases jumped from 36 per cent to 70 per cent of turnover. In parallel we see the increase in intellectual services (consultancy, market research, technical developments, etc.), which can reach up to 40 per cent of purchases in some companies, against 10 or 15 per cent in the early 1990s. Another consequence concerns the nature of the purchases themselves. Fewer separate elements are being bought, and more sub-sets and systems with a greater added value are being purchased. Consequently, the sub-contracting of parts in the automotive industry has dropped from 50 per cent to 15 per cent of the total purchases. This means that the *purchasing function* is gaining importance because of its role in the co-ordination of the internal (the company) and external (the supplier market) interface. Internally, its role is increasingly to integrate the objectives and constraints concerning the whole company's production and logistics systems. So we must distinguish between the purchasing function and the 'Purchasing Department', whose aim is to pilot and to co-ordinate relationships with suppliers. The Purchasing Department's role is to interact with other company functions both in the design of the company's offers (by looking for, selecting and motivating those suppliers that are able to integrate the activities of design) and/or the implementation (in the case of services) through their specific know-how. Externally, the purchasing department increasingly interacts with suppliers. The purchasing function therefore plays a much more strategically important role now than it did in previous years.

Purchasing Department Missions

Purchasing departments vary in size, depending on the company. Some specialists distinguish between three different development stages that correspond to different practices:

- *Supply purchasing*: dominated by an administrative logic. A large part of purchases are not handled by the Purchasing Department: for example, capital goods or service providers (advertising or training, for example).

- *Negotiated purchasing*: characterised by the start of co-ordination or centralisation of purchases which allow for pressure on price.

- *Strategic purchasing*: companies need only a few suppliers. They use external resources more often. They implement much closer buyer–supplier relationships.

Hence, from one company to another, purchasing departments have different objectives. To understand these different objectives, and their relative importance, we can refer back to the value chain described in Chapter 2. Because purchasing appears as one of the support activities, this implies that the responsibility of the department should cover the whole spectrum of the company's operational activities, including those undertaken by both the marketing functions and sales and services. Therefore, the Purchasing Department can be defined as being pivotal to the selection and management of external suppliers' contribution to the company, and hence to the creation of value. However, this is a very general definition that needs to be clarified further.

Purchasing has four major objectives:

- *Quality*: it participates in the original definition and the continuous monitoring of company quality in two ways. It contributes to the supplier quality control process (audits, certification, standards, procedures, etc.), and it also monitors the continuity of supplies, so that the production timetable and customer demands are met.

- *Competitiveness*: it negotiates the lowest prices which are compatible with the levels of quality and services expected; maintains the minimum stock level possible; avoids duplication, waste, and obsolescence of materials and machines; and contributes to the company profit margin by reducing purchasing costs or internal costs related to suppliers.

- *Supplies availability and security*: it searches and qualifies suppliers' design and manufacturing capabilities, it analyses the short-, medium- and long-term evolution of the industrial sectors concerned in order to evaluate the suppliers' power and potential vulnerability, and it manages the whole portfolio of suppliers.

- *Creativity*: it always looks for ideas, services, products and new materials on the market that could help solve problems for the company more cost-effectively.

These objectives have developed and broadened enormously since 1990. Indeed, being involved in large company projects is a new role for the typical purchaser. The need to improve the time taken to get to the market for new products forces companies into incorporating suppliers into the projects as soon as requirements have been established. This raises the notion of *co-development*. Therefore the selection of 'good' suppliers by the Purchasing Department must take place far upstream. This type of organisation structure was used, and surrounded by much publicity, during the launch of the Twingo by Renault in Europe. The following figures were given by Renault: it took just 36 months to develop the model, which resulted in 2–5 per cent savings on costs and increased by 5–10 per cent the added value. The subsequent launch of the Peugeot 406 was another opportunity to re-organise the purchasing function – almost all the parts were ordered from single suppliers, which led to savings of around 20 per cent on the initial investment.

The broadened responsibility of the typical new purchasing function means that its members are constantly in touch with all company departments to initiate and co-ordinate activities. Their objective of creativity brings them closer to design, research and development and marketing; the quality demands closer to development, quality, logistics and production; the objectives of competitiveness to marketing, development, logistics, production and finance (conditions of payment for purchases, supplier assessment, level of stocks, etc.). This interdepartmental involvement is increasing, and together with directors, the purchasing departments develop new strategies such as reducing the number of suppliers, global sourcing of purchases, co-development with suppliers, and the integration or outsourcing of certain operations. This complexity has obvious consequences for the characteristics of purchasing decision processes that we shall now examine.

Understanding Business-to-Business Buying Behaviour

Since the 1970s, this area has been the focus of much research, primarily in North America. While the research has increased our knowledge, we would argue that it has done so without dramatically changing management practices. In this chapter, we will present the main directions of this research and also refer the reader to some of the major works identified. For the interested reader, further detail can be found in Ford *et al.* (1998) and Anderson and Narus (1999).

Until the 1980s, most research was conducted on one of two levels. The first concerned trying to understand the purchasing decisions and the factors that affected the choice of suppliers for industrial customers. The second concerned the suppliers' marketing decisions, trying to understand the effect of different combinations of the marketing mix variables on industrial markets, and also how best to implement changes in the mix. It is noteworthy that both of these focused on *industrial* buying behaviour, whereas we take a broader view, looking at the more all-encompassing *business-to-business* marketing.

The fact that the research was based on two different research perspectives is a direct result of the research approaches that were being applied in consumer marketing. Although not ideally suited to understanding relationships and interactions, this type of approach allowed us to develop our knowledge of industrial buyer behaviour, either in total or partially through the detailed analysis of a specific element of the description of the purchasing process such as:

- the selection criteria used by purchasers (Dickson, 1966)
- the members of the decision making unit (Buckner, 1967)
- the stages of the purchasing process (Robinson, Faris and Wind, 1967), etc.

Or the analysis of the influence of a given variable on general purchasing behaviour, and the perception, in particular, of the risks involved, such as:

- the influence of purchasing situations (Robinson, Faris and Wind, 1967; then more recently Uncles and Ehrenberg, 1990)
- the influence of the environment
- the influence of industrial characteristics
- the influence of the characteristics of the organisation
- the intervention of marketing stimuli (salesmen, advertising, etc.), etc.

Among the purchasing behaviour models developed in the 1970s, some are particularly well known:

■ the Buygrid Model (Robinson, Faris and Wind, 1967)
■ the Industrial Product Adoption Model (Ozanne and Churchill, 1971)
■ the Organisational Buying Behaviour Model (Webster and Wind, 1972)
■ the Industrial Buying Behaviour Model (Sheth, 1973)
■ the Corporate Industrial Buying Model (Hillier, 1975)
■ the Industrial Market Response Model (Choffray and Lilien, 1978).

Other than Robinson, Faris and Wind's model which was limited to the phases and types of purchasing situation, all these models overlap to a certain degree, particularly concerning how the purchasing process is influenced by certain external variables, and also in terms of describing the different phases of the purchasing process.

Developments in the 1980s focused on the buyer's decision making unit (or DMU), seen as a group of individuals all interacting to reach a decision. Two research models can be identified:

■ the Supplier Choice Model (Woodside and Vyas, 1984, 1986, 1987)
■ the Matbuy Model (Möller, 1981, 1986).

These complete the eight models that were been developed during the 1970s. As previously argued, we adopt the position that the most meaningful stance to take is to examine business-to-business marketing from the position of buyer–supplier interaction, thereby rejecting the choice made in the above-mentioned works to concentrate on just one actor's point of view. However, let us not throw the baby out with the bath water: many do throw light on the subject and will be dealt with in the following sections.

The Complexity of Business-to-Business Purchasing Decisions

This complexity can be viewed from three different angles: the notion of the DMU (or the buying centre), the process and phases of the purchasing decision, and finally how a decision is actually reached.

In most companies, the Purchasing Department controls most company purchases, except in very specific circumstances. However it does not typically have all the skills necessary for managing such responsibility. For example, project elaboration, the formalising of customer needs, or the choice of supplier or technical developments, all require help from outside the department, either from within the company or externally. Often this wider group is not represented in the company organisation chart. However, we find that the creation of *project groups* is currently tending to promote the formalisation of such practices. For example, it is well documented that the

Peugeot 406 project brought together people from design, production, purchasing and marketing, all under the supervision of a single project leader.

Such purchasing decision complexity has several implications. First, it implies that all these people do not necessarily have the same interests at heart, and neither do they have the same role to play in the decision making process. In addition, all the people involved do not necessarily have the same selection criteria in mind, as is shown in the example of the purchase of refrigerated trucks by a transport company (Table 3.1). Traditionally, there are six roles usually identified, at least in part, by members of the purchasing DMU:

Table 3.1   Example of a buying centre: a fleet of refrigerated trucks

Purchasing management
- Pricing/price adjustment clauses
- Purchasing or renting or leasing
- Payment and financial conditions
- Service and depreciation length
- Resale value
- Economic cost during the service length
- Manufacturer's guarantees
- Drawing up of the purchasing contract
- Asking advice from an insurance consultant

Financial management
- Financial conditions
- Purchasing or renting or leasing
- Financial control

Legal department
- Support and control
- Drawing up of contracts

Transit department (and drivers)
- Volume proportions
- Cold: power, reliability, manufacturer's after-sales service
- Power, handiness
- Operating costs
- Possible modification (costs)
- Comfort/brand image
- Training

Maintenance department
- Technological audit/breakdown causes
- Spare parts (availability, cost, inventories, management)
- Maintenance strategy (periodicity, costs, guarantees) + manufacturer's after-sales service
- Repair costs (parts accessibility, diagrams, compatibility with present tooling)
- Training

Advertising department
- Marking possibilities and changes (cost, ease)

General management
- Brand image
- Return on investment
- Synthesis and final decision

Note: Based on real data, company name confidential.

- The *buyer* manages company purchases. He or she supervises all purchases made by the company, and identifies the suppliers to be used by the company. This person, however, is not automatically the one who decides. Whenever the purchase does not involve the purchasing department, the purchaser can be someone from another department within the organisation.

- The *user* receives the good or service purchased. This person is often at the origin of the demand, and can influence the initial stages of the purchase and the evaluation of the offer, and therefore of the supplier–customer relationship.

- The *influencer* influences the ultimate purchase. Such a person can be a member of the organisation or may well be part of an external organisation (engineering company, design consultant, other customer of the same supplier, etc.).

- The *adviser* suggests product or supplier selection criteria, but does not always appear formally in the DMU and therefore is difficult to identify.

- The *gatekeeper* controls communications between members of the buying unit and their relationships with the suppliers involved. This person is often also the purchaser. In many companies, we find that while the gatekeeper has the capacity to blacklist a project or supplier, they do not necessarily have the authority to make the final decision one way or the other.

- The *decision maker* is the key person. He or she has the power to commit the firm to the supplier. In all companies there are procedures for committing expenses that are usually related to the amount involved. There is however a difference between the 'technical' and 'financial' aspect of such decisions. Identifying the 'decision maker' is a major task for the supplier, which is made all the more difficult by the complexity of the organisations and the decisions to be made. And what add even more complexity is the fact that the decision makers are not necessarily the same individual at each phase of the decision-making cycle.

According to the particular situation, the reaching of the final decision within the DMU will be conditioned by a number of factors. These include the nature of the relationships between all the people concerned, their relative power in the organisation, personal objectives, the background of each individual, the experience in buying a product or a service, the extent of formalisation of the purchasing strategy and procedures, and relationships with the supplier.

Example 2   Transcold

TRANSCOLD are a transportation company. They intend to undertake a partial renewal of their fleet of refrigerated trucks. They are to call for tenders from several manufacturers. Table 3.1 identifies the various functions that will influence the decision-making process, and briefly summarises the main concerns of each of them.

Table 3.2   Comparative synthesis of different models through the purchasing phases

Phases	Founding models (1970s)	'Supplier choice model' (Woodside and Vyas, 1984, 1986, 1987)	'Matbuy model' (Möller, 1981, 1986)
A	Acknowledgment of needs	–	Purchasing initiation
B	Specifications	Drawing up the call for tenders	Definition of the choice criteria
C	Search for suppliers	Search for suppliers	Search for information from the suppliers
D	–	Short listing	Short-listing
E	Proposals analysis	Proposals analysis	Proposals analysis
F	–	–	Negotiation
G	Choice	Choice	Choice
H	Performance control	–	Implementation

The notion of a *purchasing decision process* thus corresponds to the idea that organisational purchasing varies in speed, and also that it goes through different identifiable phases, as shown in Table 3.2.

Table 3.2 highlights the sequential nature and sub-decisions that characterise any buying decision. As we shall see later, there are many types of purchasing environments that can be analysed by using analytical grids such as those shown in Table 3.2. However, this initial approach allows us to identify just what the customer wants at each stage of the process, and also the required information and the different people involved. We shall now detail each of the eight steps of the process identified in Möller's model in more detail.

Defining the need or initiating the purchase (A). Whatever the underlying reason, people are motivated within the company to solve a new problem, which initiates a relationship between the initiator and the Purchasing Department. The latter can also initiate the process when there is a change in purchasing strategy, or when the origin of the demand is external to the company, such as a change in an existing supplier's offer.

Defining specifications and quantity, preparation of the invitation to tender, and the definition of the choice criteria for evaluation (B). This gives consistency to the project and might well lead to the formation of a working party. The user and the purchaser determine the characteristics of what they will purchase, both technically and financially. This can vary in precision and detail according to the skills available within the company. Therefore, it can be both rapid and simple, when taking place in a technical environment that is well understood, and with knowledgeable suppliers. When the problem to be solved is more complex however, several people from the company are typically involved in the DMU. If the company is considering going beyond its usual field to enter new territory, for example, the suppliers may be called in to assist with the technical specifications.

The search for suppliers and collecting supplier information (C). This is the job of the Purchasing Department, which will often do it with the help of the initiator whose technical know-how is usually invaluable at this stage. This means listing all possible responses to the demand in terms of the potential suppliers' technical and economic capabilities. With some types of purchasing procedures, such as a bid for tenders, this stage is often used by purchasing departments to consult with the various potential suppliers in the market.

Short-listing (D). This means short-listing suitable suppliers (the 'vendors list'). The list may be based on the use of formal procedures for approval, qualification, or confirmation of potential suppliers. The use of these procedures depends largely on the resources available within the company and also on the means employed to evaluate quality.

The analysis of the bids and the choice of supplier (E), (F) and (G). These are the most delicate stages. They involve deciding on what basis a supplier should be chosen, knowing that the results of the choice could be extremely advantageous or disadvantageous for the company. This step is becoming increasingly rigorous to enable the comparison between several bids. It is essential when the customer treats each project separately, and very often the supplier must be rapidly integrated into the co-developments.

In Möller's model (1981, 1986), there is a negotiation stage *(F)* between the analysis of bids and the choice of supplier, which does not exist in the other North American models (Möller carried out his research in Europe). Are negotiations between a supplier and the customer the result of different business practices and cultures? Europeans tend to use negotiation after bids have been received, and this phase is thus considered as an additional one to collect more information concerning either the suppliers' bids and/or the suppliers themselves before the final choice. This is also a phase often used to reconsider the initial request. North American companies rarely do this.

Performance control and implementation (H). This involves informing the members of the DMU of the implications of their decisions and examining the consequences of a relationship with a given supplier. This involves studying how the supplier solved the problems raised by the customer. Indeed, members of the DMU frequently disagree on how to evaluate a supplier's performance, particularly when the problem was difficult to solve. For example, the fact that a supplier was late with a particular delivery because of trouble involving a specific problem could be judged favourably by some ('he has learned a lot and this could be good for us in the future'), and negatively by others ('it was obviously too difficult for him, let's call it a day now'). This evaluation process often leads to procedures that are similar to those developed for the choice of supplier.

The ultimate decision results from the combination of individual preferences. It is an extremely complex process, and involves two different perspectives: individual and collective. Examples of how this occurs can be found in Lockett and Naudé (1991) or Naudé, Lockett and Holmes (1997). We shall adopt a more pragmatic position here that we feel clearly reflects the way in which the buyer proceeds in

Table 3.3   Three requirement levels

	Characteristics	Buyer	Supplier
Veto requirements	▪ Clear definition of the requested performance ▪ A supplier may be left out on a binary judgement (yes/no)	▪ Build up the basic requirements ▪ Decide on short-listing or not	▪ Strict answer to the customer's requirements ▪ Control ▪ Immediate action in the case of a problem
Important requirements	▪ Less precise definition of the requested performance (minimum) ▪ Performances may be partially compensated	▪ Are used to make a choice between the selected suppliers ▪ Favour the development of steady relationship	▪ Key point of a differentiation strategy ▪ According to the competitive situation a minimum performance is requested on some criteria; on others an advantage has to be built
Secondary requirements	▪ Some clear very strong points may compensate for a weakness on one important requirement ▪ Play a marginal role	▪ May be used for the repartition of market shares ▪ Are linked to specific motivations of some members of the buying centre	▪ May be used to consolidate or develop on going relationship ▪ Compensate for some minor weaknesses

practice. The members of the DMU evaluate suppliers on the basis of a number of criteria. These criteria depend on a number of factors related to the product bought, to the purchasing situation, to the level of novelty of the problem, etc. They can be put into three categories, as we show in Table 3.3:

▪ *Veto (or obligatory) criteria*: only those suppliers or products reaching a minimum on these criteria will be examined.

▪ *Important criteria*: not being quite up to standard on such criteria can be compensated for by good performance on other important criteria, or even on secondary criteria.

▪ *Secondary criteria*: one or more advantages in these criteria can make up for a deficiency in important criteria. Secondary criteria help make the difference between two suppliers who are equal in important criteria.

This decision formation model combines two very different ways of thinking, but both of which we believe are realistic and necessary. With veto criteria we are dealing with what can be called a non-compensatory approach to decision making; for example, you are unlikely to buy a PC based on a 386 chip, irrespective of the delivery, service, or cost. For the other two sets of criteria, the important and secondary ones, we believe that a compensatory approach is appropriate: in buying a car, we might trade off a bit less space for a slightly lower price, for example.

The example in Table 3.4, based on the purchasing of an electrical component for the TGV locomotives, illustrates what we mean by *choice criteria*. Obviously

Table 3.4   Example of criteria grid for the choice of an electrical component

Veto criteria	■ Holding to vibrations ■ Breaking tension ■ Service length (measured in number of cycles) ■ Possibility of use in parallel ■ Absence of the creation of breaking electrical arcs	■ Delivery accuracy ■ Proximity of the supplier ■ Quality of the maintenance department
Important criteria	■ Holding to temperature ■ Temperature breaking point ■ Contact resistance ■ Holding to acceleration ■ Possibility of emergency delivery ■ Innovation capacity	■ Maintaining of the prices over time ■ Technical references under severe conditions ■ European presence ■ Technical documentation ■ Financial health of the supplier
Secondary criteria	■ Volume and weight of the relay ■ Electrical consumption ■ Regular and accurate information ■ Easy access to right people in the case of emergency ■ European supplier ■ Quality of personal relationship	■ Quickness and quality of the answers to claim ■ Capacity of adaptation to a specific request

some highly technical elements are included in the specification chart (clearly much has been summarised here). But other types of criteria are also taken into account even at the veto level. For example, the purchaser will thoroughly audit the candidates' maintenance department in order to determine if they are equipped and organised to meet subsequent requirements. Any shortcoming here is likely to place a candidate on the black list.

It is obvious that customer criteria such as those described above can change over time for various reasons, determined by both market dynamics and supplier–customer relationships. This must lead us to think about purchasing strategy and the consequences for buyers' relationships with their suppliers, which we turn to next.

Purchasing Strategies and the Consequences for Buyer–Supplier Relationships

Because of its position at the interface between buyers and suppliers, purchasing decisions contribute to the three company objectives of *quality*, *competitiveness* and *creativity* by influencing relationships with suppliers on both a macro (overall strategy) and micro (supplier relationship) level. Short-, medium-, and long-term management of these relationship resources is a key to successful company purchasing strategy. Table 3.5 in Example 3 shows an example of this: the evolution over 19 years of the purchasing strategy of a particular manufacturer of forklift trucks, and their purchase of four different types of components: the mast profiles, the engines, the forks and the gears.

Table 3.5   Evolution of the purchasing strategy

Purchasing situations	1964	1965	1966	1967	1968	1969	1970	1971	1972	1973	1974	1975	1976	1977	1978	1979	1980	1981	1982
N°1: Mast profiles Suppliers: A/B/C	A	A	A	A	A	A	A	A	A	ab	ab	ab	A	A	A	A	A	A	Ac
N°5: Big electrical motors Suppliers E/F	–	–	–	–	Ef	E	E	E	E	E	ef	Ef	fe	E	E	F	F	F	F
N°7: Forged forks Suppliers: X/Y/Z/W	X	X	X	X	Yz	Y	Z	Z	Wz	Wz	Wz	W	W	W	W	W	W	W	W
N°10: Other gear-wheels Suppliers: L/M/N/O/P/Q/R/S/T	lm	lm	Lm	Lm	Lm	Lm	Lm	O	O	lm	qrs	qrs	qrs	Tq	T	T	T	T	T

Note: The suppliers are identified by letters.
   – a capital letter indicates an exclusive or major supplier
   – a small letter, an equal or minor supplier

Example 3   The forklift truck manufacturer

This manufacturer was founded in 1960 and increased its turnover tenfold between 1964 and 1982. During this period, purchasing of 11 components came under review. We kept records of the purchasing history of 4 component parts in order to illustrate diverse purchasing strategies.

Mast profiles

- Only three suppliers were considered
- The product was designed according to the customer's specifications
- The technical requirements are very high
- It is a key component for the design of the vehicle with a considerable impact on other functions
- The necessary development and test-time to qualify a new supplier is about 2–3 years
- A, national supplier, was the exclusive or major during the whole 19-year period
- B, East European supplier, was tested for 3 years; it had poor delivery reliability and the quality was inconsistent
- To try and reduce dependency on A, a new vehicle design was considered; this was made possible through the use of new materials and in this way the number of potential suppliers was substantially increased after 1982.

Big electrical motors

- The component is purchased in a completed 'package' version specific to this vehicle
- It has an impact on the design of other components
- Many suppliers are available worldwide, but only 4 or 5 are considered as realistic alternatives
- A change of supplier would require 2 or 3 years' time for development and tests
- Two suppliers were used in some of the years, they were both carefully tested and are well known; a change from one of them to the other, therefore, will cause no problems.
- The main reason for supplier change was the necessity to keep prices down; the competition between the 2 suppliers is nevertheless strong enough to avoid considering a third possibility.

Forged forks

- Some hundreds of suppliers were identified, but many of them were small and medium-sized workshops, whose capacity was often limited; only about 20 are considered to be realistic alternatives
- In 1968 X, a national supplier, was unable to match a change in design and Y, another national supplier, had to be called in
- No other national supplier could be accepted; Z, an English supplier, was used for some time, but it proved to be unreliable in both quality and delivery time
- W, another foreign, gradually replaced Z; a change of supplier requires only 2 or 3 months' work and the substitution is easy
- A better knowledge of the international supply market allowed the company to escape from a situation of over dependence on its suppliers.

Other gear – wheels

- There are several medium-sized suppliers in a very competitive environment
- The product is adapted for each use, and a change of supplier requires 1 year's work
- The geographical proximity is important

(continued)

Example 3   The forklift truck manufacturer (*continued*)

- *L* and *M*, national suppliers, had to be chosen in spite of 50 per cent higher prices; *N* did not prove to be satisfactory
- *O*, a foreign supplier, was selected on the basis of high quality and reasonable prices, but had to be terminated because of unacceptable delivery times after 2 years of exclusivity, *L* and *M* were then taken back
- *Q*, *R* and *S* were unsuccessfully tried
- *T*, an unknown national supplier, become exclusive after a 1-year trial; in spite of the important work linked to a change of supplier and of a favourable supply market structure, 9 suppliers were used within the 19-year period. The need to find a satisfactory offer led to an instability of suppliers and to a very costly development work.

Note: Based on real data, company name confidential.

Example 3 shows how different decisions were made for the different components. More generally, these decisions on who to buy from were based on a range of different factors:

- Supply characteristics in the marketplace, expressed in terms of structure and dynamism. These can be turbulent or calm, vary in homogeneity, involve a large or small number of potential customers, and conceal or reveal substitution possibilities. Thus, for the Purchasing Department, the supply market can have varying complexity.

- The importance of the products to the activity of the company, either on an economic level (amount, importance in terms of the added value, etc.) or at a technical level (the impact of the final product).

It is important to remember that all product types bought can be evaluated from these two perspectives, both of which combine several criteria adapted to the particular environment of each company. Many purchasing departments use methods that integrate similar dimensions, even if the words vary. All the product types can be grouped in a matrix that combines these two dimensions, as shown in Figure 3.1. From this, four product types have been created:

- *Products of strategic importance* in terms of the buyer's activity. They have a high level of both impact and importance. The supply market is complex. Therefore the purchase typically involves a high level of risk. This means that the Purchasing Department closely supervises such operations.

- *Products of critical importance* in terms of the customer's activity. They, too, have a high level of impact and importance, but the supply market is typically not as complex. Therefore the buyer's risk is linked to the ability to control the use of the product.

- *Bottleneck-type products* that typically have low impact and importance to the customer's activity, but the supply market is complex. For the Purchasing

Figure 3.1   Characteristics of the supplier market

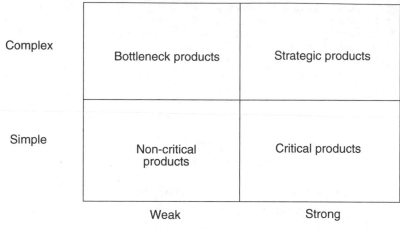

Characteristics of the supplier market

Source: Adapted from Kraljic (1984).

Department, such situations are not acceptable. These kind of situations typic-ally exist with the purchase of energy, raw materials, or in cases of supplier domination;

■ *Non-critical products*. Low impact on customer activity and the supply market is not complex. The decisive criterion tends to be price.

According to the position of any given product in the matrix, a company aims to evolve from top to bottom or from right to left whenever possible. Otherwise the company must develop its own strategies to manage the position (typically, say, by buying raw materials in bulk and manufacturing high value-added critical compo-nents, rather than incurring the risk of buying them in the open market). Through such actions, the buyer is looking to make the required resources as available and as accessible as possible.

To put these actions into effect, the company has many possible routes open to it:

■ Within its own organisation, a company may improve its own *technology* or *buying procedures* to give it a relative advantage over the different suppliers, or even when confronted by a particular supplier. The steps taken by the forklift truck manufacturer (Example 3) for the mast profiles, trying to modify the nature of the components is a good example. The company can thus gain access to a number of important suppliers.

■ On the overall plan of the *supply market*. The company can try to modify the structure of the supply market. Only a few big players have the muscle to do this – for example, some car manufacturers have managed to change the structure of the sub-contracting and parts manufacturing sector. In one example with which we are familiar, a paint manufacturer was forced to supply both paint and resin to the automotive manufacturer with whom they had a single-source relationship, in spite of the fact that they were not in the resin market at all.

■ On relationships with *suppliers*. Indeed, in order to improve competitiveness, companies increasingly involve their suppliers in their own internal planning by giving them ever more important roles to play. To attribute this role to suppliers, the company uses different approaches.

The first way relates to the *distribution of purchases* between suppliers. This means distributing the capacities and purchasing costs between various suppliers. Depending on just one supplier, however valuable that supplier may be, does represent a risk to the buying company. Thus, as an example, an aeronautical industrial group has two suppliers for relatively important purchases, and three when the purchases are of strategic importance to the production activity. No use is made of single sourcing.

However, the 1990s have unquestionably seen the number of cases of single sourcing increase, and the creation of partnerships and complex interindustrial relationships have led companies to accept such interdependence. Many good examples of this occur in the car industry.

The second is linked to the *weight* that the buyer represents to the supplier. Company history has shown that a buyer is best served when that buyer is a large or target customer for the supplier. This means that buyers attempt to gain recognition as 'target customers' by grouping their purchases, although this means reducing supplier numbers. In some cases, this can mean a company accepting one source for a given product type. However, such grouping of purchases can also make the supplier more vulnerable. Therefore, companies impose upper limits on the *level of turnover* with each supplier. For the aeronautical industry mentioned above, company policy dictates that a risk exists if the purchases represent more than 12 per cent of the supplier's turnover, and the situation becomes intolerable if this goes over 25 per cent.

The third way comes from the need to relate suppliers to *company competitiveness*. Research into cost reductions through modifying industrial operations and services, greater flexibility, investments for development, innovations, reducing response time to customers and the launching of new products and services, all require close collaboration. As these objectives are sometimes contradictory, most suppliers are given a precise role to play according to their capacity, as well as that of any competing suppliers involved.

The example in Table 3.6 clearly demonstrates this. It describes the purchasing strategy of a German automotive equipment manufacturer, who had three suppliers (1, 2, and 3) of the same product type for a particular component. Each

Table 3.6   Example of status given by a buyer to its suppliers

	Market Share (%)	Characteristics of suppliers
Supplier 1	50	■ Better prices (less 5 per cent) ■ Long but accurate delivery times ■ Weakly innovative, no technical support ■ Low service ability
Supplier 2	30	■ Intermediary prices ■ Irregular delivery times ■ Excellent technical assistance, possibility of common design work ■ Assistance to manufacturing
Supplier 3	20	■ More expansive (plus 5 per cent) ■ Quick delivery times, easily handles extra orders ■ Sufficient technical competence to adapt to modifications required by the customer

supplier was given a level of business, but also a formally recognised status in terms of competence. Three different levels of status were recognised:

■ Supplier 1 is used because of their competitiveness and logistical excellence. They were allocated 50 per cent of the buyer's requirements.

■ Supplier 2 is used because of their innovative capacity and technical adaptation. They were allocated 30 per cent.

■ Supplier 3 is used for flexibility and adaptability. They were allocated 20 per cent.

Today, and more particularly in the automotive industry that is often the initiator of new methods, operating through *project teams* means rapidly limiting the number of suppliers involved. To use the example of the Peugeot 406 once again, the ECIA company (the sole supplier of dashboards) created a project team of 12 people specifically for Peugeot. The supplier status has taken on a new dimension.

At this stage, let us step back for a moment. This is not a purchasing textbook. However, we believe that we have offered enough for a supplier to understand the purchasing environment.

We have taken the perspective of a buying company, assuming it to be the sole initiator of the process, and assuming too that all decisions were taken autonomously. We detailed the buyer's operations during the purchase (examining the phases within the buying decision), by artificially limiting the effects owing to the interaction of the buyer's organisation with any other external organisations. But the interaction mechanism outlined in Chapter 2 gave us a different perspective: the suppliers can vary their involvement in the buyer's decision process – or, indeed, even be the initiator. For example, during a management seminar at which we discussed this idea, the marketing directors of IBM Europe pointed out that changes in the supply of computers are more closely linked to technological progress than to changes in customer demands. But this does not mean that innovation is not, and should not, be developed without consulting the market and the customers. Rather, it means that in numerous marketing environments, the customer is not really at the origin of the demand, but that this is determined by the supplier who has the job of developing his customer's interest in his offer through a process of interaction. This is related to our theories in Chapter 1 concerning two types of interaction: simulated and direct. The *supplier*, not the customer, often drives the development of a technical core, with all its elements of innovation. The supplier only interacts directly with the customers at a later stage, in a phase of adaptation and adjustment to meet technical specificities (the software, for example) and social and commercial exchanges.

Consequently, procedures and methodologies are required to understand how the buyer operates, given that he or she is both interacting with the supplier and also potentially with several other actors within the broader network. In order to develop this idea further, we will now adopt the point of view of the supplier seeking to understand the buyer by looking at the risks involved, and also the supplier's position relative to the competition.

The Supplier–Customer Relationship: The Risk Approach

The supplier's aim when in front of the buyer is to understand the buyer's environment, in order to be able to anticipate demands and behaviour, or indeed to initiate such demands. This is the only way to define and to propose suitable solutions, at the right time, and to outplay the competition. Because of the nature of the activities and the problems that can arise, the buyer is constantly confronted by uncertainties that are linked to:

■ The *characteristics of the supply market*: this involves understanding how the market will evolve, and whether this allows the buyer to develop as planned over the short, medium and long term.

■ The *relationships with the suppliers* (more of a mid-term perspective) and to their ability to find solutions to everyday problems. Such problems may be related to decisions concerning the selection, deselection, or modification of relationships with a particular supplier. For example, a supplier does a good job but cannot increase the amount delivered: should we change supplier or bring in a second one? Another has reasonable quality and price, but struggles to fulfil the agreed delivery times. Another is our main supplier, and we are satisfied with him, but we cannot deal with just one supplier for such a strategically important component. We are developing a new product, so should we at the same time bring in a new supplier?

We can see from these examples that *uncertainty and risk* are at the very heart of purchasing (note that these concepts overlap very much with the IMP Group's notions of needs, market, and transaction uncertainty, see Håkansson, Johanson and Wootz, 1976). Actions by the buying centre can be interpreted as an attempt to bring the level of risk down to an acceptable and manageable level. This explains actions such as the creation of complementary tests (either internally driven or in collaboration with the supplier), specific requests to suppliers or demands for contractual guarantees from suppliers, or increasing the decision-making process or the complexity of the purchasing centre (more people, more time).

So each purchasing situation can be identified with a problem that needs to be solved, and which also involves risk. At this stage, we shall call this *incurred* risk. The incurred risk can help us to understand the purchasing situation in an 'objective' way. As we shall see below, we propose that this can form the basis for an analysis of the buying situation made by the supplier.

The way in which the buyer's DMU will try to solve the problem depends upon its own characteristics: its composition, the personalities of the people involved, the experience gained during the prior resolution of similar problems, relationships between members, technical skills, the presence of outside advice, etc. For example, a company producing mechanical parts, which has previously introduced electronic relays into its products and which has its own research department, can create competition between different offerings and even choose a relatively unknown supplier whose prices are competitive. Another company producing similar products but starting out in electronics would be more likely to approach a well-known supplier, even if the price is a little higher. Thus, we can add the notion of *perceived* risk to that of incurred risk, and which can be defined as the result of the interpretation and resolution by the DMU of a given purchasing situation. This perceived risk is interpretable by the supplier only by observing the buyer's purchasing behaviour in their relationship.

Figure 3.2 groups together all the concepts of the risk approach method and the links between them.

Understanding customer buying behaviour in business-to-business customers therefore goes through three main stages:

■ The analysis by the supplier of the buyer's purchasing environment, which enables an evaluation of the *incurred* risks

■ The analysis by the supplier of the characteristics of the organisation and purchasing centre to assess the *perceived* risks of the customer, and to detect those involved in the decision making process and to look at the process itself

■ Understanding the *differences* between incurred and perceived risks.

In approaching the buyer, the supplier must consequently make use of the notions of the incurred and perceived risks involved. The role of the supplier could be to reduce the perceived risk, through actions that would depend both on the level of

Figure 3.2   Formation of customer behaviour

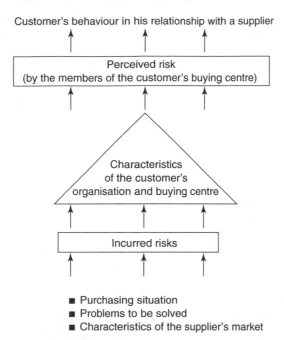

Customer's behaviour in his relationship with a supplier

Perceived risk
(by the members of the customer's buying centre)

Characteristics
of the customer's
organisation and buying centre

Incurred risks

- Purchasing situation
- Problems to be solved
- Characteristics of the supplier's market

the risk and also on which members of the DMU perceive the risk to be highest. The supplier could also stress the existence of differentials between the incurred and perceived risk.

The *risk approach* method is based on two complementary analytical perspectives. These are the *transaction*, including the characteristics of the buyer's purchasing environment in the short term (the 'problem to be solved') and the *relationship* that is formed between the two organisations during the various transactions (more of a mid- to long-term outlook). The main idea presented in the interaction model (Chapter 2) is that a transaction cannot be taken as an isolated event. It is part of a longer-term relationship and is conditioned by this relationship. In the analysis, both the transaction and the relationship are looked at through explanatory factors for the incurred risks (or where the risk comes from) and the nature of the risks (what the risk means). This is completed by the analysis of the organisation and the buyer's DMU, which allows us to both highlight those involved in the decision, and to identify the explanatory factors of the customer's behaviour when confronted by the perceived risks. The five key elements of the diagnostic analysis of the risk approach method are presented in Table 3.7.

Analysis of the Transaction

From a buyer's point of view, a transaction is characterised by a problem to be solved within a given period. Each transaction helps to build a relationship. Each

Table 3.7   The five key elements of the risk approach method

A **Transaction** analysis
   *A*1 Factors explaining incurred risks (understand the sources of perceived risks, measure what is at stake and the degree of risk)
   *A*2 Nature of risks (understand how the risks materialise in the actions undertaken by the customer and what are their characteristics)

B **Relationship** analysis
   *B*1 Factors explaining incurred risks
   *B*2 Nature of the risks

C Analysis of the customer buying centre
   Factors explaining the attitude towards perceived risks

important transaction (an order, bid for tenders, technical evolution, etc.) involves a configuration of specific risks that have to be brought into the open by identifying the explanatory factors influencing the incurred risks.

Explanatory Factors of the Incurred Risks Linked to the Transaction

A transaction can be characterised by the risks associated with it, meaning the impact of the problem on company activity. Four explanatory factors affecting the level of incurred risk can be identified: the degree of *novelty* of the transaction, the *importance* of the problem to the company's activity, the *characteristics* of the *supply market*, and the *characteristics* of the *buyer's downstream market*.

■ The *degree of novelty of the transaction*. There are three possible situations: a *straight rebuy*, a *modified rebuy* and a *new purchase*.

When a company is confronted by new problems, for example when it has little experience of either the problem or the potential solutions involved, the DMU tends to be risk averse and to take a number of precautions. These typically include searching for a significant amount of information, increasing the number of potential suppliers, close examination of the alternatives, involving more people and departments, contacting external advisers and service providers, etc. This can also apply in the case of a modified rebuy, for example when the company needs to increase the quantity purchased, since a good supplier for limited volumes can fail as volumes increase. The purchaser's time is affected by the degree of novelty, identical purchases are managed by routine and energy is devoted to little known problems.

For the customer, therefore, incurred risks will increase proportionally with the novelty of the decision.

■ The *impact of the problem to the company's activity* is measured by the degree to which it affects the production process, or more generally, the company's overall activities. The higher the degree, the higher is the risk.

Three types of situation are possible: the *routine purchase*, the *important purchase* and the *strategic purchase*.

Within this framework, it is not the object purchased that determines how it is to be classified. Rather, it is the impact of the supply of that product on the *buyer's activity*. For example, the purchase of personal computers would be routine if it improves and helps secretarial work, important if it allows the company to rationalise its production process through the implementation of a MRP system and strategic if the company expects an increase in productivity.

Therefore, for any given customer, the higher the risk that the problem represents in terms of the company's basic activity, the higher will be the incurred risks.

■ The *characteristics of the supplier's market* also weigh heavily on the buyer's decision making process. If, economically speaking, there are differences among the suppliers, the customer can choose to abandon a long-term relationship with a chosen supplier to profit from a new market entrant offering significantly lower prices/better service, even if it means dealing with a combination of long-term and one-off suppliers. This becomes evident when a supplier suddenly appears with a cheaper offer or when a technological breakthrough changes relative competitive positions. It is the same for turbulent supply markets where there is no stability among competitive positions. For the buyer, incurred risks are high when the suppliers' offers are heterogeneous and unstable, and low when offers are homogeneous.

■ The *characteristics of the buyer's own downstream market* affects the approach used to evaluating competing suppliers' offers. The following three dimensions can be used to analyse the downstream market:

– *Innovation*: the downstream market can be innovative or traditional. The incurred risks will be higher when the supplier's offer is different to the prevailing conditions in the marketplace: innovative in a traditional market, traditional in an innovative market.

– *Development*: the market may be in recession, flat, or developing. The level of incurred risk is difficult to predict in this case. With two markets in recession, one company might accept a new offer and another reject it. A market in recession will be more sensitive to immediate economic arguments, while a developing market will be more amenable to long-term investment.

– The *competitive position* (leader, challenger, or marginal player) of the buyer in his or her own marketplace can also influence the approach to purchasing. For example, a challenger will be more ready to accept innovative offers in order to be different to the other players. An important issue here is the trend of the buyer's market share, since a negative trend probably implies a buyer becoming more price sensitive.

Therefore, the incurred risks for any buyer will depend on their position in their own market and on their own strategy.

The level of incurred risk is linked to the characteristics of purchasing environment, as dictated by the above criteria. Having determined the different origins of the risks possible, we shall now consider how the buyer views them.

The Nature of the Incurred Risks Linked to the Transaction

It is possible to group the key risks into four main categories, which are dependent on the needs of each individual company: *technical* risks, those related to the availability of *products and services*, those related to the customer's *use* of products and services, and the *financial* risks (see Table 3.8).

We now have a complete grid – complex but realistic – allowing us to analyse any transaction. While we discuss later some practical conditions concerning its application, we can already see how it might be used. For example, a supplier can identify the risks involved, in terms of both their nature and their level, and formulate an offer to a buyer accordingly. For technical risks, the supplier could

Table 3.8   The nature of the risks linked to a transaction

Technical risks
- Customer's ability to elaborate specifications
- Compatibility with customer's manufacturing technology
- Compatibility with user's competencies
- Conformity with functional requirements
- Of product quality during use?
- Quality constancy
- Conformity with norms
- . . .

Risks connected to the availability of products and services
- Time allotted for product delivery
- Delivery conformity
- Delivery punctuality
- . . .

Risks connected to the handling of products and services by the customer
- Requirements in technical assistance before contracting
- Requirements in maintenance, follow-up . . .
- Requirements connected to the competence of individuals (customer)
- Availability in case of malfunction
- Speed in answering complaints
- Compatibility with user's competencies, in the case of services
- Following products in use
- . . .

Financial risks
- Level of prices
- Amount of the expenditure: cost of products and services plus extra costs borne by the customer to integrate the product and the service into the company's activities
- Terms of payment
- Price change
- Currency variations
- . . .

promote the technical part of the offer (products, technical services directly linked to the products). For risks linked to the availability of the products and services, the supplier would offer firm delivery dates, etc. As far as the buyer's use of the products and services are concerned, the supplier could stress the after-sales element of the offer, training or maintenance. For the financial risks, there would be emphasis on the price and conditions of payment. The supplier's offer could be made even more attractive by taking into consideration the explanatory factors of the incurred risks, for example, according to whether the problem to be solved has an impact on just the buyer's own organisation, or on his wider relationships with his own customers.

However it is important to widen the approach to integrate the fact that each transaction is part of an existing or new buyer–supplier relationship. Thus, the characteristics of this relationship could vary, according to how the supplier responds to a problem raised by the buyer during a transaction.

Analysis of the Relationship with the Supplier

Explanatory Factors of the Incurred Risks Linked to the Relationship

A relationship between a supplier and a customer evolves over time as both companies learn from a series of transactions. Several distinct phases of this process can be identified (Ford, 1980). In the first *pre-relationship* phase, both organisations exchange information, get to understand each other's technical competencies and common points of interest. They initiate and develop *mutual knowledge*, both individual and institutional, which, if all goes well, leads to mutual confidence and an interest in working further together. The second phase sees the beginning of the relationship: a subject of *common interest* is found, some form of initial tests are decided upon, and executed according to a prepared format. The involvement of R&D is essential at this stage of the process. This phase can last for many years and can be very costly for both companies in terms of time, the hours incurred, as well as other investments, before resulting in the next *developmental* phase of the relationship. This corresponds to the beginning of the commercial relationship with the delivery of products and/or services. At this point, the buying and selling centres increase their participation and the relationship becomes more complex. Next, (ideally) a *long-term relationship* is begun. This depends on many factors, such as learning by the buyer of the supplier's competencies, the behaviour of the current supplier (the routine of supplies, the benefits from the acquired position, the reluctance to extend investments, etc.), and other elements linked to the environment (rapid customer development, changes in standards and regulations, the reactions of other suppliers, etc.). It is important to point out that if the new relationship demands high investment from both the supplier and the buyer, it will always be costly and risky to change supplier, a fact that is often underestimated. Thus, over time, the relationship evolves and the investments of both organisations change according to the degree of freedom of each party.

When purchasing frequency is low, the existence of a relationship (if there is one) can have a limited effect on the transaction. In Chapter 12, which is devoted to project marketing, we shall look more closely at this type of environment.

In order to understand how a transaction evolves into a relationship, we need to analyse the history and functioning of buyer–supplier relationships by examining two dimensions. These are investment over time and the atmosphere of the relationship, both of which will also help us to anticipate customer behaviour. Here we are taking into account the 'memory effect' which for the supplier represents either an opportunity or a constraint (i.e. looking at previous 'scandals' or 'skeletons in the cupboard'). For example:

■ *Investments over time*. Both buyer and supplier can make these. We can look at the *absolute* level (weak, average, high); whether they are *general* or *specific*; or *application-specific* (linked to a specific supplier–customer relationship); and also the *reciprocity* (who invests the most, or is it equal?). We are therefore able to assess the level of dependence or autonomy of each company in relation to the other.

■ The *atmosphere*. We can assess the level of satisfaction that both organisations experience when working together, and this is a kind of indicator of the potential *durability* of the relationship. This can be analysed from five angles. The first and most important is the *balance of power* that exists between the two companies (from mutual dependence to total independence). The others are the degree of *co-operation* (from a partnership to a relationship based on conflict); the level of *confidence* (from short-term opportunism to confidence in the relationship); *social* and *cultural* differences (from a close relationship to a more distant one); and the level of *mutual understanding* (based on the speed with which things get done). We then need to synthesise these opinions and decide whether the atmosphere is broadly positive or negative. It is clear that from the supplier's point of view, the actions towards the buyer will vary according to the prevailing atmosphere.

The Nature of the Incurred Risks within the Relationship

Two dimensions should be taken into consideration here: the risks associated with being overly dependent on the buyer, and those linked to supplier involvement in the relationship with the buyer. The analysis of the relationship as presented above, can help to qualify the incurred risks on these two dimensions:

■ The risk of being *dependent upon the supplier*, implies not being able to take advantage of competing suppliers' offers, especially if the supplier is suspected of 'abnormally' benefitting from a privileged situation, or of involving the company in taking too many risks. This situation becomes even more dangerous when the supply market contains only a limited number of suppliers. This risk decreases the closer the buyer–supplier relationships are. It also leads to an increase in contractual relationships, giving both supplier and buyer the feeling that power is balanced enough to be acceptable.

■ The risks associated with *supplier involvement* in the relationship represent the promises made to the customer and the actions performed by the supplier to meet perceived needs and demands. For a specific project, the customer expects a certain level of service and involvement from the supplier.

Analysis of the Buyer's DMU

The buying centre consists of people of different and varying degrees of skills, different personalities and with a variable will and/or ability to 'control' the risks. Their approach to solving problems, the way DMU members interact and methods of choosing a supplier are often very different. For similar problem settings, attitudes and behaviour vary enormously from one buyer to another. In a specific purchasing environment, for example, the perception of the risks by a buying centre can be different to the 'objective' analysis of the incurred risks made by the supplier using the approach described above. According to its characteristics and approaches towards decision making, a DMU can increase or decrease the risk level associated with a given purchase. Based on their personality or their position in the organisation, the members of the DMU have access to different information, and this is the basis for their decision. This is what is known as *bounded rationality* (Simon, 1957).

The supplier's evaluation of the differences in nature and level of the incurred risks, and of the risks perceived by the members of the DMU, is one of the keys to understanding the customer, to being able to anticipate their behaviour and demands. The supplier must analyse the purchasing centre very closely from three dimensions: its *composition*, the role of the *Purchasing Department*, and the *interpersonal* relationships with the DMU.

The Composition of the Buying Centre

This is only rarely formalised (unless the buyer is working with a specific project group) and hardly ever obvious to the supplier, whose representatives have to try to identify the members for each purchase situation.

For the supplier, this means understanding the degree of centralisation and co-ordination surrounding the purchase decision, particularly for large companies with centralised buying functions. The extent of centralisation depends on a number of factors, such as the philosophy of the organisation, the type of purchase involved, the existence of central services and of the existence of formal procedures for approval of suppliers.

Identifying the members of the DMU is essential. Who are they? What are their positions? What are their functions within the company? What are their skills in relation to the problem in question? What about their motivation (personal interest in the decision)? And their ability to manage risk, their experience and relationships with other potential suppliers? What are the roles and relative influence of each person within the DMU? One way to find out or even to reconfigure the centre is to begin with the incurred risks and to identify and associate possible members from the buyer's organisation with these risks. Indeed the main mistake of salespeople is too often to think of the buying centre as consisting of their usual set of contacts, and to ignore other sources of influence. In particular, changes to the DMU, which have been ignored or identified too late, can destabilise the position of a supplier who thought that he or she was well established. For example, a new director may wish to completely change purchasing policy: whereas before this was the job of the purchasing manager, changing the head of the computer department can lead to changes in supplier relationships as the role becomes more centralised. Basically, any change in the composition of the buying centre is an opportunity for any new or marginal supplier, and bad news for the established ones. We must also remember that the purchasing centre has a particular configuration according to the particular situation. Any supplier introducing an important technical innovation or moving into a new field is likely to be confronted with a modified buying centre, given that the nature and level of risks are different. For example, in Table 3, the supplier T who was looking to supply gear boxes made from a new metal alloy, noticed that they first had to work with the manufacturer's 'advanced design office', a department with which they had never worked before.

The Role of the Purchasing Department

The Purchasing Department is a vital service provider to the DMU, but its actual role is, however, rarely decisive. While neglecting the help that can come from the department can lead to failure, so can too much influence from the department. An innovation, for example, is often perceived and valued far better by the research and marketing departments than by the buying function. At an extreme level, the buying department can act as a filter and block any proposed deal, not necessarily for reasons of power, but also because of other criteria. For example, a company's purchasing department may decide that, for strategic reasons, they do not wish to deal with a regular supplier when purchasing a new range of products, whereas the technical services staffs wish to develop closer relationships with them for reasons of mutual skills development. So we can see that two points can be raised about the centralised purchasing department. The technical and marketing skills of the buyer: what are his or her motivations and arguments to be used? Understanding the status and the power of the buying centre is also essential – the seller has to be able to differentiate between the real decision makers and the people who simply act to carry out the wishes of others.

Relationships between Members of the DMU

Relationships, conflicts and the ability to work together as a group have to be considered. The more conflicting the intragroup relationships, the longer the decision process is likely to take, and the less rational the decision will seem to the supplier. Other than normal 'conflicts' concerning differing objectives between functional areas (the production manager wants long production runs, the salesman wants greater flexibility in production, etc.), personal problems can also concern the supplier. The supplier should not be drawn into the trap whereby he or she is accused of creating conflict when in fact the problem is internal to the DMU.

Defining the purchasing centre and understanding its function will enable us to identify both the individuals who should be the supplier's target customers, and also the incurred risks.

Practical Applications

The risk approach is both an analytical framework to understand how a business buyer operates, and also a practical tool whose objective is to give help to the supplier's sales and marketing managers in defining or deciding upon their operational action. Therefore, we consider it to be a worthwhile approach to both managing important customer files and also to segmenting the market (this will be dealt with in Chapter 6). At this stage, we shall only look at the use of the risk approach in the management of relationships with buyers, and momentarily ignore the fact that the supplier can vary his or her level of involvement in the relationship, which will be dealt with in Chapter 9. We recommend using the complete approach with the sales directors – or, even better, all the members of the supplier sales centre – for a limited number of key customers and key prospects. For relatively stable and recurrent transactions, we will concentrate on those involving a high degree of innovation. The lessons learned from such an analytical exercise will then be automatically translated to less important cases, without the same degree of formal analysis being required.

Our objective here is to describe the complete approach and how to use it. The approach involves analysing a transaction with a customer in the context of an existing or new relationship. It does not replace the customer's 'sales file', but should enrich such information. The method is essentially a grid, identifying the type and order of information required for the smooth running of a relationship. The risk approach method involves three different phases: the analysis of the *factors explaining the incurred risks*, the analysis of the *buyer's DMU*, and the synthesis of the *overall risk analysis*.

The Analysis of the Factors Explaining the Incurred Risks

The supplier needs to evaluate both the *nature* and the *level* of the buyer's incurred risks, based on a systematic analysis of the purchasing situation, which in turn is based on a simple document using the elements identified above. The incurred risk for the buyer is based on a number of factors: there are four transaction-based factors, and two linked to the relationship itself. Whether judged to be 'high', 'medium' or 'low', the evaluation attempts to give a relative evaluation based on more than just subjective gut feeling. This means that an overall judgment will be reached, based on successive consideration of each type of risk, as shown in Table 3.9.

Table 3.9   Analysis of the explanatory factors of the incurred risks

Explanantory factors				Degree of incurred risk	
Linked to transactions					
1 – *Degree of novelty of transactions*					
– New buy	❐			HIGH	❐
– Modified rebuy	❐			MEDIUM	❐
– Straight rebuy	❐			LOW	❐
2 – *Importance of what is at stake in the customer's activity*					
– Strategic buying	❐			HIGH	❐
– Important buying	❐			MEDIUM	❐
– Current buying	❐			LOW	❐
3 – *Characteristics of the customer's downstream market*					
– Homogeneous	❐	Heterogeneous ❐		HIGH	❐
– Stable	❐	Unstable ❐		MEDIUM	❐
				LOW	❐
4 – *Characteristics of the customer's downstream market*					
– Innovative	❐	– Traditional ❐			
– Expansion	❐			HIGH	❐
Stagnant	❐			MEDIUM	❐
Recessionary	❐			LOW	❐
– Competitive position					
Marginal	❐				
Challenger	❐				
Leader	❐				
Linked to the relationship					
1 – *Are the supplier's investments*					
– Easy ❐	Complex ❐			HIGH	❐
– General ❐	Specific ❐			MEDIUM	❐
– Low ❐	Medium ❐	High ❐		LOW	❐
– *Are the customer's investments*					
– Easy ❐	Complex ❐				
– General ❐	Specific ❐				
– Low ❐	Medium ❐	High ❐			
2 – *Atmosphere*					
– Positive	❐			HIGH	❐
– Negative	❐			MEDIUM	❐
– Neutral	❐			LOW	❐

The Analysis of the Buyer's DMU

This should be based on those factors previously identified. There is a dual approach to be employed here. First, we need to make the link between the individuals concerned and their particular risks: they are the *supplier's targets*. At this stage, evaluations of the supplier's own position within the buying centre is important in determining possible actions. This could be done in a number of ways – for example, by looking at current personal relationships that exist between the buying centre and the selling centre. A look at the competitors' contacts within the buying centre may also be useful. Secondly, it means evaluating the *gaps between the incurred risks*, which result from the analysis that the supplier has made of the purchasing situation, and the *perceived risks*, resulting from the seller's interpretation of the behaviour of the members of the buying centre.

A good method of analysing the organisation's buying centre involves limiting the definition of the centre by linking the incurred risks and members of the centre by successive iterations. To do this means both highlighting the available information on buyer behaviour (from members of the centre, customer organisation chart, minutes of meetings, etc.), and also relying on experience of similar relationships with other customers.

The Synthesis of the Risk Analysis

We propose to make use of a grid, such as that shown in Table 3.10. The aim of this approach is to find, for each type of risk, both the level of incurred risk and the level of perceived risk, in order to simulate and anticipate probable buyer behaviour and hence to define possible supplier action to reduce that risk. It is possible to highlight a number of such possible actions:

- Actions which reduce the highest levels of perceived risks

- Actions which reduce risks where there is a gap between incurred and perceived risks

- Rapid actions, used when relationship analysis shows problems of conflict, etc.

- Actions which lead to supplier differentiation, hopefully long-lasting and difficult to imitate

- Actions that enhance the buyer–supplier relationship, involving the creation of interdependence between the two companies; this type of relationship in fact helps pay off supplier investment

- Actions having a direct impact on the atmosphere of the buyer–supplier relationship.

Table 3.10 A synthetic grid for the approach risk method

Nature of risks	Level of incurred risks	Level of perceived risks	Characteristics of the customer's buying centre		Customer's likely behaviour	Possible supplier's actions
			Names	Functions		
RISKS CONNECTED WITH TRANSACTIONS *Technical risks* ■ Customer's ability to design specifications ■ Compatibility with the customer's manufacturing technology ■ Compatibility with user's competences ■ Conformity with the functional requirements ■ Use product quality ■ Quality consistancy ■ Norms conformity . . .						
Risks connected to the availability of product and services ■ Time allotted for product delivery ■ Delivery conformity ■ Delivery punctuality . . .						
Risks connected to handling of products and services by the customer ■ Requirements in technical assistance before contracting ■ Requirements in maintenance, follow-up . . . ■ Requirements connected to the competence of individuals (customer) ■ Availability in case of malfunction ■ Speed of answering complaints ■ Compatibility with user's competences, in the case of services ■ Following products in use . . .						
Financial risks ■ Level of prices ■ Amount of the expenditure: cost of products and services plus extra costs borne by the customer to integrate the product and the service in the company's activities ■ Terms of payment ■ Price change ■ Currency variations . . .						
RISKS CONNECTED WITH THE RELATIONSHIP ■ Risk of customer dependence ■ Level of supplier's commitment						

The application of these grids represents a method for anticipating the buyer's demand, and has proven useful for providing the supplier with the ability to think ahead by 'putting them inside their customer's mind', and so gaining a real competitive edge.

The risk approach is a tool to analyse and understand organisational buyer's purchasing behaviour. It offers a solid base for the sales team in their work, and also in dialogue with their superiors and others within their company. Our examples show how this approach can help to plan innovative actions within the framework of a negotiation or relationship with a particular buyer. We shall see later, that the information obtained can be used to formulate scenarios for different relationships with buyers, and also the choice of a scenario to define and achieve a particular position with a buyer. More generally, the information gathered from customers, and also through more traditional company means, can help with market segmentation and with the definition of a competitive market position. We hope that the reader can see an emerging logic, one that takes information on customers, and turns it into a real marketing information system.

References and Further Reading

Anderson, J. and Narus, J. (1999) *Business Market Management, Understanding, Creating, and Delivering Value*, Englewood Cliffs, Prentice-Hall.

Buckner, H. (1967) *How British Industry Buys*, London, Hutchinson.

Choffray, J.M. and Lilien, G. (1978) 'Assessing Response to Industrial Marketing Strategy', *Journal of Marketing*, 42, 20–31.

Dickson, G. (1966) 'An Analysis of Vendor Selection Systems and Decisions', *Journal of Purchasing*, February, 5–17.

Ford, D. (1980) The Development of Buyer–Supplier Relationships in Industrial Markets, *European Journal of Marketing*, 14:5/6, 339–54.

Ford, D. (ed.) (1997) *Understanding Business Markets*, New York, Academic Press.

Ford, D. *et al.* (1998) *Managing Business Relationships*, New York, Wiley.

Goujet, R., Bansard, D. and Salle, R. (1992) 'L'établissement des relations fournisseurs-client en milieu industriel', *Gestion 2000*, 6, 47–75.

Groupe Ecully (1996) *Négocier: entreprises et négociations*, Paris, Ellipses.

Håkansson, H., Johanson, J. and Wootz, B. (1976) 'Influence Tactics in Buyer–Seller Processes', *Industrial Marketing Management*, 4, 319–32.

Hillier, T.J. (1975) 'Decision-Making in the Corporate Industrial Buying Process', *Industrial Marketing Management*, 4, 99–106.

Kraljic, P. (1983) 'Purchasing Must Become Supply Management', *Harvard Business Review*, September–October, 109–17.

Lockett, A. and Naudé, P. (1991) 'Winning a Large Order, a Case Study Using Judgemental Modelling', *Industrial Marketing Management*, 3, 169–75.

Magretta, J. (1998) 'The Power of Virtual Integration: An Interview with Dell Computer's Michael Dell', *Harvard Business Review*, March–April, 73–84.

Midler, F. (1993) *L'auto qui n'existait pas, management de projet et transformation de l'entreprise*, Paris, InterEditions.

Möller, K. (1981) 'Industrial Buying Behaviour of Production Materials: A Conceptual Model and Analysis', *Helsinki School of Economics Publications*, B54, Helsinki.

Möller, K. (1986) 'Buying Behavior of Industrial Components: Inductive Approach for Descriptive Model Building', in P. Turnbull and S. Paliwoda, *Research in International Marketing*, London, Croom Helm, 79–132.

Naudé, P., Lockett, A. and Holmes, K. (1997) 'A Case Study of Strategic Engineering Decision Making Using Judgemental Modelling', *IEEE Transactions on Engineering Management*, 44:3, 237–47.

Ozanne, U. and Churchill, G. (1971) 'Five Dimensions of the Industrial Adoption Process', *Journal of Marketing Research*, 8, 322–8.

Perrotin, R. and Louberu, J.M. (1996) *Nouvelles stratégies d'achat: sous-traitance, coopération partenariat?*, Paris, Ed. d'Organisation.

Robinson, P., Faris, C. and Wind, Y. (1967) *Industrial Buying and Creative Marketing*, London, Allyn & Bacon.

Salle, R. and Silvestre, H. (1992) *Vendre à l'industrie: approche stratégique de la relation Business to Business*, Paris, Ed. Liaisons.

Sheth, J. (1973) 'A Model of Industrial Buyer Behavior', *Journal of Marketing*, 37, 50–6.

Simon, H.A. (1957) *Administrative Behavior*, London, Palgrave Macmillan.

Uncles, M.D. and Ehrenberg, A.S. (1990) 'Industrial Buying Behavior: Aviation Fuel Contracts', *International Journal of Research in Marketing*, 7, 57–68.

Valla, J.-P. (1986) 'The French Approach to Europe', in P. Turnbull and J.-P. Valla, *Strategies for International Industrial Marketing*, London, Croom Helm, 11–78.

Webster, F. and Wind, Y. (1972) 'A General Model of Organisational Buying Behavior', *Journal of Marketing*, 36, 12–19.

Weele, A.J. van (1995) *Purchasing Management: Analysis, Planning and Practice*, London, Chapman & Hall.

Woodside, A. and Vyas, N. (1986) 'Microanalysis of Supplier Choice Strategies: Industrial Packaging Materials', in K. Backhaus and D. Wilson, *Industrial Marketing: A German–American Perspective*, Berlin, Springer-Verlag.

Woodside, A. and Vyas, N. (1986) *Industrial Purchasing Strategies*, Lexington, Lexington Books.

Discussion Questions

1 Why are multiple members of a firm from various functions often involved in a single purchase? And why are decisions sometimes taken just by a single person?

2 What are the differences between the concepts of the 'purchasing process' and that of the 'interaction process' as a way to analyse purchasing activities?

3 What are the reasons for a customer to change suppliers?

4 Why and how is the concept of risk of help in understanding business-to-business customer behaviour?

Chapter 1
Competitiveness, Marketing and Business-to-Business Marketing
What is marketing all about *Different marketing environments* *B2B marketing*

Chapter 2			
Business-to-Business Customers and Markets			
B2B Generic Offers	*Technological Innovation*	*Pure Services*	*Major Projects*

PART I   STRATEGY FOUNDATIONS

Chapter 3	Chapter 4	Chapter 5	Chapter 6
Understanding Business-to-Business Purchasing	**Information and Information Systems**	**Markets and Suppliers' Strategy**	**Segmentation and Marketing Strategy**

PART II   STRATEGY IMPLEMENTATION

Chapter 7			
Generic Business-to-Business Offer Design and Management			

Chapter 8	Chapter 10	Chapter 11	Chapter 12
Market Access and Customer Management	**Marketing and Technological Innovation**	**The Marketing of Services**	**Major Project Marketing**

Chapter 9
Communication and Publicity/ Advertising

PART III   STRATEGY DESIGN

Chapter 13	The Role and Organisation of Marketing
Chapter 14	Customer Position, Market Position, Marketing Strategies and Planning
Chapter 15	Issues and Specificities of International Marketing
Annex	The Internet and Marketing: Some Ideas

4 Information and Information Systems

In previous chapters we used or quoted a number of different sources of information: the textile industry, relationships in the poultry-breeding industry, supplier choice policy for a Swedish vehicle manufacturer, market segmentation criteria, and so on. The amount of information available to companies is vast. They are after all part of a system, which is open to the outside world. Through a number of antennae, the company collects information of varying importance, which is the key to effective marketing. However, this information is never perfect. *It is always tainted in some way.*

Four major questions should be raised involving the information required for effective marketing planning in a company. The first involves the value of the *existing information*. Diverging and contradictory information on the same subject is commonplace. Which is the right information? Some potentially important information is unclear: a certain major customer has begun testing a new supplier. Is this true? What is their intention? Is it because of our poor performance? The second question is linked to the first and deals with the definition of the *required information* and its availability. Many people have information of varying importance. Which is the best information? Who has it? Where can it be found? The third is based on the *people* in an organisation. Having information is a source of power, which allows the owner room for manoeuvre or the ability to allocate particular resources. If a salesperson knows he is sure to get a significant order, he keeps the information to himself in order to obtain extra resources. How can this be avoided and how can management know about such situations in advance? On the other hand, and this is our fourth issue, information can be *invented* to justify a decision which has already been taken.

Therefore the management of information is not easy. Defining the required information, collecting and sorting it to make it useful are all part of the marketing manager's job. We believe that the management of information collected for marketing purposes should be dealt with from a deontological perspective. This includes both the objective and the means used to obtain the desired result, as explained in the following definition: '*marketing research is based on the systematic and objective collection, analysis and interpretation of the information required for decision making about the successful launch of products and/or services.*' The deontological debate concerns the terms used in this definition and in particular the issues involved in 'analysis', 'interpretation' and 'objective'. Many people have highlighted the disagreement between market survey specialists on one hand, who have a scientific approach to the problem, and managers on the other, who are more tempted by pragmatic information manipulation and the use of intuition in their interpretation.

It is true that intuition, which plays a major part in decision making, and which has never really been investigated, represents a personal way of analysing information. When the information is wrong, partial or insubstantial, the decision can be disastrous. Generally speaking, business-to-business managers tend to underestimate the importance of the amount of information required for effective marketing. We remember the case of a company, which, over a number of years, had spent something like 10 000 k Euros on technical research and development and yet, had trouble finding the 100 k Euros required for market surveys to re-examine all the underlying economic assumptions behind the project. This example is perhaps a little contradictory to our opening statements concerning the abundance of information. This apparent anomaly means that it is important to utilise all *latent* information first and to assess the value of this information. Once again, the marketing planning process, beginning with market segmentation, is necessarily based on a quantity of information, and if this is in any way deficient, the marketing manager can find himself or herself badly disadvantaged.

Of course, in this chapter we are going to look at marketing information directly related to the business-to-business environment, which is very different from the more typical approach utilised in consumer marketing. In addition, other related aspects of the problem are dealt with in other chapters: data analysis and segmentation (Chapter 6), planning (Chapter 14), and special processes for special situations (Chapter 10, new technologies, Chapter 12, major projects). This chapter, after defining marketing information, the scope and the nature of the phenomena to be observed and dealing with the different sources of information, will present a marketing research method which is adapted to business-to-business marketing. Finally, we propose a structure for a marketing information system.

In order to put this chapter more into context, let us stress that this is a book about business-to-business marketing, not about marketing research – many excellent textbooks, such as that of Malhotra and Birks (1999), cover the topic of marketing research in great detail. Those wishing to cover the area in more detail should consult one of the texts indicated at the end of the chapter.

Marketing Information

Although closely related, marketing information can be categorised in two ways and classified accordingly. The first is concerned about having a good understanding of the markets and helping companies to be more acquainted with the marketplace, while the second is more operational.

Information Concerning a General Understanding of the Markets

This information comes from the company's attitude towards wanting to know and to understand the markets in which it currently or potentially operates, and to continually update this knowledge. But this information does not spontaneously materialise – there has to be a *systematic way in which to collect it*. Such data must detail both current and also potential future markets in which the company is interested. The information can be grouped as follows:

- Appreciation of *market dynamics*: the economic environment, the social and legal environment, technical developments, any changes in the structure of the industrial sector and the dynamics of the final demand

- Appreciation of *customer dynamics*: economic, technical and financial changes, different buying centres and their policies, the present level of customer satisfaction, as well as perceptions of, and attitudes towards, suppliers

- Appreciation of the *competition*: their financial and organisational structure, growth, technical developments, details of their offers, their marketing effort, their strength and weaknesses

- *Market structure*: information and analysis to give the company an overall view of its markets

- Appreciation of the *competitive position of the company*: the image as perceived by the market actors, the strengths and weaknesses of the offer (perceived relative quality).

Information Linked to the Offer and Commercial Action

It is possible to group the information as follows:

- *Sales monitoring*: per customer, customer type, region, offer type, market segment, market, sales agent, sales unit and so on. This process often leads to other types of surveys better to understand trends and changes in sales.

- *Information linked to the elaboration of the offer*: tests, ratification of the results, perceived relative quality, impact of services linked to the offer, price and financial conditions, including any impact of the particular brands.

- *Advertising and sales promotions*: choice of advertising theme and campaign, impact and anticipated impact.

- *Distribution monitoring*: evolution of intermediary distribution companies, role of distributors for the customers, distribution coverage, sales areas, price and sales conditions, importance of logistics for the user and competitors policies.

Figure 4.1   Utility of marketing information

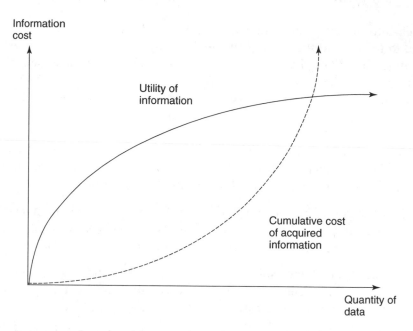

- *Promotion monitoring*: customer interest in any promotions, motivation of decision makers, policy of the competition.

This represents a lot of information. It does not imply that all companies must have all the above information available at all times. Information is sometimes extremely expensive to obtain, and hence is it necessary to choose between the necessity and use of the information, and the cost (Figure 4.1).

The *utility* of the information is linked to how it is *utilised*. It is possible to appreciate information for its *relevance*, its *accuracy* and its *timeliness*. The carrier pigeon announcing the news of the battle of Waterloo to Rothschild's in London is a remarkable example of these three qualities, even if not directly linked to marketing. The relevance can be found in the fact that the London Stock Exchange would be affected by news of either a defeat or a victory. The accuracy was announcing the 'true' information, and having done so at the right time, in other words before other traders heard of the news. The Stock Exchange was depressed, waiting to hear the outcome of the battle, and Rothschild's bought massively while others waited, then sold immediately after the victory was announced officially. If all marketing information had these three qualities, companies would be better off!

Information Horizons and Kind of Phenomenon to Watch

The example above of the pigeon and Waterloo underlines the fact that two elements must be carefully monitored. The first deals with the facts observed and how

Table 4.1 Methods of evaluation of phenomena and information collection

Time horizon \ How things evolve	Deviations	Trends	Mutations	Breaks
Immediate (week)	Invoicing	–	–	–
Short term (<6 months)	Order book Action plans Customers/ markets	Customer files Claims Customer panels Customer satisfaction barometers	Market experts (network)	–
Medium term (6 months–3 years)	–	Customer panels Market surveys	Market surveys Experts network	Marginal actors Weak signals watch
Long term (>3 years)	–	Market surveys	Marketing watch Technological watch Experts network	Delphi surveys Scenarios method Futurology

they evolve. Indeed, some phenomena can be *gaps* (in relation to forecasts) or *trends* (the introduction of 'electronics' in the mechanics industries) whose causes are easily identifiable and whose effects are obvious both in their intensity and horizon. Others have impacts on markets and the environment, which are not so obvious. The latter can affect market behaviour radically, for example laser-based techniques or ink-jet techniques completely changed the printer market. It would appear that the methods utilised to collect information to define gaps and trends are not suitable for identifying phenomena which will result in changes or radical upheavals (Table 4.1). In particular, quantitative methods of collection (invoices, panels, measures of customer satisfaction, etc.) are useless for this latter category, although they provide an illusion of security. This will be dealt with in more detail in Chapter 14.

Table 4.1 presents a classification of the methods of information collection, which is relatively good for identifying changes and phenomenon. Some of these methods already exist in companies (invoices, order books, customer files) and simply need to be organised from a marketing point of view to produce meaningful information. Others require more effort (time, skill, budget).

Relevant Information Sources

One of the characteristics of business-to-business marketing is the *multiplicity of sources* of potentially relevant information. There are many reasons for this.

Table 4.2   Sources of marketing information

Secondary sources	
Internal	**External**

■ Sales:
  ✓ Statistics
  ✓ Sales people reports
  ✓ Customer files
  ✓
■ Research and development (patents)
■ Manufacturing
■ Quality control/claims
■ After-sales service/maintenance
■ Customers accounting
■ Credit management
■ Purchasing department (suppliers)
■ Talks with competitors and other players
■ And so on . . .
	■ Trade associations
	■ Data bases (Internet)
	■ Papers and magazines
	■ General economic surveys
	■ Sector economic surveys
	■ Trade fairs
	■ www

Primary sources
= Marketing research ■ Qualitive surveys ■ Quantitative surveys ■ Customer satisfaction surveys (barometers) ■ Field observation ■ Concept/product test ■ Customer relationship management (CRM)

Dealing directly with a customer means having specific information on the customer that can sometimes be highly confidential (this information cannot be shared with others, and, if it is, it potentially loses its value), and usually only the people currently in contact with the customer can obtain it. A customer belongs to an industrial sector and to a chain of technical operations; they enter a network of agreements and sub-contractors. All these actors have information concerning the customer's activity that the supplier needs to identify and utilise. Thus, the supplier needs to identify those people who possess the relevant information and to build a system of *relationships* in order to obtain it. This is the case both outside and inside the customer's company (Table 4.2). Visits, reports following interviews and meetings at trade fairs, publications, etc. can all contain far more essential information than monthly sales figures.

Consequently, it is easy to understand why industrial groups find it harder to come by such information than companies in the retail business. Only some professions (veterinary medicines, plant-care products or pharmaceuticals, for example) have managed to do so. The reason is that these professions work with large numbers of customers which brings them closer to the large distribution markets and means that they can set up tools which are similar to those used in consumer marketing. For the majority of business-to-business markets, however, the multiplicity of sources must be taken into consideration when collecting information.

To make things clearer, we have grouped the sources into two main groups: *existing* (or secondary) and *planned* (or primary) sources such as surveys of some kind.

Existing sources correspond to the people, organisations, tools and operations whose main objective is not to supply information, but who, because of their function, possess relevant marketing information.

Existing internal sources correspond to the daily activities of the company and to procedures, which take place inside the company. The information held by individuals within the company about customers and markets is vast. Moreover, this information is vital. It is up-to-date, representing what the individuals in the company know at any given time about customers and markets. Some (accounts, sales statistics, etc.) are more concrete, more repetitive than others. This information is more *qualitative*, meaning that it has the capacity to provide managers with a better understanding of customers and markets.

We shall use the term 'qualitative' to describe all methods of collecting and analysing information with the aim of understanding a phenomenon: buyer purchasing behaviour, market segment reaction to a new offer, customer evaluation of a service and so on. This is the fundamental process whereby the information collected can be checked for its accuracy just as for any other scientific approach.

The internal sources do not spontaneously supply information. Company organisation, structure or policy may prevent the free flow of information. The information supplied may also not be suitable for good marketing decisions. Thus, as we shall see, all sources of information need to be investigated fully in the design of a marketing information system.

Existing external sources are those supplied by external organisations, without any control by the company over the methods of collection and analysis used. They vary in both nature and quality. Sometimes they are unusable, especially when searching for data on product categories that are meaningful to the company (a range of products, for example), but where much broader classifications have been published (typically by Customs and Excise, and government statistics), who generally publish their reports long after data were collected. These official sources are generally more useful when their information concerns broad areas about which the company has little prior knowledge: new customers, unexploited business sectors, unexplored countries, etc. They are more interesting here than when the company already has information available (which is generally more precise and reliable).

Some databases, through their specialisation or the area they cover, are more interesting. They are often made up of a compilation of official sources, which are then analysed differently to give more detailed insights. For example, the company data bases (Kompass, Dun & Bradstreet, etc.) are more easily accessible and efficient. The product data bases (Kompass, CCI Plus, etc.) are more difficult to use for the reasons mentioned above.

The survey organisations conduct surveys within certain sectors of activity, either for several customers at the same time (multiclient surveys) or through their own initiative to sell them later to any interested party. They are either generalists (Frost and Sullivan, Battelle, etc.) or else specialised in a particular industry or profession. They represent a category that is beginning to resemble what we call marketing research.

Marketing Research

Marketing research involves many techniques and perspectives. In business-to-business marketing, the general process is similar to that used in consumer research, however the methods used are different. The absence of panels, the non-existence of simulated test-market procedures and the less frequent use of quantitative techniques are the main differences. It is also plausible to suggest that business-to-business companies, through their relative inexperience of existing techniques and low marketing budgets, do not really exploit the full potential of marketing research. Companies are therefore going without important information, which would allow them to save time and money by making the development of new processes or techniques more efficient.

We shall look at this field by identifying several points that partly overlap. The first relates to the kind of information sought in undertaking the research: is the company seeking information that will enable it better to understand the issue in question, and/or information which makes some quantification of the issue easier? This is the debate about the choice between a *qualitative* and *quantitative* approach. The second concerns the *methods* of collecting the information, which has an influence on the nature and quality of the results obtained (for example, what type of marketing research can be undertaken by the sales force, or would it be better to use an external consultant?). The third concerns the *definition of the population* to be covered by the research and, consequently, the population to be sampled. All these questions, however, are raised only once the choice of whether to use formal research has been made, which implies the prior existence of a *decision-making process*.

The Decision Process of Whether to Use a Formal Market Survey

It is difficult to describe the exact process for companies, since it varies by organisational structure and experience. Moreover, the complexity of the problems to be studied can vary from one situation to another. We will nonetheless present a general model, which has the advantage of giving room for questions and for grouping most of the choices that have to be made in an integrated manner (Figure 4.2). It must be remembered that this is not applicable to the more innovative technologies and products, or to cases of major projects, with which we shall deal later.

Figure 4.2 needs some description. A degree of experience is required to recognise that a company lacks the sufficiently reliable information that it needs in order

Figure 4.2   General process for the study of an industrial market

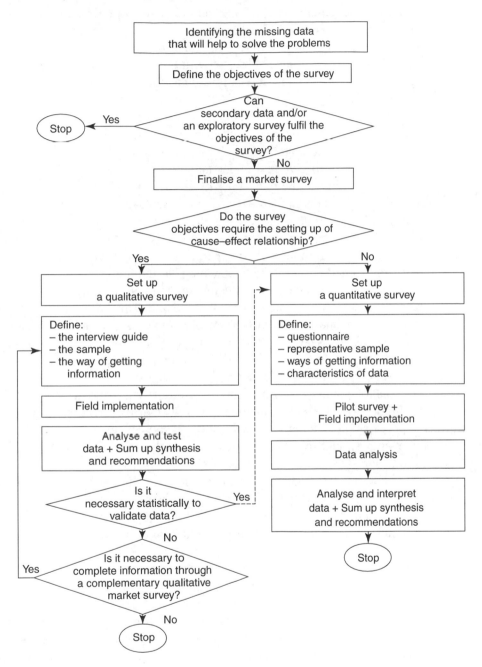

to make a decision. The typically low budget allocated to marketing research in business-to-business companies shows just how far many managers are from the required level of experience. Having reached a decision to begin a formal information search, we recommend proceeding step by step.

The exploratory phase involves identifying the relevant players, the buying behaviour and general issues. This requires two steps. The first is to identify and use all available secondary sources of information. These can vary according to the geographical scope of the survey: regional, national, European, international, etc. However the nature of the sources vary little: general economic and technical data, legal matters, general and specialised data bases, the press, previously published articles and surveys on the same subject are all available for free or at a very low cost. An examination of these sources helps to generate a certain level of knowledge concerning the market in question. It indicates types of users and uses. It outlines qualitative and quantitative developments, etc. However, this approach is not usually sufficient to give real understanding of the market and how it works. This only really begins by the interviews of *experts* or *opinion leaders* in the market(s) concerned. In each area there are skilled or specialised experts. The survey begins with the identification, usually using documentary sources, of one such expert who is interviewed. This person will then hopefully identify other experts who in turn identify other even more skilled experts, etc. (This is often called the *snowballing* approach to market research.) Depending on the complexity of the problem, 6–8 such interviews can take place to define the market, the players, their relationships, the technical and economic stakes involved, etc. This begins to develop the understanding of the market. As for survey techniques, interviewing the experts is like a *non-directive interview* (see below). One of the specific difficulties of this technique is the validation of any hypotheses. One common practice, which is similar to the validation of a journalist's sources, is to accept the validity of a hypothesis given by two experts independently – or, in case of disagreement, the confirmation by a third independent expert. For greater intellectual rigour, it is possible to combine the previous procedure to a classification of sources by level of *reliability* (*A*, *B*, *C*, for example), and to accept a hypothesis only if it is confirmed by two level *A* experts, etc. This work in collaboration with experts has given rise to a formalised methodology whose objective is aimed more towards long-term forecasts. This is the *Delphi* method, which we shall explore later.

The qualitative phase has a systematic characteristic that the exploratory phase does not have. It involves defining a sample and the method of collecting the information in order to guarantee that, as far as possible, the results represent the population as a whole.

Constructing the sample is made possible by the fact that, statistically speaking, 'the population' has been identified and defined. It is generally made up of companies. However, in business-to-business marketing, it is also important to identify the *external* actors to the companies (sectors and networks, see Chapter 2) and also the *internal* actors (purchasing centres, purchasing processes, see Chapter 3). Of course, the aim of the qualitative phase is to identify the players and to use them to understand how the market functions. However, in building a formal survey plan, one cannot allow for chance factors or for unplanned changes in direction as may occur in the exploratory phase, and thus it is necessary to have identified all the players beforehand. The sample is a 'typical sample', which represents all categories of players, but without the possibility of statistical extrapolation to cover the whole of the population.

Collecting the information is linked to the make-up of the sample and to the nature of the problem under study. The term 'qualitative' means that interest is focused on understanding the phenomenon. This assumes that the person asking the questions can adapt the line of questioning in the light of responses received while doing the interview in order to grasp the nuances and to spot contradictions without losing sight of the main objectives of the survey. The basis for this is the *interview guide* (see p. 110) that simply identifies the main issues to be discussed, rather than using a questionnaire that necessarily limits information. Using formalised questionnaires requires the researcher to aggregate responses in a way that leaves little room for understanding personal views. Collecting information can be either through face-to-face interviews or over the telephone, using a tape recorder if those questioned agree.

Writing the interview guide presupposes a certain level of knowledge of technical issues and of the vocabulary of the profession. These elements are often acquired during the exploratory phase, but the advice of a 'specialist' is often useful at this stage. In some cases a technically skilled questioner has a considerable advantage over others, as the interviewee is sure of being understood, etc. In other cases it can be a disadvantage, if the interviewer enters into a technical discussion or even argument with the interviewee. The interviewer's professionalism is therefore the key to the success of the interview. The information collected is then analysed through a *content analysis*, followed by a *synthesis* of the information, which leads to *recommendations* concerning the initial problem.

When we wish to move onto a larger survey (for example, some hundreds of interviews), although not statistically representative, we have to apply the quantitative approach. Although not typically done, it is possible to apply a range of multivariate analytical tools to a typical data set (see, for example, Morris, Berthon and Pitt, 1999).

The quantitative phase must be preceded by an exploratory or qualitative phase (Table 4.3), which helps to understand the issues in question. The aim of the quantitative phase is to measure, to estimate and to describe the issues through *numerical data*. How many customers are interested in our new technology? What is their purchasing potential? What percentage of buyers will adopt this new standard? And so on. The nature of the information sought assumes that the figures obtained accurately reflect the view of the total population questioned. Thus, questions concerning the *representativeness* of the sample are essential. As the information collected is more related to facts than to opinions, the research instrument used for collecting the information is typically no longer than the interview guide but rather a questionnaire with a number of closed questions. Accordingly, the questionnaire can be sent by the post, completed over the telephone or in person. Interviewer skills are less important, since dialogue is limited and the survey manager makes the choice of respondents.

Table 4.3   Qualitative and quantitative in industrial market surveys

Qualitative approach	Quantitative approach
Objectives:	**Objectives:**
– discovering	– measuring
– understanding	– estimating
– explaining	– describing
To set up hypothesis ——complementary views——▶	*To validate hypothesis*
Data collection:	**Data collection:**
– personal interview	– diverse data collection mode
↳ from open-ended to dichotomous questions	↳ from personal to postal
– group interview	– but an always personal
↳ interview guide	↳ standard questionnaire
Typical sample	*Representative sample*
Data analysis:	**Data analysis:**
– in-depth content analysis	– statistical analysis
↳ psychology, search for correlations	↳ univariate – bivariate multivariate analysis

The analysis of the information is dependent upon the format of the questionnaire (yes–no answers, attitude scales, numerical data, etc.) and sample size (high number of questions and individuals questioned). Specific survey analysis software may be utilised. We shall limit our remarks to uni- and bi-variate analysis. Multivariate analyses, although highly adapted to data analysis and widely used in consumer marketing, are less frequently employed in business-to-business environments. However, this is not to say that the application of multivariate tools do not find application within the arena of business-to-business marketing. For example, Hipkin and Naudé (1999), Morris, Berthon and Pitt (1999), and Naudé and Buttle (2000) all provide examples of different multivariate tools being used to advance our understanding of how business markets operate.

The *process* described above includes the recommendation of undertaking quantitative research only on the basis of sufficient qualitative knowledge. This is where the novelty of the subject for the company plays a part. In a well-explored market, it is possible to undertake a quantitative research directly. But as soon as a new issue appears, qualitative and/or exploratory phases are imperative. The understanding of issues is a prerequisite for developing a *hypothesis*, which the quantitative methods can then assess. It should be remembered however, that we have dealt separately (see Chapter 6 on segmentation) with that part of marketing research concerned with developing our understanding of the market, which may or may not include further data analysis. The strategic importance of this task puts all these methods at the interface between the specific field of market surveys and of strategic planning. Our choice is to put them in the second category.

Table 4.4 Methods of collecting information

Objectives	Interview guide		Questionnaire Structured
	Unstructured	Semi-structured	
To explore a new issue	++	+	—
To deepen the understanding of an existing issue	++	++	–
To check hypothesis	—	++	+
To quantify hypothesis	—	+	++

Relationship with the respondent — Face to face ⟷ / Telephone ⟷ / Postal ⟷ / Fax ⟷ / Internet ⟷

++: very adequate
+: adequate
–: inadequate
—: very inadequate

Collecting and Using the Information

We have mentioned several times the different approaches to or methods of collecting information and the link between the nature of the information sought (qualitative or quantitative) and the research approach. Now we must look at the nature and the use of these different approaches, which will bring us to the subject of the personal interview.

A General Process

Collecting information implies contacting the interviewee. The choice of *interview protocol* is important as it influences the design of the survey, which in turn depends on several parameters: the nature of the interviewees, the information sought and the time and budgeting constraints.

We shall look at the three different alternatives (shown in Table 4.4). In business-to-business surveys the research always follows a preparation phase that helps to define both which people to question and a general definition of the problem(s). Thus, a totally unstructured approach (the non-directive interview) does not usually form part of the armoury. The interviews are based on an *interview guide*, which can vary between being unstructured and semi-structured. The unstructured guide gives the interviewees the opportunity to express themselves in their own terms. It contains a few hints for the interviewer to make sure all the elements of the questionnaire have been covered. The semi-structured interview guide is more precise and allows the interviewer to check out hypotheses, which have already been developed. Thus, it contains much more precise questions (Table 4.5) and uses technical vocabulary appropriate to the industry concerned, while still allowing a certain degree of openness to help understand nuances and differences

Table 4.5   Extract from a semi-structured interview guide

Q5 Do you classify your customers according to the degree of credit risk they represent?

　　　　YES　　　　　　　　　　　　NO

　　If yes: ■ can you describe these categories?

　　　　　　■ what is the percentage of high risk customers in your customer base?

Q6 What is the distribution of your customers according to the amount of their overdraft?

　　　　– small　　　▭

　　　　– average　　▭

　　　　– high　　　　▭

Q7 What is:

　　　　– the average order amount?

　　　　– the frequency of orders for the same customer?

　　　　– the average customer terms of payment?

Q10 What are the sources you utilise in order to obtain credit information about your customers?

	Very much	Much	Little	Not at all
– Sales reports	☐	☐	☐	☐
– Banks	☐	☐	☐	☐
– Specialised agencies	☐	☐	☐	☐

Q11 What are the reasons for using specialised agencies?

Source: Private market research.

of opinion. Research undertaken using this kind of interview guide forms part of what we consider to be qualitative surveys. This type of interview requires interviewer training and should be reserved for trained individuals within the company. This raises the issue of the professionalism of the job – the role of the interviewer – which is one of the technical aspects of marketing.

Structured questionnaire interviewing involves a questionnaire consisting of questions which have been carefully thought up and which have *pre-coded* answers. The interviewee must respect the offered range of possible responses, which is the only way to transform opinions and judgements into numerical data (Table 4.4) that can be analysed statistically. Frequently however, a certain degree of flexibility is incorporated in the questionnaire in order to enable the collection of extra information, which the highly structured approach of the questionnaire does not typically permit. This degree of flexibility has to be treated in a specific manner within the interviewer–interviewee relationships.

Table 4.4 presents a synthesis of the different methods of collecting information, the relationship with the interviewee and the methods of presenting the data. It is obvious that the type of information collected is affected by the relationship established between the two parties. A face-to-face questionnaire gives different results from a questionnaire sent through the post. Moreover, the questionnaire must be written differently, as different kinds of bias may arise. The face-to-face interview is often replaced for reasons of cost by other more economical methods.

In business-to-business situations, it is rare to use the *focus group* form of the face-to-face method. This method is interesting owing to the possible interaction between several individuals, when discussing a specific subject under the guidance of a professional moderator. Such interaction increases creativity, permits more insights than the individual interview and improves individual performance. Other than its creative aspect, this method is particularly well adapted to the exploratory phase of research. It is little used in business-to-business marketing for practical reasons (timetabling, etc.), but also because it often means grouping people from competing companies – which often inhibits respondents expressing themselves freely.

Analysing the information is not a bias-free step in the process. The step from unstructured to more structured techniques involves substituting a formalised language – that of the designer of the survey – for the terms used by the interviewees. The risks of poor interpretation, of confusion between terms and misunderstanding thus increase. The basic principle therefore is that the designer and user must first *test* any even slightly structured approach to information collection. So, for semi-structured interviews, guides and questionnaires are first tested. They are altered whenever necessary, for misunderstanding, length, etc. The writing of an *interview guide* does not require any special skills, but must be kept simple and understandable, the questions must not be biased in any way, and must not incorporate two questions simultaneously. Table 4.5 gives an example of an interview guide.

In Table 4.5:

- these various items show the variety of questions and possible answers facilitating data collection
- this interview guide can be described as 'semi-structured'
- the text of the interview guide also allows the interviewer to write down the collected data, whatever their form
- some instructions for the interviewers can be interpolated in order to guide the interview
- there is no codification of the answers, the foreseen analysis being qualitative.

On the other hand, writing a *highly structured questionnaire* based on predominantly closed questions is more complex. The reason is the need to process the results *numerically*. It is therefore important to transform an opinion or attitude into a scale, which can be treated numerically (order, average, spread, variance, etc.). This transformation requires carefully considering the wording of the questions and how the answers are coded.

The wording of the questions is extremely difficult. The questions must be understood without ambiguity, they must not bias the answer and must allow the answer to be given in the desired format. The question *sequence* is also important, since certain questions placed at the beginning of a questionnaire can bias answers to later questions.

Using the answers requires that they are coded in a specific form which corresponds to the type of analysis that will be undertaken.

When trying to understand someone's preference for a particular supplier for example, the 'yes–no' approach is not meaningful. We have to be able to define degrees of preference, which can be done using an ordinal scale (Table 4.6). The following examples illustrate this:

- Could you describe the extent to which you are satisfied with your relationship with Supplier *A*?
- Are you satisfied with Supplier *A*?
- Could you indicate whether, in your relationships with supplier *A*, you are:

Very unsatisfied	*Unsatisfied*	*Neutral*	*Satisfied*	*Very Satisfied*
1	2	3	4	5

The first question corresponds to an open interview environment whose detailed answers are given which can then be analysed and interpreted. The second leaves no room for ambiguity but could frustrate the interviewee, forcing a yes–no response to a question that requires more complex discussion. The third gives more freedom to the interviewee but remains limited. Table 4.6 gives examples of the most common forms of scales used.

Analysing the information depends on whether the responses are *open-ended* or *pre-coded* through the use of closed questions. Basically, open responses

Table 4.6   Grading scales

- Dichotomous: Are you satisfied with supplier *A*?

    Yes ⌊_⌋   No ⌊_⌋

- Ranking: Please rank in order of decreasing satisfaction suppliers *A*, *B*, *C*.

- Differential semantic: Where do you place supplier *A* on the following scale?

    Satisfying......................................Deplorable

- Stapel: Where do you place supplier *A* on the following scale? (phase circle the figure)

    +3
    +2
    +1
    Satisfying supplier
    −1
    −2
    −3

- Likert: Please indicate to what degree you agree or disagree with the following statement: 'Supplier *A* is satisfying':

⌊_⌋	⌊_⌋	⌊_⌋	⌊_⌋	⌊_⌋	⌊_⌋
Completely agree	Somewhat agree	Marginally agree	Marginally disagree	Somewhat disagree	Completely disagree

- Semantic differential: How do you evaluate the satisfaction derived from supplier *A*:

⌊_⌋	⌊_⌋	⌊_⌋	⌊_⌋	⌊_⌋	⌊_⌋	⌊_⌋
Excellent	Very good	Rather good	Average	Rather bad	Very bad	Extremely bad

Table 4.7 Example of content analysis

Interviewee Theme	1	2	3
■ Supplier's innovation capacity	F:4 ■ Essential for us ■ Solutions are designed with suppliers ■ Lowering cost in our manufacturing process ■ Common search for lowering cost solutions	F:2 ■ Sometimes, suppliers bring in innovative solutions ■ Rather interesting but not essential	F:1 ■ We control our parts design
■ Supplier's manufacturing flexibility	F:2 ■ We place orders for long runs ■ Our forecasts are extremely accurate	F:4 ■ Our activities are seasonal and uncertain ■ We meet sharp increases in orders and turnover ■ Our customers have bad forecasts ■ We are always looking for suppliers able to meet our ups and downs	F:2 ■ Low uncertainly in our activity ■ We have an excellent forecast capacity

Note: *F*: Frequency of the appearance of the theme in the interview.

are analysed using content analysis, whereas coded responses are dealt with by statistical data analysis (un-i, bi- or multivariate).

Content analysis involves several methods: *syntactic* (structure of the response), *lexical* (the vocabulary used) and *thematic* (theme by theme and frequency). In our experience, thematic analysis is probably the most suitable for business-to-business marketing environments.

The first step is to identify all the themes mentioned by the interviewees, then the frequency with which each person raises each theme. This means that we can classify the themes in order of decreasing frequency as used by all the people interviewed. The second step is the construction of a table as in Table 4.7, which uses two different axes. One identifies the frequency of themes per interviewee and what the interviewees say about each theme and the other describes each individual through the themes used and what they say about each theme. This then allows us to compare each interviewee's responses with the others. The intersection of the two axes supplies the key to understanding the issues in question (Table 4.8).

Analysis of the data begins simply. The aim of the uni-variate approach is to identify the *mean* and *variance* of a variable. The bi-variate analysis (following statistical checks as to their independence) gives insights into the *simultaneous study* of two variables. These basic types of analyses complete a purely verbal approach to understanding the phenomenon. They can be used in both qualitative and quantitative phases. Multivariate analysis involves techniques such as *factor analysis*,

Table 4.8   Examples of single and cross-tabulation

Market survey on the presence of Computer Aided Design (CAD) within the European industry (sample of 100 firms)

- Sorting of the firms by number of employees:

▪ Is	≤100	101 to 500	≥501	Total
	60	25	15	100

Univariate analysis (sorting)

- Have a CAD software

	Yes		No		
	45		55		100

Bivariate analysis (cross-tabulation)

Size of the firms (per cent) Have a CAD software	≤100 60	101 to 500 25	≥501 15	Total 100
Yes	10	20	15	45
No	50	5	0	55

cluster and *segmentation* methods which, for us, are more related to strategy (market segmentation) than to market surveys.

Problems Related to Sampling

Generating a meaningful sample in a business-to-business environment is very difficult. We have seen that the exploratory research phase follows a process of identifying and understanding the issues through a succession of interviews, which of course all open the door for errors. At the qualitative stage, the process becomes more systematic. Let us now look at this process.

The problems begin with the definition of the population. If we return to our example of veterinary medicines for chickens (Figure 2.10), we can try now to devise a survey plan for the Veterinary Laboratory. The starting point is to identify the population to survey. Should this be limited to the purchasing co-operatives (the buyers)? Should we add the hatcheries? Or even the industrial breeders? Can we fully understand the market if we do not include the opinions of the vets? And so on. It is obvious that only an understanding of the decision-making process within the sector and its sub-sectors will allow us to define the relevant population/sample. This takes us back to the important role of the exploratory phase and the composition of the sample, as it alone enables us to acquire enough information on the players and their interrelationships. Sometimes it is extremely difficult to identify them owing to a lack of generally available statistics. No source can tell us precisely which industrial activities would be interested in an electrical cable capable of withstanding temperatures of up to 1000° for half an hour. We may be tempted to look at all industrial activities, which would give us a huge sample, and which would simply increase costs. This is one of the functions of the exploratory phase – to *define the population* concerned before beginning a more extensive survey.

Consequently, exploratory research cannot, *a priori*, define the sample, as its objective is to discover who is involved in the decision-making process, which must leave room for any unexpected results to be incorporated.

The composition of a *typical sample* corresponds to the systematic qualitative phase. While a typical sample does represent all the categories identified within the whole population, it does not allow any statistically representative extrapolation to be drawn from the sample to the population. Such a sample presents some differences, depending on whether the qualitative approach is limited to a few interviews or concerns several hundred thousand 'cases' (= interviews, in market survey jargon). The systematic nature of the process means that the identified 'population' has been defined beforehand, and that the sample, on a reduced scale, includes all the referenced sub-groups. The design of the sample will therefore always be made on a system of quotas to ensure that all sub-groups, irrespective of their absolute size, have at least some representation. Therefore, this means that there is a strong possibility that all combinations, opinions and attitudes present in the population, are present in the sample. A *limited qualitative survey* aiming to discover a relatively complex market environment can be competently executed through interviewing 20–30 people, on condition that they are spread throughout the population concerned. On the other hand, an *extensive qualitative survey* can involve several dozen or hundreds of people in order to reach a more precise measure, or estimation, or description of the market. In such cases it is possible to use profitably the methods of data analysis that we have already described. However, the construction of a typical sample, even a large one, does not allow us, in statistically valid conditions, to extrapolate the results obtained to the whole original population.

Whatever the proposed scope of the survey, the construction of a typical sample in a business-to-business environment (Table 4.9) must express the '*units*' (i.e. the companies and players: co-operatives, hatcheries, industrial breeders, vets, etc.). It is also necessary to represent the *functions* acting within each 'unit'. For example, within a breeding unit, breeding technicians, managing director, purchasing agent, and so on. Indeed, we recognise here that some particularities related to a function can affect a purchasing decision (Chapter 3).

In the mid-1980s, the Montabert Company launched a new type of hydraulic concrete-breaker, which had the advantage of being much quieter than the traditional pneumatic drills. They failed completely. This was due to many aspects. One was that during the survey phase, building-site managers were not consulted. It was later revealed that they were used to managing their sites 'by ear', the noise telling them the stage that the work was at. The arrival of silent machinery 'disturbed' them in their working habits and so was rejected. So the company failed: it had developed a 'better' product, but had not considered the decision-making process of the buyers. Other similar examples also appear in Chapter 10 concerning the marketing of innovative technologies.

Table 4.9   Design of a typical sample

A major manufacturer of computer hardware and software is undertaking a survey concerning the possible development of particular Computer Aided Design (CAD) software in the construction industry. Explanatory research led to the identification of three possible professions: architects, design offices and building firms. General data sources provided the number of units in each profession and a classification by the number of employees.

■ Classification of each profession by the number of employees:

Architects		Design offices		Building firms	
≤10	7800	≤20	10810	≤50	165
11 to 20	350	21 to 50	800	51 to 100	940
21 to 50	85	51 to 100	100	101 to 200	2500
51 to 100	16	101 to 200	80	201 to 1000	1000
101 and more	6	201 to 1000	10	1001 and more	500
		1001 and more	60		
Total	**8257**	**Total**	**11860**	**Total**	**5105**

Architects		Design offices		Building firms	
≤10	40	≤20	50	≤50	100
11 to 20	20	21 to 50	30	51 to 100	40
21 to 50	10	51 to 100	20	101 to 200	40
51 to 100	5	101 to 200	10	201 to 1000	20
101 and more	4	201 to 1000	6	1001 and more	10
		1001 and more	5		
Total	**79**	**Total**	**121**	**Total**	**210**

Total = 410 firms

■ Structure of a typical sample:

Architects		Design offices		Building firms	
≤10	2	≤20	5	≤50	5
11 to 20	2	21 to 50	2	51 to 100	5
21 to 50	2	51 to 100	2	101 to 200	3
51 to 100	2	101 to 200	2	201 to 1000	3
101 and more	2	201 to 1000	2	1001 and more	3
		1001 and more	2		
Total	**10**	**Total**	**15**	**Total**	**19**

Total = 44 firms

Table 4.10   Design of a representative sample

Following the example of Table 4.9, a qualitative survey had found a greater buying potential among the design offices. The manufacturer now wants a detailed survey of that profession giving a precise description of the existing computer equipment, the competitors' software currently in use and the attitude of the customers towards the new CAD software. It therefore becomes necessary to obtain a representative sample of the population of the design offices. The precision of the sampling relies on:

- the standard deviation of the variable under survey
- the size of the sample
- the size of the population through the sampling rate (n/N) (if the sampling rate is low (<10 per cent), the precision relies only on the size of the sample)

The number of firms is a first indication, the important point is their buying potential. A better sample is designed according to the buying potential of the firms, as the following example illustrates:

	Number of firms		Per cent of buying potential	Sample		Per cent sample/ population
	Absolute	%		Number	%	
≤20p	10810	90	33	140	35	≈1
21 to 50p	800	6	10	80	20	10
51 to 100p	200	2	12	80	20	40
101 to 200p	100	1	15	50	13	50
201 to 1000p	80	1	20	40	10	50
1001 and more	10	Σ	10	10	2	100
Total	**12000**	**100**	**100**	**400**	**100**	**≈4**

The construction of any *representative sample* of any business to business environment can include all the kinds of complexity mentioned above. The risk is that we reach such complexity that the construction of a sample either becomes impossible or leads to unnecessary costs (Figure 4.1). The most common way to limit the population to the main actors (the hatcheries, for example) is to take other actors into consideration through the construction of the questionnaire and in an exogenous way in the quantitative phase. Now, we must define what a representative sample of 'units' is, and the functions which participate in the decisions within these units (Table 4.10).

Contrary to what has just been said, the construction of a representative sample in the business-to-business world depends on the *economic power* of certain customers and the *unique behaviour* of large buying units: the law of large numbers does not apply and statistical analysis is not possible. The point is that in consumer market research, for a new soft drink for example, all potential customers are treated as being equally important in designing the research study. This is not the case in business-to-business research, as buying behaviour is not similar across all firms – there are always fewer, bigger buyers. As with the example in Table 4.10, we are led, for reasons of representativeness, to include all the major potential buyers in our sample. It is only below a certain potential capacity that sampling becomes meaningful. The reasoning so far has shown that the most common way to compose a sample is the 'quota' method: the population is divided into strata, based on general information and the aim is to give the sample a structure which is similar to that of the strata of the original population. It is extremely rare to use the pure statistical method of random sampling. We shall not discuss this here, since many pages on market surveys have already been written about the subject. However, interesting variants on the sampling process within business-to-business marketing can be found in Naudé, Lockett and Gisbourne (1993) and Lichtenthal and Long (1998).

In the example in Table 4.10, we did not look at the question of *who to interview*. We defined a sample of some 400 design offices. To have stopped there would have meant only going halfway. We were interested to understand the decision making process concerning the choice of CAD software and the subsequent investment in computer equipment. The exploratory survey showed that the managing director, the technical manager and the head of the information technology department formed the typical DMU. Therefore, in each company, three people had to be interviewed, which made 1200 interviews in all. This easily justifies the use of statistical data analysis and takes the research budget to somewhere between 80 and 100 K Euros.

Some Specific Survey Methods

In this section we introduce two survey approaches, which are slightly atypical in the broad range of available marketing research methods. The *Delphi approach* lies somewhere between a market survey and a forecasting tool. We could have dealt with it in Chapter 14, but feel that it is better suited to this chapter as it deals with an issue we have already commented upon, namely interviewing the experts. The second is *customer satisfaction surveys*, which aim to assess the competitive position of a company. We shall deal with the two separately.

The *Delphi method* was devised because of problems encountered with the use of forecasting methods based on the extrapolation of past data. When it is obvious that a market is going to be disrupted by the arrival of a new technology or by changes in players' buyer behaviour, the past cannot be used as a basis for forecasting the future. In such cases the ability to *anticipate* and to *imagine* are more useful than purely rational statistics. But the experts need to have both of these qualities, and this is what the technique seeks to exploit. It consists of:

- precisely defining the context of the survey and the problem under review
- gathering together a group of experts (scientists, opinion leaders, users, etc.) who remain anonymous throughout the duration of the survey
- drawing up a questionnaire relevant to the problem
- submitting the questionnaire to the experts

- analysing the results and noting any differences in opinion between the experts
- drawing up a second questionnaire based on the responses to the first and re-submitting it to the same experts
- analysing the results and repeating the process if required (twice is generally enough).

The Delphi method allows the exploration of mid-to-long-term developmental issues based on possible emerging trends. It is particularly well adapted to the study of *emerging* industries or techniques. Exploring future developments in this way can lead to the identification of trends as to how the future may unfold. These patterns make up for a kind of variable forecast as they are confirmed or unconfirmed over time. In this way it improves a company's capacity to anticipate when faced with an uncertain future.

Customer satisfaction surveys were the result of managers' preoccupation with two themes: the strategic impact of the concept of relative perceived quality (see Chapter 5), and the total quality management movement. Other than focusing company attention on the notion of quality, these two themes have a point in common: 'quality' is defined by the *judgement of the customer*. For a supplier, to have access to an assessment of customers' satisfaction is enormously beneficial, particularly if this includes information concerning competitors' services. Anderson and Narus (1999) provide a good example of the American approach to measuring customer satisfaction.

As such a review clearly involves undertaking a *market survey*, it is important to be able to define what is meant by the term. A customer satisfaction survey tries to measure customers' assessment of a supplier's performance, very often just a part of the whole offer. It would be wrong to question a customer about a service he does not know – or, worse, which does not interest him. This means that a customer satisfaction survey should concern only a homogeneous group of customers, a market segment that the supplier has chosen to identify. Any other broader approach and we enter the category of more classical surveys.

The second point is to define the *objectives* of such a survey. Basically, there are two. The first is to look at the whole process: the offer content, delivery to the customer, employee behaviour, etc. Thus, the aim is to identify the strong and weak points of the offer to improve them. The decisions taken following such a survey can be very general, for example reorganising the after-sales department, staff training, etc. Alternatively the objective can be more precise and concern evaluating the offer implementation and using the results as an input to future management action. For example, for a long time, Rank Xerox surveyed all their customers' rates of satisfaction in relation to its maintenance services, the idea being to give the department a tool which it could use to improve the services offered, with part of the maintenance workers' pay being related to customer satisfaction. In this case, the identities of the customers responding to the survey (almost 100 per cent response rate) were known.

The two objectives just described correspond to different survey methods. The first corresponds to a 'one-off' type survey of a typical or representative sample of the market segment and undertaken among different members of the purchasing centres. The questions are very similar to those of a classical market survey. The second is carried out at regular intervals (the term 'barometer' is sometimes used) and allows the company to build up a picture to follow trends and to be able to make changes over time. It typically involves very precise criteria: the time it takes to respond to a customer's call, the employee's skill, his or her relationship with the customer, etc. It can be made on the basis of just one person's responses as long as the person has been chosen carefully and any change will be recognised as affecting the continuity of historical data (in other words a change in the results should not be interpreted as coming from a modification in customer's attitude, but as a change in the person interviewed). The interesting aspect of this process is that market surveys based on customer satisfaction sometimes lead to firms talking to current buyers, while the marketing department itself would find this less easy to achieve. We shall look at this again later.

The Use of the Salesforce for Surveys

Sales representatives are constantly in touch with customers. It is therefore normal to be tempted to ask them to collect information about the marketplace. This is legitimate and efficient. However, one must be careful. The 'reps' should be briefed beforehand and the difference between *negotiating a sale* and *collecting information* must be made clear. Some subjects are to be avoided. Customer satisfaction surveys should be excluded, as it would be wrong to be both judge and the judged at the same time. The best themes are centred on the development of new offers or services for long-term customers. However, it is often costly and inefficient to ask reps to collect information concerning companies which are unknown to the supplier, and this time is often wasted. However, even if it is possible to question having the sales team devote time to market surveys, it is certain that they should contribute to the *design and maintenance* of a marketing information system.

The Marketing Information System (MIS)

In business-to-business marketing, everything – the diversity of sources, the multiplicity of contacts, the number of people involved – leads to a spread of the information within the company. If we add to this the tendency of some individuals in the company to keep their information close to their hearts, it is easy to understand the problems that business-to-business companies meet to gather, store and manipulate the information that is required for effective decision making. The role of consumer panels and distributors in mass marketing has no real equivalent in the business-to-business sector, but the information is just as important. The business-

Figure 4.3   Role of the marketing information system

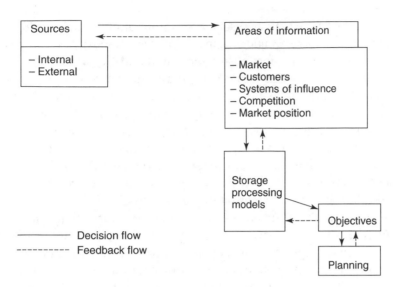

to-business sector lags behind the other sectors in this field, given the relatively late adoption of marketing and the recent realisation of its advantages. We propose here the design of a MIS adapted to the business-to-business world, in response to certain ideas concerning the role that it can play in the company.

The Role of the MIS

Figure 4.3 represents the concerns a marketing director can have about the management of information. The information system has a double function: to organise an *initial information flow*, which leads to the definition of objectives and assists in planning, and to *return and control information flow* to allow for adjustments to be made to decisions and future courses of action.

A flow of diversified information from different sources irrigates the company. But it has to be managed by defining the areas of information that make up the system. The question, for example, is whether technological monitoring is or is not part of the information system; we suggest not, as it has a logic different and complementary to that of marketing, except for the case of sectors affected by high technological turbulence.

Once the information system is defined, it must be decided what information will be stored, how, for how long, what form of updating is take used, etc. This step is very important. Generally speaking, a company does not lack information, but lacks knowledge as to how to collect it, update it and present it in an understandable way. An additional step would be to add the possibility of processing the information to *aggregate* it, to make it more easily and readily understandable and usable in the establishing of objectives and planning (Chapter 14).

The Organisation of the MIS

The absence of any established source of information, which could be related to consumer panels for example, means a business-to-business company has few outside influences imposing a structure to its MIS. Moreover, the nature of business-to-business marketing leads us to assume that any structure of marketing information which does not take into consideration the customer dimension would be inadequate. This means that the buying unit must be identifiable, processable and usable by the information system. Thus, the idea is to take the customer unit as the basis for construction of the information system. This will ensure a dual function of the system: to manage knowledge about buyers in a classical way (customer files, accounts of visits, customer action, etc.), and to proceed by aggregations to give a 'market-segment' dimension to the information thus collected.

The principle of this structure is first to define the information required for *market consolidation*, which in our view covers both the global nature of the market and the sub-divisions (segments) already established. This characteristic is essential. With segmentation (grouping of homogeneous customers) being the pivot of decision analyses in marketing, an information system that does not do this and that does not allow for its evolution would be rejected immediately. However, we still need to define the categories under which the information will be collected and processed. These categories will be the same for the customer base as for the consolidation, to allow for the planned aggregations. Information from outside sources or surveys could be added to these categories to complete or validate the information coming from the customer base (Figure 4.4).

This definition of an MIS is close to that of software packages known as 'Customer Relationship Management' (or CRM systems – see, for example, Oracle, Intentia, 1-to-1, I2, etc.). These packages aim automatically to structure and consolidate information coming from general databases. They generally process data

Figure 4.4   Organisation of the marketing information system

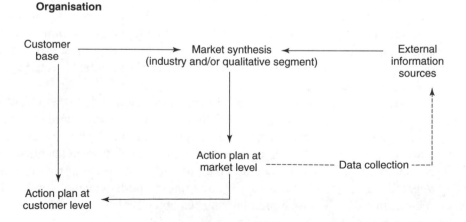

Table 4.11   Customer description

Customer base
■ **Customer description**

Headquarters	Plant *A*	Plant *B*	Plant *C*	etc.
	Workshop *A*1	–	–	
	Workshop *A*2	–	–	
	etc.	–	–	
	(Equipment)	(–)	(–)	

■ **The customers (or their units) can be gathered**[1]
– by 'industry'

and/or

– by 'qualitative segment'
Sorting on all the important criteria

Note: 1. A 'customer' can be split between several 'industries' or 'segments'.

of limited complexity over a large number of customers. Our proposal includes all the necessary complexity of information requested to understand a customer fully (Chapter 3).

Structure of the Customer Base

This structure is very similar to the recommendations given for the design of a good customer file. It is the result of all the concepts previously identified: the interaction and risk approach, purchasing centres and selling groups and segmentation. It includes three aspects: customer *description*, customer *intelligence* and *plans of action* (objectives-results). What follows is a proposal that includes many items of information. It is obvious that an efficient system can be built within a company by using only some of the items and by substituting some items for others mentioned here.

Customer description (Table 4.11) means all the elements that make up the database concerning the customer. One important point to underline here is that the word 'customer' has a limited meaning in marketing. A customer can include several distinct 'units' which belong, from a supplier point of view, to several market segments. The definition of a unit can correspond to the official division of the customer (division, department, organisation, etc.) or to a supplier identification (service, factory, workshop). In all cases, it is a unit that has a relationship with the supplier that is different from the other units, based on many possible points: type of production, manufacturing tools, organisation, purchasing centre, downstream market, etc. The consequence for the supplier is obvious; each 'unit' is the object of a distinct marketing approach and must be seen as such. One of the results of this is to be able to piece together the market segments from the sub-elements, according to the segmentation defined by the company for each of its markets. The

Table 4.12   Customer intelligence

- Who is in touch with the customer (functions – names) (headquarters, units)
- Major facts in the relationship
- Customer's strategies:
    - globally
    - general position
    - per unit (or application)
- Competition: global position
- Per unit:
    - purchase records (also per offer: volume, turnover, margin)
    - purchasing trends
    - customer's applications (list, specifications, purchases)
    - our strategy per application
    - our position for application/unit
- Call reports:
    - date
    - who met whom?
    - next call date
    - atmosphere
    - customer's evolutions (opinions)
    - evolution of our position with the customer
    - evolution of competition (facts, opinions)
    - assessment of the quality of our performance
        - products
        - services
    - summary of the call
    - usual topics – call topics
    - for each topic – proposed/decided actions

---

combination thus obtained is similar to that of the classical panels used in mass marketing, while respecting the characteristics of business-to-business marketing.

Customer intelligence (Table 4.12) utilises the elements used to understand the customer and to position the supplier at any given time. The updating of this part of the file, as for the following one, is a tedious but essential task. How many managers have found themselves in front of a customer who recalls a company action or promise which is not mentioned anywhere in the customer file?

The idea of this part of the file is simple. It involves having information that helps to understand customer changes and to anticipate behaviour. The analysis of this information, coupled with the risk approach method, gives the supplier the elements to anticipate likely behaviour and to design the actions that make up the following section.

The plans of action (Table 4.13) should be examined from two angles. The first is the supplier issues, whose implementation determines success. The second is the promises made to the customer since their *delivery* is an important point in the judgement that the customer has of the relationship.

We now have the elements of the file. Now we must examine the computer set-up (Figure 4.5) required to make our recommendation operational.

Table 4.13 Plans of action

- Realised actions:
  – Headquarters/units/applications
  – Definition/objectives/implementation/results/completion time
- Actions in progress:
  – Headquarters/units/applications
  – Definition/objectives/starting time/completion time
  – Blinking lights: late actions
- Actions under survey:
  – Headquarters/units/applications
  – Definition/objectives

Figure 4.5 Computer set-up of the information system concerning the customer base

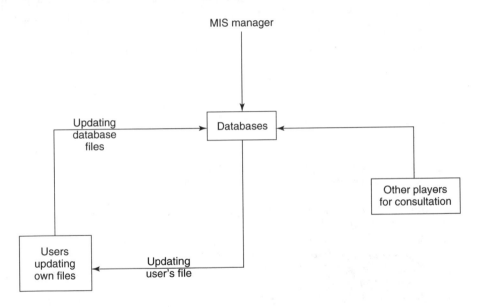

This is a very typical database set-up. Certain individuals have access for updating (or partial updating), whereas others can only access the data. A centralised function manages the database, automatically updating the files of those who address the system.

Conditions for the Implementation of a MIS

Having a good MIS does not present major difficulties on a technical basis. There is an overabundance of good software available. Designing and building the system is not really a problem. The difficulties lie in the maintenance and the requirement to constantly update the data. Problems abound in trying to introduce into the system all customers and all data at once. Updating the whole lot may prove to be too difficult and time-consuming a task. And if the system is not constantly updated, it quickly loses interest and value. Thus, the MIS is abandoned as one of these false good ideas coming from marketing. A way of solving this problem is to design the system in its entirety (all customers, all data), but to start with only a part of the whole: for example, the first 20 per cent of the customers (those realising 80 per cent of the turnover, known as the Pareto rule) and the essential data. It is so easier to prove the value of the system and later enlarge it to the complete structure.

A second danger comes from rivalry between a sales manager and a marketing manager. A MIS requires the day-to-day participation of the sales force that 'owns' a large part of the relevant data. If the sales manager does not back and support the whole operation and tells the commercial people not to be bothered with it when meeting sales problems with customers, the system quickly dies.

A MIS results from the deep understanding and support from the company management who seek to define the marketing approach within the company. And this is impossible without a sound base of marketing information. It is a true management decision that requires both tenacity and courage to make it live within the company.

References and Further Reading

Anderson, J. and Narus, J. (1999) *Business Market Management, Understanding, Creating, and Delivering Value*, Englewood Cliffs, Prentice-Hall.

Boyd, H., Westfall, R. and Stasch, S. (1977) *Marketing Research: Text and Cases*, New York, Irwin.

Curry, D.J. (1993) *The New Marketing Research Systems: How to Use Strategic Database Information for Better Marketing Decisions*, New York, Wiley.

Dibb, S. and Simkin, L. (1996) *The Market Segmentation Workbook: Target Marketing for Marketing Managers*, London, Routledge.

Evrard, Y., Pras, B. and Roux, E. (1993) *Market. Études et recherches en marketing. Fondements. Méthodes*, Paris, Nathan.

Gross, A.C., Banting, P.M., Meredith, L.N. and Ford, I.D. (1993) *Business Marketing*, New York: Houghton Mifflin.

Hipkin, I. and Naudé, P. (1999) 'An Application of Judgemental Modelling for Strategic Decision Making in International Environments', *Electronic Markets, Special Section: Globalisation and Information Systems*, 9:4, 247–55.

Lichtenthal, J.D. and Long, M.M. (1998) 'Case Study: Service Support and Capital Goods – Dissolving the Resistance to Obtaining Product Acceptance in New Business Markets', *Journal of Business and Industrial Marketing*, 13:4/5, 356–69.

Malhotra, N.K. and Birks, D.F. (1999) *Marketing Research, An Applied Approach*, Englewood Cliffs, Prentice-Hall.

Morris, M., Berthon, P. and Pitt, L. (1999) 'Assessing the Structure of Industrial Buying Centres with Multivariate Tools', *Industrial Marketing Management*, 28, 262–76.

Naudé, P. and Buttle, F. (2000) 'Assessing Relationship Quality', *Industrial Marketing Management*, 29, 351–61.

Naudé, P., Lockett, G. and Gisbourne, S. (1993) 'Market Analysis via Judgemental Modelling. An Application to the UK Chemical Industry', *European Journal of Marketing*, 27:3, 5–22.

Pinard-Legry, J., Marion, F. and Salle, R. (1996) 'Les études de satisfaction clientèle en business to business', *Décisions Marketing*, 8, 92–9.

Vernette, E. (1991) 'L'efficacité des instruments d'étude: évaluation des échelles de mesure', *Recherche et Application en Marketing*, 2, 43–64.

Discussion Questions

1 Can you stress the differences between a Marketing Information System (MIS) and a market survey?

2 Name some important data that business-to-business suppliers must possess.

3 Indicate the specificities of building a sample from a population of business-to-business customers.

4 Indicate the differences between a 'typical sample' and a 'representative sample' of a population of business-to-business customers.

5 Why is it important for marketers sometimes to split a single customer into several 'sub-customers' or units?

Chapter 1

Competitiveness, Marketing and Business-to-Business Marketing

What is marketing all about
Different marketing environments
B2B marketing

Chapter 2

Business-to-Business Customers and Markets

B2B Generic Offers	Technological Innovation	Pure Services	Major Projects

PART I   STRATEGY FOUNDATIONS

Chapter 3	Chapter 4	Chapter 5	Chapter 6
Understanding Business-to-Business Purchasing	**Information and Information Systems**	**Markets and Suppliers' Strategy**	**Segmentation and Marketing Strategy**

PART II   STRATEGY IMPLEMENTATION

Chapter 7			
Generic Business-to-Business Offer Design and Management			

	Chapter 10	Chapter 11	Chapter 12
Chapter 8	**Marketing and Technological Innovation**	**The Marketing of Services**	**Major Project Marketing**
Market Access and Customer Management			

Chapter 9
Communication and Publicity/ Advertising

PART III   STRATEGY DESIGN

Chapter 13	**The Role and Organisation of Marketing**
Chapter 14	**Customer Position, Market Position, Marketing Strategies and Planning**
Chapter 15	**Issues and Specificities of International Marketing**
Annex	**The Internet and Marketing: Some Ideas**

5 Markets and Suppliers' Strategy

This chapter has many objectives. The first is to define the links that exist between company (or corporate) strategy and marketing strategy. Indeed, as these two levels of decision are interdependent, and in certain cases inseparable, many comparisons are often made between the two, but it is also vital to make a distinction between them. To understand this overlap, it is necessary to have a clear vision of the different ways of *dividing* and *aggregating* company activity (the strategic base, the strategic business unit and the market segment), and also how they are used in strategy formulation. This has led us to produce a common understanding of principles, of methods of analysis and strategic decision making required for the understanding of the risks and choices that we will present. The reader wishing to have further information on this can refer to the references and further reading at the end of the chapter.

If the works quoted define the risks linked to the preparation and formulation of strategic decisions, we feel they do not fully deal with all the very different situations that make up the variety of *business-to-business* environments. Indeed, most work concerning company strategy adopts a 'top-down' perspective in which marketing strategy is considered as a direct result of decisions taken higher up. This usually happens through the definition of predetermined offers and interaction with selected market segments (the marketing mix model). But as we stated earlier in this book, it is unrealistic to apply the same approach to a supplier of garage equipment aiming at a potential 5 million customers worldwide and to a supplier of subsystems for the car industry that has less than 20 customers.

In the first case, interaction with the customer is often limited to *sales-orientated exchanges* (low direct interaction, Table 2.3). Interaction here is merely an issue of implementation. Strategy is determined through a global view of the market and its division between segments to which predetermined offers are directed. A *top-down* perspective may then be satisfactory. In the second case, however, buyer–supplier interaction is close and often leads to new resources and skills for both companies; for example, new technical adaptations, which could interest other customers, the joint creation of new procedures, new methods of financing projects, etc. (high direct interaction, Figure 2.8). What is developed with one customer can be considered as a kind of pilot project, leading to further operations with other customers (see Mory–Ancel, Examples). In this context marketing strategy is not just a case of implementing decisions taken at a more global level, since actions taken in the marketplace can have a considerable impact, in return, on company strategy (a *'bottom-up'* perspective). This is why our approach to marketing (Chapter 2) puts the accent on the contribution that it makes to *strategy*, and not only on its contribution in the field of information on the markets or as an executor of company policy.

The 'Applications–Resources' perspective we presented in Chapter 2 joins a debate that is at the heart of current strategic thinking (Hamel and Prahalad, 1994). Strategy results from a *two-way movement*. Part of the approach lies in understanding the rules that drive market operations and consequently the implementation of resources that respect and utilise these rules (the deterministic perspective). Therefore a firm's competitive advantage stems from their ability to play the rules (or part of the rules) of the game. However, another situation can occur via a competitor inventing new ways of playing (or new rules for) the game. This is possible only through the development of new resources and competences that they present to the market in a better way than competitors do (the constructionist perspective). The Plastic Omnium story (Example 1) describes how a firm was traditionally driven by the creation of new competences and their implementation in a market driven by particular rules. Then, at some point, they invented a new way of working with customers and acquired the necessary resources to achieve greater value added for both parties in the relationship. In this way they created a competitive advantage that was of value to customers. Chapter 10 underlines the fact that technological innovation can be described in a similar way, as it often leads to setting new rules in a marketplace.

Our idea is that these two approaches are complementary. Inventing new rules is rooted in the understanding of the older ones, and often a firm can manage some business transactions in a traditional way as well as showing innovation in other areas. This dual approach dominates our thinking throughout this book. On the one hand a minimal understanding of corporate strategy is necessary to our purpose. On the other, some concepts of corporate strategy are incorporated in the design and implementation of marketing strategy.

We shall approach the subject by dividing a firm into distinct *businesses*, which is the consequence of market heterogeneity. The nature of this division gives meaning to the *analysis of competitive areas* in which the firm is present. Having set the *bases for strategic analysis*, we shall be able to examine the *methods* adapted to the orientation of the firm's investments when faced with competing possibilities. We will then be able to consider the links and distinctions between *corporate strategy* and *marketing strategy*.

Company Activity and Competitive Position

Company activity involves identifying the markets (or parts of markets) on which it has chosen to operate, and then allocating particular resources designed to meet customer needs within a competitive situation. The different methods of strategic analysis all allow us to understand the diversity in the marketplace, given the different levels of focus. This concept of activity covers two different realities:

- The first is that homogeneous activity is characterised by a particular combination of conditions of success, the *key factors for success*, which can be described as 'all the actions that have to be made to succeed on a market, or a sub-set of a given market'. The key factors for success can be extremely varied. They can exist be technically derived (research into a specific scientific domain or a conjunction of disciplines, innovative capacity, capacity to adapt to customer demands, product range, performance, etc.), be service-based (presales or design advice, after-sales services, skill of the sales force, etc.), or be based on logistical capacity and product availability (response time), or economic performance (costs structure and price level).

- The second is to be found in the very notion of *homogeneity*. On the basis of which factor(s) can an activity be said to be homogeneous? Is homogeneity an inherent element to the market and shared by all the players concerned, or does it depend on how the supplier sees it? For example, do all customers expect delivery within 24 hours of placing an order, or are some prepared to wait a week? Are all customers interested in a high technical performance or are some satisfied with a more 'basic' product? If these differences exist, we can argue that a company can choose to use certain key factors for success and not others, or can differentiate its activities based on the intensity of importance of certain factors.

Thus, the company will have to make choices taking into consideration both the homogeneity and the heterogeneity it has found on the market. These choices, which depend on human, technical and financial resources and their dynamism, will in return have an effect on company capacity to use certain factors, and therefore on its organisation. Here we can see the close link between the *configuration* of all company activities and the planned use of certain *key factors of success*.

The process of *segmentation* covers all the operations that help to recognise the heterogeneity of activities, and determine its consequences on the firm's organisation and operation. There are several levels of segmentation, which correspond to the company recognising varying degrees of market heterogeneity, which in turn determine the level and nature of involvement that the company adopts. This decision is central to company strategy and marketing strategy, as shown by Table 5.1 in Example 4.

The way Stäubli operates here is interesting for more than one reason. It allows us to update the links in the process. First, through a repeated 'try or fail' approach, which itself is a learning process for the organisation, the company began to recognise the *heterogeneity of the market*. They understood that a single approach would not allow them to reach all their customers. At the same time, they tried to reach

Table 5.1   Stäubli: two types of customers and key success factors

Strategic features	General industry	Craft industry
Brand	Stäubli	Prevot
Customers	Large and middle firms	Small firms
Range of products	1000 references	50 references
Manufacturing		
■ Precision	Very high	Standard
■ Materials	From standard to very sophisticated	Standard
■ Production cost	High	Moderate
Type of supplier–customer relationship		
■ Nature of the relationship	Direct	Through distributors
■ Base of the relationship	'technique'	'commercial'
■ Design office assistance	Yes	No
Product adaptation	Yes	No
Sales force	Engineers/technicians	Sales people
Accepted price index	From index 150–2000 according to the type of product	Index 80
Competitors	– same –	

all customers through slight modifications to their marketing actions. For example, they assumed that a craftsman is just a company on a smaller scale, and therefore that the market was relatively homogeneous. At this point, the company thought that they were entitled to prospect such clientele on the basis of their available resources. Faced with failure, the company understood that they could reach their objectives without increasing their *involvement* over that in force in the first two steps. But the sales team, the market approach, the offer, the brand, and the organisation were all different in the case of Prevot. Less involvement meant not having to dedicate expensive resources that were poorly adapted to the characteristics and requirements of the craft market. That is the very basis of a *strategic approach*.

Management must respond to the various sub-sets in a heterogeneous market (segments): marketing, supply, brand, and general organisation all need to vary. The varying the level of involvement represents recognition of heterogeneity, the analysis of the key factors for success, and the intelligence that management brings to the analysis of such factors.

Consideration of Market Heterogeneity by the Company

Example 4 shows that any company can vary its responses to market heterogeneity, from a simple visit to a prospect to the creation of an independent subsidiary. Such different responses, operational and strategic, cannot come from the same level or the same decision-making process within the company. This suggests the

Example 4   Stäubli*

The example of Stäubli, a mid-sized firm in the mechanical engineering sector, helps to illustrate our point. Among this firm's diverse activities, we will consider only those dedicated to instant industrial couplings for industrial fluids (compressed air, gas, liquids). This activity possesses its own manufacturing, design and marketing resources.

At the end of the 1970s, Stäubli had established a leading position based on a strong presence in middle- and large-sized customers. It presented a large range of high performance devices, and sold directly to the customers at higher prices than the competition through a technically qualified sales force. Special requirements for customers would be developed if necessary. A market survey had shown that some competitors that were pushed out of the 'large industry' segment were able to establish positions in the smaller 'craft industry' segment. Stäubli management thought that this represented a threat to their activity and tried to design substantial retaliation. Several attempts were implemented prior to a successful solution:

First step: Stäubli prompted their salespeople to prospect in the craft industry, and to sell devices from the industry range. However, prospective customers would find the range too complicated to make a choice from, and the prices were far too high. In addition, Stäubli's salespeople considered the potential volume of each customer far too small, and found the customer's applications to be without any technical interest. Failure occurred quickly.

Second step: Stäubli then chose to go through industrial distributors to gain access to these smaller users. Salespeople were hired to visit them. But the distributors found Stäubli's range of products too complicated, and its prices so outrageous, that they immediately looked for heavy discounts. Stäubli's salespeople would not accept that, and ultimately judged the distributors too price-minded and too uninterested in technology. They consequently stopped visiting them and failure was again apparent.

Third step: Stäubli decided to set up a commercial subsidiary, under the new brand Prevot, exclusively dedicated to the craft industry. Prevot had their own sales force to visit the distributors and promote a limited range of products marketed at competitive prices. Design remained with Stäubli and manufacturing was sub-contracted. Success followed.

Table 5.1 summarises the main features of both strategies that, with the exception of the items 'customers' and 'competition' can be described as 'key success factors'.

*Stäubli started near the lake of Zurich as a manufacturer of machines for the textile industry. It up set a subsidiary in France in 1909 in order to develop industrial connectors (couplings), which was later transformed into a Connectors Division. A Robotics Division was created in 1989 to exploit Stäubli's expertise in workshop organisation. The three Divisions form the Stäubli Group that encompasses seven production units in Europe and China and possesses commercial subsidiaries in 20 different countries. (www.staubli.com/WEB/staubli.nsf/?Open).

existence of several levels of segmentation, which need to be defined in order to determine company responses. Most authors distinguish two types of segmentation: *strategic* and *marketing*.

Strategic Segmentation

Strategic segmentation applies to a much broader field, such as an industry or a market, than does marketing segmentation. Abell and Hammond (1979) suggest a

Figure 5.1   Method of strategic segmentation

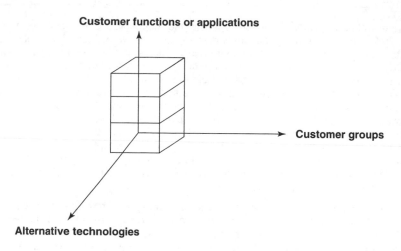

Source: Abell and Hammond (1979).

commonly accepted method of segmentation according to three axes: *types* of technology used, the *functions* (or applications) and the types of *customers* concerned (Figure 5.1). Thus, we can define an *elementary activity* (Atamer and Calori, 1993) through the simultaneous overlap of the three variables on the three axes. In practice, elementary activities are often analysed to eliminate those that do not exist, and to group together those that are highly similar, implying that they have identical key factors for success.

Using this approach, we arrive at a 'limited' number of homogeneous customer entities that can be grouped together, and that allow the company to dedicate specific resources as required (production unit, organisation system, financial resources, etc.). There is a need to allocate certain company assets to each such group, and each of these can be considered a *'Strategic Business Unit'* (SBU). These SBUs make up the relevant cornerstones of the strategy and are the focus of involvement on the part of the company. However, a company can be involved in many areas of strategic activity that constitute its *activities* (or *businesses*) *portfolio*. Therefore, company strategy can be analysed at three levels: a group level, an activities portfolio level, and also at the level of each of the areas of strategic activity. We shall look at how to analyse an activities portfolio later.

In Stäubli's case, two units of strategic activity were found. These were simple technology, standard applications, craftsmen or small companies all defined within the 'craft' SBU, while the 'industry' SBU was defined by complex technology, special applications and average- to large-sized companies. Both SBUs, even if they are based on different key factors for success, share the same resources and know-how, particularly concerning design and production. Thus, owing to their interdependence, several SBUs can form a *strategic base*, or a sort of common fund of know-how and means. On the other hand, two strategic bases are independent from each other. The strategic bases are the objects of a horizontal strategy of mutual sharing and strengthening between the SBUs that make them up.

We have presented one approach to strategic segmentation based on the three steps of:

1. Dividing into elementary activities
2. Regrouping if necessary into SBUs given similarities between the key factors for success
3. Defining strategic bases in case of interdependence between SBUs.

Determining the appropriate level of *aggregation* is an obvious next question, but it is not an easy one to answer. It will depend on the characteristics, in particular the size and diversity of the activities, and any company may find that it needs several 'notches' or 'levels' of successive strategic segmentation. It all depends on the nature of activities, the strategic stakes or risks, the decisions to be made and the structure of the organisation. In certain industrial groups, the number of successive divisions is related to the need for *globalisation* or *divisionalisation*: group, branch, company, and division, knowing that each 'stratum' can only efficiently manage about 20 entities. Thus, internal vocabulary could be different from the vocabulary we are using. Indeed, one of the industrial groups we are working with uses the following terminology: strategic families on a group level, areas of strategic activity on a branch level, strategic segments on a company level.

Even if it is homogeneous on a certain number of dimensions that have been used as the basis for performing strategic segmentation, an area of strategic activity may not, however, be a homogeneous group if we consider other characteristics, such as customer behaviour and demands (Chapter 3). Thus, it is necessary to accept this second degree of heterogeneity, which makes up the object of marketing segmentation.

Marketing Segmentation

We shall not linger on this subject here as Chapter 6 deals with it in detail. The previous section led us towards a distinction between company and marketing strategy. In both cases, the fundamental logic is that of strategy – in other words, of allocating resources according to previously identified issues. *Company strategy aims at allowing for the adequate allocation of resources between areas of activity, organisations and functions. Marketing strategy is a process of allocating resources between markets and customers.* For us, both are obviously complementary in both directions: *'top-down'*, and *'bottom-up'*.

Marketing segmentation is the instrument (the technical device), which controls the allocation of resources for commercial use between the markets and customers according to market dynamism, individual customer purchasing behaviour and specific demands. Therefore, marketing segmentation, in its different forms, (descriptive, explanatory, normative) is an instrument that can explain company decisions concerning both how the offer is adapted and the broader market environment. Marketing segmentation therefore identifies market sub-sets that are all distinct, and that all present an acceptable degree of internal homogeneity, and that are subject to specific treatment from the point of view of the offer and/or commercial action. In some cases, one customer can represent a whole relevant sub-set (Chapter 2). To illustrate, in the 'industrial' SBU of Stäubli, three 'market' segments were identified: the General Industry, the Weapons Industry and the Nuclear Industry, which led to the construction of offers and adapted commercial action.

From the Definition of Company Activities to Competitive Analysis

We have just made an essential distinction between company and marketing strategy, which can help to clarify the difference and the link between these two complementary approaches to an organisation's global strategy. Our aim now is to present the different fundamental concepts that are used in approaching strategic management. We can do this in many ways: with a sequential approach through strategic logic, an approach based on assessment of the techniques, or in a way that integrates the approaches. We favour the last-mentioned approach, indeed we feel it is essential. In the present economic context, we think that the most pertinent approach is the analysis of the *competitive systems*. Understanding the main mechanisms of competitive rivalry is one of the major issues of modern-day management. However the choice of this approach means that we first need to clarify what we understand by the notion of a 'competitive system'. The problem is complex. Generally speaking, three perspectives can be used: the *economic* logic of industrial activities, which is the perspective mostly used by strategic management specialists; the logic of the *dynamism* of industrial systems and the complex networks of relationships of which they are made up (between all actors whatever their status and function); and the logic of *supplier–customer relationships* and *direct competition* in defined markets. To a large extent, these three perspectives are complementary. However, they require different logic and methods of analysis. For example, if the last two are adopted, as we have, it is impossible to present a unique vision of competitive reality. In examining relationships between actors, (including between competitors), it has been shown that reality is often more of a continual combination of competition and co-operation ('co-opetition') depending on a particular situation. The classical competitive approach of the strategic management analysts does not really take this essential dimension into account. This is true despite the increasing number of works devoted to alliance strategies in the field of strategic management.

To reconcile these different approaches and to focus on the most important elements, we shall present the main concepts and the major methods of analysis of the field of strategic management. The reader is invited to read Chapters 6–8 for further information (networks and supplier–customer relations). Chapters 10–12 also deal with this question (technical innovation, company service activities, project marketing).

Authors of strategic management texts argue that to appreciate the value of its activities, and to identify the threats/opportunities with which it must deal, the company must adopt a viewpoint which is both larger and more stable than the SBU, since it can possibly disappear, merge with other SBUs or split up during the period covered by the strategic review (Atamer and Calori, 1993). Thus, it is important to study the competitive game of the different players to understand the *competitive system* as seen by strategic management, in other words as 'a sub-set of a larger economic, sociological, and political whole' (Atamer and Calori, 1993). The concepts and methods used by the authors of strategic management texts are presented and detailed in the following section.

Analysis of Competitive Systems

The concepts and methods to be used here are systems of analysis which, for most of the authors involved in strategic management, all have the same aim: to judge the attractiveness of industries in which the company is currently or potentially active, to evaluate the chances of success in situations of direct competition, and to determine the strategic path for the company to follow in order to reach its objectives while using a minimum of resources. From the manager's point of view, understanding the functioning of competitive systems, with which most company activity is concerned, involves seeking the answer to several questions: the relevant *definition* of the market, the appreciation of the *forces* involved and the dynamics of their evolution, and the evaluation of *competitors' positions* and the identification of their *strategies*.

The first thing is to decide on a framework for the competitive systems directly related to the perspectives of this book. Many authors have offered their own models. We have decided to use a model which is both all-encompassing and general and which has two virtues: the first is that it takes into consideration the notions of the industrial sector and networks (Chapter 2) in defining the 'strategic arena', and secondly, it gives a dynamic representation of competitive forces active in a given competitive field.

The whole of this section will be devoted to the analysis of competitive systems and organised in the following way:

■ *Step 1:* presentation of a general model of competitive analysis and of the elements that help in defining the field of reference (competition between sectors, competition within a specific industry, geographic delimitation of the competitive field).

■ *Step 2:* presentation of the bases for strategic analysis (product, technologies and industrial sectors life-cycle, the related impacts of experience and market share, the relative perceived quality).

■ *Step 3:* analysis of the position of competitors in a given competitive system (classification of possible positioning strategies, notion of strategic group).

We shall then look at the question of choice of the relevant strategic path for a company and the related methods of analysis.

The General Model and the Definition of the Field of Reference

Based on the work of Rothschild (1984), this model offers a wide and dynamic view of the competitive environment (Figure 5.2), which is particularly adapted to the business-to-business world. It incorporates the fact that some companies are often faced with competition coming from completely different technologies from their own and operated by sectors which are separate from the one within which the company is operating. Therefore, this idea of competition includes that of other sectors and that of the sector 'close' to the company, defined by Porter (1980) as an 'industry'.

Figure 5.2   The strategic arena

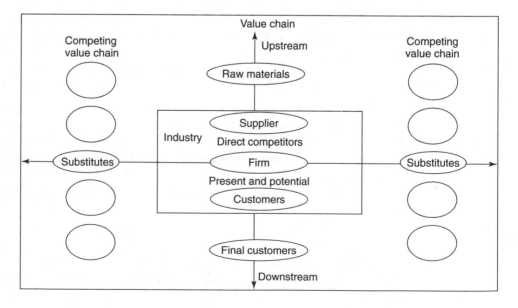

Source: Bidault (1988).

Competition between Sectors

The *strategic arena* is defined as all the actors who are directly or indirectly in competition for an application or the execution of a given function. Its definition can be very wide or more precise. Thus, we can talk of the competition of the steel, aluminium and plastics sectors for applications in the car industry. However, it may be more interesting to limit the analysis to the bodywork and to analyse the respective situations of the steel, plastics and composite materials sectors for car bonnets. We know for example that the glass, aluminium, steel, paper (cardboard) and plastic sectors compete against each other for the packaging of drinks, yet differ according to the applications (table wines, wines, mineral water, milk, soft drinks, etc.). The relative competitiveness of a company depends on that of its sector, which is based on a number of factors: the characteristics of the companies, the relationships between them, the degree of vertical integration, cost evolution for raw materials, quality of technical evolution, cost dynamics, etc.

Competition within the Industry

If the competition between companies takes place from one sector to another, they also compete within the same sector as defined by Porter (1980) as an *industry*, meaning a group of companies which are relatively stable in the mid-term and which have the similar technological stakes. For Porter, the aim of the structural analysis model of an industry is to appreciate the potential attraction of a competitive system and the related difficulties for a company to establish, maintain or develop a given position. For Porter, the attraction for an industry depends on the competitive intensity that itself is a function of the pressure coming from five sources: the rivalry between direct competitors, that of potential entrants and substitution technologies, and the negotiating power of both buyers and suppliers (Figure 5.3). The pressure of these five competitive forces has an impact on the profitability of an industry.

One of the most interesting points of view obtained from this method of analysis of the competitive structure concerns the *barriers*, which means that a company or a group of competitors can block the entry of new competitors into the industry. Another is the identification of *upstream* and *downstream* barriers, which mean a company or group of competitors can continue to impose and to enjoy a certain degree of strategic autonomy.

It should be pointed out that competitive intensity depends on two other factors: the degree of concentration of the industry (an industry with a low concentration has more strategic options), and its degree of maturity (a mature industry has fewer possibilities than a new or developing industry). This last factor related to maturity will be examined in more depth later.

Figure 5.3   Forces governing competition in an industry

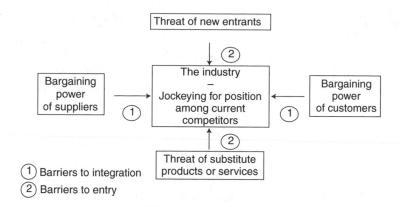

Limits of Previous Concepts

The limitations behind the models just presented were hinted at when considering the 'Applications/Resources' matrix (Figure 2.3). Both concepts (Figures 5.2, 5.3) are based on an explicit or tacit assumption about the *continuity of competition* between technologies and of the firms that exploit them. If one of the competitors, such as Plastic Omnium, changes the rules of the game by changing technology, the pressure of substitution technologies is no longer relevant. In Example 1, the company presents itself as an integrator able to cover all aspects of the application with all the available technologies and their developments. This mastering of the technologies comes from internal resources as well as from alliances with competent partners. The strategic key to this approach was the mastering of the technology traditionally undertaken by the customers. As we indicated before the success of this strategy was made possible by a parallel modification of the customer's behaviour. It delegated to a third party a share of the competences and responsibilities it had previously undertaken and controlled. This delegation also included a radical change of the usual concept of power- and price-based relationships between buyer and supplier. Both parties embarked on a co-operative perspective that was likely to produce a significant reduction in the overall cost of the application for the customer. This is a direct consequence of the transaction cost theory we investigated in Chapter 1.

However, any 'integrator' supplier still meets competition from other firms (Table 5.2). This comes either from more traditional suppliers that provide the customers with other alternatives, or from coalitions or alliances of firms trying to present the customer with the same type of approach and relationships. A coalition is led by one firm that deals directly with the customer (in the car industry: 'first-tier suppliers'). The other firms ('second- or tier-rank suppliers) are nevertheless

Table 5.2   Towards mastering the customer's application

Supplier's position*	Technologies used	Activity with the customer	Nature of competition
Product supplier	Basic technologies	Helping the customer with an application	Competition on the same technologies or on substitution technologies
Supplier of design engineering and complete function	Group of relevant technologies ↓ Complete reorganisation of internal and external resources	Mastering the complete application at and for the customer* ↑ ⌐ Reinforcement of the supplier's position with the customer	Forms are: – as above – other design engineering

Note: * The new position of the supplier is the result of a co-production between the supplier and the customer. The supplier reorganises and realigns its internal and external resources. The customer delegates activities, redeploys forces and integrates the supplier within its organisation.

approved by the final customer to whom they have only an indirect access. Coalitions and the players driving them are in direct competition at the final customer. Plastic Omnium rather 'stepped out of its sector' for an application in the car industry. It is no longer a plastics transformer aiming at applications in the car industry. It is a 'provider of industrial services and products' within a focused sector of the car industry. In the long run it may consider applying its new competences and resources to other sectors.

This perspective is very similar to that traditionally in use with major projects marketing (Chapter 12) where dealing with consortia or syndicates is day-to-day practice. The reader will find a discussion of developments in this chapter. One difference, however, is that for major projects the customer is very often a one-off project, although here the customer is a highly stable entity that requires regular delivery for the length of the contract. A new development by the customer may well start new consultation with coalition members. The new question will present new aspects, but some others will remain stable. In particular, the buyer's purchasing behaviour will still conform to the model developed in Chapter 3. Such a strategy is meaningful only for large buyers where each customer is *per se* a strategic issue. A firm may play on both strategic models. Plastic Omnium is a resources integrator for the 'petrol tank circuit' application and remains a traditional plastics transformer for the other customers that they keep serving. We shall incorporate this duality within the model of marketing strategy that we shall present in Chapter 6 (Figure 6.2).

Geographic Delimitation of the Competitive Field

In Chapter 1 we mentioned the characteristics of a company environment and underlined the issues of international competitiveness. We also highlighted the constraints that an increase in the geographic field of exchanges (globalisation of markets, etc.) can have for companies.

Indeed, all competitive systems, or 'industries', as Porter puts it, are not yet 'globalised'. Many companies are in fact subject to conditions of competition in rather limited geographic areas, countries or regions. In such conditions, the methods presented are still valid, but the nature of the competitive conflict needs to be analysed differently. Take, for example, the glass industry. Just because there is a powerful glassmaker in Japan does not automatically imply that the company operates in the same competitive field as such companies as Saint Gobain Emballages or Pilkington in Europe. On the other hand, the industrial lubricants industry is moving towards internationalisation. Many essentially regional companies have been joining larger conglomerates with a broader, worldwide outlook. This shows that the geographical delimitation of a competitive system is a dynamic notion, which can change over time, even in the short term.

This example brings us to our second point. Even if, at a given time, a company feels its competitive field is limited to the companies that exist in a precise geographic zone, then analysis of its competitiveness can still be made only on a world scale. If they do not make the analysis on a global scale, they will fail to develop a capacity of anticipation for the survival of their company. This geographic approach to the competitive analysis of the company is too often either ignored or taken as fixed. If one of today's main strategic tasks is to be ready for tomorrow's competitive environment, it is also true that the most frequently used analytical methods are more concerned with the dimensions developed by Abell and Hammond (1979), for example (Figure 5.1). We shall try to draw the corresponding perspectives in Chapter 15.

The Bases for Strategic Analysis

Any company's strategic issues are linked to its capacity to exploit and strengthen its competitiveness in relation to its customers within an environment. Facing these challenges today means that it is impossible to have too many separate activities, as it would be difficult to generate sufficient resources to maintain competitiveness in each. This has meant many companies over the years have 'concentrated on their base industry'. One of the aims of strategic analysis must be to provide ways of *prioritising investment opportunities* given this new context. In this light, we have retained three classical notions of strategic analysis that can shed light on this problem of investment selection, each of which focuses on a particular characteristic. These are the *life-cycle* of products and groups of technologies, and includes the notion of maturity of a given industry (an explanatory factor of the dynamism of the competitive system); *experience curves* (whose consequences are to be found in the cost structure and the relationship with market share); and *relative perceived quality*, which helps to understand the competitive position of the company from a buyer's point of view.

Figure 5.4   Life-cycle of a product or technology

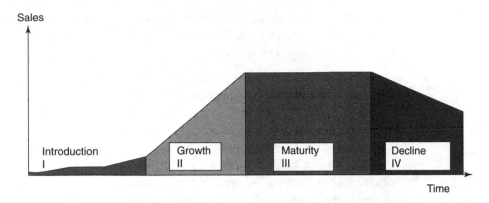

The Notion of a Life-Cycle

This idea (Figure 5.4) is not based on a scientific law, but on experience. A product, a technology, or an industry all mature differently: they develop, grow, mature, then decline under the effects of scientific and technical evolution, the behaviour and the ways of living and thinking of the players. These changes influence the competitive situation, and at each stage of the evolution, typical strategies are appropriate for the company. Although this notion was created originally for consumer goods, the notion of the life-cycle can also apply to business-to-business environments. Following phase 0 that involves no commercial activity, four other are recognised in the life cycle: *introduction*, *growth*, *maturity* and *decline*.

■ *Phase 0*. This is the time of very heavy *investments* and research *expenses*. It can last many years, almost 20 for the digital reading of sound or optoelectronics, 10–12 years for certain medicines, 6–8 years for a system of electronic sensors to calculate speed. It would be wrong to believe that this phase involves only technical activity. Indeed, we shall see later how efficient research demands a specific form of marketing to accompany and guide the technical development (see Chapter 10 on technological innovation).

■ *Phase I*. For us, marketing has already begun in the previous phase. However, much effort must be made to develop applications, accept and integrate alterations and customer suggestions, reduce risks, etc. The innovator also has to gather precise information about the advantages and disadvantages of the innovation in relation to existing methods, and to begin *explaining to and convincing the potential customer base*. Even if all the applications are not yet fully developed, there is still work to be done with the customers to ensure a transfer of technical know-how and to obtain approval for the solution. Here the innovator has a choice to make, which is particularly important, between large-volume markets, which will guarantee long-term development, and other applications that are more reactive to innovation and can ensure its profitable launch and promotion. The lucky innovations have both. This phase is characterised by the acquisition of the skills to master all economic and technical parameters, and by a competitive battle with the marketers of previous technical solutions (substitution competition).

- *Phase II*. Growth comes from the conjunction of two phenomena. On the one hand, the progressive development of all the possible applications for the innovation in phase I translates into an increase in the sources of *sales volume*. On the other hand, the sales volume for each application is developed by an increase in the *number of users* and/or by a positive increase in the *rate of use*. It is during this phase that the company proves its capacity to conquer new markets. Our observation shows that this capacity is not obvious and that at this stage it has to be developed within the company. Both competitors and new technical solutions based on different technical procedures often appear, owing to the attraction of the sector that is now visible through the volumes reached. Patents and alliance strategies between competitors become commonplace.

- *Phase III*. The *growth rate slows down*. The previous reasons for growth cannot be maintained in the long run. Competition becomes even stronger. Customers have by now mastered the techniques and are increasingly watchful of prices. Once patented products fall into the public domain, more competitors are attracted who are better equipped to face the original competition. The initial innovator has to rethink the role of the technology in the activity (manufacturing productivity, expected profitability) and to upgrade either/or technology and products, or even to renew them.

- *Phase IV*. The *replacing of the technologies or products accelerates*, and sales volumes fall. Only a few users remain. But only a few producers, too, which, paradoxically, allows those remaining to increase benefits and continue profitability despite an apparently negative environment.

This classic model has its uses. However, it is not always clear, appearing perhaps a little mechanical and deterministic. First, we must clearly define the context. Is it the demand linked to a particular application (for example, textile flooring); a specific response (polyamide textile flooring); or the position of a company in a given territory (flooring made with a fibre produced by a specific company on the European market)? By closely examining this question, we see that we have life-cycle curves that express different ideas: the total demand, the demand for a precisely defined response, the position of a company or a technology or a product within a company.

Another question related to the life-cycle concerns its effect on managers. In the early phases, the effect could be one of mobilisation of resources, and demobilisation towards the latter phases, especially if they are unplanned and not anticipated. Indeed, there may be no point in fighting against an obvious decline, but it can be

Figure 5.5   Life-cycle of Intel microprocessors

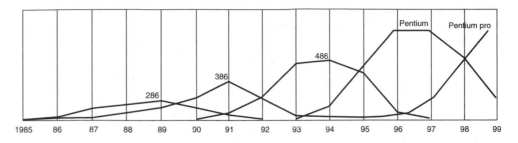

Source: *Le Nouvel Economiste*, 1026 (8 December 1995).

organisationally dramatic to amplify this decline while other complementary innovative possibilities still exist. For example, it was thought at one time that composite materials and aluminium would replace steel in the car industry. The innovative reactions of the steel producers concerning product improvements and weight management have proved the opposite. We shall develop this further in Chapter 7. With this in mind, Figure 5.5 illustrates the case of the life cycle of Intel microprocessors.

Another criticism concerning the life-cycle is linked to the fact that it is related to changes in demand, whereas certain authors (Atamer and Calori, 1993) believe this is not enough to explain the evolution of competitive systems. They prefer the wider notion of *degree of maturity of the sector* or *industry* as formulated by the consultants Michael Porter and A.D. Little. Indeed, maturity of a sector is the result of the permanent interplay between several interdependent influences (the market, the competition, etc.). According to these authors, the sectors themselves pass through several phases of maturity: emergence, growth, maturity and decline. Even if this broader notion includes more explanatory factors for the evolution of the structure of the competitive system than that of the life-cycle of products, it, too, has its critics. For example, it has been proven that within an industry, sub-sets can exist at different stages of maturity. Thus, the formulation of global strategic recommendations for an industry according to maturity is not always easy.

Experience and Market Share

First observed in America in 1925 by the commander of an air-base who observed that experience meant that less time was spent servicing planes, the 'law' of experience curves was adopted by economists, and then later by the Boston Consulting Group (BCG) consultants. It argues that 'the unit cost of the added value for an homogenous product, calculated in constant monetary units, diminishes by a fixed percentage each time the cumulative production doubles'. The notion of *unit cost for a company* means, for example, materials, components, incorporated labour,

Figure 5.6   Representation of the experience curve

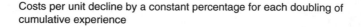

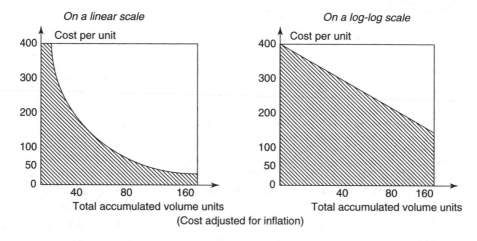

distribution costs, payments to pay off investments in equipment, after-sales services and administrative expenses. The origins of the experience benefits are numerous: training of the workforce, improvements in the conception of the product, innovations in the production process, incorporation of economies of scale and supplier efforts in productivity and so on. The effect is not the result of a natural process, but of regular and repeated efforts throughout the company value chain: research and development investments, industrial investment, staff training or the use of new technologies. The graphic representation of the experience is a curve using linear co-ordinates or a straight line using logarithmic co-ordinates (Figure 5.6). The slope of the curve is determined by the percentage drop in unit cost with each doubling of production. It varies depending on product type: 50 to 60 per cent for semiconductors in the world, 80 per cent for aluminium in the USA, 70 per cent for the production of steel in Japan, etc.

Company economists have made a link between cumulative production and the market share of a company at a given time. They confirm that a company that at a given time has a higher market share than its competitors (the notion of *relative market share*) will normally have better costs than competition, and consequently, and for a given market price, could have better profitability. They propose a strategic logic (Figure 5.7) that argues for building a market share advantage to obtain a reduction in costs, this reduction leading to a reduction in price as market share progresses (see Chapter 7 for more information concerning price fixing). All of this being accompanied, of course, by improved profitability. This strategic logic is known *as domination through costs* and relates to what we mentioned in Chapter 1 concerning company global competitiveness (Figure 1.2).

Figure 5.7 Domination through costs

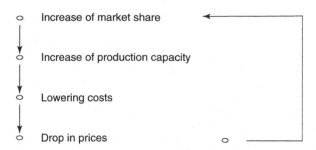

The relationship between profitability and market share has long been debated among management scientists. This centres on the definition of the limits of the market concerned. BCG consultants have always been vague on this point and have let it be believed that, for example, the excellent results for Mercedes during the 1980–90 period despite a low market share were an exception. The PIMS project researchers believed, on the other hand, that market share must be calculated on a narrower definition of the notion of market, which they called the '*served market*'. PIMS once again underlined the crucial problem of defining the relevant strategic arena to allow for an analysis of the environment, the evaluation of the position of the company, the allocation of resources and the evaluation of results. The 'served market' is defined by taking into consideration the following elements: the products and services involved, the customers affected by the marketing efforts of the company, a group of particular competitors and a geographic area. Thus, to come back to the car industry, Mercedes' market share must be calculated in the world luxury car market, in which its competitors are Jaguar, Porsche, Saab, BMW, Acura, Lexus, Infiniti, but not Renault, Ford or Fiat.

Mercedes has a large part of the luxury car market, which explains its good profitability. Indeed, the work undertaken by PIMS has shown a 'constant and strong' link between company market share in a served market and profitability (Figure 5.8), without however confirming the mechanical relationship that the BCG group led us to believe in. In its contribution to company strategic management, PIMS also highlighted the role played by factors other than relative market share to explain the level of profitability reached. This will be developed further below.

For us, the conclusion to be reached is that experience is an important economic 'law' that leads to the establishment of a relationship between a company's relative market share for a given product and profitability, even if this relationship cannot be reduced to the purely mechanical linear function as proposed by BCG. However, it is important to note that experience has no effect in certain markets: for example, when the market does not react to price changes, or when technical breakdowns allow poorly experienced competitors to get better costs than their bigger-volume competitors, or when other factors (personal motivation, current assets, cost of labour or capital) have more influence on profitability than experience.

Figure 5.8   Relationship between market share and return on investment

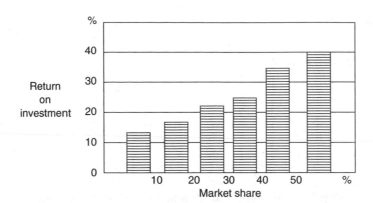

Source: Buzzel and Gale (1987).

Relative Perceived Quality

We highlight the results from the PIMS project concerning other factors that explain differences in profitability. These include aspects such as capital intensity, output, served market growth, relative market share, efforts in research and development, vertical integration, pressure on costs and the role of time in the strategy process. The reason for our stressing these is that they are also the factors that fully participate in the definition of relationships with customers. So a marketing policy also illustrates the link that the marketing function must establish with the functions of technical design, manufacturing and company logistics (Chapter 1). This notion has already been used in Chapter 4 (customer satisfaction), and will be mentioned again in Chapter 7 (the offer), and Chapter 11 (services marketing). *Quality* is thus a major transition issue between customers and company investment in technology. Indeed, the definition of relative perceived quality is a measure of the quality of the company's global contribution to customer activity, as perceived by the customers themselves relative to that of the competitors. What the PIMS project does is to relate relative perceived quality to profitability (Figure 5.9).

Another interesting point is the *dynamic* aspect of this idea. Customer perception is continually affected by the customer's learning process, and by all the efforts made by competitors concerning all the parameters related to quality. Thus, any company can find itself suddenly in a weaker competitive position simply because the competition evolves faster. Watching over all aspects related to relative perceived quality is therefore essential. The PIMS report supports this and also points out other aspects concerning qualitative superiority: given an increase in market share, customers should find improved quality, and the quality permits higher prices. This allowed the PIMS researchers to put forward a strategic logic, which is different from that of domination through costs. Quite naturally, this is based on the search for better *relative perceived quality* (Figure 5.10). Here we find, in

Figure 5.9   Relationship between quality, return on sales and return on investment

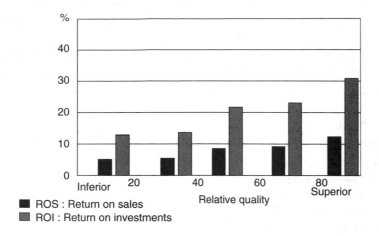

ROS : Return on sales
ROI : Return on investments

Source: Buzzel and Gale (1987).

Figure 5.10   Strategic logic of relative perceived quality

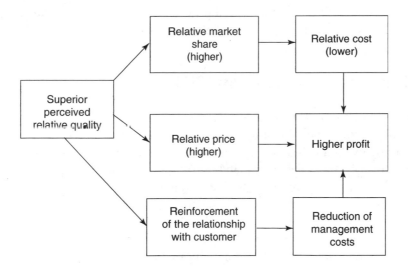

Source: Buzzel and Gale (1987).

another form more directly based on company management, the conclusions we reached in Chapter 1 after examining the notion of competitiveness by insisting on the interest of a 'marketing of value' approach (Figure 1.5).

The perspective of quality we have underlined raises the question of its role in firm management and competitiveness. Leading firms met changes in defining quality and the ways it orientated management thinking. The first step is setting and meeting quality norms and standards, and responsibility lies mainly with manufacturing. A second step is marked by the concern about customer satisfaction, and manufacturing is joined by marketing and research and development. But this stage may lead to intra-company turf wars, and avoid solving the major issues linked to the delivery of world-class quality. A third step is necessary where market and customer value is the focal point for firm strategy. This is made possible through inter-functional management who understand the issues of competitive strategies and utilise the common tools of *performance assessment*. These tools are built on the hypothesis that financial results are a direct consequence of a policy of quality (perceived relative).

The three notions we have just examined (life-cycle, experience and relative perceived quality) are three basic elements for the determination of strategy. The first represents the company market(s) maturity. Later, we shall see that although limited, this notion is useful in strategic thinking. The other two offer a representation of the company position in relation to the competition, either on cost or the quality of the offer. To conclude, there is a double approach to strategic thinking: *confrontation with the competition* and *market appropriateness*. Thus, the company can position itself in the strategic arena (battle field), and identify the 'fields' in which it can best succeed considering the attraction they represent for it, its assets, and the strategies of competitors. To complete the elements of this analysis, we will now examine how companies develop their strategy in a determined competitive system and identify the various possible options.

Competitive Positions in a Competitive System

The notion of *strategic behaviour* refers to the global options a company can choose from depending upon its strategic aims and its characteristics. Updating these options by using an empirical typology based on the observation of real behaviour allows for the global but simple and useful identification of the orientations of the competitors who are present in a given strategic arena.

A competitive strategy is always based on either superiority, which is at least partial (quality, costs, etc.), or the imitation of the best competitors present. Company competitive strategy in a given competitive field can be approached on two levels: on a *global* level (the activity or the industry), or on a more precisely defined level by dividing the field into *homogeneous groups*. Here, we shall look at the former approach; the latter will be dealt with in Chapter 6.

A Classification of the Strategies of Position: Leader, Challenger, Specialist and Follower

It is often useful to position the various competitors in an industry by retaining only the dominant characteristic of their strategic options, in other words the general option chosen to approach the market. In many ways, this approach is similar to the notion of *company image* (or *profile*). Our classification will be based on the distinction between three types of competition to be found on the market: those who look to attain a position of dominance over the whole market, those who look to maximise their partial superiority and those who look to imitate the behaviour of the market's main competitors. The choice of strategy depends on an appreciation of the real capacities of the company when confronted by opportunities that at the same time expresses the degree of involvement (investment) that the company is prepared to make, given the attraction of the market for the company.

- The '*leader*' of a competitive field has built up an important market share in relation to the competition. Owing to its role as leader (Chapter 2), the issues are twofold. First, it must, as the leader, develop or at least maintain demand. Secondly, it will try to conserve or enhance its position, which means fighting on many fronts: maintaining a high rate of relative innovation and technological development; having a high level of relative perceived quality; being able, through experience, to maintain market price or even in some cases to withstand a price war; covering all market segments and presenting a large range of offers; covering distribution, reacting to competitor manoeuvres, and maintaining the effect of power linked to its commercial investments (sales force, communication, etc.).

- The '*challenger*' tries to build up market share. Thus, the challenger is fighting against the leader(s). To do so, the company must have specific assets (partial superiority), either concerning quality, or organisation (innovation, productivity, commercial investments). In fact, the challenger has two generic forms of strategy to achieve this: an open attack on the leader, which can be considered as risky and expensive, or by getting round the leader by exploiting his weak points: market segments, distribution channels, types of application, etc. One important criterion for challenger success is the capacity to anticipate the leader's *reactions* and *form of reactions*.

- The '*specialist*' concentrates limited resources on precise market segments in which they can develop their competitive advantages, which for the main part are based on technological innovation and quality. This choice of strategic option generally involves the creation of ways to reach targeted market segments (for example, a different way to gain access to the customers' purchasing centres through the technical functions, see Chapters 3 and 8). In these segments the leader or challenger may neglect those customers demanding small volumes, thereby opening possibilities for a more specialised approach. It is nevertheless important that these segments have enough potential to give the specialist real development possibilities, as it will be difficult to move to other segments where the partial superiority does not have the same value for the customer.

- The '*follower*' is a company that acts in the main segments without expecting high market share. It often offers lower prices for a 'normal/standard' value, which means that it limits its offer to the key elements in order to reduce expenses and be able to keep up with technical evolutions.

This typology allows us to forecast the most likely competitor behaviour, if we believe that they behave in a stable and coherent way that corresponds to their strategic choice. This typology is obviously more relevant for mature industries than for new and emerging industries where competitor position is unstable and less predictable.

The Concept of Strategic Group

The classification proposed in the previous paragraph is based on market share and, as such, does not necessarily take all the phenomena that are at stake into account. Thus, it is useful to complete it with a second classification based on the notion of *strategic groups* that are defined as a sub-set of competitors who develop similar strategies in a given industry (for further details, see Atamer and Calori, 1993). Grouping together companies in an industry that work on the same applications, we can find:

■ The *generalists* who are present in most applications and who have a large range of offers

■ The *multispecialists* who are also interested in all the applications, but who look for particular ways of operating linked either to different technologies, or to original service offers

■ The *specialists* who are interested in only one, or at the most two, market segments.

The identification of strategic groups allows us to list the competition and to define their intentions and their potential. The use of the notion of strategic groups paves the way for further areas of research, in particular, to identify how the costs are shared between different applications for the same group of technologies and to analyse the resulting competitive advantages. It leads to incorporation into the analysis of decisions concerning the various applications of new technologies. In addition, analysing customer purchasing behaviour when confronted by the different offers, application by application, (see Chapter 3) makes it easier to move from the notion of application to that of market segment and thereby enrich the analysis of the industries (Chapter 6). Whether customers prefer *global offers* (generalists and multispecialists) or not, is likely to limit the number of their suppliers, or result in a policy of partnership with them (specialists and multispecialists). Some of them will prefer one supply policy rather than another. This takes us to the problem of multicriteria segmentation of the markets, which we shall look at in Chapter 6.

This, and the notions and classifications mentioned above, show clearly that a company must always make choices according which areas it wants to invest in, and the resources that it has to commit clearly affect this decision. Whatever the mode of definition for these entities – application, market segment, SBU, competitive field, etc. – management must think about the following question: How and why is it profitable to invest in one entity rather than another? Many methods have been devised to analyse the possible choices and to make the best decision. This is the subject of the following section.

Methodology of the Strategic Choice

It is unthinkable to talk of suppliers of industrial goods strategies without mentioning the methods of analysis of the company portfolio, most of them having been designed by large consultancy firms. Widely published and used, they have often been unjustly criticised. They are guides for the decision-making process and should be considered as such. They do not replace the decision maker and are there only to help analyse the competitive fields. In this sense, the methods have proved their worth. Even today they continue to be the most efficient way to 'decipher' the strategic environment of a company and to help in the formulation of a systematic and reasoned analysis. They lead to simplified and yet acceptable representations of reality. The various methods give something essential to the strategic analyst: to simplify the complexity of the real world in order to make a decision possible.

We shall present three methods: that of the Boston Consulting Group (BCG), of McKinsey and of A.D. Little (ADL). For greater detail the reader is invited to study the works found in the References and Further Reading. The idea behind the methods is to get the decision makers to think about the attractiveness of an industry (or a sub-set of the industry) in which the company operates, and also to assess the assets of the company in relation to the competition in each field of activity. The graphic presentation of the results clearly outlines the choices available. In some cases it may be useful to combine at least two of the methods when thinking about strategy and even to create one's own method of reflection, if it appears necessary to look for a greater adaptation to the specific characteristics of a trade.

The BCG Method (Growth Rate/Market Share)

This was elaborated at the end of the 1960s and is based on two simple criteria: the attractiveness of an industry is expressed by its *growth rate* and company performance by its relative *market share* (Figure 5.11). The choice of these criteria is based on the existence of an evolution in costs through experience, a notion we looked at earlier.

The choice of the industry's growth rate (vertical axis) is inspired by the *life-cycle curve*: company activities which correspond to developing industries with a

Figure 5.11   The BCG matrix

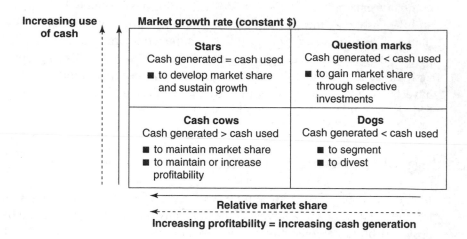

strong growth rate require large investments to continue the development, while those which are more mature (low growth or stagnation) free assets which can be reinvested in other activities, and those in decline need more attention to avoid loss making investments. Market growth rate is measured by the increase in market volume or value from one year to the next. The median of the vertical axis is determined either by the average growth rate for all company activities or the average growth rate of the industries it is operating in, or by a rate that has been determined by the directors.

Relative market share (horizontal axis) is linked to *experience*. Higher market share than the competition means a better position on the experience curve that is itself the source of favourable profitability. The relative market share calculation is made either by comparing company market share in volume with the market leader, or by comparing with a competitive index (average market share of the first three competitors).

The BCG method has a strong financial element to it. The recommended strategic paths are those that optimise *financial flow* and permit allocation of resources to the most *profitable fields* for the company. Thus, we can distinguish four types of activity or strategic positions:

■ The '*stars*' are activities that are characterised by growth and a favourable competitive position. They absorb increasing amounts of cash flow but also generate cash flow through their intrinsic profitability. In theory, they are self-balancing in the short term and can lead to prospects of surplus of cash flow in the mid- to long-term.

■ The '*cash cows*' are activities that will no longer grow, they generate more cash flow than they require owing to the strong market share already reached. Such activities give rise to an immediate cash surplus, which can be used to finance investments in other activities. The investments that are required to maintain profitability (productivity, for example) and market share should not be forgotten, however.

■ The '*question marks*' express the ambiguity of positions of activities that are not clear. These industries are attractive because of their growth potential, but because the company has not yet acquired a sufficiently high relative market share this means insufficient profitability. This problem can be solved only through investment designed to build a better competitive position. The problem becomes more complicated when the company invests in several such growth activities and does not have enough resources to support them all. Thus, it is necessary to make choices that the BCG method does not really describe.

■ The '*dogs*' are activities where the combination of low relative market share and low growth only rarely lead to a satisfactory level of profitability. The solution for the company is to either abandon the activity or to concentrate its efforts on a market segment. In some instances (ongoing demand/abandonment by the main competitors), 'dog' activities can lead to positive results. This is rare, but should be remembered. In other words, it is not always a good thing to apply the methods too mechanically, whatever the case.

Together, these can create a *balanced portfolio* (Figure 5.12).

Owing to its simplicity and easy interpretation, the BCG method has many advantages compared to other methods. Its main drawback is linked to experience, whose field of application is essentially related to volume industries. Therefore, to explain the profitability of a given activity by only market share is insufficient; there are lifeless 'cash cows' and profitable 'dogs'. As demonstrated by the PIMS research, this

Figure 5.12   The BCG matrix: a balanced portfolio

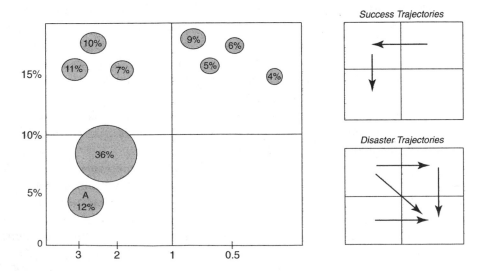

Table 5.3   Example of attractiveness and business strength criteria

Industry attractiveness	Business strengths
Example of criteria:	*Example of criteria:*
– Size	– Market share
– Growth	– Mastering of basic technologies
– National/European/international scope	– Possibilities for technological innovation
– Business cycles vulnerability	– Relative offer quality
– Scale economies possibility	– General image
– Importance of entry cost	– Advertising and promotion effectiveness
– Competitive structure	– Logistic capabilities
– Customers' bargaining power	– Position with major customer accounts
– Threat of new entrants	– Sales/distribution effectiveness
– Threat of substitute technologies or services	– Etc.
– Influence of technical norms	
– Influence of legal issues	
– Energy impact	
– Market diversity (segmentation possibilities)	
– Etc.	

means that other factors have an influence on profit: capital intensity or quality, for example. Also, we must not forget that the definition of the reference market (calculation of market share) is not given by the method, whereas this can be a decisive factor. To apply the BCG method to a large heterogeneous market would be ridiculous, the definition of the competitive world lacks relevance. On the other hand, to apply it to a well-defined market sub-set is very often more accurate, which reinforces the attention to be given to the relevance of strategic segmentation.

The McKinsey Approach

This method, that was produced during the 1970s for applications with Shell and General Electric is, through its inherent variability and capacity, representative of the multicriteria methods. In order to break away from the 'simplistic' BCG method, the McKinsey consultants devised a method based on the integration of multiple criteria to orient company choice in a particular competitive field. These sub-sets have been divided into two: the attractiveness of an industry and the company's competitive advantages (Table 5.3).

The evaluation of the advantages is made by using the criteria to measure the *intrinsic value* of the industry for all the competitors and its *relative value* for the company in question. The criteria can be classified in order of importance by using factors that express the strategic issues facing the company. If we consider the two following criteria, market volume and potential profit margin, allocating importance to one or the other gives an indication of the strategic path of the company. Then, for each criterion, a system of scoring allows us to compare the different markets between themselves and to formulate a hierarchy of attractiveness (high, medium, low).

Figure 5.13   The McKinsey matrix

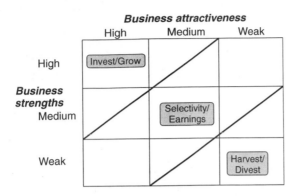

Appreciation of the company advantages is made similarly. A list of criteria allows us to define the essential conditions for success on all markets. A subsequent weighting for each market leads to a hierarchy in advantages (high, medium, low).

The combination of the two sets of criteria defines three zones of strategic involvement: *development*, *maintenance* and *abandon* (Figure 5.13). This approach has some advantages. It allows a better understanding of the prospective elements, advantages which have been developed by the company that give it access to new fields or the possibility to act with new means on known markets. This prospective capacity stimulates management creativity and imagination that can therefore integrate these elements into a more rational approach and make it easier to explain the judgements that would otherwise remain subjective. Thus, the McKinsey method facilitates management reflection and the creation of agreement between participants. However, its flexibility can be a disadvantage. This is based on the sensitivity to the weightings used. In other words, by varying the weight given to each criterion, the positions on the grid of the different fields change. In fact, this apparent instability is also the opportunity more precisely to discuss and understand the strategic issues facing the company.

The ADL Method

Elaborated by another major international consulting firm known for its research into company technological issues, this method is based on the same basic idea of having two axes describe the *internal efficiency* of the company and the *external attractiveness* of the industry. The horizontal axis represents industry maturity and shows whether it is worth investing resources or not, and the vertical axis presents, on the basis of a multicriteria matrix, an evaluation of the competitive position of the company.

The resulting matrix helps to isolate four zones that are the result of different strategic choices: natural development, selective development, recovery and abandonment (Figure 5.14).

Figure 5.14   The ADL grid

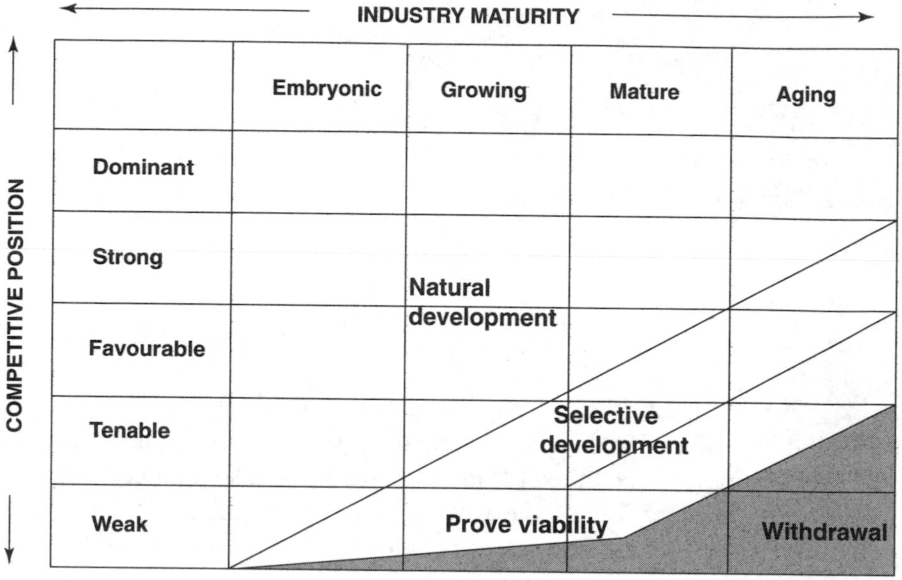

The ADL method is particularly well suited to competitive environments when technology has a strong influence on company activity. This is why it is often used in companies to evaluate technological portfolios, replacing the 'industry maturity' axis by 'technological maturity'.

Links Between Company Strategic Choices and Marketing Strategy

Without wanting to denigrate the above-mentioned methods, we feel it is necessary to point out our conception of the strategic process. This will enable the reader better to understand the links between the elements to be found in this work which concern global company strategy (Chapters 1 and 5) and those which detail our approach to marketing strategy in the business-to-business world (Chapters 6, 7 and 8).

Company Strategy and Marketing Strategy

We begin with a hypothesis based on experience and our own work in business-to-business environments. This hypothesis assumes that an efficient strategic process for a modern company is both the result of a 'top-down' process, and a 'bottom-up' process. It is also compulsory to take into account the *building of resources*, with a capacity to modify the competitive rules. This is based on several observations:

■ Whatever the method used, a global strategic analysis of the kind mentioned in this chapter cannot offer the detail required to make it (1) 'totally' coherent with the functioning of the markets, customer demands and the rules of the real competitive game, (2) internally credible for those in charge. The strategic route chosen for a given activity can therefore be considered only as a general orientation, simple and definitive over the decided period, but lacking in detail to lead directly to commercial action. The old expression of company 'general policy', now a little out of date, clearly explained the idea, according to which one simply has to cover a number of steps to move from global strategic choice to its operational interpretation.

■ The missing elements to complete the move from global strategic choice to commercial action can be considered only as complements designed to ease operating. These details (for example, analysis of customer purchasing behaviour and demands) are the result of an analytical process that is distinct from the global strategic analysis. They are the result of a different approach to the activities and the most obvious result is market and clientele segmentation (Chapter 6). Because of this difference, this dual process often leads to differences of opinion about reality, and even contradictions. For example, a certain market segment choice which is considered to be growing following the application of a BCG-style analysis and whose general orientation is to acquire market share, appears, following marketing segmentation, to be made up of six different market segments: five of which are growing (one of which is at the early stages of growth), one is declining because a substitute technology is more economical for the customers with relatively little drop in quality (from their point of view). Among the four growth segments, two are concentrated markets with strong customer negotiating power, which makes a market share acquisition strategy impossible without a minimum of changes to the offer. This type of case is typical and frequent. Company strategists saw a homogeneous activity whilst 'marketers' saw heterogeneity. Thus, it is clear that for the sake of efficiency, these two representations of the market environment be confronted, which subsequently leads to an adjustment in global strategy. This can even result in a change in objectives. If this confrontation does not happen, the global strategy becomes a simple exercise of little interest and impact on daily activity because it is judged as ill-adapted by the actors involved.

■ The global strategic analysis also presents two disadvantages: it promotes direct competitive rivalry in the analysis and neglect the characteristics of the systems of influence that usually shape the markets (Chapters 2 on networks). By promoting the competitive confrontation between clearly identified companies, global strategic analysis also promotes a simplistic view of reality. In the creation of a marketing strategy to dominate market share based on the offer of particularly advanced services, the company can call in help from the outside through a strategy of an alliance that can modify its advantages dramatically. Global strategic analysis does not normally take into account these *external resources*, while the skilled marketer does. Therefore, it is important not to inhibit what can be called 'entrepreneurship spirit' or the *creativity of internal company thinking*. Also, the functioning of the systems of influence in a given market (or a network of relationships) can upset the introduction of a strategic choice that has been elaborated rationally. This is frequent when global strategy is used to conquer foreign markets to extend the geographic base of the activity. A direct competitive analysis has shown for example that the company in question had clear partial superiorities over its local competitors in an export market. With company advantages being high, it is normal to set high objectives concerning market penetration, the objectives being realistic as they are based on the market survey as part of the strategic analysis process. In complex industrial systems (Chapter 2), networks and working habits of the actors who have been operating for many years and trust each other are difficult barriers to overcome. Inertia and resistance to change are elements which even partial superiorities find difficult to break down. In such cases, our experience shows that it is not the objectives that are unrealistic, but the time allotted in the global strategy to reach them.

■ We must now underline the possibilities open through the building of new resources. This approach may stem from a technological innovation or a clever decision made by the Chief Executive Officer. It may also surface from the attention paid to sometimes limited and uncertain modifications in customers' behaviour or issues. If the firm is able to spot such moves and to realise the corresponding learning progress, it may open considerable perspectives. The Mory–Ancel case (Example 5) gives a remarkable example of this happening.

All these elements have led us to adopt a completely systematic conception of strategy, involving successive iterations between the global analysis and the detailed analysis function by function, in order to clarify choices made by the managers and to limit the risk of choice errors. This does not mean one of the strategic processes (either global or functional) is wrong; both are useful and legitimate. In our perception of strategy, strategic choice is not a programmed part of the life of a company, but a gradual construction based on interaction and a number of exchanges of opinion and information internally. The usual strategic process leaves no room for such exchanges owing to its organisation of restrictive and fixed dates. This does not mean that strategic processes cannot be organised and planned.

Figure 5.15 is an attempt at formalising the above ideas. The fact that the diagram is based on marketing is obviously linked to the central theme of this work. It could certainly be replaced another company function.

The left-hand side of the diagram shows the different steps of the global strategic process as presented in this chapter. Its result is expressed in detailed choices made for each field of activity and the resources allotted. This result can be used as a framework of involvement of the strategic marketing process that is on the right side of the diagram. Marketing has helped in the preparation of global choices by supplying information and the analysis in the form, and with the required

Figure 5.15 Global strategy, a double process: 'top-down' and 'bottom-up'

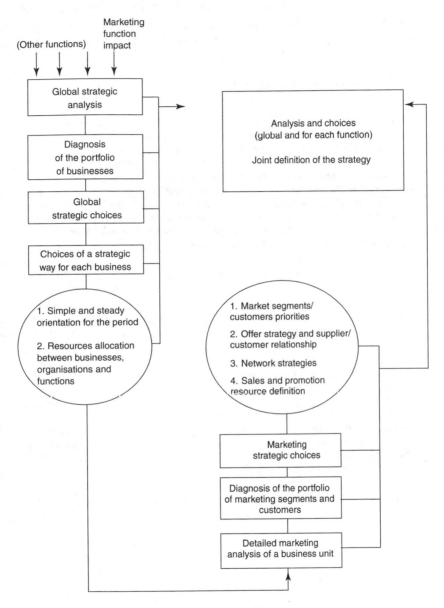

precision, of the strategic analysis method chosen by the company (BCG, McKinsey, or another). Marketing is also involved in the analysis and decision process with enough detail for the efficient orientation of its operational action. This functional strategic process, as stated in Chapter 2, is based on the same stakes and reasoning as the global process. Only the methods are different (see Chapter 6 for more details on these differences). The result can either be compatible with the orientations of the global strategy, or lead to new discussion concerning these orientations.

To simplify, Figure 5.16 presents the different steps of reasoning. It does not mean we are talking about successive chronological sequences of analysis and decision that would only lengthen the global strategic planning process. We consider it as a *systematic process*, both iterative and permanent, which can be used

Example 5   Corporate Strategy and Marketing: Mory–Ancel*

In 1982, Ancel, a middle-sized firm and subsidiary of a large German group located in Strasburg, specialising in food preparations (custards, creams, etc.) decided to expand their offer with salted and sugared snacks. These products were to come fully packed from the countries of production, namely African and Caribbean territories. As a result they had to be delivered to some French Mediterranean and Atlantic harbours, which was inconsistent with Ancel's present logistical organisation. So they started looking for solutions. They then approached Mory, their major supplier of logistics and transportation. From this point the development of relationships between Mory and Ancel illustrates the systemic and iterative relationship in progress between marketing and corporate strategies. From now on we shall adopt the point of view of Mory, the supplier:

1. Mory makes a proposal to Ancel, including customs clearance, storage and delivery to Ancel customers (large chains of hypermarkets and supermarkets). This is merely an *offer adaptation* inside the usual range of service provisions from a freighter and customs agent.

2. Ancel indicates their satisfaction to their supplier and transfers a requirement from their own customers, price marking on packing. Having given some thought to the requirement, Mory decided to organise (small investment and extra labour) to ensure this new service provision. This move can be described as an *offer broadening towards a target customer*.

3. Ancel then asks their supplier to provide overpacking allowing the realisation of promotional offers, essential for this kind of a market. This represents a more significant investment on Mory's side in both machinery and labour. Potential sales to Ancel do not seem to be sufficient to ensure profitability. Mory then embarks on a search among their present clientele and possible customers to identify firms interested in this type of a service provision. And they find firms interested whose characteristics are mid-sized firms specialised in dry grocery and suppliers of the food distributors. Mory consequently designs and markets a new offer: customs clearance, storage, overpacking, price marking and delivery of dry grocery products to the French food distributors. There it is a *new offer targeted towards a new market segment*.

4. Mory, when servicing their customers with this new offer, soon realises that their delivery men can also ensure some tasks usually undertaken by the product supplier: shelf-supplying and management, watching the orders flow, gondola heads assembly and so on. This new and enlarged dimension of the offer requires other resources: a highly precise logistical organisation in order to meet the distributors' requirements, a better qualified and trained personnel, specialised warehouses and workshops, own lorries, and so on. Mory's traditional transport organisation is not able to cope with these new *key success factors*. They now have to build a completely separate activity under the form of a subsidiary with their own capital, personnel, resources, budget and balance sheet. Thus, Mory created a new Strategic Business Unit, separated from its classical transport organisation. Within a few years this subsidiary employed more than 3000 people.

Source: Adapted from the Symposium, 'Les synergies tertiaires' (1987).
*Mory was founded in Boulogne, France in 1804 to carry mail out of and to France. It quickly developed as a carrier between France and the UK. It followed this with the development of transport activities with maritime, road and rail routes as well as airfreight. It presently (2000) achieves a turnover of around 5 billion Euros, employing 3500 staff through differently defined transport based activities. Mory TNTE www.mory-group.com/fr/identite/hiscont.htm

progressively to create a better global strategy, by incorporating both global reasoning linked to overall company strategy, and detailed reasoning that takes market reality into consideration. We believe such a method gives more room for *company reactivity* to changes within its environment. At the same time, the usual decision and collective action processes can continue to function normally. They will be interrupted only when a consensus is reached concerning the need for partial or total reorientation of the global choices.

The question now raised concerns the internal organisation of dialogue so that the improved global strategy mentioned above can be produced. The creation of permanent informal groups, across functions if possible, generally allows for the creation of the conditions for this discussion (strategy committees, and company marketing committees could fulfil such a mission).

Having clarified our conception of strategy in companies which produce and market industrial goods (product, services or projects), we feel it necessary to end this chapter with an example to illustrate our ideas and that highlights the specificities of the industrial world and the consequences on strategic thinking/reasoning.

The Consequences of Adaptations Carried Out with Customers

One of the major strategic places for the industrial company is the particular context of the buyer–supplier relationships that it is involved in. The events that take place within such frameworks are often strategically important for the company. They can include the creation of new resources, which can influence the evolution of the company's global strategy. This can be seen in the example of the Mory–Ancel relationship (Example 5).

This example shows the potential of supplier–customer relationships as a generator of strategy evolution for the company. There are many such examples. This potential, which has been generated by the direct interactive process between a supplier and customer, is often present when the relationship is long-term (the notion of partnership and environment of trust). With time, the relationship develops, deepens, even grows and creates new added values. All a company's supplier–customer relationships are not always like this, but those that are as important as technological capital or company market share. This cannot be forgotten in the industrial world and it is normal that it is marketing strategy that takes it into account. At the same time, it should be pointed out that in order to remain efficient, this involves the creation of the iterative marketing strategy/global strategy process presented above.

To end this chapter, we have to imagine the company as both a rational organisation in which the global strategy process offers the basis of a general orientation of action, and a 'learning' organisation where actions and subsequent results can be exploited and generalised in order to produce new strategic orientations. To think and to organise the links between the 'top-down' and 'bottom-up' processes, even 'lateral' interfunctional processes, for us, is one of the major tasks for the industrial company for the years to come. The rigidity of structures built up over the years based on Taylorism then matrixes, etc. mean this is difficult today. However, it is necessary in the name of the search for global competitiveness mentioned in Chapter 1.

References and Further Reading

Abell, D.F. (1980) *Defining the Business: The Starting Point of Strategic Planning*, Englewood Cliffs, Prentice-Hall.

Abell, D.F. and Hammond, J.S. (1979) *Strategic Market Planning: Problems and Analytical Approaches*, Englewood Cliffs, Prentice-Hall.

Actes du Colloque (1987) 'Les synergies tertiares: qu'attendre d'un prestataire de servies', Paris, IRE.

Agence Nationale pour la Valorisation de la Recherche (ANVAR) (1992) *Histoire(s) d'innover ou comment l'innovation vient aux entreprises*, Paris, InterEditions.

Atamer, T. and Calori, R. (1993) *Diagnostique et décisions stratégiques*, Paris, Dunod.

Bidault, F. (1988) *Le champ stratégique de l'entreprise*, Paris, Economica.

Boston Consulting Group (1981) *Les mécanismes fondomentaux de la compétitivité*, Paris, Hommes et Techniques.

Buzzel, R. and Gale, B. (1987) *The PIMS Principles: Linking Strategy to Performance*, New York, Free Press.

Karim, R., Mehajan, V. and Varadarajan, P.R. (1990) *Contemporary Perspectives on Strategic Market Planning*, London, Allyn & Bacon.

Metais, E. (1997) 'Intention stratégique et transformation de l'environnement concurrentiel', IAE d'Aix en Provence, Université Aix-Marseille III, *Thèse pour l'obtention du Doctorat de l'Université non-publiée*.

Millier, P. (1999) *Marketing the Unknown: Developing Market Strategies for Technical Innovations*, New York, Wiley.

Porter, M.E. (1979) 'How Competitive Forces Shape Industry', *Harvard Business Review*, vol. 57, no. 2, 137–45.

Porter, M.E. (1985) *Competitive Advantage: Creating and Sustaining Superior Performance*, New York, Free Press.

Rothschild, W.E. (1984) *How to Gain (and Maintain) the Competitive Advantage in Business?*, New York, McGraw-Hill.

Valla, J.-P. (1991) 'Options stratégiques en marketing inter organisationnel: un nouveau modèle à partir d'une nouvelle compréhension de l'environnement', *1ère Conférence Internationale de Gestion Stratégique*, 'Les options stratégiques', HEC Montreal.

Discussion Questions

1 Discuss the relationships between market segmentation and key success factors.
2 What are the main factors underpinning a strategic analysis in business-to-business marketing?
3 What are the strategic consequences of achieving better relative perceived quality?
4 Identify some of the issues that are really specific to designing a strategy in business-to-business marketing.

Chapter 1

Competitiveness, Marketing and Business-to-Business Marketing

What is marketing all about
Different marketing environments
B2B marketing

Chapter 2

Business-to-Business Customers and Markets

| B2B Generic Offers | Technological Innovation | Pure Services | Major Projects |

PART I   STRATEGY FOUNDATIONS

Chapter 3	Chapter 4	Chapter 5	Chapter 6
Understanding Business-to-Business Purchasing	**Information and Information Systems**	**Markets and Suppliers' Strategy**	**Segmentation and Marketing Strategy**

PART II   STRATEGY IMPLEMENTATION

Chapter 7
Generic Business-to-Business Offer Design and Management

Chapter 8
Market Access and Customer Management

Chapter 9
Communication and Publicity/Advertising

Chapter 10	Chapter 11	Chapter 12
Marketing and Technological Innovation	**The Marketing of Services**	**Major Project Marketing**

PART III   STRATEGY DESIGN

Chapter 13	The Role and Organisation of Marketing
Chapter 14	**Customer Position, Market Position, Marketing Strategies and Planning**
Chapter 15	**Issues and Specificities of International Marketing**
Annex	**The Internet and Marketing: Some Ideas**

6 Segmentation and Marketing Strategy

In Chapter 5, we highlighted the essential concepts of a company's global strategy and the main methods of strategic analysis available. This led us to wonder about the link between global strategy and marketing strategy. To answer this, we explained the concept of strategy that this book is based on, while underlining the need for a systematic and iterative link between a company's global strategy and its localised marketing strategy. Both processes are strategic and affect strategic priorities and the allocation of specific resources. But they do differ on two points: the vision of the markets concerned (general versus local), and the methods used. In Chapter 5 we analysed the potential negative consequences of such a double vision of industrial systems. It produces a lack of credibility concerning global strategic choices for those directly involved, incoherence between the formalised general orientations and the local action put into operation. We also proposed a first hint on how to confront this problem.

This chapter is devoted to the methods that are associated with a company's marketing strategy operating in business-to-business markets. For reasons of clarity, we shall use a logical step-by-step approach. As we adopt a slightly pedagogical approach, this does not mean to say that we believe this to be the case of decision making in practice. It simply suggests that logical and rational reasoning can be used, based on the incorporation of everything we know about business-to-business market dynamics and buyer behaviour. All the concepts mentioned in previous chapters are included here, but not necessarily in a sequential way. Thus, it is recommended that you read Chapters 1–5 before starting on this one.

The three approaches to global strategic analysis examined in Chapter 5 (BCG, McKinsey and ADL) lead to the evaluation of a company on both the global level of its portfolio of businesses and the level of each strategic business unit (SBU). This global evaluation indicates the value of all company activities that allows for the setting of priorities and the recommendation of a relevant strategic orientation for each SBU. The strategic paths which are recommended, according to the type of activity, are generally quite similar from one method to another. To simplify, they can be listed as follows:

- to *gain market share* (through cost, differentiation or both);
- the *defence of market* share (through cost, differentiation, or both);

- maximisation of *assets*;
- maintenance of a *position without investment*;
- *disinvestment*.

These global strategic orientations for each field of activity make up the framework of marketing strategy as shown in Figure 5.14. Any marketing strategy is then the result of this dual orientation. One is the *implementation* of the chosen strategy within a given SBU. The other is checking the coherence between the *designed strategy* and the corresponding *market dynamics*. That is how marketing can contribute to and orientate corporate strategy. We shall try to integrate both perspectives in a model for a marketing strategy that we call Multistrat.

Thus, marketing strategy must involve more information than just that required for the determination of global strategy. This more detailed analysis must clearly involve the following:

- buyer demands and purchasing behaviour
- market dynamism and the reasons behind this
- the characteristics of the sales channels (direct or through an intermediary)
- the competitive rules
- the functioning of the systems of influence (relationship networks).

At this stage it is important to have a clear idea of the strategic logic behind business-to-business marketing before going further. There are three elements to this logic. Marketing strategy in a business-to-business environment means:

1. *Choosing a position in a competitive field.* This implies a first level of reflection on the respective dynamics of the firm's resources and the applications in the market. The issue is to understand both the attractiveness of the application and the firm's corresponding competitive position. That is the only way to discover the possibilities of resource modification leading to the upgrading of the competitive position. This first level of reflection is likely to produce three types of results and objectives, qualitative or quantitative:

    - a definition of the necessary *resources* in a given market (or market segment)
    - a position on the *demand market*: how does the firm want to be viewed by its customers (desired image, see Chapter 9)
    - a position in the *offer market* (market share desired).

2. *Designing formalised choices* for each relevant group of customers (resources, technologies, offers, supplier–customer relationship types, competitive advantages, position within networks and so on).

3. *Creating a marketing system* adapted to the implementation of these choices (human and financial resources, sources of information, communication, organisation, planning).

The entire strategic logic of business-to-business marketing can be found in these three categories of decision. This is very different to the strategic models linked to the 'mix marketing' concept. Therefore, we need a new tool to help in the decision-making process hence the introduction of the Multistrat model. We shall now look at the main elements of this model (Dorey and Valla, 1984). The heart of this model is a method of *business-to-business market segmentation*.

Market Segmentation: Some Introductory Elements

Segmentation in marketing is an old and well-known technique. As early as 1956, W.R. Smith put forward the following definition which is still appropriate today: '*segmentation is based on the observation of evolution in demand and represents a more precise and rational adaptation of the product and the marketing effort made to meet customer or user demands.*' Since then, increasingly sophisticated techniques have been proposed and are now frequently used in consumer marketing. However, the transferral of these segmentation practices to the business-to-business environment is hampered by the particularities of marketing situations that imply interorganisational trade exchanges. We do not propose to offer a synthesis of the works carried out on the subject, but rather to put forward our own thoughts on the subject. Then we shall explain the segmentation method used in the Multistrat model, developed to help companies solve problems with the segmentation of business-to-business markets.

In more recent works, the usual argument to justify the importance given to marketing is the recognition of the heterogeneity of markets. Indeed, if customer demands within a given *accessible market* (see Chapter 2) differ, it is unlikely that a single offer can satisfy them all at the same time. Thus, the supplier may wonder how to recognise the diversity of customer expectations and to organise information in such a way as to be able to provide satisfactory answers. Segmentation techniques make up the main response of marketing to this question.

It must be mentioned that the company's capacity to respond to market heterogeneity is limited. It depends on the resources that are available and can be mobilised (mainly technical competences), on the potential profitability of adapting to customers' demand, and also on the issues linked to company objectives and the competitive position in the business in question. Segmentation techniques are very useful for management to design the best possible standardisation/adaptation compromise of its offer for each market segment, given its own objectives and constraints.

The Relevance of Segmentation

From the above, it might be thought that market heterogeneity is a characteristic of all industrial markets, and that it simply means knowing whether a company wants to (or can) adapt to it. We know that this is not the case. To think seriously about the use of the application of a sophisticated segmentation process for a given activity, we should remember the following two points: the *dynamism* of markets and also their *nature*.

Indeed, the degree of market heterogeneity varies over time. A growth in heterogeneity is the result of a convergence of the effects of the diversification of customer demand and supplier efforts to meet them in different ways. On the other hand, a reduction in heterogeneity (or homogenisation) is the result of limited customer requirements linked in general to the learning process or economic pressure, and also to supplier strategy (the result of offers becoming commonplace due to imitation – see Chapter 7 – and efforts of cost-competitiveness that lead to the standardisation of products). Market heterogeneity in a specific market can be considered within the framework of current evolution dynamics. Generally speaking, market heterogeneity tends to diminish with the evolution of the activities life-cycle (the progressive normalisation of products follows the same path). This distinction exists in current vocabulary – for example, there are 'stable' and 'unstable' or 'turbulent' and 'calm' markets. In fact, it would be right to say that depending on a particular situation, the relevant usefulness of advanced forms of market segmentation varies. And in addition, it becomes necessary to reconsider the segmentation approaches in use within the company about every three years.

Moreover, in business-to-business markets, two particular situations require approaches that are specific to market segmentation: the case of *emerging technologies* for which we cannot honestly say there is a market, and *major projects*. These are particularities that are linked to the nature of the markets in question.

The Notion of Segments and of 'Good' Segmentation

Technically speaking, segmentation means grouping together similar customers. The results of segmentation performed by a given company depend on the quality of the information available and on the company's own characteristics (in particular, technological and organisational abilities), and the type of decisions it wishes to make. Thus, market segmentation can vary according to how the company sees the market, and whether it is for the present or a future offer. Indeed, we find that two competitors in the same market can produce two different market segmentations. Above all, segmentation helps to recognise closely related (similar) customer groups. Statistically speaking, the aim is to minimise intragroup variance (to create sufficiently 'homogeneous' groups) and to maximise intergroup variance (to create groups which are different from each other). This means it is also an intellectual process (and/or statistical, if statistical data analysis techniques are used), which aims to give the company a simplified representation of its market, by incorporating the aspects of customer behaviour and the market dynamics that can affect it. Such a representation is always a simplification. This is necessary to make the market understandable and the segmentation usable. Therefore, the process must lead to a well thought-out and controlled summary of the initial information.

Thus, the segment is by convention a group of 'customer units', although a market – a population – can be divided into an almost infinite number of segments. Each segment must have an operational 'reality' for the company, meaning that the company can define a suitable, autonomous and coherent marketing strategy for each group. The process depends on the market in question. The complexity of the segmentation is proportional to market volume, value and heterogeneity which command the number of variables taken into consideration by the process. In other words, the quality depends on the work performed and how this complexity was managed and 'summarised'.

Thus, we can talk of '*good segmentation*' as having led to the creation of *homogenous segments*, all *different between themselves*, with a *specific and identified competition*, large enough to be *profitable* and *operational*. It thus justifies a differentiation in the offers, and/or in access to the market, and/or in the marketing process. It therefore affects both the supply strategy and customer approach, making it the key to the marketing process.

The Problem of Segmentation in the Business-to-Business World

Between the CEO of a major group and a sales engineer from one of this group's divisions, the difference in perspective towards the market is surprisingly important, and yet defined by the same word. To take decisions, the former uses general aggregates (SBU) or global information, while the latter uses only a few dozen customers or even sub-sets of companies (purchasing centres) in the case of key customers, and far more specific and precise information. Between these two extremities, global coherency and compatibility can be obtained only if a series of intermediate aggregates are established to make a link between the two. The whole of a company's segmentation process can do this by linking SBU, market segments and customers.

Segmentation and Offer

We can formulate an approach to link the marketing segmentation inside a SBU with a strategy type established in accordance with its relative position in the portfolio of activities (the result of the global strategy diagnosis). In this framework, and according to the degree of heterogeneity highlighted by the analysis, three ways of designing the offer exist:

■ (1) Either the SBU is a homogeneous group in the marketing sense of the term (one market), and therefore requiring *one identical offer* for all customers.

This is rare. It can be found in the field of simple and everyday products (or 'commodities'). In this example, partial superiority can be obtained only through pressure on costs (output, experience) and/or distribution and logistical excellence.

■ (2) Or the SBU is made of a heterogeneous group of markets, and therefore demand varies. When confronted by this situation in its analysis, the company can react in two different ways:

Average Offer

It is possible to consider that the differences are not too large and do justify the use of an *average offer*. In this case, the offer must meet all the veto customer requirements (see Chapter 3), which presupposes that such requirements are in themselves homogeneous. For other customer requirements (important and secondary criteria), this is possible only if buyers' purchasing behaviour shows that they will compensate poor performance on some requirements with advantages on others. It is easy to understand that the competitive situation does or does not allow for the adoption of this type of strategy according to the choices of the competitors. It all depends on the importance given to the 'price' (or purchasing cost) criteria by the customers when they compare possible suppliers. If the price criteria are secondary to technical criteria, it will be difficult to maintain such a strategy for a long time without losing market share, especially when other competitors adopt different strategies based on greater segmentation with more adaptations. This kind of approach to the market has one advantage and two disadvantages. The decision to respond through an average offer to slightly different customer demands has the advantage of giving the supplier greater productivity through volume. On the other hand, a company that decides to market an average offer risks not satisfying those customers who have specific requirements, thereby losing high added-value market share to the competition. Also, the same company risks oversatisfying customers whose demands are lower than others', thereby increasing costs unnecessarily. This can therefore have an effect on the profitability of a company that markets an overdimensioned offer but cannot get all its customers to pay for it, as they do not need this superior performance. However, in several major industrial sectors (steel, aluminium, glass, etc.) the characteristics of production tools (low flexibility, etc.) mean that companies have to adopt this policy to have enough volume available to make it worthwhile. In this instance, production advantages can compensate the potential loss of profitability owing to the relative overperformance of the offer.

We have seen in the above section that decisions concerning the relevant segmentation methods for a SBU, and decisions concerning offer strategy, are closely linked. Understanding the links of interdependence between the different aspects of marketing strategy in the business-to-business world is vital for the marketing efficiency of a company.

To illustrate this, Figure 6.1 highlights the questions raised by the choice of an average offer strategy for a specific SBU – or, more globally, at any level of

Figure 6.1 Market heterogeneity and average offer

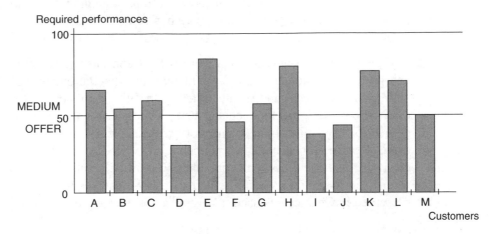

segmentation. The horizontal axis lists the customers belonging to the SBU. The vertical axis gives the levels of expected performance. The horizontal line showing the medium or average offer helps to indicate differences in relation to customer demands. Theoretically, the supplier who adopts this type of strategy should fix the performances of his offer at the level that minimises such differences. We can clearly see that the optimum minimisation of the differences between offer and demands can be reached only by segmenting the customer portfolio into several sub-sets.

Specific Offer

One may consider that the differences are too great for a single offer to be efficient, and that a customer group (or each customer in cases of a concentrated market, see Chapter 2) justifies a specific offer. There are two different possible answers:

■ The first one is the design of a modular offer, built in such a manner that it can allow the presentation of an *adapted offer* to each customer. The implementation of this strategy raises the question of how far the company should go concerning adaptation. Any supplier can be asked by each customer for specific developments, whose costs are evident, even if profitability is often far from clear and closely guarded. This logic can prove to be dangerous. It corresponds to a 'sales' approach that consists in answering positively to all customer demands. Is it not a 'sound marketing approach' that gives satisfaction to a customer? Except that it may turn out just the opposite of this very satisfaction, if the supplier does not master all the consequences of this choice. There is many a difficulty linked to an enlargement of the offer: shorter production runs, therefore management of manufacturing planning, resulting in increases or decreases in customer orders, maintenance of a security stock, keeping a constant and homogeneous level of quality. Such a solution is adapted for major customers presenting large volumes. Another way has to be considered for other types of customers.

■ The alternative is suggested in Figure 6.1. It consists of the 'construction' of sub-groups of customers (market segments) whose requirements are sufficiently similar to be served with the same offer, with only minor adaptations. A specific offer is to be designed for each segment. A supplier is then entitled to make the choice to serve only some segments (target segments) and to leave the others aside. Reasons for abandoning segments are varied: difficulty in designing an offer, the cost of access, unfavourable competitive position, volume too small, insufficient potential profitability and so on. We can see that the strategic logic presented in Chapter 5 is used here at a much finer scale.

We can conclude this section with the assumption that segmentation produces ambivalent results. A lack of segmentation leads to reduced efficiency towards customers. Too complex an approach may increase costs to a level with which the firm cannot cope in the long run. For segmenting a market involves costs, as well as maintaining a position on a given application. And these costs are necessary. A supplier must ensure a level of investment necessary to maintain its competences and productivity on each 'part' of the market. If it does not do so in a regular way, its position will deteriorate in terms of both volume (market share) and profitability.

Three Interwoven Levels of Segmentation: Business Unit, Market Segment, Customer

We began by presenting the problem of segmentation for an SBU and by indicating the different ways of considering the differences in characteristics and requirements within a given market (single offer, adapted offer, average offer). At each of the three levels of segmentation possible (SBU, market segmentation and customer), the reasoning to be used is the same and involves making the same compromises, based on more or less precise information and on the company capacity to include it in its decision making process. It is important to mention at this point that segmentation in the business-to-business world does not simply involve the mechanical application of a technique. At all stages of its elaboration, the segmentation of business-to-business markets involves both choices and understanding the company's strategic intentions.

Generally speaking, as mentioned in Chapter 2, business-to-business markets have a natural heterogeneity, which is linked to the numerous explanatory factors of an individual buyer's purchasing behaviour (Chapter 3). The probability that two customers have exactly the same expectations and behaviour is therefore very low.

This intrinsic complexity can be expressed by the numerous possibilities of business-to-business market segmentation, owing to the number of possible segmentation criteria. Thus, to be efficient and operational, segmentation should be based on a clear choice of relevant dimensions of heterogeneity (the segmentation criteria chosen) and the order in which they will be considered (criteria hierarchy). Through these choices, the supplier allows a certain degree of heterogeneity to influence its decision, and then designs the offer and the accompanying commercial approach. Thus, the resulting segmentation is not a perfect representation of the real market heterogeneity, which would suit all suppliers operating on these markets. It is the result of an appreciation of 'reality' made by one supplier who must assess the level of differentiation judged appropriate, in accordance with each strategic situation (the attraction of the activity, the advantages of the company, the desired strategic objectives, the competitive situation). Thus, the supplier builds up its own relevant representation of the markets it is examining. This representation will then help formulate its marketing decisions.

These questions raise the classical standardisation/adaptation dilemma and the way to best combine the two elements. The main difficulty in the business-to-business world is to find a balance between the productivity demands, which promote standardisation (single or average offer) and a market 'reality' which highlights different customer requirements and promotes adaptation (adapted offer). The 'operationalised' process can be found in the segmentation methods and again in Chapter 7 dealing with the elaboration and the driving of the offer.

To conduct the complex operation of segmentation efficiently, it is first necessary to clarify the relationship between the three levels of segmentation mentioned above – i.e., the areas of activity, the markets and the customers. Indeed, the quality of these relationships contributes largely to better integration of the global strategic perspective (the company's areas of activity), the perspectives that are linked to the formulation of the basic offer (the company's markets), and the perspectives that are linked to the process of commercial action (the customers). Table 6.1 presents the three levels of analysis to consider, their bases, the adopted perspectives in the analysis and the expected results of the segmentation.

Table 6.1 proposes a progressive aggregation approach ('*bottom-up*') and refining approach ('*top-down*') of the information in an integrated system. As indicated, it is up to the company itself to choose the level of refinement that it wishes to give to its marketing segmentation in accordance with its strategic objectives. The particular characteristics of the market can determine the required level of refinement, in particular in concentrated markets with a limited number of customers. However, this is not very common.

In two levels of marketing segmentation in Table 6.1 (markets and customers), the notion of homogeneity needs to be clarified. Strategically speaking, segmentation aims to create groups that have the same *key success factors*, which allows the supplier to elaborate a clear and coherent strategy. The homogeneity of a group can be determined by the following:

Table 6.1   The three levels of analysis of segmentation in the business-to-business world

Scope	Perspectives	Expected results
The BUSINESSES of the firm	Medium- and long-term business trends	Homogeneous SBUs
The MARKETS of the firm	Medium- and long-term market trends	Homogeneous market segments
The CUSTOMERS of the firm	Characteristics and trends of the buying behaviour of customers	Homogeneous customer groups

- the individual members of a group have the same *needs* and *requirements* and/or

- the group presents a *dynamism* based on a criteria which can be applied to all individual members (growth, innovation, etc.) and/or

- the *environment* (particularly the systems of influence) is the same for all members of the group and/or

- the *purchasing behaviour* of the individuals is the same (particularly the choice criteria used to evaluate suppliers, purchasing strategy and processes) and/or

- the same *competitive process* operates for each member of the group.

Depending on the level of segmentation, a certain view of homogeneity can be adopted in accordance with the company's objectives. Basically, the homogeneity of a segment is linked to the characteristics that lead to a certain type of marketing action (for example, a certain type of offer strategy, investments in relationship of a particular kind, etc.). The homogeneity criteria for a segment therefore must not be confused with the segmentation criteria themselves, see Table 6.2 (p. 182). This final remark brings us to the final element of clarification by distinguishing the different types of segmentation that can be utilised, and their respective usefulness.

Descriptive, Explanatory and Prescriptive Segmentation

We are sometimes asked to give an expert opinion on a company's segmentation process. Our reaction is basically the following: 'Before answering the question, can you tell us why you segmented the market in this way?' In fact, until now, we have considered segmentation as having one goal: to help the marketing function of the company. This now needs to be developed.

Among the numerous options for a company to justify market segmentation, there are three principal ones:

- to *analyse* and *describe* the markets linked to the company's businesses to discover their main characteristics

- to *understand* and *explain* the behaviour of different members, either individually or as a group, to be able to plan in accordance with future evolutions

- to *choose*, within a market, one or more *sub-groups* whose demands correspond to the company's expertise and to which the company will prioritise resource allocation.

All of these aspects contribute to the main objective outlined above. Each of these aspects represents an unavoidable step in the segmentation process. In fact, by outlining the above aspects, we have established the steps of the segmentation process that can be defined as a succession of three forms of distinct and useful segmentation (Dorey and Valla, 1984).

- *Descriptive segmentation* aims at describing company activity and creating sub-groups with identical descriptive characteristics. The most common form of descriptive segmentation is the segmentation by industrial sectors (e.g. SIC codes). The advantage of this is easy quantification through the use of the statistics that are available (from Eurostat, for example).

- *Explanatory segmentation* helps to understand the dynamism of markets and the behaviour of the market players by identifying and analysing their causes. It helps define sub-groups from these causes by transforming them into segmentation criteria. Unlike descriptive segmentation, explanatory segmentation favours a certain level of forecasting market evolution and actor behaviour. For example, we can explain that a group of customers putting pressure on suppliers for more innovation is linked to the nature of their own customers and the competitive issues on their own markets. The company could thus use the 'nature of downstream markets' criteria, whose groupings could be expressed by sectors of industrial activity, as a criterion of segmentation.

- *Prescriptive segmentation* aims at selecting, from the sub-groups formed by the previous forms of segmentation, those that merit the allocation of the most resources, either in terms of volume or quality. Prescriptive segmentation therefore sheds light on the differences in value for the company between the different market segments that have been identified. Thus, prescriptive segmentation generally comes from the strategic orientation chosen by the company for the activity in question. For example, if the strategic path chosen for a particular SBU is the growth of market share, prescriptive segmentation will identify those market segments that present the highest annual growth rate.

The questions raised in this chapter concerning the segmentation of business-to-business markets represent the basis of the Multistrat model. In the next section, we will look at Multistrat Segmentation, which is fundamental to the model, as the segmentation process corresponds to the foundations of any decision-making procedure related to marketing strategy.

Multistrat Segmentation: A System of Business-to-Business Market Segmentation

The Multistrat model takes its name from the principle of breaking down into stages the marketing strategy for a business-to-business company. This involves the need to formulate the marketing orientation on two levels of relevant analysis: that of the *markets* (the intermediary level of aggregation) and that of the *individual customer* (the most precise level of the analysis). These two levels of strategic marketing decision making must also be linked to the global level of company strategy per area of activity. This integration of three levels of strategy relative to the market position of the company is designed to produce greater coherence than when the three are treated independently.

Our observations outlined the need for such an approach as a substitute for existing practices, which generally reflect an absence of integration concerning the three perspectives identified above. The Strategy (with a capital 'S') is reserved for major decision makers within the company, marketing strategy being conceived of as a simple functional implementation of company strategy and the absence of customer strategy. The Multistrat model was thus created on the basis of new know-how acquired through our research into business-to-business market dynamics and the critical analysis of existing practises.

Definition of Multistrat Segmentation

The definition of marketing segmentation used in the Multistrat model is the following. Marketing segmentation is the process which relates market heterogeneity and the present or potential resources of the firm with the objective being to divide the accessible market into homogeneous categories (market segments). This identification of homogeneous categories will allow the firm to define the intensity and modalities of its engagement towards each category:

- SBUs
- Market segments for which a particular offer can be designed
- Choice of customers and of the types of relationships and access.

In Chapter 2 we gave a definition of an 'accessible market'. The notion of offer in the Multistrat model is better adapted to the business-to-business world than to the typical product/price combination found in the 'marketing mix' model. The model includes a tangible form to which a large set of services is associated (Chapter 7). The methods of access to markets refer to the organisation of the sales/service function, to the nature of direct relationships that have been developed with each end-customer, or to the choice of suitable distribution channel, and also to the position of the company in the systems of influence (networks) of the given markets.

Figure 6.2 Multistrat: a guide for marketing strategy

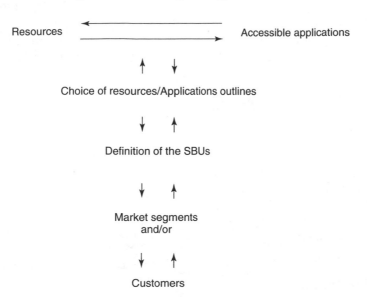

The approach that we suggest with the Multistrat model (Figure 6.2) has been built on the preceding facts, reflections and propositions. It aims to facilitate two essential movements. The first is the establishment and maintenance over time of coherence between the choices of target customers, operational actions and the firm's resources. Secondly, it is important that strategic evaluation integrates a vision of the customers and markets dynamics in such a way that makes possible the identification and use of strategic opportunities. Mory–Ancel (Example 5) illustrates these two movements (Figure 6.3). The opportunity discovered and built with its customer Ancel led to the discovery and the construction of a new 'application' that ended in the requirement of a new SBU. Simultaneously the necessary resources were gathered and organised.

The Segmentation Process in Practice

Segmentation is an operation of classification. It aims to provide management with a representation of the markets that is designed as help to make choices. This representation is the result of a process founded on a simplification of the initial data. The result depends on the variety and quality of available data. This may mean that market research has to be undertaken before final decisions are taken. Market research does not 'naturally' produce any segmentation, which requires a particular approach. But it often leads us to give up a very simple way of segmentation, the sector-based one, that proves to be more and more ineffective (Figure 6.3) in Example 6.

Figure 6.3   From a sector-based segmentation (descriptive) to an explanatory segmentation

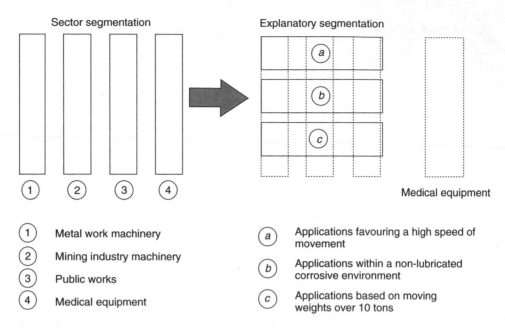

The practical setting up of a detailed segmentation process operates around the three phases as shown above:

■ Phase 1: analyse and describe
■ Phase 2: understand and explain
■ Phase 3: make choices.

For reasons of efficiency, phase 1 involves the simultaneous identification of all possible segmentation criteria (all variables). Some such criteria will turn out to be relevant for explanatory or prescriptive segmentation, while others will not, and will remain simple descriptive criteria of the markets and customers. Some of the latter could be eliminated while others help in the elaboration of a permanent bank of marketing information and in the creation of links between the company's database and the official statistics available.

Phase 1: Analyse and Describe

■ Define the *objectives* of the segmentation.
   What do we want to know? What are the decisions to be made? Segmentation is a representation of a market as defined by a supplier. Therefore, it depends on its objectives. A new offer from a supplier will not arouse the same level of

Example 6   The Limits of Sector-Based Segmentation

Numerous firms think that relevant segmentation can be based on the customers' sectors of activity (for example, the building industry, public works, mining, pharmacy, etc.). This is true as long as a sector presents a homogeneous group as far as the supplier's offer is concerned. But it often happens that customers belonging to different sectors present the same requirements to a supplier. The danger then is to stick to the sector-based segmentation and to consider that these emerging demands in each sector are too small to be considered. In fact, they can appear as real opportunities only if they are linked together through what we may call 'trans-sector segmentation'. But then the direction of the segmentation is turned upside down, which is not easy to realise in a firm.

This remark illustrates the transition we shall explore further on. It means moving from a *descriptive* segmentation (for example, sector-based) to an *explanatory* one, founded on criteria 'explaining' customers' behaviour and requirements. Figure 6.3 presents the segmentation realised by a roll bearing manufacturer. Roll bearings are mechanical parts used to transform a rotation movement into a translation one. The initial sector-based segmentation showed different sectors: machines for metal working, machines for mining, machines for public works, machines for medical use. A market survey showed that inside each sector specific demands were emerging: applications based on the speed of the movement, those based on over 10 tons weight to be carried, those based on working within a corrosive non-lubricated environment. They made up three segments based on the type of use (or application). For many customers the technical conditions of the application were more important than their belonging to the same industrial sector or not. This led to a different segmentation approach where the conditions of the *application* constitute a sound basis for marketing decision making. Conversely, the medical sector still presented a high degree of homogeneity and could be counted as a fourth segment, the sector and its characteristics still being the basis of the marketing decisions.

Note: Based on real data, company name confidential.

interest from the customers. This is likely to modify any segmentation based on a former offer. Equally, segmentation can lead to thinking about the outline of a new offer as it helps to find the emerging trends and dynamics which will not be satisfied by the existing product and service offering.

■ Determine the *limits* of the 'offer–customers–competitors' combination to be segmented.

As shown in Chapter 5 and the beginning of this chapter, marketing segmentation takes place within each SBU in accordance with its characteristics and the implemented strategy type. However, most companies know something about their markets and could therefore begin with smaller areas than the SBU itself. In reality, most companies begin the segmentation with pre-identified sub-sets. This in itself can include some problems that are to be identified.

For example, a company producing cutting and tempering oils decided to carry out two separate segmentation studies for each activity. One single study would have revealed the two activities to be completely different. And a very simple reflection among the people in charge showed immediately and at a very low cost that it was necessary to design two separate studies. Therefore, any company can 'save' stages in the segmentation process through internal discussion before any fieldwork.

On the other hand, analysing market sub-sets with similar characteristics in the same segmentation study, but that are in fact independent from one another, can lead to the identification of segments that are too general or too heterogeneous to allow for decisions to be made. This is usually the case when *a priori* groups are formed according to company size. If it is true that large multinational companies have some similar character traits, (for example, administrative purchasing policies), they are often so different that it is dangerous to put them together for segmentation analyses.

Finally, the inclusion of non-users of the service or product in the sample used for study must be considered. If care is not taken, including their opinions and judgements can make the results unnecessarily complex, or even impossible to understand. Generally speaking, it is important to give limits to the field of marketing segmentation, just as it is important to define objectives before beginning.

■ Identify the *criteria* that help to describe the markets and customers of the company.

This essential phase is often based on intuition and empiricism. A number of individuals within the company receive and interpret information and so create their own view of the market structure. They then base their actions on this view. Therefore it is important to compare these different market representations and to identify the criteria being used in order to qualify the different actors' behaviour and the global market dynamics. Thus, any segmentation begins with the identification of such criteria from experience and knowledge from inside the company.

The identification of these criteria must be exhaustive and detailed. If there are doubts about this internally, it can be completed with a qualitative study

Table 6.2 Possible segmentation criteria

- Type of activity (sector)
- Nature of customers
- Type of market (public, private)
- Function ensured by the supplier's offering
- Type of the customers' downstream markets
- Degree of complexity of the customers' problem
- Size or buying potential of the customers
- Nature of the customers' manufacturing process
- Composition of the customers/buying centres
- Importance of the price as a buying criterion
- Importance granted to the nature and intensity of the proposed services
- Position of the customers on their markets
- Profitability expected from an order or from the customer
- The customer as a reference
- Disposition to innovate

(Chapter 4). The aim is to be sure of customers and market forces. Table 6.2 gives some relevant segmentation criteria that we have seen from our experience of applying this technique.

Phase 2: Understand and Explain

- Selecting the *determining criteria*.

    Among the criteria above, some are more explanatory than others of the differences in requirements and purchasing behaviour, or of the variations in market dynamics. Our aim here is to reduce this mass of information to produce an explanatory diagram that can help with managerial decision making. In this phase it is often impossible to achieve the desired objective without using classical techniques of data analysis. These techniques, on the basis of quantitative analysis, help to measure the relative weight of each criterion used in the descriptive phase. The application of these techniques means we can list by order of importance the criteria upon which the segmentation is based.

- *Building the segments*

    The objective here is to group together customers who are close in relation to the discriminating criteria, and yet who differ from other customers on the same criteria. The question then is how to do it. A first way is to utilise the statistical methods of data analysis. These methods (Belson method of segmentation, factor analysis, correspondence analysis, cluster analysis and so on) provide the researcher with a statistically processed and controlled hierarchy of the criteria and a classification of the players according to this hierarchy (see Hipkin and Naudé, 1999, for an example). They usually require use of expert consultants who use the internal data of the company or the results of a formalised market research. In business-to-business environments they are utilised when large numbers of customers are concerned, which is normal, as these techniques were developed for consumer marketing (see the References and Further Reading for this chapter).

    However, many cases are characterised by a limited number of customers or players. This facilitates the use of a simple approach founded on an 'intelligent' classification of the criteria. The method used is the '*segmentation tree*' which classifies criteria through a successive dichotomy, in a similar way to the Belson method. The segmentation tree method is a simple adaptation of Belson's idea that does not call for the use of statistical techniques and data analysis. Intelligent people using their brains and a sound understanding of the concept of segmentation can employ it. Figure 6.4 in Example 7 provides the reader with an example of the use of the segmentation tree method.

The segmentation tree method allows the *identification and hierarchical classification* of the criteria that 'explain' the fact that two customers will not present the same behaviour (requirements, interest, etc.) towards a supplier's proposal. Crite-

Figure 6.4   A segmentation tree

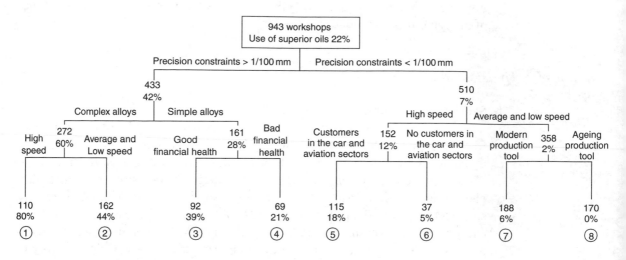

Example 7   Segmentation of the Market of Industrial Oils for Metalworking

A survey concerned the utilisation of 'cutting oils' in mechanics workshops. They commonly utilise several types of oils that for the survey's sake were grouped into two categories: 'superior oils' and 'standard oils'. In the 943 workshops surveyed the average consumption of superior oils was 22 per cent of the total consumption.

The objective of segmentation was to define the characteristics of the workshops whose consumption was over or under average. The variable to be explained was: 'the percentage of superior oil consumption'.

The highest consumer group (1) works at high-speed complex alloys with precision constraints superior to 1/100 mm and uses superior oils for 80 per cent of total consumption. The non-user of superior oils group (8) has ageing production tools, works at low or average speed and with precision constraints under 1/100 mm.

The method shows the explanatory variables at each level of segmentation. The first one is the precision constraint superior to 1/100 mm. It allows determining two groups whose consumption is significantly different: 42 per cent for the left-hand side group and 7 per cent for the right-hand side one.

For the left-hand side group, the second explanatory variable is the nature of the alloys employed (complex or simple). For the right-hand side group, the second variable is a different one: the working speed (high speed as opposed to average or low). And so on.

Note: Based on real data, company name confidential.

ria are classified along a simple criterion (first, second, third, etc.) by order of importance. A first level of segmentation can be defined with the first criterion. If this segmentation is not satisfying, the second criterion can be put forward to divide in a finer way the segments of the first level. And so on. This process results in market segments inside which it is possible to identify 'customer–application' ensembles. Practically, only a limited number of segments can be useful. This limits the number of criteria to be used. Therefore, what is important is not the refined character of the segmentation but its usefulness for marketing decisions. For those more familiar with multivariate statistics, the same is achieved via AID or CHAID analyses.

For example, a manufacturer of electric engines segmented the market in the following way: *A* (first-level) operations requiring the driving of a complex trajectory against simple movement (2 resulting segments); *B* (second-level) requirement for high dynamics against standard dynamics (sub-division of the first 2 segments into 4 segments); *C* (third-level) working in a constraining or non-constraining environment (resulting in 8 segments). This result of 8 segments proved to be satisfying for the firm for targeting customer–application groups (segments) and defining the corresponding offers.

It is not always necessary to make use of the same criterion at each level. As Figure 6.4 shows, different criteria may be used at the same level for the segments formed at a preceding level.

■ To acquire a *better understanding of each segment*

We must remember that the resulting segmentation has its origins in a simplification of the information that was gathered during phase 1. This simplification or reduction of the information helped to build a clear 'map' of the market. Based on a simplification of the initial data, this 'map' does not generally supply us with a very precise description of each segment. Thus, we must return to this initial information for a better understanding of the segments.

■ *Quantifying* each segment

The quantification of the segments described above raises many problems. Indeed, identifying the customers in the official statistics is usually done by a system of coding based on industrial sectors. When there are few customers (the car industry, for example), or the final segmentation coincides with a freely available classification, it is not difficult to quantify the segment. The problem deepens when the two classifications do not coincide. Either the result is a segmentation grouping players coming from several industrial sectors, or players within an industrial sector are grouped in several segments that do not correspond to generally available data. One first solution could be to make an approximate assimilation between a segment and a given classification. Another, and this is our choice, would be to recognise that the resulting segmentation is the real basis of marketing strategy and that many decisions and actions will be based on it. Therefore, one must consider that segmentation is the most important factor of marketing strategy and that efforts have to be deployed in order to base quantification on the segmentation and not the other way round. This means giving the company its own information system, in other words, based on a structure that is *adapted to identify segments* (Chapter 4).

It must be remembered that it is essential to be able to quantify the market segments in order to check their operational characteristics, to categorise possible actions according to their potential profitability and finally to define company strategy in terms of market share.

Phase 3: Make Choices

The market description supplied by the completed segmentation will enable the company to determine the parts of the market upon which it wishes to concentrate: the target segments and customers. Earlier on in this chapter we called this the *prescriptive segmentation* phase. It involves taking the company towards market segments where it can best use its resources and skills, in accordance with customer demands and the competition, and also the type of the particular SBU.

In Example 7, the engine manufacturer, their manufacturing capacities and competitive position dictate that they will potentially overlap best with the high-value segments, in spite of the smaller volumes. They will then target segments defined as complex trajectory + high dynamics + constraining environment (4 target segments out of a possible 8).

Determining *target customers* involves the same procedure. However, it would be better not to select customers on the basis of just two variables: target customers and the others. This is too direct and brutal. Classifying the customers according to several preferred classes is a better method. This will be analysed in Chapter 8 when treating the subject of the portfolio of customers.

Segmentation and Demand Concentration

Typically, the whole or only a part of this segmentation system is usually utilised by a firm. All the suggested levels of segmentation are not necessarily relevant in all environments. A segment, according to the degree of demand concentration and the type of segmentation utilised, can consist of one customer only, or of several major identified customers or of differentiated groups of customers (Figure 6.5). It is useful to consider that in a highly concentrated market (the car manufacturers' industry, for example) *one customer is one segment in itself.*

Figure 6.5   Segmentation and demand concentration

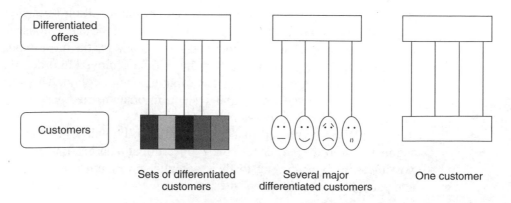

Sets of differentiated customers	Several major differentiated customers	One customer

We raised this issue in Chapter 2 (Figure 2.4) and more precisely in Chapter 4 (Table 4.11). It plays a major role in recognising the diversity inherent in business-to-business environments and the relevant types of marketing strategy. A very large customer is both an entity of its own and a bunch of differentiated units. As far as segmentation is concerned, this ambiguity cannot be escaped, but there are two ways to handle it.

The first one is to consider that, from the point of view of segmentation, a customer is a *group of distinct customer entities*. While a global customer is often recognised from a commercial point of view (Chapter 8 on key account management), this is not usually considered as an input to the segmentation process. Only distinct customer entities are considered. However, a very large customer can simultaneously belong to several market segments. And all the very large customers should be treated the same way. A second way is to treat the very large customers as part of a double approach: the customer as a commercial entity, and the various possible applications on which a supplier can position itself, as we shall see in Figure 6.7 (p. 195).

To conclude this development of the segmentation process, let us underline once again that the only objective of segmentation is to provide management with a comprehensive and efficient understanding of their markets, and a solid base from which they can devise 'good' marketing decisions. It defines the most attractive or the most open (accessible) segments and those that should be given priority. It allows managers to determine the conditions that the company must fulfil to succeed in each segment. The methods of strategic analysis we have mentioned in Chapter 5 are too broad to help define the daily commercial action of the company. This must be more precise to ensure that such action corresponds to the company strategy. This is the reason behind the creation of the Multistrat method, which aims to give greater coherence to the methods of global strategy, introducing intermediary levels of decision to help link the three dimensions of strategic thought of the marketing function: *technology*, *markets* and *customers*. The final part of this chapter will deal with this Multistrat model – its global logic and the relationships between its different dimensions. Further chapters will then look at each dimension in greater detail.

Marketing Strategy: The Multistrat Model

An Original Strategic Approach

The aim of this model is to present a strategic process adapted to business-to-business marketing environments that takes into consideration all the aspects previously described. Two major elements can be put forward for its justification. First is the fact that the resources available (implemented know-how and techniques, design of the manufacturing plant, ability to provide services) are fundamental to the business-to-business marketing approach. So there is a two-way process between understanding the (external) markets and the design of the (internal) investments that produce the necessary resources. But the availability of resources is prior to any implementation of marketing actions. Second is the recognition that business-to-business customers (corporate bodies made up of individuals) constitute a basis for strategic thinking as well as the object of commercial action. That recognition may also provide dynamics for suppliers' strategy, as Mory–Ancel (Example 5) shows. Thus, it is necessary to give it the place it deserves in the supplier strategic decision strategy.

It must be remembered that our strategic marketing process is based on a specific view of marketing (Chapters 1–3) and of a particular understanding of the marketing function within the company (Chapter 13). Its role is to manage the interfaces between the company and its markets. It thus involves managing complex internal and external interfaces with other company functions, partners, customers and the players in the systems of influence. This role is both strategic and operational. In collaboration with management, the marketing function is responsible for marketing strategy (global, targeted market segments and customers), for justifying its strategy, for sales volumes, for the market position of the company in the relevant networks for its global performance (systems of influence operating in the markets), and for the return on commercial investment. To fulfil its role, it must convince the different functions within the company to act according to customer demands and to motivate them into taking into consideration the competitive forces influencing the company.

Marketing in the business-to-business world is essential and demanding in as much as it is at the heart of the system for global performance. Indeed, the marketing function has to manage, either alone or in collaboration with other services, the position of the company in the value chain, the offer portfolios (adaptations to products, prices, delivery dates, services, etc.), customer portfolios (the main asset for the company), the competitive position and all marketing means (or investments devoted to commercial action).

But we once again find it difficult to apply the same approach to all business-to-business environments in a non-differentiated manner. In particular, the strategic process presents variations according to the degree of concentration of the buyers. Therefore, we present two forms of the Multistrat model, one for *dispersed* and one for *concentrated* customers. A third form adapted to the major projects situation is described later in Chapter 12.

The Multistrat Model for Dispersed Customers

The Multistrat model is not a mechanical or mathematical model (Figure 6.6). Our aim is to provide managers with a system that rationally and pedagogically integrates the different aspects of our research. It can stimulate thought by both clarifying the different dimensions of strategic decision making throughout the organisation, and also by helping to identify the coherence that is essential for the efficiency of the planning process.

Figure 6.6　　The Multistrat model: dispersed customers

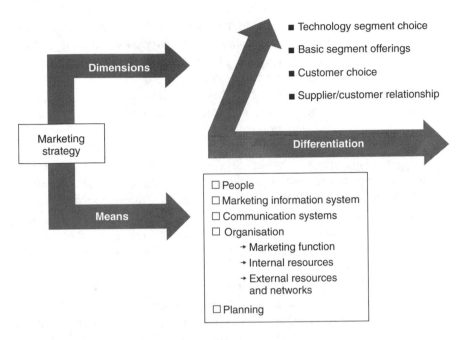

- Technology segment choice
- Basic segment offerings
- Customer choice
- Supplier/customer relationship

The model is composed of two parts: the *dimensions* of marketing strategy of the company (the top part), and the *marketing means* that are required for the preparation and implementation of decisions. The reader may be wondering about the double arrow on the left. We believe that working first on strategic decisions and then implementing the decisions is wrong, even if some books on management strategy think otherwise. With a complex system such as a company, such a process is bound to fail (the '*top-down*' perspective detailed in Chapter 5). The efficiency and coherence of marketing in a company is as much a condition for the production of 'right' decisions as for the efficient implementation of such decisions. Company marketing must be adapted to both these conditions; otherwise not all the material support required will follow. A critical analysis of company practice shows a frequent problem. On the one hand, the marketing system may be adapted to supply the required information for strategic decision making, but the organisation of the system is not adapted for the implementation of the decisions taken (particularly concerning the sales force when there is too large a gap between a functional marketing service and an operational sales management). Or else the system is efficient and adaptable, but the information system does not provide the data required to take rapid and relevant decisions. In the business-to-business world, the desired balance between these two aspects and the efficiency of the marketing system is, in practice, rarely present. Progress can be almost always be made here.

We shall now look at the different elements of the model and their internal logic.

Coherence Between Resources – Applications – Markets – Customers

Referring to Figure 6.2, the highest part of the model presents an articulation between the key marketing decisions and proposes decision logics founded on the links between resources–applications–markets–customers. In Figure 6.6 the model is based on previous choices made in order to define an SBU within which a marketing strategy has to be designed. Thus, a particular setting of resources (manufacturing technologies, technologies incorporated in products or services, diverse know-how and competences) is decided, which defines an *accessible market*. But the definition of the 'accessible market' can vary over time, particularly if customers within the SBU embark on divergent evolutions. Thus, the company has to redefine resources in order to maintain them adjusted to each new definition of the market. In this way the firm maintains its capacity to propose offers that are both differentiated and that create value for the customers. The same question arises when the firm approaches new markets. The following example will help in understanding what we mean concerning this first decision step.

As indicated previously, seeking a resources–market adjustment is not easy, even if it is so important that it determines the characteristics of the firm's position in the market. The performance level or design of the production technology defines the material form (product) of the offer (performance on many dimensions, range, quality, etc.). The level of manufacturing cost indicates the market price. The degree of manufacturing flexibility impacts both the product range and the capacity to answer some customer's requirements. Thus, part of marketing management in business-to-business environments is dedicated to adjust or rearrange the resources–market relationships. This is often done through *segmentation*. In fact markets usually evolve through regular dynamics along a period of some (3–5) years. Exceptions are the new technology markets where technology evolves so quickly that it creates new market structures at each step of evolution (Chapter 10) or the major projects situations where the offer is renegotiated for each deal (Chapter 12). For more traditional markets, this incremental evolution has the consequence that managers often de-couple their thinking on technology from the marketing task, the latter being limited to the offer–market adjustments in the rather short term. And marketing often considers technology as being stable on a 3–5 year horizon, which may be well true for numerous markets. But another consequence is that decisions on technology – managed by the technical function – and customer expectations evolution – managed by the marketing and sales function – may diverge, leading to an uncoupling of the offer–segment, which may be the consequence of a lack of integration between resources and customers' demand. The uncoupling produces difficulty in designing offers correctly positioned in terms of performance, time and price. We can note, however, that such uncoupling can have other origins not linked to technology: customer targeting, competitive action, choice of channels of distribution, quality or extension of the range of services accompanying the product and so on.

Example 8   The Glass Company

To illustrate this, let us consider the example of a glass company (Varlet, 1982). It is simple and yet full of pedagogical richness. Management noticed a difficulty being faced by the company, losses being equivalent to 10 per cent of the turnover. The sales and marketing director's report concluded: 'Our production is non-differentiated, we produce a bit of everything on all the machines. The markets however are very differentiated: perfumes, cosmetics, pharmacy, spice bottles. There is a large range of models for our activity.' This report recognised the gap between the characteristics of manufacturing tools and the market. A four-step method was used. The first three centred around segmentation and the adjustment to chosen target segments. The fourth integrated these choices to define the different offers and restructure the production accordingly.

Step 1: Market Segmentation

Management identified, as an example of significant differences, the pharmacy and the perfume activities. They involve very different issues for the customers. The pharmaceutical industry is characterised by the existence of long production runs, the importance of price and the requirement for a standard level of quality, the recipient playing practically no role in the marketing process of the product. The perfume industry, on the other hand, is characterised by shorter runs, a lower importance given to price, a strong requirement for innovation, an extremely high definition of quality for the containers, as shape and size of the bottles are a major facet of the marketing. Thus, the key success factors are significantly different in the two activities and they constitute in fact two different SBUs, even if they share the same strategic base (Chapter 5).

Step 2: Segment Characterisation

This step focused on qualifying the segments: detailed requirements of the customers, competitors' technology (tools, lines, processes), volume, expected growth, evolution of direct and substitution competition and the company's position. For each segment, managers therefore had quantitative data. They were able to assess for each segment the degree of vulnerability of glass in relation to other materials and the company position.

Step 3: Selection of Market Segments

The objective was to define target market segments and the criteria for development on each of the chosen markets. The choice was made on two criteria: vulnerability of glass against other materials and the attractiveness of the segment (volume, expected growth rate, possible margin). For example, a segment may show a high rate of growth and an important vulnerability. In this case, growth may well go to substitution materials and therefore be unattractive for a glass manufacturer.

Then it was useful to think about the consequences of the company's decisions on its position in a segment. For example, what effects would a strong productivity increase and a consequent price reduction produce on the company's competitive position in this segment? Going through this process allowed the company to select target segments and to define the developmental criteria for each of the chosen ones.

Step 4: Revision of the Manufacturing Organisation in Accordance with the Selected Segments

This step involved defining the offers adapted to the requirements of the selected segments. It was then necessary to modify the characteristics of the manufacturing plant in order to produce these new offers.

The two main elements to be considered were the *price elasticity* and the *ranges of products* to be marketed. In this way, it was possible to define the level of price required in

(continued)

Example 8   The Glass Company

each segment, and consequently to identify the objectives of cost assigned to production. Simultaneously the characteristics of the ranges of products and their main features were defined. As the sales and marketing director said 'If we were to be in sectors where price elasticity is close to zero, we need to have the best production unit with the lowest possible level of cost and to seek for constant improvement in productivity.' To sum up the results of this process of decision making, the design of two very different offers led to the definition of two *specialised production facilities*:

■ The first had a high output suited for long production runs, based on productive, powerful and fully automated machines. It was more specifically adapted to the requirements of the pharmacy segment.

■ The second was more flexible and could handle shorter batches. It could easily and at low cost be altered, but required a higher labour involvement. It was more specifically tailored to meet suit the *perfume industry*.

Note: Based on real data, company name confidential.

In our example we have highlighted the production technology/market–customers relationship. In business-to-business environments we can say that the design of resources very often takes place prior to the definition of new offers. The characteristics of the production technology impact directly upon some characteristics of the core parts of the offer: products (range, technological level, performances), price, flexibility towards customers' orders and availability (delay, punctuality). Two significantly different offers often require the design of two different production facilities. But the offers a company formulates for different market segments are not just the result of technological know-how and competences. Other know-how and competences not directly linked to the technology can be involved. For example, for the sale of capital goods, the supplier has to offer solutions to finance the sale and this condition may be as decisive for the customer as the characteristics of the machine itself. Or, the supplier may possess logistical competences that will better its offer in terms of delay, punctuality and delivery costs. Such know-how and resources can be available within the company or acquired from other more specialised partners. This idea of a 'network firm' is usual for major project issues and it becomes more and more common in other business-to-business environments (capital goods, services, etc.). Companies increasingly build access to other companies to complete their offer. This type of organisation avoids companies having to integrate activities which are only required occasionally and/or maintaining a level of competences in these activities that are not really part of their business definition. Most computer companies use this method, which means that they pay a lot of attention to the management of their partners ('external resources' in IBM definition) and are constantly seeking new partners to adapt their offers to constantly evolving markets.

The Dimensions of Marketing Strategy

A given resources configuration allows the firm access to a market (or a market segment), which very often corresponds to the internal definition of an SBU. It also defines the position that the firm may build on this market and the corresponding strategic path. Thus, this jointly establishes coherence between corporate and marketing strategy, the latter having contributed to the definition of the former. The issue is then to optimise in this market the potential contained in the resources, in which technology plays a major role.

With the accessible market still being a heterogeneous group, the first approach is *segmentation* in order to constitute homogeneous groups in terms of key factor success or customers' requirements. The selection of *target segments* permits a concentration of the firm's means of action. Then decisions must be made concerning the *global offer* that the firm wants to present to each selected segment. This kind of offer definition corresponds to a basic offer plus eventualities of adaptation, along a process that will be examined in Chapter 7. The issue is to define the best possible coherence (and then profitability) between the firm's offers and the resources capabilities, taking into account customers' requirements and the firm's competitive position in each segment.

Preceding chapters, particularly Chapters 2 and 3, showed that business-to-business marketing still faces another step and must integrate an 'individual customer' perspective, in order to meet the issues presented by all or some of them. This last part of the Multistrat model implies that the supplier has to consider the individual characteristics of each customer to adapt the offer and dedicate resources to invest in a sometimes rather complex buyer–supplier relationship. These investments may be important (Table 2.2) and cannot be allocated simultaneously to all customers. Therefore, a method for allocating customer-dedicated resources has to be integrated into the marketing strategy. Thus, *target customers* have to be identified. The firm may then define for each customer a particular offer adaptation and a level of relationship investment. These choices are elaborated within the *customers' portfolio management* approach (Chapter 8).

All this approach is elaborated with the perspective of a competitive environment that orientates towards a systematic research of *differentiation* elements. On what, with what and how a supplier can make itself identified by its customers, acquire customers and build their loyalty against competition. The Multistrat model indicates that differentiation may come from a large variety of sources.

The Means for Marketing Strategy

The elaboration and the implementation of a marketing strategy require specific means and commercial investment (for example, the building of the firm's awareness and image, or the organisation of logistics and of a distribution channel). The necessary marketing means (the bottom part of the model in Figure 6.6) come from different sources. The first and more important is *human resources*. The firm unquestionably needs marketing personnel educated in business-to-business marketing, understanding all its aspects, as well as being aware of its methods and approaches (Chapter 13). Second comes the *marketing information system*. No firm can claim that it follows a marketing approach without a sound definition, acquisition and management of the information necessary for decision making (Chapter 4). The *communication system* allows the firm to build and manage its desired image towards customers and players in the network, as well as to promote its offers and their distinctive features (Chapter 9). Decisions of *organisation* concern the marketing people, the selling groups (including the sales force), the channels management (Chapter 8) and the internal interfaces with other functions of the firm, among which are the technical functions (Chapter 13), as well as the use of external resources and the management of the firm's position within the broader system of influence. And finally, the design and implementation of a *planning and budgeting system* are the ultimate element of a marketing strategy (Chapter 14).

A Multistrat Model for Concentrated Customers

The model presented in Figure 6.6 is relevant for fairly or largely dispersed customer bases. When a supplier potentially deals with a very small number of customers (say from 1 to 20) worldwide, this model has to be rearranged in order to meet the characteristics of the market structure and working (Figure 6.7). In this case the marketing strategy concerns the following dimensions: resources, ability to adapt the offer and capacity to establish a relationship with each customer. The means of marketing described in Figure 6.6 remains relevant, but their content has to be adapted. For example, a customer as a global entity has to be identified as such (letters $C1$, $C2$, etc. in Figure 6.7). But a 'marketing customer' is defined as well by the type of application on which it is working with its supplier. So there are as many marketing customers as 'customer–application' couples. The weight of each customer and also of each application at a given customer may well be a 'market segment' in itself. The issue for a supplier is whether to enter into a relationship with a single customer for a precise application and then to expand the offer into other areas of application, or whether it is better to concentrate on a specific application initially with one customer, and then to broaden the effort by selling the same (or similar) offer to other buyers. The cost of both operations is huge and requires the dedication of specific resources in order to gain a new customer or develop a new application. So a supplier may look at two strategic paths:

- One is derived through the establishment of a relationship with a customer and the development of the corresponding resources to design an offer on a precise application, then a second offer for a second application, and so on. This is the development of the supplier's position with a customer. The word 'spreading' is

Figure 6.7   The Multistrat model: concentrated customers

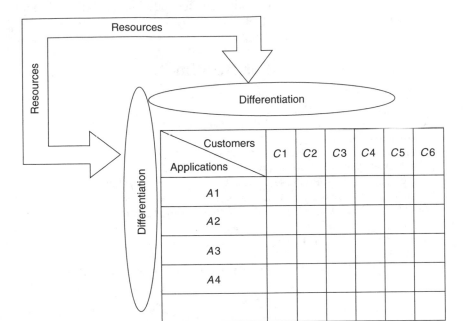

often used to describe this kind of a strategy. It is dominated by the importance of the management of the relationships with the customer (the concept of key account management, Chapter 8). It tends to favour the adaptation of the offer in each case through the combination of *internal and external resources*. It is sometimes seen as a total adaptation strategy. Its basis is the fact that building and maintaining the relationship with a customer is more costly than the development of a new application. Then this leads the supplier towards profitability.

■ In some cases the necessary investment to develop an application is huge and cannot be amortised with one customer only, whatever its potential. In this case, and it constitutes the second strategic path, an application is developed at one customer, then at a second, and so on. This allows the grouping of the applications in market segments or SBUs. It leads more towards *standardisation*, since the supplier draws profitability from developing its solutions with as many customers as possible.

In practice, observation of suppliers shows that they use both paths and combine them in a variety of ways. Whatever the weight they give to one or the other path, the main point is that a business-to-business marketing strategy, even in the case of concentrated customers, is based on the consideration of the market (or market segment) and individual customer dimensions. The application in this case is more market-driven. The previous single-customer approach has more to do with individual customer management. But both have to be taken into account in the design of a marketing strategy, and both can be accommodated within our proposed Multistrat model.

References and Further Reading

Bennion, M. (1987) 'Segmentation and Positioning in a Basic Industry?', *Industrial Marketing Management*, 16, 9–18.

Bonoma, T.V. and Shapiro, B.P. (1983) *Segmenting the Industrial Market*, Lexington, Lexington Books.

Cova, B., Mazet, F. and Salle, R. (1995) 'Approche de marketing stratégique dans la grande industrie', *Revue Française de Gestion*, 106, 22–37.

Dorey, F. and Valla, J.-P. (1984) 'Pour une système de segmentation adaptée à l'entreprise industrielle', 11ème séminaire international de recherche en marketing, IAE d'Aix en Provence.

Evrard, Y., Pras, B. and Roux, E. (1993) *Market. Études et recherches en marketing. Fondements. Méthodes*, Paris, Nathan.

Frank, R.E., Massy, W.F. and Wind, Y. (1972) *Market Segmentation*, Englewood Cliffs, Prentice-Hall.

Hipkin, I. and Naudé, P. (1999) 'An Application of Judgemental Modelling for Strategic Decision Making in International Environments', *Electronic Markets, Special Section: Globalisation and Information Systems*, 9:4, 247–55.

Hooley, G. and Saunders, J. (1993) *Competitive Positioning: The Key to Market Success*, Englewood Cliffs, Prentice-Hall.

Laughlin, J.L. and Taylor, C.R. (1991) 'An Approach to Industrial Market Segmentation', *Industrial Marketing Management*, 20, 127–36.

Millier, P. (1995) *Développer les marchés industriels. Principes de segmentation*, Paris, Dunod.

Smith, W.R. (1956) 'Product Differentiation and Market Segmentation as Alternative Marketing Strategies', *Journal of Marketing*, 21:1, 3–8.

Valla, J.-P. (1984) 'The Marketing Strategies of the Industrial Firm: A New Approach', Congrès EVAF, Paris.

Valla, J.-P. (1990) 'La segmentation en milieu industriel', Document IRE.

Varlet H. (1982) *Les conséquences industrielles d'une segmentation marketing*. Working paper 82–07. Lyon, Ecole Supérieure de Commerce de Lyon.

Discussion Questions

1 What are the different levels of segmentation in business-to-business marketing?
2 Give some rationale for attributing two different forms to the Multistrat model.
3 Why can segmentation in business-to-business marketing lead to a revision of the basic resources of the firm?
4 How does segmentation in business-to-business markets differ according to the degree of concentration of the customer base?

Part II Strategy Implementation

Chapter 1
Competitiveness, Marketing and Business-to-Business Marketing
What is marketing all about
Different marketing environments
B2B marketing

Chapter 2
Business-to-Business Customers and Markets

B2B Generic Offers	Technological Innovation	Pure Services	Major Projects

PART I STRATEGY FOUNDATIONS

Chapter 3	Chapter 4	Chapter 5	Chapter 6
Understanding Business-to-Business Purchasing	Information and Information Systems	Markets and Suppliers' Strategy	Segmentation and Marketing Strategy

PART II STRATEGY IMPLEMENTATION

Chapter 7	Chapter 10	Chapter 11	Chapter 12
Generic Business-to-Business Offer Design and Management	Marketing and Technological Innovation	The Marketing of Services	Major Project Marketing

Chapter 8
Market Access and Customer Management

Chapter 9
Communication and Publicity/ Advertising

PART III STRATEGY DESIGN

Chapter 13	The Role and Organisation of Marketing
Chapter 14	Customer Position, Market Position, Marketing Strategies and Planning
Chapter 15	Issues and Specificities of International Marketing
Annex	The Internet and Marketing: Some Ideas

7 Generic Business-to-Business Offer Design and Management

The design and management of the offer lie at the very heart of business activity. Offer design is the result of the interaction between the skills of the company internally on one hand and those externally available through alliances with other companies, taking into account the characteristics of the marketplace, the customers and the competition. By placing offer design within the realm of marketing, it automatically becomes linked to segmentation. Thus, offer and segmentation are connected in an iterative way, even if we have presented them in two distinct chapters.

We shall not come back to this necessary iteration between segmentation and the dynamics of the firm's resources. In this chapter we start from two assumptions: a firm with a stable resources capability and the choice of the firm to occupy a position within a segmented market, for which it designs the best possible offer.

The repositioning of a company's market segment position can be made via the definition of the offer that combines several elements:

- Fixing a performance and quality level, which represents the understanding of customer expectations

- The spread of the range and the flexibility of the offer that represents the response of the company to the variety of market segment demands; this flexibility also represents the inability of the supplier to anticipate demand and its acceptance that it will have to manage changing demands from its customers

- The material form of the offer in accordance with customer use

- The nature and range of accompanying services

- Delivery dates following receipt of the order

- The determination of prices and conditions for the whole offer, and possible flexibility thereof.

Later in the chapter we shall elaborate on these different elements in order to define the offer of a company for a given market segment. The customers judge all of the aspects listed above. In spite of a supplier having some negative points, they can still be chosen by a buyer. A buyer might make up for deficiencies through using multiple sources (Chapter 3), by bringing in service providers from the outside to complement the offer of a given supplier (in the case of servicing and maintenance, for example), or by performing some of the operations themselves (storage, for example). Developments in customer activity, and moves made by the competition, can alter the supplier's relative competitive position for one of these points and hence lead to a modification in the customer's requirements and judgement criteria. This is the reason why *relative perceived quality* (Figure 5.10) plays such an important part in the issues we are dealing with. This relates to the question of customer satisfaction surveys that can help to unravel the connection between a supplier's offer and the customer's expectations.

Another element that results from these developments is the phenomenon of the offer becoming a *commodity*, linked to the customer learning about what the supplier is offering. Indeed, in the interaction with the supplier, the customer learns to master the technologies in question. In some contexts and situations, the customer may concentrate on finding the lowest price possible without paying any great attention to the ongoing relationship with the supplier. It is not rare to find very opportunistic behaviour from customers.

A particular case concerning the offer happens when the offer integrates what is known as a *professional standard*, in other words when questions on specific compatibility and functioning are raised. We shall look at this aspect later in the chapter.

The Relationship Between Technology and the Offer

We underlined the point in Chapter 6 that a firm combines both *internal* and *external* resources to gain access to specific applications with customers. In business-to-business environments, we must note that technological resources (production technologies and technologies incorporated into products) make up the foundation of marketing strategy. We observed that the relationships between supplier's and customer's technologies are a key point to understand the relationships between both organisations. The interaction model supports this perspective. That is the reason why we insist on the relationship between technology and market in this chapter. But other resources combine with technological resources, particularly when the intangible content of the offer becomes important. We shall deal with this subject when detailing the question of the service part of the offer, or Chapter 11 when giving a brief overview of service marketing.

For over 50 years the industrial world has developed its production and management methods. This movement began earlier in the USA than in Europe, and then was reinvigorated by the Japanese, only to be taken again into American and European hands. The economic situation of the 1970s generated an optimised production system and tightly controlled management methods that led to the development of a self-centred industrial model. It became, from the 1980s onwards, a little out of touch with the arrival of a multiform demand, both capricious and demanding, and a Japanese style of competitive system composed of much more flexible companies. To this rigour, the companies added flexibility; they developed *reactivity based on internal motivation* (in other words, auto control) rather than a hierarchical system.

The 'productivity/flexibility' dilemma now confronting companies comes from numerous sources. The progressive fragmentation of demand and the increase in buyer's expectations have led to a proliferation of offers. In almost all world markets, the potential supply is greater than the demand, which automatically increases competition (Chapter 1), which leads in turn to diversification and differentiation in the offers. And this, of course, stimulates demand even further. These developments are coupled with accelerated technical advances and renewal of products that impact supply and demand in the same way. Even more influential is the fact that company growth and increase in market share are related to their capacity to offer greater variety. However the manufacturing systems of the 1970s were very sensitive to output and flexibility, with any increase in the latter automatically leading to the breakdown of the former. Consequently business systems promoted the maintenance of or increase in output levels. In addition, some strategic thinking, such as the methods proposed by the BCG (Chapter 5), also pushed decisions in this direction. There was thus a simultaneous increase in direct costs linked to wages, and in indirect costs linked to the development of industrial investments. This double movement produced two types of consequences: to raise the break-even point and to decrease flexibility in the production system. Greater fragmentation in demand created an imbalance between business organisations and the marketplace. New production management procedures were required, and it was at this time that the West realised that Japan had already achieved some interesting improvements: 'auto-activation', worker versatility, just-in-time, *kanban*, *andon*, *poka yokē*, etc. Thus, in just a few years, firms had to integrate new concepts and new ways of considering markets. This led to the appearance of new words in management language: 'local markets', 'mass-markets', 'segmented markets', 'market niche', 'made to measure markets' and so on.

In this light, as Coriat (1991) says, 'it is not mass production as such which is condemned, but rather the mass production of non-differentiated products'. The challenge is now to combine mass production with manufacturing batches of numerous product variants. And all manufacturing organisations have begun searching for the ideal combination while remaining competitive. This involves managing both product design and production. This corresponds to our notion of joint development used in Chapter 1: competitive advantage can be developed only by paying close attention to both value for the customer and to the human, technical and economic conditions of its creation and renewal.

From a technical point of view, many adaptations were brought to the company's logistics and value chains to meet the new challenges. For more information, the reader is referred to the References and Further Reading for this chapter. The challenge is twofold: to respond to demand variety and time to market required by the marketplace, while retaining the advantage of the effects of scale and experience – in other words, to combine *productivity* and *flexibility*. To do this, many potential solutions exist, based both on company resources (production technology, products, structure of the organisation and so on) and on external players (suppliers, intermediaries, partners, buyers).

There are several ways to meet the demand for variety and adaptation while yet remaining competitive:

- The *modular design* of products, and the possibility of swapping sub-assemblies increases the variety of products while limiting the number of sub-assemblies from which economies of scale and experience effects can be obtained. Advantages can be found in the cost price, production and inventory management, all of which improve company competitiveness. Moreover, reducing the number of sub-assemblies means using a limited number of suppliers producing larger volumes at lower cost, which also has a positive impact on competitiveness.

- *Increasing the functions* that can be performed by a given product allows the users to find more uses. For example, trucks equipped with hydraulic platforms and cranes can perform a variety of loading and unloading operations. Here the way to answer the variety of requests is *polyvalence*.

- *Delayed differentiation*, which applies to several elements of the value chain activity: within the company's production process, or even externally with intermediaries such as distributors and/or customers. Delayed differentiation in production implies *finalising the products as far downstream as possible* to limit upstream variety. For semi-processed products (steel, aluminium) this can mean dedicating heavy and very productive investments to the first stage of the transformation process with more flexibility for the completion of operations of the second stage. The manufacturer can transfer this second stage to intermediaries. For example, steel stockists prepare orders (cutting, treating, etc.) and create the variety required by particular customer demands. These stockists buy and stock the steel in its most common form, and in the minimum volumes imposed on them by the steel producer. Another example: lorry manufacturers do not manufacture the bodywork. Rather, independent coachbuilders who design and fit the bodywork once the lorry has been completed do this. This partition of activities enables the latter to limit the variety of vehicle plus bodywork combinations. It should be pointed out that the number of vehicles (cabin and chassis), with all possible combinations (cabin, chassis length, engine size, etc.) could reach 3000 for certain manufacturers. If the number of coachbuilders is added to this figure, it becomes easy to understand the interest in delaying differentiation through the use of intermediaries. In some cases, customer participation in the finalising of the product can allow the supplier to 'delay' the internal finalising by transferring it to the customer. The client finishes the work using sub-assemblies provided by the supplier.

- The *dynamic flexibility of the manufacturing process* aims to reduce the *costs of variety* (reduction of stocks for lower cost, reduced delays, increased output of different products per machine, improvement in quality) while easing response to changes (variations in quantities ordered, easier integration of technical modifications, reductions in response time).

We have indicated some methods that help to develop a company's capacity to increase variety by focusing on the technical dimension of the offer (the products) and on the manufacturing organisation. The company seeks to ensure a better fit between its technological characteristics (production technology) and increased customer technical needs and decreased response time. This fit materialises through an offer (production technology perspective) on a given market segment (market–customer perspective).

This search for increased flexibility while maintaining competitiveness can also take other forms: the offer of services linked to the product (the firm relies then more on human resources than on technological ones), the use of external sources and customer participation. We have given some examples of this under delayed differentiation above. Some steel makers, for example, have rationalised their large product range that were too adapted to specific customer uses. To keep their customers despite this rationalisation, they have intensively worked on technical support to integrate customer requirements into their reduced range of products. Thus, rationalisation of the range has increased the productivity and reduced production costs. The result is a policy that compensates for an apparent reduction of adaptation through the development of services (technical assistance) to the customers and involving the customer in the process. Through this example, we have shown the compensatory role of services in the supplier's offer. Sometimes a standardisation or a reduction in the variety of products could be compensated for by an improved service offer that can be designed to help the supplier to respond to the variety of customer needs. This idea will be developed in due course.

The Offer Process

The complexity of the marketing of business-to-business products can be found in the need to make coherent choices at several levels. On the one hand, the competences and technological skills mastered within the company, or acquired externally, must be fully understood, and on the other hand, so must the characteristics of the marketplace. We must underline here the concept of 'the network of the firm' that we have already mentioned. Long used in the major project environments, it exists too in all the business-to-business situations. The increased strategic use made of suppliers (externalisation) largely contributes to this approach being used in many business-to-business sectors. This type of network helps to prevent the firm from maintaining competences for which it has a low rate of use, and on which it becomes difficult to build and upgrade quality and competitiveness levels. We can thus better understand the Multistrat model (Figure 6.2) and define a typical process of offer design in business-to-business marketing (Figure 7.1).

Figure 7.1   The offer design process in business-to-business marketing

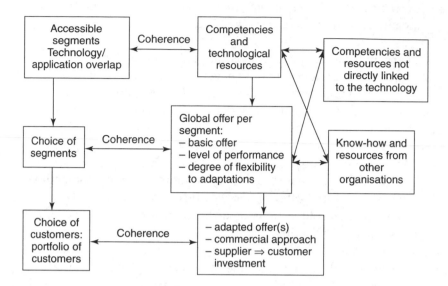

To utilise this approach, many successive horizontal and vertical iterations are required. At the upper level, given a specific technology/application overlap, the company can potentially gain access to *accessible market segments* based on its competencies and technological resources (Chapters 5 and 6). This first level of segmentation based on the definition of the interface of technology and applications allows the firm to define the technical part of its offer. This is followed by a succession of segmentation exercises, depending both on the degree of market heterogeneity and also on the company's capacity to respond with suitable offers. The aim is to identify *target market segments* for the company (Chapter 6). For each segment, a global offer per segment is designed, requiring decisions related to the basic offer, the level of performance and the degree of flexibility. These global offers per segment make up the different bases that then enable the company to adapt to each customer's requirements. The degree of adaptability in turn often depends on the nature of the portfolio of customers and on strategic choices made by the company. The adaptation of the offer for a given customer is one of the elements of supplier investment in its potential relationship with the customer.

Decisions Concerning the Basic Offer and Performance Level

The *basic offer* is, in a way, the minimum offer that a potential supplier is required to consider. Defining the *performance level* is at the centre of this process, and results from the company's understanding of its markets and segments. A segment is composed of a group of customers (from one through to several thousand) who

Table 7.1   Example of demands for plastic films designed for foodstuff packing

	Veto	Important	Secondary
Technical	■ Easiness to print ■ Admitted for packing foodstuff ■ Adapted to be used at the customer's ■ Film width	■ Range of thicknesses/quality ■ Physical characteristics ■ Aspect ■ Packing of film drums ← ■ Film cleaners	
Financial	■ Price	■ Payment terms	■ Geographical origin (change rates)
Services		■ Technical assistance ■ Availability ■ Commercial response ■ Salespeoples' technical expertise	
Delivery terms	←	■ Ability to adapt to late order changes ■ Geographical proximity ■ Delay ■ Punctuality	

Arrows indicate the direction of an evolution

present homogeneous characteristics and requirements in relation to a given purchase. The adaptation of the offer to these characteristics and requirements is the direct consequence of the selection of the segment. This includes setting a performance level for the technical and financial dimensions, product availability and also the associated services. This performance level responds to two objectives: to correspond to basic customer requirements in the segment, and to allow for (at least) partial superiority or significant differentiation over the competition.

But customer expectations are not all identical. Some demand more than others. As explained in Chapter 3, this is owing to the perceived risks on different attributes. To make the notion of a global segment offer easier to understand, we shall use the three-level classification of expectations that we used in Table 3.4: *veto* requirements, *important* requirements and *secondary* requirements. In this approach, the basic offer must fit the veto requirements perfectly. A superior performance on other dimensions of the offer can in no way make up for weaknesses in the response to any veto criteria.

Our example is that of a producer of plastic films used in the packaging of foodstuffs (Table 7.1). The film is made by transformers and utilised by the food processing industry. The films are transported via the food distribution channel before reaching the final customer. The listed demands are presented in order of importance (veto–important–secondary) for a given market segment. The performance level of the offer must be coherent with this hierarchy of demands.

The Response to the Variety of Demand

As already indicated, the response to the variety of demand can be achieved in two ways: the *variety between the offers* (the extension of the products and services range) and the *inbuilt degree of adaptation* (variety within the offer).

The different requirements existing in the marketplace mean that the company had to find a two-level response: the variety of the product range and the flexibility of their offer.

Extending the Range

A company's product range is the result of *strategic choices*: its objective in terms of market share, and its recognition of the variety in the demand.

For example, let us call Lubrimet the company that undertook the market survey described in Example 7, Figure 6.4. The first decision level concerns determining whether it wishes to market only top-of-the-range oils or the more standard ones as well. If it decides to specialise in only the best, it can decide to cover the 7 segments that use the oils or to select some segments only. If the segments have been well identified, this means the company must prepare 7 different offers. However, should Lubrimet decide to concentrate on just segment 1, it may be required to produce an even greater range of products for very precise uses; for example, different oils used for the different alloys manufactured by the customer.

Example 9   The Leman Company

For example, the Leman Company produces materials using pneumatic energy: electric screwdrivers, drills, grindstones, etc. The company was reconsidering its offer of screwdrivers. Each model had the following attributes: a motor, speed control, torque, screw direction and shape of the handle. Each attribute had a number of different variants available; for example, there were a number of different motor powers. The company had the choice of whether to list the exact attributes of the full range of all the final products it could assemble for each customer, or else to define a more limited range of product combinations from all those possible. The first alternative corresponded to a market characterised by a wide range of operations performed by the customers, low-volume orders for each model, difficulty in forecasting sales, no strict delivery terms and yet the possibility to demand high prices. This choice would require sophisticated organisation of supply deliveries and of manufacturing, a large stock of sub-assemblies, versatile workforce and machinery and technical back-up for the sales team, particularly concerning the definition of the specifications. The second choice was worth considering only if the company could define the operations and customers who would consider a limited number of machines, delivered rapidly according to reliable forecasts. It would mean a production system with long product runs, with a relative specialisation of the workers, machines and stocks of finished products. Clearly, Leman could opt for a mix of the two solutions, to have a range of products for some specific customer–application combinations, and a made-to-measure offer for others.

Note: Based on real data, company name confidential.

The composition of the range will be decided depending on different customer requirements, the company's capacity to meet these requirements through one or several offers and also the achievable volume in each of the segments or sub-segments. The decision concerning the composition of the range must take all the elements of the supplier's offer into consideration: products, services, deliveries and prices. For example, in the case of maintenance, some companies have developed ranges with different types of contracts according to delays and pricing. For lorries, maintenance contracts range from the normal garage-type service through to contracts based on mileage, and so on.

All the possible combinations can lead to an important variety and complexity of the offer that are difficult to manage, particularly for the sales team. This is typified by the computer industry, where the offer is constantly evolving, which raises problems of management linked to the mastering of the variety of offers. Some companies go so far as to offer only preassembled packages of the product plus services to certain selected segments.

Offer Flexibility

This second way of responding to diversity of demand consists of not finalising the offer until the sale has been concluded. In other words, tailoring the offer as closely as possible to the customer's demands. This choice is obviously the opposite of offering a standardised, preconceived configuration where flexibility is limited to just a few elements. For example, a very standardised offer in terms of product, service and delivery can have price flexibility. However, beware of 'hidden flexibility'. The sales representative for a major American chemicals industry revealed that he had identified almost 1300 different payment terms for their customers. It is obvious that in such a case, even if the offer is technically standardised in order to reduce manufacturing costs, administrative complexity has had a negative impact on administrative costs. It should be possible to agree to limit the number of payment terms, and so reduce overall costs. These differences in payment terms are often the result of the sales team's decisions or concessions. If company policy is 'to never mention product flexibility in order to protect production productivity', the sales representatives often have to allow for certain flexibility in other elements of the offer. For example, we have heard sales managers of a lorry manufacturer and aircraft manufacturer claim that any extension of the guarantee would be so costly that it is better to agree to a reduction in pricing. However, the sales people were not aware of this and were going on with proposals of guarantee extensions. The point of these examples is the necessity to take into account the interdependence of all these facets and the need for *intelligent offer piloting*.

As Example 9 demonstrates, the policy of flexibility is often built around a *modular design* of the products, as is often the case for the components or capital goods industry. On the other hand, in the case of semi-processed goods (steel, aluminium, plastics, etc.) or in the computer industry, this offer flexibility cannot be anticipated by means of 'prefabricated' sub-assemblies and the flexibility of capacity is rooted in the characteristics of the production technology in one case and in human resources in the other one. Sometimes, the uncertainty is such that the supplier cannot define the sub-assemblies in advance. This requires producing on the basis of orders received, since one does not know customer's requirements in advance. For example, a large boilermaker working for engineering firms has to adapt its work according to the equipment ordered. It does not know in advance the dimensions, the types of alloys, the conditions of use and so on. In such a case, the very idea of an 'offer' is difficult to formulate. The issue is more to sell a *group of competencies and manufacturing capacities* readily available to respond to a particular order. This corresponds to the sub-contracting position where it is not really possible to formulate an offer.

The logic applied to the technical attributes of the offer can also be applied to the other dimensions, in particular to services.

The service can be either *complementary* or *compensatory*. As indicated, a large range of services can increase the supplier's flexibility. It must be remembered that services cannot be stored, so the idea of 'prefabricated' modules cannot apply to services as it can to products. We shall deal with service characteristics in more detail in Chapter 11.

In Chapter 2 we saw how situations in business-to-business marketing involve a degree of interaction between supplier and customer, plus a varying degree of offer flexibility. Any offer leaves room for a degree of negotiation. Even in the case of a very standardised offer – photocopiers, for example – negotiation between the supplier and customer can involve discounts, terms of payment, or the inclusion of free servicing over a given period. The supplier must consider the importance of the flexibility of the offer when dealing with the customers. Figure 7.2 describes the process involved in formulating a business-to-business offer. It provides both an overall perspective at the segment level and a specific perspective at the customer level.

The *overall offer per segment* has all the elements that can be included in the supplier's offer for a given market segment at any given time. Part of the overall offer segment, the *basic offer*, will become the common element of all transactions concluded with the customers of this segment. The basic segment offer is designed according to customers' veto requirements. On the other hand, potential offer elements are designed to meet the secondary and important customer demands. They make up the attributes which, when added to the basic offer, will allow the supplier to deliver 'package offers' or to introduce offer flexibility ('solutions'). Two important elements have to be taken into account. First, we must keep in mind the fact that numerous competencies are built during interactions with customers. Some potential offer elements evolve and are enriched by these interactions, and may eventually become part of the basic offer. The bottom part of Figure 7.1 sheds light on these elements, identifying customers' choices and investments realised during the interaction process. Secondly, we believe it is necessary to formalise a structured and complete inventory of all these potential offer elements, utilised in par-

Figure 7.2   The industrial offer and interaction

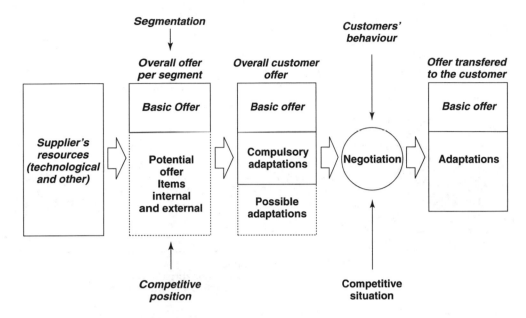

ticular relationship. It is a kind of *best-practice* work. Surprisingly, many companies find it difficult systematically to identify and make use of all the resources developed in this way. Thus, offers which have been developed during transactions with each individual customer end up relatively independent, even if there is very often possible synergy and transfer from one customer to another. We feel this task of experience structuring within the marketing department is important, and should form part of their task.

The *overall customer offer* includes the basic segment offer plus the unavoidable adaptations (fatal adaptations) without which the customer cannot use the supplier's offer. They correspond to the veto demands at a given customer. For example, for Lubrimet it could mean delivering the oils in 50 litre barrels rather than the usual 200 litre barrels. Delivery times are another example when there are tight constraints on when lorries can be accepted in overcrowded discharge areas at the customer's factory. These flexible elements help to create the final offer that will have been adapted to each particular customer at a particular time.

The *offer transferred to the customer* is dependent on the contents of the overall offer, the behaviour of the customer, the competitive situation at the customer and the strategic importance of the customer for the supplier. The result of the transaction, when successful, is a particular picture of the overall segment offer. This picture is largely linked to the importance of the customer and the supplier, and to the power balance active during the negotiation. Therefore, if the degree of potential adaptation, as examined before, is the means chosen by the supplier to respond to the variety of the demand, an actual adaptation may be the result of a power balance favourable to the customer during the negotiation.

Figure 7.3   Variety of the offer and industrial constraints

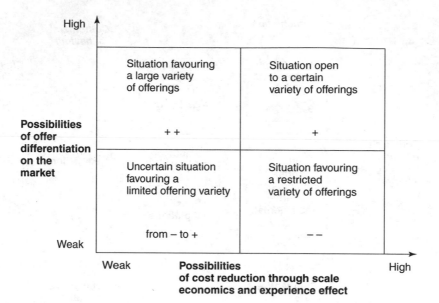

Variation in the offer can be considered as both a direct result of customer demand heterogeneity and the outcome of a process of interaction, and our aim is to integrate the constraints of the design processes and production techniques. Some customers can accept product standardisation because of greater regularity and reliability, better reaction to changes in the market, economies of scale and experience, better stock management, and so on. Figure 7.3 shows the conditions of choice and the compromises to be made in order to reach the best possible balance between flexibility and the respect of production objectives and the renewal of competitive advantage.

The Tangible Part of the Offer

The tangible part of the offer is its most obvious and most visible aspect. It results from the company's know-how and technological resources, complies with the specifications and allows the customers to use it. There are two main points to remember: the user's point of view and the flexibility involved in the design of the final offer.

The user's point of view involves the supplier's understanding of the customer's 'way of operating' when using the offer. The analysis of this includes the material conditions of use (tasks to perform, expected performance, user training, etc.). An excellent technical definition is not enough, the supplier needs to know by whom, why and how the product is used. This classical concern of industrial design is only beginning to enter the industrial world and the progress already made in certain

Example 10 Schlumberger Technologies' Reflectometers

A reflectometer is a measuring apparatus designed to check and measure different elements of an optic fibre connection: fibres, links, connectors.

The control of optic fibre connections can be divided into four different applications: in *laboratories* the tests of new components and new architectures; in *manufacturing* the tests of the fibres or cable during the production process; for *installations* the measure of solderings, connectors and connection efficiency; for *maintenance* the spotting of defaults and the measure of degradation.

Schlumberger estimated that the two last applications were handled by the same operators and that they could be merged into a unique segment ('installation–maintenance': IM), which represents 85 per cent of the total market for reflectometers.

Facing competitors that, in 1987, presented a sophisticated type of product, always requiring qualified specialists and with slight differences according to applications, Schlumberger thought they should approach the IM segment with a particular offer.

First offer: Item SI 7727 (non-visible technological gap).

Aimed at *field operators*, the product realised measures automatically without human intervention. It was designed to be very simple to use, with a direct screen display of the results. Particular attention was paid to handiness (volume, weight, design of the front face, conditions and instructions of use) and to resistance in difficult environments. The screen displays were easy to read, showing directly the type of default and its localisation. Field technicians could easily use the apparatus after a short training. The SI 7727 was completely non-adapted to the two other segments.

Second offer: FLASH

Control operations on optic fibre connections developed. Applications diverged: Installation and Maintenance showed different requirements. Each one became more demanding in terms of definition and precision of the measures to be performed. The logics of the requirements normally led to two different machines.

Schlumberger's solution was to design the same measuring apparatus (laser source, measure functions) differently outlined through dedicated software cards, one for maintenance, one for installation. This manner of responding to demand variety gathers two types of advantages. It well meets the exact requirements of each segment. But it does so with a core product that respects the objectives of a productive manufacturing process (long runs of production, no changes of tools, reduction of the number of production lines allowing a limitation of investments, and so on).

Note: Based on real data, company name confidential.

fields (cars, motorbikes, skiing, electrical appliances, etc.) should allow us to improve these processes, as shown by the design by Schlumberger Technologies of their 'Reflectometers' in Example 10.

The possibility of including a certain degree of flexibility in the offer's design and its tangible form is one response to the request for variety. Flexibility occurs in offer design in two ways. The first is to delay finalising the total offer until as late as possible in the development process. Too early a finalisation can lead to a partial, but decisive, condition that makes the product unfit for some uses. The second is to identify the different possible uses and to give the final product a design that can be used in different ways, following slight adjustments made by the user. The 'Reflectometers' example is an excellent illustration of this.

The Services Linked to a Tangible Offer

The definition generally given in marketing a product (particularly in North American textbooks) includes both the tangible parts and the associated services (packaging, operating instructions, etc.) that allow the customer to use the product. In business-to-business marketing, where we have substituted the term 'offer' for the more common 'product', the services are so much part of the offer that they should be dealt with at the same level as the tangible part. Indeed, the customer evaluates the whole package he receives from the supplier. We shall examine later (Chapter 11) the marketing of business-to-business services (computer services, consultancy, publicity, industrial maintenance, cleaning, and so on). But words are deceptive, because for these services the term 'product' is often used to describe 'ready-to-use' packages such as software. Numerous concepts developed for 'pure' services are useful to our present concern, that is services associated to an industrial offer focusing on the use of an industrial good or component.

In the field of services, there is often support material involved (for example, computer equipment for a computer services company). The support material cannot, however, be related to a 'product' as defined in this paragraph, as it is not the real object of the exchange.

The Variety of Services

Services cover an enormously heterogeneous group from one sector or company to another. They can be grouped in different ways, each approach having its merits depending on what the seller wishes to achieve.

The first involves defining services according to the chronological aspects of the sale during a transaction. Table 7.2 shows the services offered by a company supplying industrial plant.

A second approach involves separating the services directly linked to the product and those that are not. Those directly linked concern services that facilitate operation at the customers' site, such as delivery, start-up, guarantees, maintenance and training. Other services can be more directly linked to customer activity. For example some industrial groups give customers (mainly small and medium-sized enterprises (SMEs)) the benefit of their sales networks. Many packaging suppliers (glass, cardboard, metal) offer services aimed to help customers optimise their packing lines. They may even intervene as engineering consultants for the design of new installations.

There has been a development in the design of contracts where the supplier agrees to results linked to the *conditions of the use* of the equipment by the cus-

Table 7.2   Four levels of services

– *Services before the sale:*
■ Help to define the customer's technical demands: size and performance of the machinery in accordance with expected results, quality, production speed, running costs, etc.
■ Preliminary tests with the customer, demonstrations

– *Services on delivery:*
■ Factory acceptance tests, packaging
■ Transport, installation, start-up
■ Staff training

– *Sales conditions:*
■ Guarantees
■ Price and reductions, terms of payment
■ Financing

– *After-sales services:*
■ Breakdown and repairs under guarantee
■ Breakdown and repairs not covered by the guarantee
■ Telephone or Internet hot-line
■ Servicing and maintenance contracts
■ Supply of accessories and spare parts

tomer. For example, the PPG company (industrial paints) signed a contract with one of its customers, a maker of car wheels, where the price was not based on per kilo of paint delivered but on the cost of the painted wheel at the end of the production line. PPG technicians, whose cost is invoiced to the customer in addition to the price of the wheel, ensure the correct functioning of the production line. Similarly Houghton, the American group, is committed to 'chemical management' by ensuring the complete management of industrial oils used by specific customers. This trend is similar to the type of service known as 'facilities management' whereby the supplier is committed to ensuring a global service at an agreed price and in accordance with a predetermined result. In this case, the company enters the 'pure service' area (Chapter 11). The important point is that some companies move from an offer of a product plus services to a pure service offer that in some cases represents diversification. This means being confronted by new competitors and the need to acquire new skills and resources. Thus, it is important to differentiate between services that are directly linked to the product and those that may take the company away from its original focus.

The Definition of Services

The definition of the offer of services can take two routes. One is founded on a good knowledge of customer characteristics stemming from various surveys. The company is thus able to master and control the development of a service policy. To define possible services, the risk approach applied to a customer segment (Chapter 5) can be used. Customer activity can thus be broken down. Technical risks, linked to the availability of products and services, can be identified. This can be linked to customer know-how and use of the products and services, and also to the financial risks that should be listed in order of importance for the customer (veto, important, secondary). A range of services can be presented for each risk thus identified. As this work is conducted on a group of customers (a market segment), risks are defined by the fact that they are common to all concerned customers. We may then speak of 'generic risks', which more or less corresponds to the concept of incurred risk (Chapter 3). The concept of perceived risk is not used here, as it refers to the situation of an individual customer only.

The second approach to define the service offer involves leaving as much room as possible for the development of interaction with the customer. The choice of developing a particular service happens case by case. A structuring and reinforcement of the developed skills follows in order to build a capacity to offer the new service to other customers. The aim is to create a service offer through a pilot operation, which the company will then rationalise. In this instance, the company chooses adaptation as a development strategy.

Services in Supplier Strategy

Services have many roles to play in suppliers' strategy:

- They can be seen as a means to give certain *flexibility* to a standardised basic offer. They give the company greater adaptation and adjustment capacity to allow it to meet customer demands without disrupting productivity too much. The service can use varying amounts of company resources, depending on the importance of the customer in the company's portfolio.

- They help the supplier/customer relationship by *creating value for the customer*, thereby ensuring that price is not the only negotiable element of the offer.

- They are an important element of any *differentiation strategy*. Services are less visible than products and thus less easy to imitate. A company can always obtain samples of the competitors' products. It is much more difficult to understand how essential or useful a service provision is for a customer. Offering a large range of services and some quite 'advanced' ones adds to the company image, even if they are not always available to all customers.

- They involve taking over of some of the customer's tasks and activities, and thus *enrich the supplier's position* (supplier involvement). For example, a transport company agreeing to a maintenance contract with a truck dealer is thus freed from the garage activity it was performing before.

Today, many companies producing industrial products are investing heavily in service activities. They are seeking greater differentiation from their competitors, and looking to increase interdependence with their customers. However, this interdependence can go too far and the customer may try to put an end to it. This raises the following questions concerning services in an industrial environment:

- What *price should be used*: a bundled price for product and services or one for the product and one for the services? There is no rule here. It is maybe easier to sell at one price than to have to negotiate two prices. In our example of trucks, a salesman will negotiate the sale of a truck, but the manager, or dealer, will negotiate the servicing contracts. We shall return to this when we discuss pricing below.

- Should a specific *organisational structure* be set up to offer the services? This would seem to depend on whether the services are performed by the company itself, or by a partner. There are advantages and disadvantages to both choices. The choice is related to who holds the skills required and the ability to develop them cost-effectively. Another element concerns the importance of incorporating services into the offer for the global strategy of the company. Some computer manufacturers have developed partnerships with other companies (information technology companies, for example) or with the designers of software. However, when these companies saw their profitability fall in the hardware department, they sought to develop their own services dimension either through the acquisition of service companies or through planned internal development.

When the choice has been made not to use a partnership to offer services, the company must decide on different issues. Which department will be in charge of the services? Will this department be considered as a part of the company sales centre, or is it a profit centre in its own right? The choice is not clear between the two alternatives, and it is truly a strategic choice. Choosing to be part of the sales centre is valid when the service is directly linked to the product and when trying to aggressively gain market share. It gives the sales team room for flexibility. If loosely controlled and/or without limitation, it may lead to an inflation of costs and accelerate the banalisation of the offer. The profit-making entity is more often used for capital goods, and when the services are not directly linked to the products.

In the case of a partnership between a principal and a secondary supplier, a problem can arise about the quality of service to the customer from the 'external' company. The principal supplier is in charge of quality control and management.

What is the use of services linked to product offer? The trend is to increase the service component in order to improve company flexibility. However, this raises many questions. What and who are the services for? What is the logic behind the offer? Does the customer understand it? How much does it cost and how much does it earn? How far should the service offer go? Can we limit the service offer to just a selection of customers? In fact, we can consider the possibility and validity of setting up strategies to limit service through standardisation of the offer by turning it into a basic offer.

Does the company have a service 'culture'? We shall look at this issue in Chapter 11. Many companies are moving towards an offer including a large range of services that are, or are not, linked to the product. In many cases they can anticipate the technical characteristics of the product and eliminate any problem before it arrives. Buyer–supplier co-operation in the elaboration of services means that the final characteristics of the offer are the result of this co-production. If it is possible to stop delivering a product that presents unacceptable defaults, service provision does not allow the same policy. If there is a problem, very often the problem has already occurred. Therefore, a true service culture is not easily attained for product oriented companies, mainly because the services are simply a means to sell the product. This is the case for computer manufacturers who have a 'hardware' culture and who have little by little added services to their offers (they may amount to over 50 per cent of the turnover) whose culture is different. And these 'product oriented' firms meet their competition from specialised suppliers, such as the Information Technology Services ones in the computer industry, who have for long integrated and implemented this service culture. Customers can easily tell the difference between the two approaches. Thus, the choice of an external partner or the internal creation of entities dedicated to services is a way around the inherent problems of a product culture. It is often the choice of capital goods suppliers.

Delivery Time

There is no need to remind the reader of the importance of delivery times. There is no point in a company altering sales policy or product design if production does not allow it to meet market requirements, which are the result of customer demands and competitors' capabilities. On the other hand, if a company can shorten delivery times, this can lead customers to modify their production schedule in a way that can give them a competitive advantage.

More important than the elapsed time is the management of *delivery schedules*. A customer can usually cope with longer elapsed times if these are arranged in advance and are accompanied by other supplier advantages. Currently, the drastic reduction in delivery times and stock levels has led to the setting up of *intra-company* and *intercompany* organisations. These new ways of organising have been made possible through the fantastic development in information technologies that allow a real synchronisation of the information flow. The Internet particularly allows a considerable improvement in the management and delivery service of spare parts (see the <southco.com> website for an excellent example). This field is so large that we suggest the reader refer to the numerous books published on these themes as well as those dedicated to logistics and supply chain management.

The Financial Dimension of the Offer

We have looked at the different ways in which the supplier can elaborate its offer. The financial dimension is, *a priori*, an action lever that is both identical to and different from the other dimensions of the offer. It represents the possibility of differentiating the offer and can be approached from the financial service angle (guarantees, dates, replacement value, etc.) that gives even more opportunities for flexibility during negotiation. It is particularly important when the other dimensions of the offer lack flexibility. The financial dimension can also possibly be used as a compensation for another element of the offer that seems to be too costly for the supplier. Here, fixing the price will be a key element in the response (see below).

Fixing the Price

Pricing policy in business-to-business marketing is different from that usually adopted in consumer marketing. The fact that demand for an industrial component is based on the demand for the end product automatically means there may be considerable variations in its pricing. For example, let us take the notion of price-elasticity of the demand, which argues that the quantities sold will increase as price decreases. But this does not hold in business-to-business markets that have regular demand patterns. A reduction in price for gear-boxes, for example, will have little effect on the total number sold, which is of course controlled by the sales of cars. However, a drop in the price of ABS braking systems, which are fitted in only certain categories of cars, will affect the quantities sold. Such a drop might well allow the addition of ABS systems to lower car-price categories either under the form of options, or included in the basic price list. The difference in the two examples comes from the level of equipment in the cars, which is the exact expression of a demand. Although basically solid as a theory, care must be taken with the conditions under which it is employed and the definition of certain terms. On the other hand, in the case of an expected increase in prices, customers can anticipate by bringing forward their orders and thus building up their stocks to reduce the effects of future increases. Such behaviour leads to a kind of reversed notion of the price-elasticity effect on demand that has not been well researched so far. With these preliminary remarks, let us examine some issues in more detail.

Pricing Policy in Business-to-Business Marketing

Fixing the price in a business-to-business offer is the outcome of many factors, based on both constraints for the decision maker, and the options available. To fix a price requires managers to synthesise opinions, objectives and interdependent constraints. This requires examining simultaneously the following points of view:

■ The price represents the *position and strategic objectives* of the company
■ It expresses the *value of the overall offer* in the eyes of the *customers*

- It allows for the *creation of profitability* and depends on the methods of calculation of the cost
- It is influenced by the *market and the competition.*

Company objectives are influenced by the competitive situation and have to take into consideration the value of the offer for the customer and the positions of competitors. However, it is important to position these elements in a more precise context, which in turn will affect our thoughts on pricing strategies.

Price and Strategic Objectives

In Chapters 1 and 2 we have analysed the strategies of *cost domination* and *differentiation*. The choice of one or the other of these strategies automatically implies thinking about the pricing policy that is associated with it.

Domination through costs is linked to the notion of *experience*. If this law applies, its consequences for prices are fundamental. If costs are set according to the experience curve, two approaches are possible for fixing prices (Figure 7.4): one in which prices follow the reduction in costs, and another in which the price curve can, for a while, be independent of the drop in costs.

Graph (a) shows how competitor *A* uses market price to eliminate competitor *B*, who does not have the same capacity to reduce costs. Therefore *B* must change strategy and differentiate to survive. *A*'s choice of strategy depends on an evaluation of their industrial capacity (product design and production) to reduce costs faster than the competition, and the fact that a drop in price for the same product is attractive to the user. The link between an increase in market share and a reduction in costs becomes clear. This type of approach explains the aggressive strategies developed by companies attacking new technical fields and who want to gain market share as rapidly as possible. For this strategy to work, prices must be low enough to replace the current products and competitors.

Graph (b) shows a different evolution, known as the 'umbrella' phenomenon, where the price is first used to make a profit for the company and then, layer by layer, to let the market profit from reductions in costs.

The choice between these two approaches is related to the concept of *relative perceived quality* (Figure 5.10) where advantage can either be used to build increased market share or to make immediate profits through higher relative prices.

Both strategies are linked to different market characteristics. The first strategy is characteristic of markets with *relatively homogenous customer expectancies* centred on the *price*. In such a case, the market can be approached globally with little segmentation immediately to launch preconceived offers with little flexibility and concentration on output and cost reduction. The second concerns more *heterogeneous markets*. The market is segmented. The company begins with that segment which gives the highest value to the supplier's offer. Gradually, as experience increases

Figure 7.4   Price and experience curves

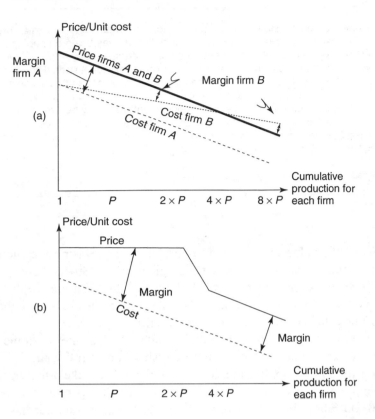

and costs decrease, the supplier can present his offer to other segments in turn. This approach is quite common in the plastics industry, where one can begin with the aeronautical sector and move into larger markets with lower prices to end up in the car or electrical appliances markets, etc.

The strategic choice is related to the ideas of building market share (a *penetration* strategy), which supposes long-term profit, and short-term maximisation of profits (a *skimming* strategy). The choice depends on the size, ambition and abilities of the company.

Offer Price and Value for the Customer

Strictly speaking, this is the only perspective that is really the result of marketing, since customer opinion guides the design of the offer. However, since the customer is both the aim and the means of existence of the company, the price is a compromise between what the two parties want under the threat of the competition. If the company is not totally free to fix its prices, the attention it must pay to the value of its offer to the customer is even more important. For consumer goods,

Example 11 The Houghton Company

The Houghton Company studied a new product for one of its customers in a very interesting way. To make washing machine drums, the customer was using a shaping and drilling operation on a very powerful metal press. The press required heavy-duty cutting oil. When complete, the drums were then stacked and transported through an aerial conveying system to the production line. During conveying, some of the drums began to corrode owing to the atmosphere. A protective coating was required. However, the drums had to be cleaned before applying the product because of the incompatibility between the coating and the cutting oil. Thus, Houghton studied the problem and offered cutting oil compatible with the coating. Because this meant the elimination of the cleaning phase and a consequent saving, the supplier was able to offer the new oil at a higher price.

Note: Based on real data, company name confidential.

estimation of the value of a product or service is made using techniques such as the 'appreciation of the acceptable psychological price' (Stoetzel and Adam, 1958) or conjoint analysis (Green and Wind, 1975; Cattin and Wittink, 1982). The equivalent method used in business-to-business marketing is the analysis of the economic impact of the offer, often known as value pricing.

This means assessing the conditions under which the customer uses the company's offer. A manufacturer of plastic resins knows full well that to replace a competitor for a given application, their customer must make a number of changes before being able to use the new product. The cost of this operation is, say, typically 100 000 Euros. If, in their price structure, the new supplier has no plans to compensate this cost, they will find it hard to convince their customer despite any obvious technical advantages.

This approach requires preparing a detailed report of the advantages that an offer presents for the customer and of the costs involved of incorporating the offer into all stages of the customer's activity. One way is to follow the production of the product from the beginning to the end of its production line and even further downstream (the customer's customers) and to assess the *process costs* involved. These costs can be very diverse, from material costs that are easy to calculate, through to staff training and the cost of production time lost during the learning process. More than allowing the supplier to fix a price, it also enables it to establish arguments to promote the offer and the price. This takes us out of the perspective of purchase or sales price, to a perspective of *economic* or *value–in–use cost*. A detailed analysis of the customer's use of the offer will help to clarify the design of the offer and to place the sale price at the heart of the design, rather than as a separate issue. This is why we place the pricing policy at the centre of this chapter devoted to the offer, rather than dealing with it separately. The risk approach (Chapter 3) is an interesting element in the definition of the price. Other than the analysis of incurred and perceived risks that allow us to identify the key points to be watched, the analysis of how the customer's purchasing division operates also allows us to judge the feasibility of a pricing strategy. Indeed, in many cases, the supplier tries to promote the idea that a more expensive product can cost less in terms of total usage over a number of months ('payback'). This involves convincing the members of the decision making unit (DMU) who are typically the most receptive to such arguments. This is not always easy and depends on how the customer operates. For example, the type of accounting system installed by the customer may act as a block: cost allocation approaches, budgets, etc. The relationships between those involved may also act as a block, such as when the person who benefits from the increased value may not necessarily be the one who pays for it, which may create problems.

Pricing based on a marketing perspective, in other words taking into consideration the value of the supplier's offer for the customer, must be updated continuously as *customer expectancies evolve*. Let us take the example of a company called Advantelec.

Example 12 shows the efficiency of novel solutions following a detailed and creative analysis of customer purchasing behaviour. It also underlines the importance of an approach to *customer profitability*, rather than being merely offer or product focused. Costs are not simply linked to the design of a traditional accountancy system, and a more global view of the issues becomes more and more necessary.

Example 12 Advantelec

It manufactures electronic components in large quantities for most industrial sectors. It is very efficient, possesses the most sophisticated technologies and has developed a customer support service including a design office to study buyers' component needs. These components are most often a combination of standard and original elements. Faced with increasingly strong competition, the company had to look closely at its sales results. Their study showed that it was losing sales of a particular component – without, however, losing these customers for other products. These lost sales corresponded to a particular period in the customer's product life-cycle in which the component in question was incorporated. A detailed analysis of the situation revealed that during the early stages of the product's development, the customer demanded that the supplier guarantee the product's reliability and undertake complementary developments. During this period of product launch, the customer perceived risks to be at their highest level and appreciated Advantelec's help, whatever the price of the component. Following this period, the customer, by now having mastered the component, approached the competition. Advantelec's pricing policy was to fix a basic price in relation to the variable costs and to pay off the costs of development throughout the product's life. The price decreased by about 10–15 per cent during the supply cycle. However, the production of a similar component by a competitor, with lower development costs, meant prices between 20 and 25 per cent lower. Advantelec then reassessed its variable costs in comparison with the competition; the costs involved in acquiring new customers, and related development costs. Finally, they calculated the loss of sales and margin linked to such a loss of a supply, and realised that it was probably more efficient to stabilise customer relationships by automatically applying a price reduction when business begins to fall. This proved the right solution, as customers were pleased to see prices fall and were less tempted to approach the competition for what had become a smaller difference in price.

Note: Based on real data, company name confidential.

Price and Profitability

For the supplier, the price invoiced must allow them to make a profit. Thus, there is a minimum price that represents the costs involved. Below this price, the producer loses money for each unit sold and such a policy cannot be sustained for long, even if it may be a strategic way for some companies at a given point in time.

The *break-even point* determines the level of activity *where a company makes neither a profit nor a loss*. It is calculated by dividing costs into two categories: *fixed* costs and *variable* costs. The calculation is simple. For a given price and for a unit produced and sold, there is a difference between the price and the variable costs involved: the margin above unit variable cost. By multiplying this margin by the number of units sold, a mass margin over variable costs is obtained. The break-even point is obtained when the margin above variable costs is equal to that of the fixed costs involved (Figure 7.5).

Figure 7.5 The break-even point

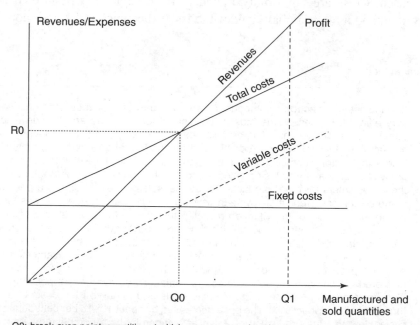

Q0: break-even point, quantities at which revenues equal total costs
R0: turnover break-even point, turnover corresponding to Q0 quantities
Q1: quantities bringing a global profit for a certain price level
Selling price per unit = SPu
Variable cost per unit = VCu
Margin on unit variable cost MUVC = SPu − VCu
Fixed costs = FC − Variable costs = VC

$$\text{Break-even point} = \frac{FC}{MUVC}$$

$$\text{Turnover break-even point} = \frac{FC}{MUVC} \times SPu$$

Obviously, the break-even point depends on the *sales price*. Thus, a relationship must be established between the price and the volume it is possible to sell on the market and to determine the point Q1, which represents the sales objective (and market share) for a given sales price.

The *level of return on investment* (*ROI*) can represent a company's objective according to the offers that it markets. The aim is to generate a sales level so as to reach an appropriate level of return on investments dedicated to the offer. In relation to the calculation of the break-even point, this means increasing variable costs by a value corresponding to the desired level or the fixed costs by a sum that corresponds to this objective of return on investment. This very Anglo-Saxon method can penalise the strategy of using a very low price to gain market share, but corresponds to a certain 'philosophical' objective in company management.

This brings us to the question of how the different forms of calculation of profitability can affect pricing. The problem begins with cost calculation. With multi-purpose production units, the fixed costs are spread over different production lines or processes. Depreciation is calculated according to activity forecasts that can obviously be erroneous either globally or in an item-per-item allocation, and the whole cost calculation system can become ineffectual. When a company performs several transformation operations, the internal rules concerning the transfer and spread of costs can lead to an accumulation of methods of calculation whose results often appear debatable. According to the system used, downstream activities can be either profit making or in deficit, without knowing the exact economic reality. This shows just how difficult pricing is when based on costs and illustrates the precautions that must be taken.

Price and the Competition

When determining prices, a company must take into consideration the prices charged by the competition in a number of ways. In Chapter 1 we indicated the major reasons for the internationalisation of competition, and showed that some competitors operated on the basis of costs – particularly labour costs – being much lower than those prevailing in the developed world. Thus, how to compete varies depending upon the labour input in competitors' products. Competition on prices is therefore unbalanced for those sectors incorporating intensive labour costs, such as clothing, basic electrical appliances, footwear, etc. Moreover, whatever the competition, knowing their cost structure is a major element in anticipating their future policies or their reaction to changes in prices on the marketplace. Some prices, which may seem initially absurd, can be explained either by a better use of certain resources, or by recourse to a different logic of cost calculation.

Our example in Table 7.3 shows the effect that the use of a certain type of cost calculations can have on market prices. There are two comments to be made. The first concerns the precautions to take when determining prices. The second concerns the care to be taken when a company notices abnormal market prices.

Table 7.3   Cost calculations

	Firm *A*				Firm *B*		
	Aluminium	Magnesium	Stainless steel		Aluminium	Magnesium	Stainless steel
Materials costs	250	600	150	Materials costs	250	600	150
Variable costs	53	50	80	Variable costs	17	38	11
Total cost	303	650	230	Variable labour costs	43	28	68
				Selling expenses	10	10	10
				Margin on variable labour costs	134	118	212
Price with a 33 per cent margin on total cost	454	970	343	Selling price	454	794	451

Note: Based on real data, company name confidential.

Example 13 Two Structures of Costs Calculation

> This example permits a sound understanding of all the difficulties mentioned so far. Two manufacturers produce an aluminium-based tool and sell it for $454. Both decide to manufacture this tool with magnesium or stainless steel. Firm *A* bases its price calculation on the objective of keeping the 33 per cent margin they achieved on the aluminium tool. Firm *B*, however, sets its selling price through the definition of a margin on variable costs.
>
> This difference in accounting leads to very different levels of price. This simple effect of accounting methods places the competitors in very different situations. If *A* and *B* sell the aluminium tool at the same price of $454, *A* seems to be very price aggressive on stainless steel and *B* on magnesium.
>
> *Note*: Based on real data, company name confidential.

These can correspond to competitors basing decisions on different pricing structures or using specific methods of cost calculation. The knowledge of these differences is essential to give a meaning to price responses in retaliation to competitors' pricing actions.

Offer Profitability or Customer Profitability

This debate, briefly raised above, is beginning to seriously concern supporters of modern management techniques. The principles of the profitability of the offer, meaning the product or product line, are widely known. By taking into consideration several elements that are relevant to the customers themselves (the importance

Table 7.4   Establishing customer profitability

Turnover	a
Margin on goods and services sold	b
Costs linked to a customer – Selling expenses – Other expenses (development, technical assistance, maintenance, claims, etc.)	c
Marketing contribution	**(b–c)**

of the price, problems in dealing with certain customers, the services expected by others, etc.), it is legitimate to wonder whether establishing customer profitability is not the required complement to, or the intelligent substitute for, product profitability. Research has shown that there are large differences in profitability from one customer to another (Turnbull and Zolkiewski, 1997). In particular, we have already shown that investments for a given customer are important and they must be offset over time. Keeping customer loyalty is less costly than gaining new customers. Different customers do not generate the same amount of cost from their supplier, and therefore the selection of customers is important to the overall profitability. The principle of establishing customer profitability is shown in Table 7.4.

The comparison of the different levels of 'marketing contribution' from several customers enables us to have an additional view to that of the profitability per family of offers or products, and consequently to orientate the company's commercial strategy.

Determination of a Pricing Structure

In considering a company's pricing structure, one should also bear in mind two other aspects. The first concerns the *invoicing of services* linked to the product offer. One method involves bundling products and services in a total invoice and thereby supplying the services without necessarily promoting them individually. This has two disadvantages: the range of services risks becoming overwhelming and their supply to the customer becoming difficult to control. Such an approach, particularly in a situation where the competition is strong, requires strict control as to which services are supplied to which customer and of the profitability of these operations, which boils down to careful consideration of the segmentation and profitability of the customers. The opposite approach is unbundling all or part of the services offered and *invoicing them separately* according to customer use. This approach is more difficult to defend commercially, as it leads to negotiation concerning each element of the offer.

This second method leads us to our second aspect, which concerns the *flexibility of the pricing structure*. If a particular offer is only considered from a cost point of view, it can be invoiced only at a set price (with small adjustments for quantity and delivery times). On the other hand, if the competitive environment and the value of the offer to the customer are also considered, greater adjustments are possible. For example, airline companies offer prices per kilometre that vary according to the destination, the class or the booking time. The most competitive flights have the lowest prices. A new technology may be invoiced at the same price as the old system to a high-volume segment on the basis of future cost reductions, owing to expected experience effect, and therefore prices. In a low-volume segment, the same new technology could be invoiced at a higher price, as it cannot justify the same economic dynamics. Such a policy of flexibility requires that the market segments (geographic, customer, or other) be relatively resistant so that 'grey' markets will not be created beyond the control of the company.

Banalisation and Differentiation: Offer Dynamics

Customer expectations evolve over time for a number of reasons. Therefore, the company's analysis of the 'assessment of the heterogeneity of the market–segmentation–definition of an offer per segment' sequence must be regularly updated.

Understanding of a fundamental dynamic that affects offers in the business-to-business world in particular must complement our previous concepts: that of *banalisation*. By this we mean the constant pressure on suppliers that is brought about by their customers treating what was once an innovation (and could be charged accordingly) as an 'ordinary' offer, with no justification for higher prices. There are two causes of this phenomenon. Customers perceive risks attached to the adoption of any new technology or offer, even if they see the advantages, and accept the guarantees offered by the supplier and the relatively high price. At this point, trying to obtain the best of the advantages of the novelty, such customers are more preoccupied by the resolution of their particular problems and how to integrate the new solution into their activity than by a purely financial aspect. Thus, there is a strong interaction between the two parties. Eventually, the technology becomes stabilised and trusted. The customers master the technology through the learning process they have been through with their supplier, and begin to question the guarantees and the price. This movement is accelerated by the behaviour of competitors who rarely let a new technology dominate the market for long. They counter-attack with identical or substitute offers that bring alternative choices to the customers.

A second factor inducing the banalisation of an offer comes from procedures of standardisation and approval from authorities, which are perceived as a sort of guarantee by the customers. Such procedures contribute to the creation of 'veto' criteria that are shared by all the customers of an industrial sector. This forces the suppliers to integrate normalised responses in their basic offer. For example, in France, the 1975 law concerning veterinary medicines made compulsory the granting of a permit to market a product (PMP) prior to commercialisation. The market leader,

Rhône Mérieux, had to lower its prices for certain products. The advantages of some vaccines (no side effects, for example) no longer justified their higher price than for competitor approved, and therefore 'guaranteed', products. The fact that these products were of perhaps a lesser quality was in several cases no longer relevant.

The banalisation of offers means changes in customers' purchasing behaviour. They gradually tend to marginalise the criteria linked to risk and concentrate on elements linked to the price. This means the importance of price moves up in the listing of attributes (secondary–important–veto). A supplier's efforts to differentiate their offer by basing its design on 'important' or 'secondary' expectancies can no longer compensate for a higher price. For the customer, this movement coincides with changes in the purchasing process, which becomes increasingly administrative (for example, annual procedures of generalised consultation or tenders for bids). At this point, the competitive conditions also change. Customers are more likely to change suppliers, to adopt multiple source strategies, and to continually question prices. Competitors who are most likely to succeed are those who have adopted a strategy of domination through costs which is accompanied by reduced sales costs and, if the customers allow it, a transfer of sales towards distribution channels, the control of which then becomes an important element. Situations of progressive banalisation of offers require a detailed analysis and a strategic response. There can be three phases:

- First, a *diagnosis* of the banalisation of the market or the segment must be made according to the unit of analysis chosen. We suggest the use of a two-dimensional grid: the importance of the issues for the company and the degree of banalisation of the market, or segment, offers. The importance of the issues to the company can be measured in terms of volume, turnover, profitability, etc. The degree of banalisation can be categorised as being not banalised, becoming banalised, banalised (Figure 7.6). If the analysis concerns a given offer on a given market, there will be segments or groups of customers. If it concerns several offers, we would have offer/segment combinations.

- Thus, we can position both the *hierarchy of priorities* linked to the importance of the issues for the company and a *chronology of the priorities* that depend on the urgency of the situations to be dealt with and the reaction time. Therefore, in Figure 7.6, the priorities concern boxes 6, 8 and 9 of the matrix.

- Finally, to orientate company investment, it is necessary carefully to evaluate the position of the offers corresponding to the cases to be prioritised. For this, a grid positioning the offers/segments in relation to the expectancies of each combination could be used (Table 7.5). Furthermore, the position relative to competitors has to be considered (final column in Table 7.5).

This grid means that we can evaluate the *relative performances* of the offer and take the necessary decisions: disinvestment when company position is weak in relation to the rate of banalisation or investment, towards domination through costs, or towards differentiation, or a combination thereof.

Figure 7.6   Grid for the diagnosis of the degree of banalisation

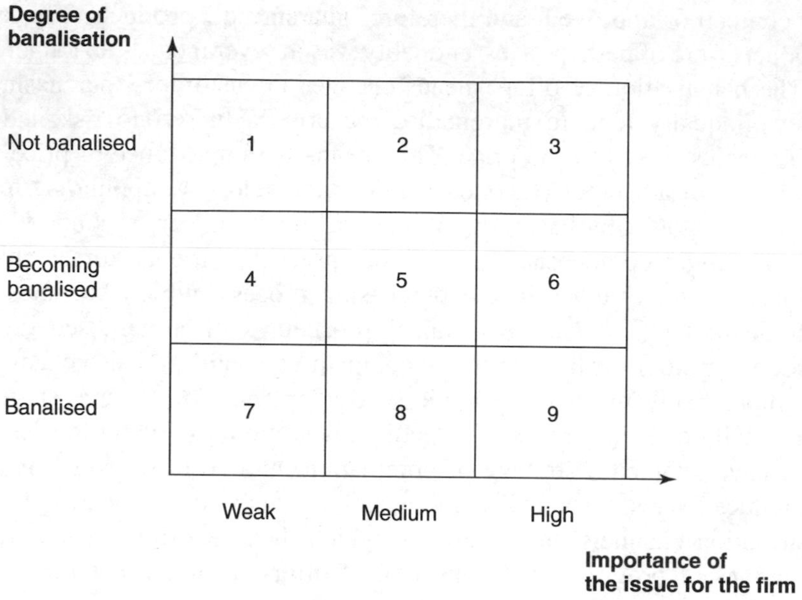

Table 7.5   Evaluation of the relative position of the offer

Requirements	Elements of the suppliers' offering	Adequacy of offering/ requirements	Relative performance of the offering
Vetos	–	Good	Superior
	–	Medium	Identical
	–	Weak	Inferior
Important	–	Good	Superior
	–	Medium	Identical
	–	Weak	Inferior
Secondary	–	Good	Superior
	–	Medium	Identical
	–	Weak	Inferior

This is an important element of the strategic process as it seeks to evaluate and to strengthen the competitiveness of the company. It is important to base the process on a detailed analysis of customers' behaviour and of the market dynamics. This is the only way to discover possibilities of debanalisation, whether it means a change in resource allocation, in offer design or in service policy.

The Relative Perceived Quality as a Function of Synthesis

We briefly mentioned this notion and its strategic importance in Chapter 5. Now we will look at its conditions of application, which are related to another element, customer satisfaction surveys (Chapter 4) whose objective is to get customers to measure the *relative quality* of the supplier's services. Other than its strategic aspect, this notion coincides with the perspective of *total quality* which has entered industry as a lever to motivate people and to drive the design and production of both products and services. Total quality management (TQM) underlines the importance of customer satisfaction and of the focusing of company attention on this task, which acts as a means for the company to reach its objectives of profitability and survival.

Various definitions of quality exist. We prefer that given by the American researchers on the PIMS programme (Table 7.6). This definition states that quality is made up of a number of items that represent the *attributes* from which the customers form their judgement of quality. Some consultancy firms specialised in quality management itemise up to 300 possible attributes. A selection must therefore be made for a given market to make the analysis possible. This is a classical process similar to a market survey. In order to make a sound selection of criteria, a qualitative selection may prove satisfactory. If not, we can proceed with the data analysis techniques mentioned in Chapters 4 and 6.

Once chosen, PIMS recommends listing the attributes into three groups: the *product* or tangible form, the *service* and the *image*, and then isolating the price criteria. Each non-price criterion is given a score indicating its relative importance in the eyes of the customers. Or else we could use the previously mentioned method of identifying 'veto', 'important' and 'secondary' criteria. The customer is asked to give a mark for performance of between 0 and 10 for the said supplier and for a relevant selection of its competitors. Depending on the scores, these marks give an overall score for each criterion; and the total score gives an indication of the relative performance of the company as perceived by the customers. The company now has information on the *priorities on the marketplace*, the position of several *competitors* and on its *own performance*. It can now act accordingly.

The method includes a *correction factor*, which is the relative importance of the quality (both tangible and intangible) versus price. This is important as it permits arbitration between several axes of development. It helps to define the economic framework within which the changes must be made and to remain realistic about the economic advantages that could be gained from any improved quality.

The measure of the relative perceived quality can be made only with groups of homogenous customers (segments or the 'served market' to use PIMS vocabulary). Heterogeneous groups of customers will lead only to errors. Segmentation is the key to the marketing process and is vital when using operational tools such as this.

We can now calculate the relative importance of quality and price in the buying decision for a market segment (= served market) (Table 7.7).

This approach examining the relative perceived quality and price is enlightening. On the basis of a certain level of relative quality, a company can apply different pricing policies. The combination of a level of relative quality and a price which has been fixed in relation to the average market price, permits us to establish a kind of appreciation of the 'value' of an offer. To each value of the offer,

Table 7.6　　Measuring the relative perceived quality

Purchase criteria (excl. price)	relative importance (%)	Performance appreciation (0–10)							
		Firm		Competitor A		Competitor B		Competitor C	
		N	Nx%	N	Nx%	N	Nx%	N	Nx%
Linked to the product									
1									
2									
3									
4									
5									
6									
7									
SUB-TOTAL									
Linked to services									
1									
2									
3									
4									
5									
6									
7									
SUB-TOTAL									
Linked to image									
1									
2									
SUB-TOTAL									
TOTAL	100%	Fq		Aq		Bq		Cq	
		10		10		10		10	

Source: Unpublished documents from SRI International.

Table 7.7　　Quality versus Price

Quality	
Price	
	100 per cent

Figure 7.7   Value marketing

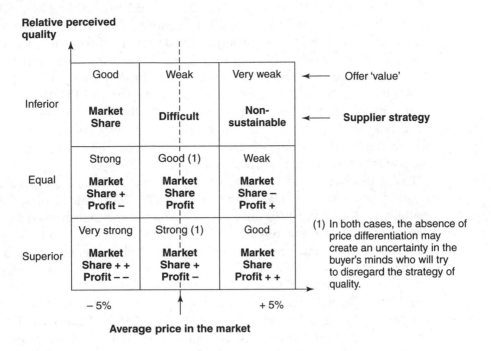

a strategy can be associated according to company objectives: market share growth, profit maximisation, or a combination of the two. Figure 7.7 presents the 'values' that correspond to the possible strategies.

The Particular Case of Compatible Standards

The development of certain offers follows a number of rules that combine to create a particular economic arena: the offers associated with *compatible standards*. Standard compatibility defines the design and interface norms that allow different base products to use additional services and goods and/or to be connected in a network. The aim of this internal coherence is to preclude the use of offers which are based on different norms. The question becomes tricky when, for example, a new offer requiring standard compatibility appears on the market, as was the case for the PC industry.

Many problems are raised when a number of manufacturers appear on the market at the same time with different and incompatible offers based on new and similar technologies. Potential customers who are initially interested in the new offer become wary when they see the diversity and incompatibility of the different propositions. They hesitate to invest (material, training) in a proposition which is not necessarily the best and which may not survive the market competition. The other extreme situation would be the monopoly of only one manufacturer. This situation could give rise to a fear of being too dependent on just one supplier.

For PCs, the market really began to develop with the arrival of IBM's PC in 1981. It had many advantages, immediate credibility, continuity, wide-ranging compatibility, etc. The success of IBM's proposition was due to the strength of the company, but also to the support of the designers of software and accessories. The customers thought they had sufficient choice (hard disk, screen, keyboard, printer, software, etc.) and could count on the competition for lower prices. Only Apple was able to remain 'independent' from the standard PC. In 1987, IBM was losing market share and decided to launch PS/2 that was based on a different and 'reserved' IBM standard, and the coalition and support did not follow. The technical advantages of the PS/2 were not strong enough to make the users leave the powerfully supported MS/DOS standard.

Given this example, we can sum up the particularities of the development of an offer based on a standard compatibility. The development of standard compatibility is linked to its openness to all or part of the industry concerned. When two standards are competing, the winner is the one gaining the most powerful support and following, despite possible technical imperfections. It means that the winner gathers a very strong coalition of players able to install a customer base at a very high speed. Credibility of the new technology stems from the mutual reinforcement of choices from as many users as possible. And many reasons can block the process. For example, we know the Dvorak keyboard can save 20 per cent in time for users of Latin keyboards, but hundreds of millions of people using Qwerty keyboards would need to be retrained. The size and cost of the operation prevent any further initiative in this direction. Two standards can coexist only if they concern totally different market segments. Finally, the speed of development of the standard and the availability of products and services using it is vital. Any delay can cause customers to hesitate – or, worse, change standard. SNR Roulements (Example 16 in Chapter 10) is a good illustration of a marketing strategy process based on this concept.

References and Further Reading

Bansard, D. (1991) 'L'offre en milieu industriel: des typologies aux stratégies', *Working Paper*, 9130, IRE EM Lyon.

Buzzel, R.R. and Gale, B. (1987) *The PIMS Principles: Linking Strategy to Performance*, New York, Free Press.

Cattin, P. and Wittink, D. (1982) 'Commercial Use of Conjoint Analysis: A Survey', *Journal of Marketing*, vol. 46, 44–53.

Chevalier, M. (1977) *Fixation des prix et stratégie marketing*, Paris, Dalloz.

Coriat, B. (1991) *Penser à l'envers: travail et organisation dans l'entreprise japonaise*, Paris, Bourgois.

Gabel, L. (ed.) (1987) *Product Standardisation as a Tool of Competitive Strategy*, INSEAD Symposium, Paris, Amsterdam, North-Holland.

Giletta, M. (1990) *Les prix: politiques, stratégies et tactiques d'entreprises*, Paris, Eyrolles.

Green, P. and Wind, Y. (1975) 'New Way to Measure Consumers' Judgments', *Harvard Business Review*, 53 (July/August), 107–17.

Grindley, P. (1990) 'Winning Standards Contests: Using Product Standards in Business Strategy', *Business Strategy Review*, 1, 71–84.

Hague, D.C. (1971) *Pricing in Business*, London, Allen & Unwin.

Stoetzel, J. and Adam, D. (1958) *Les reactions du consommateur devant les prix*, Paris, Sedes.

Tarondeau, J.C. (1993) *Stratégie industrielle*, Paris, Vuibert.

Turnbull, P.W. and Zolkiewski, J. (1997) 'Profitability in Customer Portfolio Planning', in D. Ford (ed.), *Understanding Business Markets*, New York, Dryden Press.

Discussion Questions

1 Comment on the fact that this book uses the word 'offer' rather than the more usual term 'product' that can be found in many marketing textbooks.
2 What are the different forms of adaptation of an offer in business-to-business marketing?
3 What are the respective roles of the marketing function and the commercial function in the design and implementation of an offer in business-to-business environments?
4 Why are services so important in the design of an offer in business-to-business marketing?
5 Comment on the issues of product profitability and customer profitability for a company's successful strategy.

Chapter 1
Competitiveness, Marketing and Business-to-Business Marketing
What is marketing all about
Different marketing environments
B2B marketing

Chapter 2
Business-to-Business Customers and Markets

B2B Generic Offers	Technological Innovation	Pure Services	Major Projects

PART I   STRATEGY FOUNDATIONS

Chapter 3	Chapter 4	Chapter 5	Chapter 6
Understanding Business-to-Business Purchasing	**Information and Information Systems**	**Markets and Suppliers' Strategy**	**Segmentation and Marketing Strategy**

PART II   STRATEGY IMPLEMENTATION

Chapter 7
Generic Business-to-Business Offer Design and Management

Chapter 8
Market Access and Customer Management

Chapter 9
Communication and Publicity/ Advertising

Chapter 10	Chapter 11	Chapter 12
Marketing and Technological Innovation	**The Marketing of Services**	**Major Project Marketing**

PART III   STRATEGY DESIGN

Chapter 13	**The Role and Organisation of Marketing**
Chapter 14	**Customer Position, Market Position, Marketing Strategies and Planning**
Chapter 15	**Issues and Specificities of International Marketing**
Annex	**The Internet and Marketing: Some Ideas**

8 Market Access and Customer Management

We have previously argued that a number of managers in business-to-business firms pay too little attention to the notion of *commercial efficiency*. For them, a superior offer, which usually means technical superiority, creates such an advantage that productivity and sales efficiency, or even marketing value, become of secondary importance. Low marketing budgets and poor levels of commercial investment in these companies are a direct consequence of this kind of approach.

The problem is a complex one, and our aim is not so much to oppose it as to complement it. A customer's order is just the tip of the iceberg, the visible part of company's efforts to create value and conclude transactions. It cannot be attributed to just one salesman. The problem lies in identifying all those other people involved. The design office, production team, marketing and sales divisions, switchboard operators and so on, are all part of the process. How do they co-ordinate their action? Our objective in this chapter is not to answer all the questions that need to be examined when dealing with the marketing function (Chapter 13). Rather, our aim here is to look at the decisions that a company has to make in order to optimise its commercial efficiency. This depends on two groups of factors. The first covers external factors: customers' expectations, constraints surrounding the access to markets and the corresponding costs. The second involves the internal marketing strategy adopted by the supplier, its level of interaction with its customers and consequently, its willingness to offer adaptations. We will present the different options available to managers and the conditions under which they should be used. The choices to be made will be placed in a strategic perspective in Chapters 14 and 15.

Our argument is that the objectives of market access and customer management are, as in any other company function, *efficiency* and *productivity*. They are also, as we shall see, contributors to the achievement of company profitability. These objectives concern two aspects: the management of the customer base, including the establishment and maintenance of customer relationships, and the response to logistical necessities and constraints.

To fulfil these objectives, different approaches are possible. Companies have many possibilities open to them, including that of sub-contracting or outsourcing certain tasks, which raises some interesting issues. Two extreme approaches can be where (a) the company performs all commercial tasks, via a sales force that is

236 STRATEGY IMPLEMENTATION

directly in contact with all customers and via its own logistical resources (transport, warehousing, delivery, etc.); or else (b) the company sub-contracts the whole of the function to one or more third parties.

Other than these two extremes, a range of other possibilities is possible. The sales force can be shared either between several companies, or by using an independent sales force (e.g. agents). It can act directly towards customers or manage inter-mediaries (wholesalers, distributors, etc.). These intermediaries themselves may or may not be responsible for managing the relationship with the customers. Finally, the range of choices open to the company can be influenced by market conditions that are impossible or ineffective to bypass.

We shall attempt to clarify these various routes to market by pointing out alternatives offered by the different types of 'channel players'. By this, we mean all the professions active in a broad definition of the ways to gain access to markets and customers. We shall examine indirect means of access to the market, the condi-tions of direct access and the building of a sales force. These elements will enable us to present an overview of the reasons for choosing between indirect and direct access. We will also look at the case of key accounts. We will end with the presentation of an overall framework, that of *customer portfolio management*. This approach makes it possible to identify the importance of different issues to the customer, with a view to bringing coherence between the choices of customer-dedicated investments, the market and segment strategies (see the Multistrat model, Chapter 6).

Indirect Means of Access to the Market

In almost all economic sectors, there are organisations that offer customers a wide variety of services. We will focus on just two types of intermediaries: the distri-butors, who buy from the manufacturer to resell, and the sales representatives, who at no time take title to (i.e. ownership of) the object of the exchange.

The Distributors

This is a large category, which includes very different types of companies who have very different perceptions of their role in the market. It could range from a local company employing just a few people and operating in a limited geographical area through to international groups such as Sonepar (almost 1000 sales outlets through-out the world with a turnover of 8 billion Euros in 1998) or Bearing Service Limited (part of the SKF group). group). SKF in the UK also have a range of different distributors (see <http://www.skf.co.uk/skfuk/_skf_uk_frames.htm>). Further afield, large dealerships in America are identified at <www.manufacturing.net/scl/yearbook/giantsdistributors.htm>. Some of these major international groups remain unknown to the general public: they do not operate in the more visible consumer markets, and are often the result of mergers or takeovers between average-sized local companies. This diversity, however, can be described according to a number of dimensions, of which we look at three. These are the type of *specialisation* (the result of a process analogous to that of segmentation), the integration of *added value* (similar to the definition of the offer) and the type of *service* (equivalent to the market position sought).

The type of *specialisation* is the first interesting characteristic. Business-to-business distributors are generally specialised according to industry sector in which they operate: chemicals, metrology, electronics–computers, mechanical industries, electrical equipment, etc. Only one category, that of 'industrial supplies', groups different companies whose offers are general and spread over numerous industry activities. In some sectors (chemicals, for example), specialisation remains rigorous. In others (industrial supplies, heating and plumbing), there has been an extension in activities and product ranges to several sectors. This is also the case when groups have diversified out of sectorial specialisation by buying or creating companies with larger sector coverage. (Rexel, for example, and its CDME and GDFI units). There has also been an increase in the globalisation of industrial distribution achieved through the merging of national and regional companies in order to achieve either volume advantages in negotiations with suppliers, or to reach customers who themselves are international.

There is a second type of specialisation of distributors depending on the customers that they chose to serve (the industrial sector) and the offer range (see Figure 8.1).

Bearing Service Limited is a good example of the first case of specialisation in just one technology. This group (represented in France by Roulement Service and in the UK by BSL <www.bsl.co.uk>) distributes ball bearings to users, be they industrialists, garages, maintenance or servicing companies. Its range consists mainly of SKF products with, in some cases, additions from other manufacturers, and their customers belong to different industrial sectors.

The second type of specialisation in customer activity can be illustrated by the example of the building industry. Many distributors (Dubois, Brossette, Gedimat,

Figure 8.1   Classification of distributors

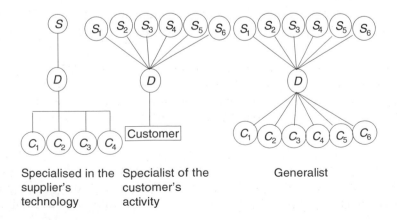

Specialised in the   Specialist of the   Generalist
supplier's   customer's
technology   activity

Point P in France) and companies such as Travis Perkins and Jewsons in the UK (see <www.travisperkins.co.uk> and <www.graham-group.co.uk>, but also the Industrial Exchange and Mart <www.iem-net.co.uk> for an online list of suppliers) buy from a selection of suppliers, offering everything that a construction company could need, such as cement, sand, reinforced concrete, paving stones, tools, security shoes, working clothes, etc. In this case, however, the specialisation remains within one industrial sector.

General distributors are usually local companies (Codima of the Brossette group, Jewsons as part of the Graham Group) that manage diverse products (construction, industrial supplies, electricity, etc.) for companies that are geographically close and belong to different industrial sectors. They could almost be called 'industrial supermarkets' and are difficult to manage with the variety of technologies, product ranges and commercial issues involved.

The *integration of added value* is a second important characteristic. Some distributors perform only 'logistical' functions (availability and delivery) of products that they buy and then sell. Others can add various functions that include transforming the product (cutting beams or reinforced concrete, polishing and preparing sheets of corrugated iron, etc.) or offering advice and training. The distributor can also undertake operations that are traditionally performed by the customer itself (heat treatment of metals, etc.). In this case, where the manufacturer does not offer some valued element, it is advantageous for the customer to benefit from the distributor's services, as long as the work is performed more efficiently than if the customers did it themselves. A good example of this type of service can be found at <www.chemstation.com>. This is extremely important, as it is one of the major reasons for a reversal of power in relationships between suppliers and distributors. If the latter, through their services, manage to attract their customers, they are no longer an alternative choice for the supplier, but a *compulsory intermediary*, because to a degree they hold the key to the access to the whole or a part of the customer base. This also means that modes of interaction are created between the distributors and the customers that can be analysed using the same methods as those that govern the direct manufacturer–customer relationships (Chapters 2 and 3). Other than geographical proximity and added value, the distributors often have a strong social interaction with the customers and in the networks. The directors of these companies are often involved in local social life, which is often an important advantage.

The predominant type of *service* corresponds to a distributor's strategy based on a very precise definition of their relationships with their customers. This will consist in offering a limited range of services rather than embracing them all. Here, excellence is the key success factor. We can identify a number of ways in which this strategy can be implemented.

- Response time to a tender can be a distributor's *raison d'être*, a way of outperforming the manufacturer. It is very often linked to the importance of geographical proximity. The distributor's sales people must be readily *available* to visit customers, a factor more decisive than achieving a daily high number of visits.

■ The technical skills of the distributors' representatives underline the technical orientation of industrial distribution, and the essential character of technical competence in establishing relationships with the customers. This means helping to define the products and their specifications, occasionally being involved in installation and implementation and more rarely in staff training. The distributor is the holder of information about all possible offers, which can mean saving time and limiting risks for the customer. The customers also know that, through the distributor, they have the support of the manufacturer, and often with better conditions than if they had approached the manufacturer directly. This takes us back to the idea that a manufacturer may or may not become involved in a relationship with a customer, and that they may prefer to lend their support to a distributor rather than having to deal with small or medium-sized companies (SMEs).

■ The distributor's *product range* is also essential. This encompasses breadth (the range of products), depth (the number of items per category), and availability of supplementary products, accessories and spare parts. Some distributors have more than 50 000 items in stock, even if many try to limit the number by defining a list of items that are available upon request. All this requires good *stock control* (centralisation, geographic location, transfer between warehouses), most often in co-operation with the manufacturers, and also networked information systems. Seeking improved productivity leads the distributors to develop their performances in logistics and information systems to accompany a reduction in the number of sites and the importance of stocks.

■ The level of *after-sales service* is an important element of certain strategies, whether performed at the customer's premises or, more rarely, at the distributor's.

It is possible to classify distributors using a different typology, based upon the type of services offered:

■ *Group 1: after-sales specialists* give greater importance to breadth of the range and to services linked to maintenance and breakdown, rather than to depth

■ *Group 2: technical assistance specialists* place importance on the advice they give to their customers, on the basis of a level of technical competence not mastered by their customers

■ *Group 3: logistics-based businesses* are always looking to make their products readily available to their customers

■ *Group 4: sales representatives* base their strategy on an aggressive sales approach; highly active, they offer a large range of not very technical products (the 'industrial supermarket' mentioned earlier).

This brief categorisation shows how diverse the world of industrial distribution is, and also the possible strategies for the distribution companies. What about the links that can exist between a distributor and a '*supplying manufacturer*'? One approach is for the distributor to be completely independent, free to stock whatever it wants to. A second approach is the practice of '*authorised distributor*' that contains certain obligations for both parties, formalised in a contract. A third, '*franchised dealership*', allows both parties to establish the conditions of a reciprocal exclusivity within a given geographic area and the distributor to use the manufacturer's label. The ultimate phase is the *legal integration of the distributor by the manufacturer* (often used by major industrial groups, ABB, SKF, etc.). Once integrated, the distributor is most often in charge of performing adaptations for the customer. The objective of such a separation of the roles is the protection of the manufacturer's productivity on the one hand, as well as providing the customer with the required adaptations. Distributor–manufacturer–customer relations enter a new phase with this kind of approach.

Other than distribution companies, who buy to sell, there are many other types of intermediaries who make market access easier. For example, transport companies can also provide intermediary storage and delivery facilities and other services (see Mory–Ancel in Example 5), in the same way as servicing and engineering companies can sometimes replace the distributor for some types of products. Several examples developed throughout this chapter show that some companies act as the distributor for players placed upstream in the value chain, even if this is not their primary role. For the manufacturer, these intermediaries – information technology firms or consulting or engineering companies – represent an additional opportunity to increase both flexibility capacity and access to certain customers. Thus, we shall treat them according to their role of distributor, even if their contribution to added value is much higher than that of an 'ordinary' distributor.

Commercial Agents

These are either individuals or companies acting on behalf of others to take orders, for which they are paid, usually in the form of a commission. A commercial agent can be a company employing several trained people, thus being in the market with its own objectives and strategies (type and level of activity, types of suppliers represented, investments, profitability) and also with a certain power of negotiation with their suppliers and their customers. They are under contract, which indicates the obligations of both parties that are legally independent. The representatives usually establish their own customer portfolio, depending upon both their competencies as well as the suppliers whom they represent. This asset allows them to play an important part in introducing any new manufacturer into the area. In some circumstances, where there are problems with importation and customs clearance, the commercial agent is often the first step used by a manufacturer to setting up abroad.

It would have been possible to deal with commercial agents in the chapter devoted to sales forces. However, we have chosen to include them here in the chapter devoted to intermediaries, as they are 'free' agents with no direct dependence on the manufacturer.

Indirect access to markets is possible through a range of intermediaries. But the choice may be not to use intermediaries at all. *Direct access* is another way, and we need to look at it further in order to explore the full range of possibilities open to any company.

Logistics and Direct Market Access

In business-to-business environments, direct market access is almost a natural development. The nature of supplier–customer relationships would appear to require this practice. However, the presence of a number of powerful intermediaries with excellent logistics systems may alter this initial approach. It is necessary to understand the conditions under which direct market access can be made: creating the logistics infrastructure required and then securing the orders. It may not appear logical to do things this way round, but what is the point of having orders if the company's organisation does not allow it to fulfil them to the satisfaction of the customer? Having observed several companies experiencing extreme difficulties in performing these tasks, it seems that setting up the logistical process is the first requirement. It is the first sign of an understanding of the market's expectations.

The design of external logistics depends on three factors: the market position sought by the company (standardisation or adaptation), customer expectations in terms of delivery (can it be the source of a competitive advantage?) and the general organisation of production. From these three factors comes the ultimate objective: delivery times promised to and accepted by the customer. Markets have their own 'rules', the result of technical constraints, forecast demand and the general organisation of the economy and the profession. These rules or conventions have developed over time: in 1955 the very basic Citroen 2CV took 18 months to deliver; in 2001, a 3-week delay for a car is definitely too long. Managing this *'time to market'* has almost become a question of survival for many companies. For others it has become a way to strengthen their competitive position. At a given moment in any company, the accepted promise of delivery is at the very heart of the logistical organisation. Such a promise concerns the product as much as the accessories or spare parts. While an aeroplane may be delivered months or even years after the order is placed, the spare parts have to be delivered in just a few hours (4 in general) anywhere in the world over a 20-year period following the original delivery.

This has many consequences for the supplier's organisation that need to be noted:

■ The organisation of the *production* itself, including the range and product design, supplier supply times, production tools and methods (in Chapter 6 we saw how marketing was concerned with these issues)

- The *level of stocks* required and their geographical distribution

- *Transport management* in terms of reliability, delays and cost

- A *'commercial' organisation* whose role is to link customer expectations (agreed delivery times) with the organisational possibilities: the setting up of delivery priorities, finished products and parts stock management, relationships with production and planning

- A *supply of information* between supplier and customer, for example based on the exchange of computerised data (Electronic Data Interchange or EDI, Internet-based).

A range of diverse studies (owing to the problems of comparing very different situations and accounting methods) have shown that the cost of the operations mentioned above, calculated as a percentage of turnover, can vary from 4 per cent (pharmaceutical products) to 14 per cent (chemical products). And, of course, there are variations between companies within the same sector. While this is obviously influenced by the value per kilogramme of the products, the figures do show that *rationalisation* of the operations is an important factor of productivity.

The second aspect of direct market access is the taking of orders. As mentioned at the beginning of the chapter, this is the result of work involving a number of individuals in the company. Among them, there are those whose task it is to deal with customer relations, and therefore taking the actual orders. We shall see that their activity is a complex one, which is the subject of the following section.

The Composition and Management of a Company's Sales Force

This involves many different points of view: for example, whether the sales force intervenes directly with the end users or intermediaries, and whether it is a integral part of the company or is shared among several companies. We shall begin by examining the questions raised when the sales force (either dependent or shared) deals directly with the end user.

A Dependent Direct Selling Sales Force

The *mission* of the sales force is that the company optimises its sales performance given its competitive position. In other words, this mission is closely related to the definition of the company's marketing position and the strategy surrounding it. Most of the problems we have encountered in firms have occurred because of a lack of clarity concerning the role of the sales force versus the company's marketing position. Being closest to the customers, salespeople who have not been given clear instructions normally determine their own ways of doing things, which could well diverge from company strategy. This strategy is very often defined by the invest-ments in research and development and manufacturing assets. Differences between commercial choices and the technical orientation of company strategy are one of the main causes of poor profitability in companies. Thus, we will stress the impor-tance of *customer portfolio management* in the second part of this chapter, and its role of clarifying the company's strategy to the sales force.

The above argument leads us to complete the definition of a sales force's mission, in as much as this raises questions concerning the relationship between commer-cial activity and the technical, and then market, potential of the company. In fact, the sales representatives have a strategic role to play owing to their contact with the customers. This is all the more true as companies seek to adapt to specific customer demands. Thus, we can define the sales force mission as follows:

- To *recognise* and *exploit* a company's *sales potential*

- To *manage* the responses a supplier must give to *customer expectations* and the activity of the different internal and external players involved in this

- To inform the company of changes in both *customer behaviour* and *demands* and in *competitors' behaviour* to help the company maintain and/or modify its competitive position

- To perform 'cold-calling' activities (to convince potential customers to enter into negotiations), to negotiate (to persuade potential customers to become part of the customer portfolio, and current customers to remain) and to *follow the clientele*

- To conclude operations correctly (to conclude the negotiations) with a *signed order.*

The *composition* of the sales force is influenced by both qualitative and quanti-tative factors. There are no definitive rules here, as each situation is different. However, we would like to put forward the following ideas. First, there is the choice to be made of the people and their level of qualification. If the relationship with the customers is based on technical grounds, then the salespeople must have the requisite technical expertise. This is different if the relationship concerns under-standing the customer's management system, as is the case for information tech-nology, general organisation problems, marketing organisation and so on. In technical environments, this would mean choosing representatives who have the same or even higher levels of expertise than the people with whom they are expected to negotiate.

One peculiarity of the business-to-business sales force is that it often includes people that have gained professional experience, often of a technical nature (design offices, laboratories, production, maintenance, etc.) before moving onto a strictly commercial function. This explains the term 'technical sales force' that is frequently used. This means that when hiring someone with a technical background, attention must be paid to other more qualitative abilities, such as ability to listen, empathy, intellectual flexibility, persuasive capacity, etc. It is common practice to define a function profile and to select staff accordingly.

The size of the sales force is typically determined in a classical fashion by establishing an average yearly time to allocate to each customer and by dividing a representative's time by this average to calculate the number of customers he or she can deal with. This is easy to calculate, based on the number of visits per year per customer and the potential visits in a year of a representative. In business-to-business environments, time spent with a customer is often short (about 20 or 25 per cent of real working time); the rest of the time is dedicated to preliminary studies, estimates, price calculations, internal contacts, travelling, etc. Thus, the calculation becomes less precise, and more qualitative elements enter the definition of the number of customers that can be assigned to a sales representative. This approach is supported by an estimate of the expected *turnover* (and/or profit margin) for all customers and the calculation of the ratio between the cost of the sales representative (nearly 100 000 Euros/year approximately) and the results obtained. The usual cost ratios of a sales force in the industrial world are between 1 and 2 per cent of the turnover, except in the computer, electronics and office materials industry where they are somewhere between 2 and 15 per cent. Obviously these figures are only indications. Finally, whether a supplier–customer relationship is continuous or intermittent can affect the ratios and the way of managing a sales force. Environments where continuous relationships are the rule suggest adopting a time-based system, whereas intermittent selling environments are more typically turnover-based. We shall return to this categorisation later in this chapter.

The *organisation* of a sales force involves two aspects, its managerial staff and its organisation structure. The managerial staff of a sales force of less than 10 people can be limited to a sales director who is responsible to the marketing director. Once we get beyond about 10, intermediary managerial staffs are typically required to look after the activity and control of the salespeople. This support was traditionally regionally managed (an office and a secretary). Recent developments in information systems, the possibility to store customer accounts, invoices, stocks and so on have led to changes. Regional directors and sales representatives work from home; they have fax machines, telephones (video conference facilities will soon be everywhere), computers, and Internet and extranet connections. Physical encounters are less and less frequent (yet there is a minimum frequency to be respected), but the content and availability of information have vastly improved.

However, for forces of over 50 people, regional managers are a kind of essential layer for leading sales action, and the trend is to provide them with a *regional marketing team* in order to implement national strategy at regional level. This means determining a potential regional turnover and a strategy that takes into account the particularities of the customer portfolio, or else introducing regional specialists of a specific technology or industrial sector. This means the role of a regional sales manager is threefold: to define a regional marketing policy, be in contact with customers in certain circumstances and motivate the sales force.

The distribution of the force is usually done according to two criteria: it must be sufficiently close (geographical criterion) and sufficiently skilled (specialisation criterion). For example, when the nuclear industry requires a technically advanced sales approach, then a generalist will not be suitable. The solution is to 'remove' the industry from this field of normal sales action and to place it in the care of a specialist who is usually based at the head office. This person therefore has a double role, sales and marketing, and as such an industrial sector is in fact a market segment in itself, which justifies a specialised offer and sales approach. The question of key account customers often requires a similar approach, as we shall see later in this chapter. Moreover, it is also possible to place such specialists in the regional teams to act purely as sales representatives or for marketing support, as mentioned above. Two issues influence the *motivation and control* of the salespeople. These are management's creation and upkeep of good relationships within the team, and a satisfactory management system. The two are obviously inseparable. The first gives the salespeople the required peace of mind to operate effectively – their work is often lonely, and physically and mentally demanding. The second offers the necessary rigour in an environment where the 'personal coefficient', if important, must not be the explanation for everything.

Without going into the details of the issues and methods involved, some points can be identified. Efficient sales force management is based on two dimensions, the ability to act and the will to act. The development of the ability to act is based on training (technical knowledge, working methods and tools, negotiation skills), thereby allowing each individual to develop competencies. The will to act depends on motivation, which itself depends on the relevant use of three means:

- To clearly define the missions, jobs and expected results; *continuously assessing* results and objectives is essential for motivation
- To recognise the efforts, performances and results by coherent systems of *stimulation* and *remuneration*
- To evaluate the salespeople in terms of the previously agreed qualitative and quantitative objectives.

A system of motivation and control has to be based on objectives, means and results. To achieve this, it must be possible to define a *potential turnover* for the individual's customer base, time-based objectives in terms of market share or turnover and other related means of action. This sequence is a necessary condition for sales force efficiency. This means a salesperson can be evaluated on three points: the gap between results and targets, quantity of work and the quality of this work. The gap is mainly an indicator. Explanations can be influenced by a particular competitive position in one area (this must be carefully informed and checked) or individual reasons. The causes linked to the salesperson can be twofold, a lack of activity (hence the need to check the number of visits, travel, wasted time, etc.) and poor quality of activity (poor negotiation skills, insufficient technical competencies, incorrect identification of the purchasing centre, lack of knowledge of the customers, etc.). Customer understanding and information are so critical for efficiency that a salesperson in the industrial world must have good training in business-to-business marketing and the methods that have been developed on a sales level. They must master the procedures that can allow them to use efficiently the methods of the risk approach as well as the keeping and updating of customer files and the management of the customer portfolio.

Shared Direct Selling Sales Forces

The commercial agents described above would strictly speaking not be considered as a sales force as there are no hierarchical links between them and the company that gives them a mission. However, there is another group of actors who are similar in many ways: the 'representatives working for several firms', or sales reps. These are individuals who, with a particular legal status, represent several firms simultaneously in a specific area or for specific customers. Even if they operate for several firms, they are company employees (their pay being based on a percentage of turnover, no expenses included). They have customer portfolios and work according to their own objectives and the converging imperatives – and sometimes contradictory ones – of their different employers.

The management of this category is very different. Despite legal ties between them and the employers, we must remember that they are also in a relationship with several employers and therefore have a greater degree of freedom than a normal member of staff. The 'objectives–means (training and support)–results' sequence is thus vital and is enriched by the quality of human relations between the management and the sales reps.

We would add that some organisations have been set up to 'rent' sales forces either on a geographical basis or for a clearly defined clientele. This is known as a 'back-up' sales force. They help to solve problems of access to either a geographical territory or specific customers. They can be used for either the whole offer or a part of it – for example, customers not normally solicited by the sales force. In France, there is the Districom Company, for example: the cost for a sales rep is around 250 Euros per day plus expenses. With expenses, the cost of a visit comes to somewhere between 150 Euros for two visits per day, and 80 Euros for four visits per day. Two or more companies can also share a sales force, whereby either a sales company is created to operate for partners, or a company markets the offers of another company under contract or even based on other forms of contract.

How to Deal with Intermediaries

The management of commercial agents or of intermediaries raises the same questions as that of a sales force. The differences are due to the fact that they are autonomous and have their own strategies and respond to specific constraints and competitive situations. Their management must integrate any differences that have to be accounted for in order to build efficient relationships between the manufacturer and its commercial network.

Many points must be taken into consideration:

■ A manufacturer is confronted by the need to make sure its commercial partners and also their staffs are *constantly interested in the relationship* and show a positive attitude towards the person

■ The intermediary needs *technical support, training and marketing tools* just like an integrated sales force

■ The intermediary's constraints and objectives can be considered as supporting elements for the relationship to gain in efficiency in the eyes of the end user; for example, there could be agreements concerning the spread and level of stocks, the regularity of deliveries or the upholding of guarantees – the common aim is to *satisfy the end customer and to get both partners to make money*

■ This has to involve the staff of the commercial partners; but it cannot be done without the agreement of the company's management, which can come in the shape of *annual motivation and support plans*.

Choosing Between Dependent or Shared Sales Force

There are many reasons in favour of the solution of a shared sales force. The first concerns the type of offer and the relationship sought with the customers. The lower the interaction and offer flexibility, the more it becomes possible to use a shared sales force. Conversely, the more company strategy is based on high interaction and offer flexibility, the more a dependent sales force is used. Management should be concerned about the relative efficiency of the two methods in different marketing situations. We need to analyse the situations from the point of view of the relationships with the customers, but also concerning the internal management of the offer flexibility.

The second reason is a question of cost: a shared sales force represents for its largest part a variable cost and lowers company risk as pay is only due once the turnover has been achieved; and this usually represents a predetermined percentage. A dependent sales force represents a fixed cost, whatever the turnover achieved. New companies often tend to prefer variable costs and begin with a shared sales force whenever possible. Later, they can change their options: variable costs can become such that they are higher than the cost of a dependent sales force. As the feeling of risk related to turnover disappears at the same time, the creation of a dependent sales force would probably appear a more efficient and less costly alternative. It should be added than getting out of a commercial agents system can be costly as many European countries' legal systems ensure statutory protection that gives them the right of ownership over their customer base that the company has to 'buy back' when it separates from the reps.

To conclude, our intention is not to replace existing works on sales force management. Our aim has been to highlight some specific issues involved in the management of sales forces in the business-to-business world and to reposition the sales force in a more general perspective of the relevant marketing process.

The Choice of a Method of Market Access

The choice is not simple, nor always obvious. There are also different opinions among practising managers. On the one hand, customer preference is most often for a direct relationship with the supplier, in order to obtain the information and technical skills required. On the other hand, distributors have other skills, they perform services that manufacturers cannot, and sometimes they are the ones who finalise negotiations with a customer, making their presence almost compulsory. In addition, when determining a manufacturer's marketing strategy, it is the structure of the portfolio of customers that explains the type of relationship to establish with customers. So is it a voluntary choice, or is the choice imposed on the manufacturer? We will examine first the reasons to use intermediaries, before presenting an overall synthesis on strategy design.

Reasons for Choosing Intermediary Distributors

This is the result of the convergence of several different and mainly independent points of view.

■ The first is to evaluate the manufacturer's *freedom in relation to intermediary distributors*. This is limited if the distributors dominate customer relationships to an extent where they become compulsory. Information technology consultants – even if not really distributors – often have this role for manufacturers concerning the most important clientele. They define the computer system and the software and hardware that are required. So the manufacturer can only accept this and therefore is dependent on the intermediary to sell its machines. Such an operation, however, cannot be merely a one-shot action and requires upstream collaboration between the manufacturer and the service company to be successful. And this takes us to the question of the definition of a long-term distribution policy that we shall look at later. In other professions, like the building materials trade, there is a clear distributor domination of the relationship with the end users.

■ The second is to look closely at the importance of the *direct relationship between the supplier and the customer*, from both their points of view. How does the customer benefit from the direct relationship with the supplier, in comparison to a relationship with a distributor or other intermediaries? Who – the supplier or the distributor – is the best placed to offer the customer the advantages of strong interaction (product flexibility, advice before and after delivery, maintenance, etc.)?

■ The third is based on the issues raised in the second point but seen from a different angle. A manufacturer's offer is only one element of the response to the *global problems of the customer*. When IBM changed its marketing strategy, moving from the sale of products to a complete service ('we no longer sell computers, we sell solutions') including the design of computer systems, software packages, equipment and the starting-up of the system (training, support, etc.), it noticed that a 'per professional sector' approach was more efficient than a general 'computer-based' approach. The customers, particularly SMEs, who lacked any real internal computing skills, were appreciative of the IBM people's know-how of their profession and the flexibility of the solutions on offer. How is it possible to satisfy customers who work in such different sectors as the pharmacy industry, mechanics, the wines and spirits trade, architects, etc.? IBM developed a network of agents and distributors who were specialised in different trades and named 'External Resources' to be able to offer customers the required skill and adaptation. And this is a point of view that we have already expressed in many ways, when presenting the choice between internal and external resources.

■ The fourth is based on the contradictions generated by the issues involved in a *diversification of the offer* (segmentation, adaptation) and the search to *improve productivity*. The adaptations that result from a manufacturer's strategic choice usually weigh heavily on manufacturing productivity, provoking the need to create means to protect it. One of them is that the supplier maintains a strategy of standardisation but, concerned by the need to respond correctly to customer expectations, transfers the corresponding operations of adaptation to the intermediary. Here we have the problem of sharing the added value of an offer throughout the value chain. A manufacturer's choice could be to modify their offer towards greater possibilities of adaptation and to maintain a direct relationship with customers. As this evolution leads to a difficult and costly reorganisation of industrial production, so the manufacturer prefers (often unwillingly) to abandon part of the final added value of the offer to limit investments and maintain productivity. This means that they have to change strategy on two points. First, they have to make sure that the basic production can subsequently support transformation procedures (delayed differentiation). Secondly, they transfer part of the know-how to the distributor to enable them to operate correctly. Sometimes it is the manufacturers who ask the distributors to equip themselves to take over part of the clientele and the corresponding technical operations, which is like assuring the level of interaction required by the customer through a network. We feel it is obvious that this can apply to a customer, a group of customers, a market segment or all the market. Such a strategy can lead a manufacturer to take over the control of the distributors. The Usinor Group, for example, has integrated a number of distributors (in France: Nozal, Longometal, Merlin; in Germany: Ancofer; in America: Edgcomb; in the UK: ASD, etc.) that perform operations of finishing and technical assistance. This has led to such concepts as: 'steel service centres' and 'technical distribution'. The Group has also created specialised sales companies (Le Fer Blanc, Le Matériel De Voie, Ugine-Service, etc.) or generalists (Valor, Daval, Francosteel, etc.) to develop its assistance to key account customers.

■ The fifth involves considering the *average importance of the customers to the supplier* (potential annual turnover, average order size) and the *cost of direct market access*. For numerous and widespread customer bases, and even more so when the supplier represents only a small part of the customer's supplies, the use of intermediary distributors is an efficient, economically sound solution. For example, it would be out of the question for Schneider Legrand, the world leader for low-tension electrical equipment, to seek direct access to the 300 000 European electrical fitters that are their customers for low-tension equipment. As most of these fitters are small/very small companies, the use of distributors such as Rexel or Sonepar facilitates solving logistical and relational issues. Thus, the aim is to *optimise the market access cost/efficiency ratio* in accordance with a given clientele structure.

Elements of a Market Access Strategy

While remembering that the choice depends for a large part on the extent to which the supplier's strategy is based on standardisation or adaptation, we can summarise the pros and cons of direct market access in Table 8.1.

While the choice of direct access is clear when the manufacturer pays for everything, the choice of access through an intermediary is more complicated. We have seen that relationships between a manufacturer and the intermediaries can vary and the examples of Schneider, IBM and Usinor demonstrate this well. We have to examine this phenomenon more closely. One can observe several types of distribution policy:

■ Intensive distribution involves looking for the *greatest possible coverage of the market* by any means available. The result is that the manufacturer has little control over the development of competition among the distributors. This can lead, particularly for new products that generate gains in market share and profit for the distributors, to conflicts owing to price differences for the end customer proposed by the competing distributors. This problem often raises the issue of the structuring of the manufacturer's conditions of sale.

■ Selective distribution concerns the desire to limit distribution to *distributors of a certain quality*. This policy has been deemed anti-competitive in the European

Table 8.1 Pros and cons of direct market access

Advantages	Drawbacks
■ Complete marketing control + Direct relationships with the customers (proximity) ■ Control of the interaction with the customers	■ High cost ■ Difficulties of coping with a large number of customers with weak purchasing potential ■ Giving up to competition of – customers loyal to distributors – market share held by distributors
■ Technological control	■ Rigidity, difficulty to provide answers to new or abnormal requirements ■ Difficulty and cost of adaptations requested by the customers
■ Logistic control	■ Centralisation and rigidity ■ Importance and cost of inventories ■ Importance of customers' credit ■ Cost of approaching numerous and dispersed customers ■ Cost of approaching minor customers (weak purchasing potential)

Community and banned except in very special circumstances. The criteria can be, for example, the possession of a specific material, the presence of specifically qualified persons, etc. The advantage for a supplier is to limit, without actually suppressing, the competition and the conflicts between distributors as they are less numerous and closer to the manufacturer.

■ Exclusive distribution goes even further in the search for *competition-free distribution*. It involves the creation of extremely strong links with the manufacturer. Selection can be geographic (a given sector), clientele (garage mechanics) or based on a precise offer or a combination of the three. The principle of exclusivity is its reciprocal, with the manufacturer promising not to create new competition within the 'area' given to the 'exclusive' distributor. Société Pepro (Rhône Poulenc Agrochimie, now Aventis) adopted such a system in the 1970s. The company had suffered from competition between distributors for both their new and original products. The distributors adopted a policy of price reductions to beat the competition. This meant reducing profit margins that, when they became so low as to be of questionable profitability, the distributors moved away to look for other new and original products. The consequences for the manufacturer were conclusive: a drop in profit margin owing to the distributors' policy of price reductions, then more importantly, a drop in the market life-cycle of the new product. The new policy meant selecting distributors for different crops (cereals, vines, trees, etc.) according to their skills and their actual position in the crop in the geographical area in question.

■ *Franchise distribution* takes the selection procedure even further. The manufacturers authorise the distributor to use their brand as a sign, and in return they

Table 8.2   The allocation of distribution tasks

List of tasks	To be executed by		
	Manu-facturer	Distributor	Third party
Marketing and sales			
■ Offer design			
■ Negotiation of the content of the offer			
■ Finishing of the offer to customer's specifications			
■ Drawing up estimates			
■ Price and payment terms definition			
■ Handling of the customer			
■ Prospecting new customers			
■ Technical and market information			
■ Information on the customer's financial situation			
■ Assistance on design of the customer's specifications			
■ Specificiations design			
■ Assistance in putting into service			
■ Training of customer's personel			
■ Maintenance and care			
■ Repair			
■ ...			
Logistics			
■ Packing			
■ Finished products warehousing			
■ Spare parts warehousing			
■ Orders management and planning			
■ Commercial planning			
■ Transport and delivery			
■ ...			
Finance			
■ Customer's credit			
■ Customer's credit management			
■ ...			

transfer part of their know-how. There are a lot of similarities with the system used with car dealers.

These various ideas, however, do not mean that to gain direct access to customers the manufacturer must choose one and only one of the above possibilities.

The Distribution of Tasks Between the Manufacturer and Their Partners

A company determines its policy of access to markets depending both on its strategy and the possibilities open to it. Table 8.2 presents a simple method to think about these choices. This approach, however elementary it may seem, allows management to define a sales organisation by integrating all the possibilities that exist in a diversified and dynamic economic environment. The central aspect is for the manufacturer to determine carefully *what constitutes the heart of its activity and to define its exact role within the value chain.* Secondary tasks are then those undertaken by the distributor rather than being performed by the manufacturer itself. Careful examination of these activities in terms of productivity and capital expenditure often reveals that intermediaries could most often manage them more economically. Thus, Rank Xerox transformed part of its sales teams into legally independent agents who were given part of the customer base and product range; however, it kept control of the entire after-sales service. Let us refer to the Mory–Ancel relationship (Example 5) that also sheds some light on this subject. Thus, it would appear that the choices made are not only the result of deliberate decisions, but also the seizing of opportunities and of various learning processes.

The diversity of its customer base and strategic positions can lead a company to adopt several solutions simultaneously. However, before looking at this point, we must first examine the case of customers who represent a major stake for the company – the *key account customer*.

The Special Case of Key Account Customers

Major customers who represent huge business volumes and are difficult to manage have always confronted suppliers. Large administrative organisations, semi-public companies and certain industrial groups belong to this category. There are two factors that have contributed to the growth in number of these key account customers. The *speed of industrial concentration* occurring in almost all sectors means most suppliers, whatever their size and geographic area of activity, are affected. The second factor is the spread of professionalisation and the rationalisation of purchases in this type of company (see Chapter 3). It is becoming less and less feasible for companies to base their strategy on exploiting local relationships only, or to rely on historical personal links.

A key account is a large company with a complex purchasing centre and decision-making process. Added to this, these organisations combine both a varying degree of centralisation or co-ordination and a set-up linked to the existence of a number of geographically dispersed units (or decision centres).

For the supplier, such accounts represent major stakes, particularly in concentrated markets. They make up the core of their customer portfolio. They require special attention owing to their importance, and demand particular management methods that can deal with their specific requirements. The problem is twofold: to understand and follow the customer, and to mobilise enough internal human, technical and financial resources. The complexity of the structure and customer organisation is such that a member of the sales force dealing with a particular unit (a factory, division, subsidiary, etc.) is unlikely to grasp all the ins and outs of the negotiation he or she is conducting. It is almost impossible to identify all the actors of the purchasing centre. The solution is to name one person responsible for identifying and understanding the customer's decision process and strategies. This is the price to pay for working together. Simultaneously, the relationship with the customer requires the mobilisation of many *internal resources* for the creation and setting up of these actions. The risks of underinvesting, overinvesting, or inadequate investing all increase. It is vital to define, activate and closely co-ordinate the required internal resources. This demands a specific organisation, one that is usually called the '*key account function*'.

The minimum level of co-ordination offered by the supplier would deal with the information concerning the characteristics of the key account exchanged between the different individuals and functions involved. The most important co-ordination is the setting up of an organisation and a key account strategy based on the methods outlined in this book: the risk approach, customer file, information system and action plan. Thus, it may be relevant to consider a key account customer as a *market segment*, as shown in Chapter 6. Two forms of organisation can be identified for the key account function, the 'mixed' form and the 'dedicated' form.

The 'mixed' form involves a member of the sales force, whose activity includes a major unit of the key account, *managing the key account in addition to other relationships*. This solution limits the costs and involves the sales function. Moreover, the importance of the part of the key account in the sales representatives' customer portfolio means that they are deeply involved in its management. There are problems, however. The person responsible must learn more about the plans and global understanding of the customer, develop its contact capacity and organisation skills. They must be prepared to devote a lot of time and energy and to rally support so as not to simply accept price reductions. Moreover, they must be able to muster their sales colleagues to work on common issues that do not always correspond to an important individual objective. Experience shows that this type of organisation is interesting when the management is not excessively complex and the customer does not have unreasonable expectations. If such were the case, the 'dedicated' form would be more appropriate.

The 'dedicated' form corresponds to the creation of a '*key account manager*' responsible for specific tasks concerning the customer and the co-ordination of the relationship. This person is dedicated full-time just to the management of this one relationship. The success of this job is not necessarily related to a mere detailed description of the work involved. Indeed, it is difficult to define and determine *a priori* all the tasks involved. Thus, Pardo (1995) defined the task as the 'unclear function'. There is no hierarchical link between the manager and the sales force, and therefore their capacity to direct the actions in a precise direction depends more on their *internal legitimacy* than the technical means used. This legitimacy depends on a number of factors. These include their background, experience (usually they are over 40 and have spent their whole career in the same company), the support of the hierarchy and their position in the company set-up and their knowledge of the decisive actors and decision process in both the customer's and their own company. The choice of person for the job requires careful thought. Often, problems are related to a lack of legitimacy.

Apart from the computer industry, key account managers are a relatively recent development, and there is little information available. Such forms of organisation are currently the subjects of research (Pardo, Salle and Spencer, 1995; Naudé and McClean, 1999). Several months, or years, are necessary for the company and actors to integrate this new profession (Millman and Wilson, 1995, 1996). Let us now look at how this function can be incorporated into the sales organisation.

The Sales Organisation of a Business-to-Business Company

Here, we will look at the questions concerning the organisation that are directly related to sales. Chapter 13 will deal with marketing in general, which will allow us to position sales in marketing and to define its contribution to the design and implementation of marketing strategy. Three specific aspects must be considered in the sales organisation of a business-to-business company:

- The recognition of having to deal with very different customers, with diverse structures and expectations

- Consequently management has to find solutions mixing direct and indirect access to these customers

- The position of technical support functions that are necessarily involved before, during and after the sale.

The first of these three points is the most important. A company that has to deal only with one marketing situation will easily solve problems concerning the sales organisation with its own sales force. The problems occur from the moment the company recognises the variety of marketing situations it has to deal with, and accepts the challenge to adapt its sales organisation accordingly. Companies are too often reluctant to make this effort. This is understandable in as much as the increasing complexity of a sales structure is costly, and managers are not very keen to accept this as an investment. And we must recognise that it is not always easy to prove the profitability of such an organisation – and certainly less easy than proving it for a new manufacturing capability.

To look at this further, let us take the example of the Roulements SA (RSA) company (Table 8.3 in Example 14).

The organisation of RSA shows a certain level of flexibility to the demands found in different marketing environments. It results from the complexity that needs to be recognised and dealt with. Indeed, one cannot always ask individuals to go from one extreme to another without it affecting their efficiency. If, nevertheless, that is what they are requested to do, some end up making 'non-official' choices, such as not paying full attention to some categories of customers. These may well lead to dropping a complete activity while this has never been expressed as company strategy. It is thus important that the choice of customers is a major strategic decision and that this is treated in terms of objectives and means, particularly those that pertain to the sales organisation.

Table 8.3   Roulements SA: sales organisation

Automotive division

Sales manager	Technical assistance manager
Sales engineers	Technical assistance engineers
10	10

- Sales engineers live in their customers' country
- Technical support engineers are with headquarters
- I sale engineer and I technical support engineer are allocated to I major customer or to 2 or 3 less important customers
- The sales engineer of the country of one customer's headquarters plays a pilot role to other sales engineers dealing with this customer

General industry division

Sales managers

5 area managers

Standard department	Special products department
■ Industrial distribution channels	■ 20 sales engineers
■ 20 sales engineers	■ 10 assistance engineers
■ General public distribution channels	■ 10 after-sales technicians
■ 10 agents	
■ Commercial subsidiaries in other countries have a similar but reduced organisation	

Example 14 Roulements SA

> The company is a large European producer of ball bearings used in almost all industrial activities. It has a large range of standard products (several thousand) and also makes specific models when necessary.
>
> This example is not a general model of commercial organisations, but it does illustrate how one company dealt with these questions at a given moment of its development:
>
> - The company has recognised that the car industry demands special skills and a degree of flexibility such that, for potentially important customers, the car manufacturers (10–20 million ball-bearings for a car model with large sales during its life-time), it is necessary to create an autonomous sales division.
>
> - The salespeople are technically competent; however, they are supported by a team of technicians linked to a technical back-up structure that assures internal relations with the design, quality and production divisions.
>
> - Because the key accounts are so important, sales representatives–engineer combinations are given 1 such customer or at most 2 or 3 to provide availability, and very precise knowledge of their specific ways and requirements.
>
> - The 'key account management' function facilitates the solution of the problems linked to the international co-ordination of relationships with largely international manufacturers. Other than a national duty to perform, the sales representative in the company's country of origin has to co-ordinate actions undertaken by colleagues in other countries, and, in return, they must keep them informed of any changes in the relationship with the customer, etc. This is an example of the mixed form of key customer account management.
>
> (continued)

Example 14 Roulements SA

- The existence of a car division with certain autonomy is the recognition of the importance of the sector for the supplier's activity and of a high level of flexibility for the customers.

- The existence of the 'general industry division' is the result of the decision concerning the car division. Its structure is evidence of the fact that it manages heterogeneous marketing situations in terms of both the customer relation and the nature of the offers.

- In the 'general industry division', the distinction between the standard department and the speciality department is due to the differences between the two approaches. One customer can purchase standard RSA ball-bearings from a distributor and also study a particular problem with the specialities department. This organisation needs the back-up of a good marketing information system (see Chapter 4).

- In the standard department, two different situations exist: the sale by catalogue of standard products to industrial distributors (including car bearings for garage mechanics for maintenance and repair) and the sale to the general public through specialised distributors of bearings bought by people who repair their cars themselves.

- For the general public, the products sold are the same as those marketed to the car producers, but packed differently with more detailed instructions.

- As RSA's offer to the specialised consumer distribution channels is limited, a specific sales force could not be justified. Also, the type of relationship involved is less technical than the salespeople's usual profile, which has led to the introduction of multicompany representatives to deal with these more commercial orientated customers (price, availability, possible reductions, etc.). The use of a distribution network requires a well-built sales team designed to manage the distributors. The mission, the composition, the size, the organisation and motivation of this kind of sales force should be thought about as much as if it were one's own dependent force.

- More than just commercial relationships, the technical sales people in general industry assure technical support to the distributors of the end customers, the training of storepeople and the distributor's sales people.

- The existence of these two teams in charge of different distribution circuits leads to the creation of 2 jobs, 2 sales managers, and 1 for each circuit.

- The specialities department was designed as an autonomous unit, able to cope with all of a customer's demands. It is responsible for customer satisfaction from before the sale to after the sale.

When examining RSA, we realised just how many marketing situations are possible for one basic product. RSA and the car manufacturer design the bearing, which is delivered and installed on the car for which it was designed. The standard department delivers the same bearing to its industrial distribution network to supply garages. The manufacturer itself under their own brand name could also deliver it. The same bearing is delivered, in different packaging, to the general public distribution network, etc. This just shows how important it is to control all the offers based on the same product and to check the prices offered and the sales conditions. This variety also leads to serving customers with different sales structures, which also raises problems.

Customer Portfolio Management

This important phase of marketing strategy is based on three main elements: the type of customers, the mobilisation of resources to be used in the relationship and the specificities of strategy in business-to-business marketing. The *potential market* that is accessible for a company given its strategic choices is made up of easily identifiable customers. The number is generally limited or most of the potential is represented by just a few accounts (the Paneto 20/80 rule applies). Thus, it is a perfectly normal procedure to consider customers individually, and to make comparisons between the major company customers or all of them.

The positions held by a supplier have certain stability, as do those of the competitors. The threat of risk is an efficient antidote to rapid changes. However, not all customers are of the same interest to a supplier, some are more open to change, others are faster in their decision making, etc. Moreover, to win over a potential customer takes *a lot of time* and requires *mobilising internal resources* (involvement of the hierarchy, public relations, demonstrations, tests, etc.) which are scarce and costly. It is often argued that the creation of a new customer costs around 4 or 5 times more than the managing of an existing relationship. So the investment is huge. The resources used for one customer will not be available for another, and so it is necessary to judge the importance and possibilities offered by customers and potential customers.

Implementing the strategy means finding customers who will really favour its value. Once the segmentation has been accomplished, the target segments chosen and the base offers defined, the salespeople must not waste resources on uses other than those identified in the priorities. How can they know whether a particular customer belongs to a particular segment? The Multistrat model (Figure 6.2) clearly shows the links between the decisions, but another method to treat the information would be helpful to make the right choices. Indeed, the closer we get to the reality of supplier–customer relationships, the more important the details become. Busy with the everyday tasks with each customer, a salesperson can lose touch with the issues related to the customer base and be far from optimising commercial investments. If their managers cannot or do not check on this, the danger of poor competitive positioning increases and consequently a drop in profitability is possible. The coherence between the strategic choices looked at in previous chapters and the present and potential customers approach begins to make sense. The choice of a degree of involvement in relation to certain customers is as strategic as, for example, defining a path for technical research or a major manufacturing investment. We have seen many situations in which salesmen were bringing to their company customers whose expectations were so very different from the company's normal strategies: low production runs for a high-production-run tool; a simplified offer and low price for a strategy of high performance products supported by a policy of sophisticated services, etc.

This involves certain requirements. The company must have a strategy that is clear, understood and shared. Chapter 14 looks at the issues of planning and formalising the strategies. One or two points need to be mentioned here. The salesmen must know and understand the strategy to be able to make clear choices among the potential customer base and to defend their choice with their management. This discussion may centre on agreements to carry out 'pilot' studies with certain customers and the latitude to give to this initial exchange. This practice characterises the company that is learning to recognise and seize new opportunities. Such discussion is possible only if a 'rule' exists and if procedures and methods are designed in order to identify such opportunities 'honestly'. See Chapter 14 for the contribution of the management of customer portfolios to strategic thinking. Let us now describe the standard operational tool it represents for the salespeople, a useful tool of synthesis for the directing of sales action.

The Principles of Customer Portfolio Management

As seen with RSA (Example 14), the principles we have chosen to develop are quite general. However, their application differs according to the structure of the customer base. For example, for a very concentrated market with limited customers (automobile manufacturers), the application of portfolio management as such makes no sense, even if one tries to determine whether the supplier should invest in one manufacturer rather than another. As explained in Figure 6.7, these choices are simultaneous in both perspectives, strategic and commercial. Therefore, the method is more generally directed towards relatively dispersed market structures.

Let us now focus on a defined unit. The method is adaptable to different definitions (geographic sectors, customer types, etc.) and to different sizes (region, country, continent, etc.). It is based on a principle that is close to that of the activity portfolios matrix in Chapter 5 – in other words taking a look at two independent sets of criteria, and making use of yet another 2 × 2 matrix. The two axes are not predetermined. They represent issues that are important to the company in dealing with a number of customers. They can be defined in different ways, as long as the two axes are relatively independent. However, it is not possible to give just one definition to cover all the marketing situations. Let us now present some versions that are based on the distinctions that we have looked at previously.

First, let us distinguish those customer–supplier relationships based on *continuous* supply as compared to *intermittent* supply. In the first case, we must identify the situation of current and potential customers separately, the issues being very different for the supplier. In the second, having been a customer's supplier 3 or 5 years ago is an advantage, but in reality the situation is similar to that of a potential customer with no previous sales. Intermittent supply corresponds to the marketing of capital goods for example. Thus, it covers the area of major investments (factories, civil engineering, building, etc.), which, because of their volume and low renewal rate, shall be dealt with in Chapter 12.

In the case of *continuous* supply, the two axes might be:

- *Current customers*. First, the customer's *structural attractiveness* ('structural' meaning the most inherent or permanent elements – structural – of customer selection) for the supplier, which means a customer's suitability to a supplier's strategy. Secondly, we might consider the *vulnerability of the supplier's position* with the customer, (meaning the level of investment required to remain with the customer). Depending upon company strategy, this axis can be changed by renaming it *supplier development possibilities*. The dynamics of the supplier–customer relationship will determine which of the two possibilities is chosen.

- *Potential customers*. The *structural attractiveness* again comes first, but here associated with *entry possibilities* to the potential customer, which expresses both the level of openness to the supplier and the amount of investment required.

For an *intermittent* supply environment, it does not appear appropriate to make the distinction between customers and potential customers, but rather to examine the *structural attractiveness* of the customer and the *interest of the business* for the supplier. These two axes represent the supplier strategy on the one hand and on the second a double evaluation of the opportunity (Is the customer attractive? Is the business interesting?) Another possibility could be to distinguish between *the structural attractiveness of the customer* **and** *the business* from the *required level of investment*.

It is obvious that the method is both flexible and versatile. The company can adapt it to its particular situation and issues by studying the possibilities presented in Figure 8.2. The application of the method requires following particular steps: the definition of the customer entity, the choice of two criteria for the axes, the weighing and measuring of the criteria and the definition of actions according to present customer and potential customer positions on the matrix.

The *definition of the customer entity* was presented in Chapter 4, in other words, the unit that has meaning from a marketing point of view (identification, allocation of resources and evaluation of results). The choice of the *criteria for the two axes* depends on actual company strategy. A customer that is not very attractive for a company using a niche strategy, could be very interesting for a volume-based strategy. The criterion of *structural attractiveness* (customers and potential customers) represents the basis of the supplier's strategy, and involves establishing a ranking between the customers by estimating their score on this criterion. The criterion of customer financial health is probably the only criterion that can be given 0 or a veto score at the very beginning of a relationship. The *vulnerability of the position* criterion includes several aspects: an inadequate supplier offer for new issues involved, the consequences of claims, of difficult relationships, the efforts made by

Figure 8.2 The axes of a customer portfolio matrix

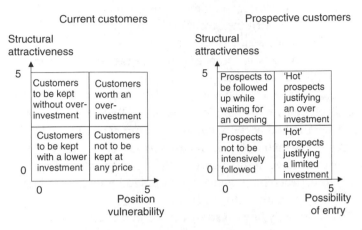

Case of a continuous supply

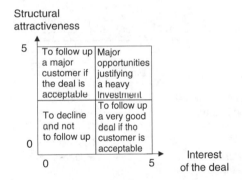

Case of an intermittent supply

the competition, changes in the purchasing centre (always dangerous for the present supplier), etc. The *entry possibilities* criterion expresses the probable chances for success for the supplier with a potential customer: offer advantages, new possibilities of price reductions, problems with the existing supplier, changes in the purchasing centre (always an opportunity for new suppliers), etc. The *interest in the business* criterion includes turnover, expected profit margin, problems involved, the advantage in relation to the competition, the freedom of choice for the purchaser, the creation of a reference, etc. Some of these criteria can be cyclical: for example, they can be linked to the production schedule.

The process that we propose is based on a typical multiple-criteria decision making procedure. This involves three steps: determining the *attributes* to use, scoring them (out of 5) and then scoring the potential customers on the same set of criteria (again out of 5). *Evaluating the criteria* involves scoring them. For example, among the criteria of interest for the business, 'the expected profit margin' could be given a score of 3 out of 5 and 'turnover' a score of 1, thereby describing a strategy where the company is looking to maximise profits. This weighting operation is delicate and often requires testing several times. A score of 0 for a company on one of the attributes means a veto mark, and is generally used only concerning the financial health of a company. Using this approach, a company might classify the 'changes in the purchasing centre' criterion on the 'entry possibilities' axis in the following way when evaluating potential customers: 1 (no change), 2 (slight change), 3 (major change), 4 (changes that could lead to a change in supplier), 5 (changes that include elements potentially favourable to us). This illustrates that the method accepts *subjective judgements* in evaluating a customer. But it also tries to normalise the degree of seriousness of these events and to give a *quantified form* to these judgements so they can be compared from one case to another. Thus, it respects the judgement expressed by its author and forces the user to supply precise explanations to support it.

Table 8.4 shows exactly how to construct a criteria grid. It shows the criteria used by a supplier of industrial automatons. The nature of the chosen criteria expresses

Table 8.4   Grid of criteria for the evaluation of a customer or potential customer portfolio

Criteria for prospect attractiveness		Grade	Criteria for possibilities of entry		Grade
Potential annual turnover	>20 000 Euros	5	Level of technical investments within 5 years	Very high	5
	10 000–20 000 Euros	4		High	4
	2000–10 000 Euros	3		Medium	3
	1000–2000 Euros	2		Weak	2
	<1000 Euros	1		Very weak	1
Importance of price in buying decision	Low importance	5	Degree of sophistication of investment projects	Very high	5
	Little importance	4		High	4
	Medium importance	3		Medium	3
	Important	2		Weak	2
	Very important	1		Very weak	1
Technological level	Local networks	5	Position of main supplier	Important claims	5
	Logic modules softwares	4		Secondary claims	4
	Software supervisors	3		Satisfying	3
	Software communication	2		Strong	2
	Automatons	1		Very strong	1
Manufacturing competence	Very high	5	Supplier change	Very low cost	5
	High	4		Low cost	4
	Medium	3		Average cost	3
	Weak	2		High cost	2
	Very weak	1		Very high cost	1
Financial situation	High profit	5	Delay for a decision	Immediate	5
	Profitable	4		Less than 1 year	4
	Balanced	3		1 year	3
	Losses	2		2 years	2
	Important losses	1		3 years	1
	Veto	0			

the fact that the company prefers a high level of customer (or potential customer) technicality, which is a characteristic corresponding to its strategy and could add value to its offer. It should be noted that for a potential customer, the financial situation is the only possible 'veto' criteria. It is obvious that this analysis could be made before adding a potential customer to the portfolio. However, it is not certain this that would be relevant, as a potential customer scoring well on other criteria can see its financial situation change rapidly for one reason or another (a takeover, etc.). For an established customer where large investments have already been made, any worsening of the financial situation leads to concerns over the supplier's further involvement.

Determining plans of action takes place on two levels: for the whole portfolio, and for a particular customer. Determining the action for a given customer depends on both its position on the matrix and the positions of the other customers. Figure 8.3 gives a very general indication of the strategies to pursue for positions that correspond to a given quadrant. Over and above these main strategies, precise action could be determined and pursued by relying on the risk approach, as presented in Chapter 3. Consideration of the overall structure of the portfolio must include its spread and – most importantly – the potential that the customers in the upper quadrants of the matrix represent. The evolution of this spread over time is another interesting area to consider. Changes in supplier action make the structure evolve, in as much as it affects its vulnerability or its development possibilities. This also concerns customer volatility. If supplier–customer relationships are unstable, a portfolio of qualified potential customers is required. On the other hand, a stable portfolio means seeking to develop positions with each of the present customers. Finally, the aim of the method is to lead to the creation of priorities rather than exclusions.

The Advantages of Customer Portfolio Management

These are numerous. Using this approach makes it imperative to integrate customer choice or the generation of tactical plans into strategic thought and at the same time, to explain the formulation of the strategy. This is a factor of both orientating and of strengthening the strategic choices. The elaboration of the customer and potential customer evaluation grid sums up company strategic thought. The work should be done with the marketing and sales divisions (possibly other divisions too). This is an important stage in relationships between the functions that interrelate with the customer.

Example 15 completes our thoughts on the use of applying a customer portfolio management method. The use is twofold. It optimises the execution of company strategy and gives food for thought concerning the relevance of the strategy. It is also an important method for the salespeople in their analysis of the potential opportunities in their areas and for action design and planning. It is obvious that such a tool must be incorporated into the process of defining the sales force objectives and

Example 15   Glass Bottles in the Wine Industry

The positive outcomes can be better stability of the positions acquired, a better resistance against price changes, an improvement in the success rate of prospecting new customers, and often an improved profitability of the portfolio, as shown in Figure 8.3. It shows the case of a new sales representative of a producer of glass bottles active on the market segment of the wine industry. The producer has approximately 40 per cent of the national market share, similar to its main competitor. Their objective was not to increase this percentage but to maintain or improve profit margin. Realising that his area was not being exploited in the best way, the salesperson involved sought to change the composition of the customer portfolio. He focused on those dealers and co-operatives marketing top-of-the-range products and therefore selling at relatively higher prices. Such customers are more open to developments than others, to specific models, special operations, technical assistance, etc. On the other hand, other customer types were more interested in volume and therefore seeking lower prices. This modification in the composition of the customer base led the sales representative to value other items within the large range of products available. He consequently modified the composition of the portfolio of products sold in his area, developing the share of the higher-margin items. This was the underlying reason for the improvement of the sales margin. This orientation, implemented by the salesperson, can be positive only if it coincides with that of the company, which could be summed up as follows: promote profitability without losing volume and, consequently, sales with the types of customers known as the most price-concerned.

Note: Based on real data, company name confidential.

Figure 8.3   Influence on profit margin of a change in the composition of a customer portfolio

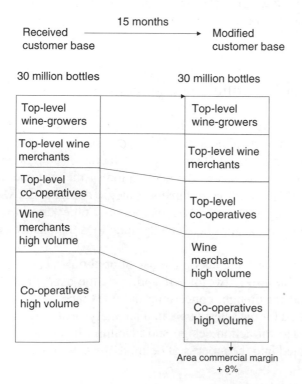

into the reward schemes. In Chapter 14 we shall see that the marketing planning method we recommend is very similar (to join strategic thought to market reality) to this one and integrates precise consideration of the supplier's positions with the customers.

References and Further Reading

Corey, E.R., Cespedes, F.V. and Rangan, V.K. (1989) *Going to Market: Distribution Systems for Industrial Producers*, Boston, Harvard Business School Press.

Davis, K. and Webster, F. (1968) *Salesforce Management*, New York Ronald Press.

Diamond, W.M. (1987) *Distribution Channels for Industrial Goods*, Colombus Ohio State University Press.

Jobber, D. and Lancaster, G. (1997) *Selling and Sales Management*, London, Pitman.

Millman, A.F. and Wilson, K. (1995) 'From Key Account Selling to Key Account Management', *Journal of Marketing Practice*, 1:1, 9–21.

Millman, A.F. and Wilson, K. (1996) 'Developing Key Account Management Competences', *Journal of Marketing Practice*, 2:2, 7–22.

Naudé, P. and McLean, D. (1999) 'Watching the Concert: How Global Account Management Developed within the Concert Alliance', *Journal of Selling and Major Account Management*, 2:1, 13–30.

Pardo, C. (1995) 'Le gestionnaire de compte clés en milieu industriel: entre logique économique et logique symbolique', *Les Cahiers Lyonnais de Recherche en Gestion*, 12, 191–225.

Pardo, C., Salle, R. and Spencer, R. (1995) 'The Key Accountisation of the Firm', *Industrial Marketing Management*, 22:1, 123–34.

Salle, R. and Rost, C. (1993) 'Une méthode de gestion des portfeuilles de clients en milieu industriel', *Gestion 2000*, 2, 69–87.

Webster, F.E. (1983) *Field Sales Management*, New York, Wiley.

Discussion Questions

1 What are the different reasons for a supplier to use indirect access to a market?
2 What is the role that distributors may play in the adaptation of a supplier's offer?
3 Why is the concept of the management of the portfolio of customers a part of the design and of the implementation of a marketing strategy in business to business marketing?
4 How can good management of a portfolio of customers contribute to the formation of the profitability of the firm?

Chapter 1

Competitiveness, Marketing and Business-to-Business Marketing

What is marketing all about
Different marketing environments
B2B marketing

Chapter 2

Business-to-Business Customers and Markets

B2B Generic Offers	Technological Innovation	Pure Services	Major Projects

PART I   STRATEGY FOUNDATIONS

Chapter 3	Chapter 4	Chapter 5	Chapter 6
Understanding Business-to-Business Purchasing	Information and Information Systems	Markets and Suppliers' Strategy	Segmentation and Marketing Strategy

PART II   STRATEGY IMPLEMENTATION

Chapter 7			
Generic Business-to-Business Offer Design and Management			

Chapter 8	Chapter 10	Chapter 11	Chapter 12
Market Access and Customer Management	Marketing and Technological Innovation	The Marketing of Services	Major Project Marketing

Chapter 9
Communication and Publicity/ Advertising

PART III   STRATEGY DESIGN

Chapter 13	The Role and Organisation of Marketing
Chapter 14	Customer Position, Market Position, Marketing Strategies and Planning
Chapter 15	Issues and Specificities of International Marketing
Annex	The Internet and Marketing: Some Ideas

9 Communication and Publicity/Advertising

I don't know you.
I don't know your company.
I don't know your company's products.
I don't know the philosophy of your company.
I don't know your customers.
I don't know your company's results.
I don't know your company's reputation.
Now what is it you would like to sell me?

Moral: the sale begins before your salesman's visit with an advertisement in a special-
ized publication. (Advertisement for McGraw-Hill Magazines, quoted by David Ogilvy,
1983)

The above quotation, with its typical advertising provocation, has a message that goes far beyond the words used. In previous chapters we have highlighted the importance of *confidence* in the creation and maintenance of relationships between a supplier and a customer. This Ogilvy advertisement raises the question about the creation of confidence between two organisations, and the possible contribution of advertising to this objective. A company director, when questioned about the difficulties of canvassing for new customers, said that the salesman had first to sell himself: 'If the person is not accepted, the company never will be.' Another noted, 'Our salespeople don't know how to sell the company.' Even if we begin to understand *to whom* we want to sell, it would appear that we do not really know *what* we must sell. If, when hired, a salesman is given the mission to sell the 'company philosophy', what will his reaction be? If a salesman begins an initial appointment by saying 'First, I would like to explain who we are, how we operate, and how we have succeeded with various other customers. Then I would ask you to outline your issues and the problems you have so that together we can work to finding solutions and to improving your activity', what else is he doing other than selling his company and company 'philosophy'? Would it help if he had known that the person had already learned about his company through an advertisement that he had read?

From the remarks above, we can find almost all the questions that business-to-business managers ask themselves when thinking about communication. What exactly is communication? How does it concern business-to-business companies? Are our salespeople not paid to do this for us? Should we talk of the company or of what it offers? Nothing can match a good technical demonstration. According to what the advertising industry show to us on TV, what can they bring to business-to-business marketing? Once the customer arrives at the factory gate, we've got him. As long as the staff remain motivated, everything is fine. And so on.

Intellectual rigour (the scientific training of many managers is not always adequate when trying to understand the phenomenon of communication), *moral prejudices* (advertising creates unwanted needs) and *misunderstandings* (do advertisers always try to understand their industrial customer?) are all obstacles in the definition of the role of communication in business-to-business circles. And when it comes to defining criteria to help managers choose between several types of communication, the landscape becomes even mistier.

Communication Between Organisations

Communication is a social phenomenon that is usually studied by taking an individual's perspective and trying to understand the mechanisms in the relationships between two or more persons (in negotiation, for example) or between an organisation and a group of people (for example, advertising for the general public). Interorganisational relationships occur between people, but also between the organisations they belong to.

Whether we like it not, a *company communicates*. The switchboard, the president appearing on television, a strike, technical achievements and failures, what spokesmen or journalists say, advertisements that appear in various documents and other media events, all are forms of company communication. Many people, who vary between having close or distant relationships with the company, receive such communications from or concerning the company. These receivers form a representation (or image) of the transmitter (i.e. the company), either directly or indirectly, through the messages that are spread in an organised or spontaneous way. This is exactly what is meant by *image*. Brand image or company image is the construction and interpretation in a person's mind, from the communications received – which obviously include the use of its offers – of a representation of what the transmitter is. This image will determine the person's *attitudes* (opinions) and *behaviour* (buy, reject, expect) in relation to the company.

The company must consider its communication on several levels. First, it must define what image it would like other people to have of it. As these people are numerous and varied, there may be several definitions. A company communicates to several 'markets': *internal* (staff), *sales* (customers, influencers, distributors, competitors, partners, etc.), *financial institutions and people* (investors, analysts, banks, shareholders, specialised press, etc.) or the *public* (general public, potential staff, general media sources, etc.). Therefore, the choice of just which public to aim

Figure 9.1 The flow of company communication towards markets

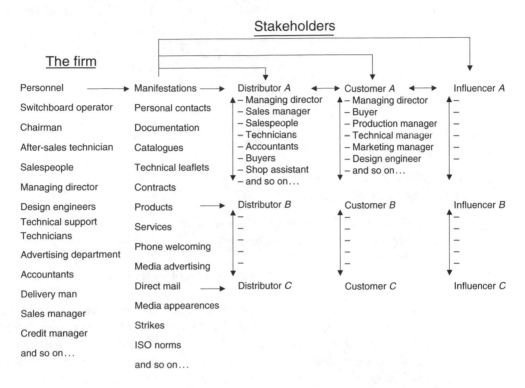

at is a second issue. The third is to determine how to contact that public, according to the message to be delivered.

Business-to-business markets are complex environments upon which firms have to act (Figure 9.1). Company communication is made by both the personal action of different staff members and by a variety of different media. The individuals being addressed by the advertisements of a company are all different, and each of them has a particular and different relationship with that supplier. In addition, they communicate among themselves and with other players in the industry about that supplier. The company must therefore address a number of different people, and it must decide whether the message has to be adapted for each different public. If the firm wants to control its image in the eyes of its different publics (to the extent this is possible) it has to take into account this complexity. Therefore, we shall try to define in more detail just what we mean by an *image*.

The Notion of Image

Any dictionary will give several definitions of the term, according to the context, whether scientific or abstract. We have identified three definitions of the term:

Figure 9.2   Corporate and product advertising

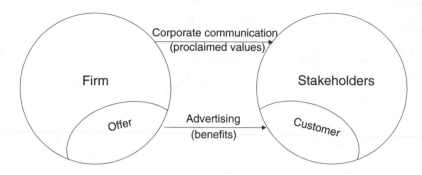

1. Reflection of an object in a polished surface
2. Mental representation of an idea or impression in the absence of the object in question
3. Internal (more or less accurate) vision of somebody or something.

All three definitions use the idea of *reflection*. But the company must 'build its image', 'brighten it' and even 'reshape it', if quotations from directors are to be believed. These contradictions lead us to think that it is useful to make this definition even clearer. First, let us distinguish between two levels: company communication or 'corporate advertising', and communication aimed to promote the company's offers. The two notions are often overlapping. For example, IBM's image is not identical to that of the AS 400. However, the AS 400 has its own image that in turn contributes to that of the company that, in its turn, helps to attract a number of customers to the machine (Figure 9.2). Consequently, any company can simultaneously support its company image (Dupont de Nemours), brands associated with some of its offers (Lycra) and products with no identified brand (yarns X or Y).

Let us return to our dictionary definitions to study the reflection process that is related to all these notions of communication, by distinguishing between what the company meant to say (the *desired* image) and what has been understood by the receivers to have been said (the *received* image), in order to see whether the *gap between the two* is not also the result of how it was said (*transmitted* image) (see, for example, Kotler, 2000).

The Desired Image

We can see this as the expression of the desire of the management of the company, concentrating on *defining the identity of the company*. This, in turn, is the combination of the value system of the people who work there, and the way of defining how the exchange and the relationships with external partners is implemented.

The *content of the image* is the translation of this desire, defining what those involved – notably the customers – can expect from it. The source of the definition of the content is the same as the strategic position of the company. It describes the use of company resources, given market and competitive activity, allocated to optimising its position in the short to long term. The desired image translates the strategy. If the communication design is not clear, it is often because of an absent or unclear strategy. This is an exercise that is at the meeting point between *customer expectations* and *company intention*. The company tries to promote its capacity to innovate, to progress, its product range, etc. When IBM moved towards being deeply involved in providing a full service to their customers, more than merely selling them machines ('boxes', as the internal jargon called them), they sent the famous message: 'We no longer sell computers, we sell solutions.' What is expected from such a message is that customers are favourably prepared to listen to new proposals from the company.

The choice of the elements of the image upon which the communication is based come from the assessment of the competitive strengths and weaknesses of the company and their *perceived importance* in the eyes of the customers. An advantage highlighted in any communication becomes a promise, a commitment by the company concerning a particular point, which must correspond to a company reality. To base any communication on an issue of secondary importance is worthless. To highlight a relative weakness, in the hope of compensating it in the eyes of the customer, only increases the distance between the promise and the reality, and adds to the final deception. A communication can try to rectify an error, but it cannot transform mediocrity. If the salespeople are seen as incompetent, while customers are sensitive to this shortcoming, the will to improve the image takes place first via training or new recruits, and only then via suitable communication. This implies that thinking about the image must also consider a second notion, that of the *received image*, which reflects what is in the minds of the people who have been exposed to the communication.

The Received Image

As mentioned above, all companies communicate either willingly or unwillingly, whether because of delivery delays or an advertisement in the press. All signals transmitted by the company will be interpreted and organised by those interested in such a way as to be able to form an image that will enable them to adopt a defensible behaviour. Indeed, the procedures of evaluation and comparison of the suppliers are often extremely detailed and precise, and subsequently leave little room for interpretation. However, many purchasing directors believe a site visit is enough to have an idea of supplier's capacity. This is typical of the image-forming process. We have already had the opportunity to indicate that several people can have different opinions. These differences are based on favouring certain attributes (the use of different evaluation criteria) or differing appreciation of the facts (a delay in delivery is looked upon differently by the director of a research lab and a production manager). These are the inherent problems of customer satisfaction surveys as described in Chapter 4. The surveys concerning the received image are largely overlapping, as many judgement criteria are identical. The practical difficulty of distinguishing the two types of survey means we have to clarify the framework of a received image survey, considering the case of corporate image. The elements can also be used for brand or product image surveys. There are two parts: *company awareness* and *image evaluation*.

The *awareness* is the level of knowledge of the company by those interested in it. It is different from the content. One can be well known but poorly appreciated, and vice versa. Reputation, concerning all those really interested (meaning those who the company needs to be interested) is the basis for the beginning of company action. McGraw-Hill's advertisement at the head of the chapter is a good example of this: if I do not know you, there is no reason for me to trust you. A European company director recently complained to us that non-customers rarely consulted his company spontaneously, whereas it had great technical skills and were very reliable. Having sold the company to an American group that had abandoned any direct operation in Europe years before, but had maintained its awareness in the profession, they noticed that the number of consultations increased rapidly. The level of awareness calls upon the memories of those who are asked. According to the people who are interested and/or the offers, supplier recall can vary in such a way that an 'I don't know' answer does not mean they have never heard of the company in question. Thus, two definitions of the term are used.

Spontaneous awareness is the response to the question 'which industrial oils supplier companies do you know of?' The order of the names given is interesting, the first are obviously the most well known, which is positive for this supplier. On the other hand, *aided recall* answers the question: ' Which among the following companies supply industrial oils?' The question typically includes one or two 'trick' names to check the honesty and integrity of the responses given. The idea is to jolt the interviewees' memory and to measure the degree of overlap between the company name and its production.

Awareness is therefore a *relative notion*. It is interesting to compare a company's awareness with that of its competitors. The results could be surprising for managers, and explain certain weaknesses on the commercial level (the lack of consultations, for example). This can change the ideas that they have of the benefits of advertising company activity, or redirect expenses towards increased communication.

The content of the received image uses the same elements as for the desired image. It involves measuring the image characteristics as seen by those interested, either verbally where they give their opinions about a certain supplier (qualitative phase) or as answers to a questionnaire (quantitative phase). In this latter case, the answers can be shown as in Figure 9.3, providing a summary of the received image of a company. It can be compared either to an ideal profile, or to the profiles of chosen competitor. Careful study of the received image allows us to measure the

Figure 9.3   Example of the measure of a received image

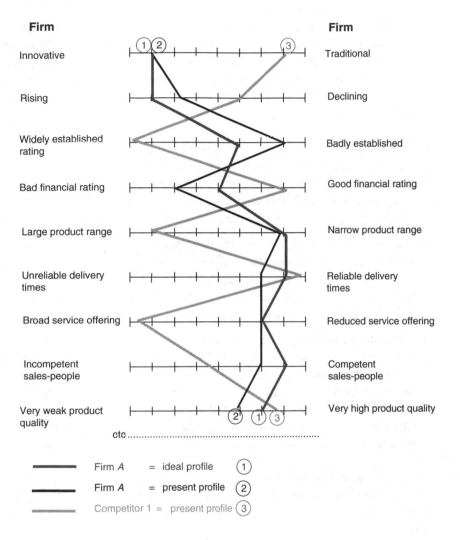

gaps between customers' perception and managers' ambition or the positions of the competitors. These gaps indicate what needs to be changed. Figure 9.3 shows that the judgement of quality is inferior to that sought by company *A*. One of two routes may now be chosen. If the 'real' quality is that which is sought, then the gap is due to pure opinion, and a communication campaign has to be designed, advertising, for example, the fact that the company has obtained the International Standard Organisation (ISO 9001) certificate, brochures given to the salespeople on the same themes, etc. If quality is not up to standard, it needs first to be improved. On the other hand, opinions concerning the sales team are better than the objectives, which shows that they have been achieved, even if continuous efforts must be made to maintain this level. These gaps can be due either to a distinction between reality and perception, or indeed be the result of the communication itself.

Transmitted Image

Some of the issues mentioned earlier have shown that gaps can be reduced through communication. Yet all companies communicate, either willingly or unwillingly. Company control over communication varies. It is typically high when concerning basic advertising, but low over what a dissatisfied customer says externally. The danger for the company is the divergence of signals that it transmits and the language it uses:

- The efficience of a communication is related to the degree of coherence between the unit's strategy and the three levels of image that we have defined. In particular, incoherence affecting the *transmitted image* affects the impact of the image. Much rigour is required in this area, the conception and execution of communication strategies, where creativity is sometimes given too much freedom.

- The wish to summarise all the strategic positions with only one communication strategy can be confusing for the person who receives it. One single manoeuvre can create doubt as to the strategy itself and work against the objectives. Once again, strategic thought must precede the communication, which can be efficient only if it *accompanies* and *reinforces* the strategy.

- The issue of coherence between a company's strategic choices and its communication (the transmitted image) means paying attention to the problems that can arise when a company changes its relationships with its customers. This can happen following the takeover of another unit whose strategic position is different from the original, or the definition of a new offer that requires altering supplier–customer relationships, or other reasons. The customers see potential *risks and confusion here*, and communication can help to clarify the situation.

To come to any concrete conclusions concerning the above, we have to look at the means of communication that exist and are available to the company to build and transmit its image. This will enable us to measure the issues and difficulties of coherence.

The Different Approaches to Interorganisational Communication

The multiplicity of means best distinguishes interorganisational communication from general public communication. During its development, a company such as Wonder Bra could concentrate its entire communication budget on television and billboards and ignore other means. This would be unthinkable in the industrial world. It is true, for the understanding of communication phenomena, that the heterogeneity of marketing situations in business-to-business also has a role to play. The lower the degree of interaction with the customers (photocopiers, for example), the closer the communication policies will be to those used for the general public, in other words using the media. The higher this degree of interaction, the more important direct relationships will be. The range of different approaches is therefore very large. It is possible to group them into 7 groups: personal contact, company offers, information supports, media and direct marketing, direct sales promotion, general media and trade fairs and exhibitions.

Personal Contact

This is the traditional approach in business-to-business environments, which allows for the realisation of the interaction. It must be remembered that all members of the company staff in contact with the customers or a member of the industrial sector carry information that characterises the company. Training the staff in communication to facilitate these relationships is the first step in the *professionalisation of communication*. This can include switchboard operators, secretaries, the design office, the CEO, the salespeople, after-sales technicians (this category is very important, when they convey to customers comments such as 'who sold you this?' or 'who put this together for you?), etc. Everybody is concerned. We shall see that this is closely linked to internal company communication. For now, let us concentrate on contacts between the company and the environment. These include:

- *Sales visits*

- *Demonstrations* and *technical or sales tests*

- *Trade fairs and exhibitions* whose preparation, procedure and use (contacts, file creation, contact follow-up, evaluation of the number of contacts and the results, etc.) represent, for some companies, a major part of their communications budget

- *Congresses, seminars and conferences*. These fall into two groups: those organised by the company for its own publics (customers, public authorities, the financial world, etc.) and those set up by general organisations on a specific theme. This latter category includes scientific groups (to strengthen technical image), professional groups (to reinforce the image of the sector in the network of influence) or general groups (to embellish the global image in the financial, political and economic environments, the international, national, local or student scene, etc.).

- *Company visits* (head offices, laboratories, production facilities, etc.) that are often decisive for some categories of persons, particularly buyers.

The last two are known as 'public relations'. We have not mentioned the media yet, which can be considered not as advertising supports but rather as conveyors of information and journalistic opinions. Whether or not managers know how to respond during an interview, especially on the television, hold a press conference, or lead an information campaign, all this is part of their job and a necessary skill.

Company Offers

It may seem odd to include the offers of a company here, but if all companies communicate, then their offers are signals. When Maco Meudon started up again in 1984 after several years of problems and financial difficulties, one of the first major decisions taken by the new board was to redefine the *design* of all the products (concrete breakers, mobile and fixed air compressors). This covered the materials used, the colours and shapes to reinforce to the distributors and users a definitive break from previous strategies, and a complete technical overhaul of the whole range. All the visible elements of the offer were involved: the writing of the offers and estimates, material forms and packaging. All these design elements are representative of an awareness that is slowly entering the industrial world, having already conquered the general public (As reinforced by the title of Raymond Loewy's famous book, whose title translated as *Ugly Does Not Sell*, 1953). Other than these aspects that concern the use of the products and their practical characteristics (see Chapter 7), the design means that we can take into consideration the significance that new shapes and colours can have for the users. Why would people not be sensitive to such ways in their professional environment, when they are in their private lives? Why deny oneself such an apparently marginal advantage, if it can be decisive?

Information Supports

These include catalogues, technical and sales documents, audiovisuals, demonstration material, instruction manuals, advertising about the place of sale, company presents, etc. These documents and objects have a double function of technical information and communication. When one consults an IBM document, one also learns about the company's corporate graphic norms. Other companies often present such a variety of presentations, of graphs, of typeface and colours that they could come from several different companies. Not to speak of the boring videocassettes that give details on how to operate production tools without ever bothering to present advantages to and for the customer. This is why the visual and nominal company identification elements (the logo, colours, etc.) and its offers (design, marking, etc.) must be based on a general framework (such as the book of corporate graphic norms) in order to preserve *coherence*, whatever the nature of the message.

Media and Direct Marketing

This term is widely used, but also wrongly used and badly chosen. The reader will have understood that the tasks of marketing are numerous and cannot all be executed in a direct way. On the other hand, the expression means that communication is ensured by the company directly to those interested and not through general media, and via several means, such as mass mailing, telephone, fax, telex or Internet.

Such media allow for direct contact with a precisely designated individual. The information is addressed to 'Ms Smith, Purchasing Director for the So and So Company.' There are several advantages. The first is economic. Secondly, efficiency: who knows whether Ms Smith saw the ad in the paper that she is supposed to have read because of her position in the company (90 per cent of purchasing managers read the *Usine Nouvelle* in France or the *Financial Times* in the UK). However, we can be surer that she would have looked at the catalogue sent by the post. Thirdly, exploitation: we can calculate precisely the result of a campaign as shown in Table 9.1. Thus, the return of a direct marketing operation can be measured fairly closely. It is possible to compare the returns of several campaigns: for example, that of a message on different categories of persons, and that of several messages on the same category. The quality of the results depends on that of the *database* used as the basis of the campaign. It is possible to buy such databases from specialist organisations. We shall see below just how important it is for a company to have up-to-date customer and other files.

Table 9.1 Evaluation of direct marketing operations

Nature of the operation	Operation implementation					Cost[d]		
	Date	Object	Contact base[a]	Number of positive contacts[b]	Number of qualified contacts[c]	Expenditure (Euros)	Cost/ positive contact (Euros)	Cost/ qualified contact (Euros)
Direct mailing	02/94	Offer Y	2000	40	20	5000	125	250
Direct mailing	11/94	Offer Z	8000	30	10	6000	200	600
Seminar	03/95	Offer Z	300	25	5	6500	260	1300
Trade fair *A*	05/94	General	20000	150	50	30000	200	600
Trade fair *B*	04/95	General	100	1	1	7000	7000	7000
Telephone selling 1	04/94	Offer W	200	40	5	5000	125	1000
Telephone selling 2	10/94	Offer V	250	25	3	5500	220	1833
Total				311	94	65000	8130	12583

Notes:
[a] The 'contact base' is built either from the files used for direct mail or phone calls or by the number of visitors to a trade fair.
[b] A 'positive contact' is a firm with whom sales people had a direct relation (personal or by phone).
[c] A 'qualified contact' is a firm that was recognised as genuinely interested by the offer.
[d] The firm realized 7 operations during the period, spent 650000 Euros, getting 311 positive contacts and 94 qualified contacts (average cost of 6915 Euros per qualified contact).
■ Although the above figures are realistic, they do not represent national averages.
Source: From a private survey.

The documents used in direct marketing operations may have been specifically designed for the purpose (which is a good solution) or found in the basic documentation (not as good but cheaper). Company newsletters, whether for internal or external use, also convey the image and therefore must be used as all other documents, in other words with the *care of controlling the transmitted image*.

Direct Sales Promotion

The aim here is to give the buyers a *reason to buy immediately*. It stimulates sales in the short term. In business-to-business marketing this is mainly reserved for low-interaction situations (non-negotiable offers). It involves presenting an exceptional advantage (reduced price, special offer, a free service – for example, an estimate or a technical audit, etc.) over a limited period. Maco Meudon used this technique to incite customers to replace their concrete breakers rapidly. The technique they used was to offer a refund on the old equipment for the purchase of the new model.

General Media

This includes all media forms: the daily press and magazines, posters, radio, cinema and television. The common point to all of them is that they have access to a *large audience* and thus are at the disposal of advertisers.

The use of the media in industrial communication is a much less powerful lever than in consumer markets. The people addressed are typically better defined and less numerous. Here, we must distinguish between 'professional' (or vertical) and general (or horizontal) media. The aim of some media is to be an information and exchange centre between the actors and the economic life in general (*Financial Times*, *Les Echos*, *Fortune*, etc.) or inside a professional sector (*Banque, 01 Informatique, Banking*, etc.). With the latter, business-to-business communication has a way of entering into contact with the potential customers it hopes to reach, whose definition corresponds with that of the audience of a medium. The use of a particular medium is the result of thought concerning the characteristics of the target people, the audience of the medium and the costs related to the various means available.

Trade Fairs and Exhibitions

These are not limited to the business-to-business world. Most professions organise an annual get-together on an international, national or even regional basis. They are the time to meet all those concerned with the profession in question: cars, building and public works, gardening, etc. They are all the more important for business-to-business marketing as they represent a 'neutral' meeting place. They are the ideal place to launch a new product, technology etc.

Participation in a trade fair can be seen as an access to a specific medium form. A look at the number of visitors, direct and indirect participation costs and expected results can be translated in the same way as for the selection of classical media. However, the trade fair is basically a place in which to profit as much as possible, that calls for careful preparation (people present, documentation, position of the stand, demos, participation at fair conferences, etc.), efficient presence throughout the fair, and using the information that has been gathered correctly (customer contacts, other contacts, etc.). Trade fairs are also an efficient place for finding elements for the marketing information system (see Chapter 4).

Media Cost

Establishing a media budget means that a choice must be made between the different media and supports. This means that the costs must be known. That a page in a magazine costs 5000 Euros does not tell us that this is better than another which costs 10 000 Euros. The advertising profession has subsequently set up some concepts to create an economic approach to the choice of media, known as *media planning*.

In defining a campaign, a support is characterised by:

■ The *audience*: how many people see or read the support during a given period. This audience is most often described in qualitative terms that mean we can define the characteristics.

■ The *useful audience*: that part of the audience that corresponds to the target of the advertising campaign. For example, a medium that has 50 000 readers, of which 5000 are purchasing directors, the target.

■ The *power*: the part of the target reached by the support. There are 20 000 purchasing directors, the medium reaches 5000, or 25 per cent.

■ The *saving*: price paid to reach 1000 useful people. If the price is 10 000 Euros per page in a magazine with 5000 useful readers, the saving of one copy is 10 000/5000, or 2 Euros per individual reached.

■ The *rate of duplication*: the part of the useful audience that is also reached by another medium or a second copy of the same medium.

These few notions will be useful for the creation of the campaign, the definition and budget allocation. In particular, they will permit a *comparison between the different media*, like magazines and direct marketing. However, it should be pointed out that the certified readership and the audience of some media are less well known, which makes it difficult to apply the above rules.

Designing a Communications Campaign

A communications campaign must be based on objectives to be reached via certain means. It takes into consideration the possibilities and limitations of these means, and seeks to optimise their use according to particular sub-objectives. As indicated above, communication is not a way to mask reality. If the customers consider salesmen technically incompetent, technical training is the only way to remedy the situation. Once the results have been obtained, it would be worth announcing this to the same customers.

The Questions to Ask

A number of questions exist. Basically speaking, they boil down to identifying *what* we want to say, to *whom* and *how*. The first term concerns the *message*, the second the *targets*, the third the *media* to be used for the above. And the three are obviously interrelated.

Promote the company or its offers. The question is often raised in advertising communication, particularly in industrial marketing. Looking at the status of the brand (Marion, 1989) can help us to understand the complex relationship that is created between the brand and the company name, which, when used as a means of communication, can help promote the fundamental qualities the company is based upon. Thus, it is common to see that large industrial groups communicate the fact they have obtained the ISO 9001 certification (CSC Computer Sciences, SpringCo, etc.). Hence, the naming of a product often becomes simply practical references that are most frequently either letters or numbers without any real meaning. Another communication strategy involves giving an offer a certain degree of autonomy in relation to other company offers. For example, SNR Roulements markets its industrial sensor bearing under the name 'Sensor line', whereas all the others are simply given figures as references.

The choice between these two strategies, which can be either *exclusive* (we communicate only the company name, or the brands which are associated with the offers) or *complementary* (we communicate on the company name and the brands), means considering several criteria, as shown in Table 9.2.

Thinking about this will lead the company to use one or other of the approaches. Both can be used simultaneously, or one after the other, according to company's objectives in terms of reputation and image. Over time, the development of a range of non-adaptable offers can go hand in hand with the creation of a brand covering this range and be the object of a specific advertising campaign, underwritten by the company.

The *choice of communication 'targets'*. The definition of what we want to communicate is related to those who receive the communication. There is a need to take into consideration the two different groups that the purchasing decision depends upon: the whole industrial sector (including their broader network of influence) at which the offer is aimed, and also the purchasing centre. If we return to the example

Table 9.2   Communication based on brands or company name

Communicating exclusively on the basis of brands corresponds to:	Communicating exclusively on the basis of the company's name corresponds to:
– Standard offers with limited adaptations	– Offering designed as basis for solutions for the customers
– Spreading risks throughout the various brand images	– The acceptance of a more direct impact of the defaults of a given offer on the firm's image
– Building awareness for a very precise offer	– A more complex argument according to the diversity of addressees and objectives
– A rather simple argument easily mastered by advertising people	

of the chicken farming sector (Figure 2.10), we can imagine a specific communication being addressed to each of the players involved: the agricultural ministry, health and hygiene advisers, veterinary experts, purchasing co-operatives, the hatcheries, the breeders, etc.

To implement the strategy towards the *players of the industrial sector* needs thinking about on two points. The first involves the *information* for the players. Efficiency comes from the adaptation of the information and the language used. In our example, food outlets are not as interested in the practical side of the operations as the breeders are. The information concerning public health, which is more important for them, cannot be given using the veterinary adviser's scientific jargon. The second is to use the understanding of the sector and the networks to *organise the communication*: Which player should we begin with? Who are the most influential players? Are some not important? In some cases, the manufacturer may feel it more important to approach the general public, or the end users. In some sectors such as textiles (Dupont for Lycra, Gore Tex, etc.) or food packaging (Tetra Pak for Tetrabrik), manufacturers try, through communication, to develop the reputation of the technology. This can orientate the networks' players in their favour, and the action can be designed and performed in collaboration with units positioned downstream of the industrial sector and people in contact with the end users. For example, in France, in 1994, the Swedish company Tetra Pak relied on a number of well-reputed brands such as Liebig, Lipton, Candia, Lactel, Materne, Nesquik, Gervais, etc. This does not constitute a recommendation for all industrial communication, but an example of the consideration of purchasing processes and the dynamic elements within an industrial sector.

Communicating to the *purchasing centres* of each customer means exploiting the knowledge that the company has of its customers (Chapter 3). Who is really concerned by the information: all the members of the purchasing centre, the research engineers, the production methods engineers, or the purchasing agents? Each one needs specific information and is receptive to specific arguments. To communicate with managers or meat department managers of food stores would be irrelevant in our example. Probably, only the central buyer is concerned, so the question now is: How and what do we communicate to that person?

The *choice of media.* Each of the above choose their own reading material, go to different trade fairs, go to conferences, or are interested in specific themes. A survey of these habits can define which message should be transmitted by certain media to each individual, who is often found through their position in the company or organisation. It is necessary to underline the importance of creating and maintaining files, to be able to establish a database of qualified contacts and to limit losses. This can represent a significant competitive advantage for those who have such files.

The Budget

It is not possible to give a clear definition of a communication budget, but certain aspects do permit us to estimate the amounts involved. Several points of view can be taken into consideration simultaneously. First, the approach of setting the objectives allows us to define the *targets* sought, the *type of message* to be transmitted and the *media* to be used. The combination of these factors gives a total amount, which constitutes a first approximation. Using the *internal ratios* is a means of fixing the communications budget at a certain percentage of the past or forecast sales turnover. This requires that the company consider that this part of its turnover represents both what it can allow for and what is required to meet its objectives. This is generally a simple and efficient rule of management, unless of course the mistake is made of forgetting that some objectives can be reached only through overinvestment – for example, the launching of new offers, particularly if they are different from the normal company offer. Thirdly, the approach of using experimentation (the notion of a 'test market') or *competitors' actions* ('share of voice') is not very useful in business-to-business marketing compared to consumer marketing. The reason is the one that we mentioned earlier: in business-to-business marketing, advertising does not represent a mechanism as effective as in consumer markets.

The Communication Plan

The aim is to produce, within the budget limits set, a synthesis of objectives in terms of messages and targets to reach using chosen advertising media. The conclusions of our ideas can be seen in Tables 9.3 and 9.4. They represent a way of defining the objectives, targets, media and expenses required to efficiently set up and manage a communications budget. The addition of dates helps to establish the schedule and to avoid overbooking, particularly concerning the use of direct marketing action. The question is how to control expenses, and to assess their relevance and efficiency.

This is part of good management. Communication is a difficult field to manage. As has been said, most managers know that they waste half their advertising budget;

Table 9.3 Example of a synthesis of communication objectives

	Buyers	Design office executives	Manufacturing executives	General managers	Engineering offices	Distributors	Financial circles
General press				Increasing awareness: 6 shots ①			Increasing awareness: 6 shots ①
Professional press		Launching product A: 18 shots ②					
Direct mail			Building Interest for our technology B: 2 shots ③				
Trade fairs ① conferences		Strengthening our image as a specialist Frankfurt/Atlanta ④			Strengthening our image as a specialist Frankfurt/Atlanta ④		
Promotion						Accelerating the replacement of product range 2 Discount for the purchase of new products ⑤	

Table 9.4 Example of a communication budget

	Buyers	Design office executives	Manufacturing executives	General managers	Engineering offices	Distributors	Financial circles
General press				① 30000 Euros			Budget 1, same as for General Managers
Professional press		② 60000 Euros					
Direct mail			2 × 15000 = 30000 Euros ③				
Trade fairs conferences	①	④ 130000 Euros			Budget 4, same as for Design Office Executives		
Promotion						65000 Euros ⑤	

they just don't know which half. Humour might be a manager's gift, but not a management rule, and we have to go somewhat further. In previous pages we have already looked at much of what follows. The specificities of business-to-business marketing lead to orienting control more to the attainment of objectives than the direct impact of advertising (achieving unaided recall, recognition, or favourable competitive position, for example). This is a delicate process, among which communication is only one tool whose consequences are often difficult to isolate. A few suggestions can be made, however:

- To measure regularly the *company's awareness* in certain target markets is an indication of the efficiency of the global communication.

- To evaluate the *image*, according to regular criteria and for the same targets. This is slightly more ambiguous owing to the large number of actions that can lead to changes in the competitive position.

- For these two indicators, a *comparative evaluation with the competition* is a useful complement to make comparable measures over time and in competitive arena.

- Most actions related to direct marketing can be the object of fairly precise control (see Table 9.1) by measuring *results* and *objectives*, insofar as they express customer or potential customer contacts (real or qualified, initiated or terminated deals). This is the same for requests for information in the specialised press.

When all these means of control are used regularly together, the company creates a database that aids reflection and improves the professionalism of the communication process.

Thoughts Concerning the Choice of Media

The use of a particular medium depends on the people to be contacted, the message to be transmitted and the aim of the communication. We have already studied these problems from different angles. Now let us look at some specific points.

The *size and spread of the target* is the first element. The general media has traditionally treated large and widely-spread customers. Technological progress in computers now makes it possible to deal with important databases on relatively cheap and easy-to-use machines and software. This creates the possibility of reaching such populations through direct mail. The availability of a database is not the answer to all these problems, as the costs of maintenance, updating and use can be very high. However, using the Internet and the launch of new 'Customer Relationships Management' (CRM) software are increasing as costs tumble.

The *message type* is another element. Here we can contrast the search for aware-ness or image and precise action. If image is fed by all type of communications, the general media remain a preferred way owing to the large distribution and the reassuring effect they have. A page of advertising in a magazine that is appreciated by its readers has a greater effect of proximity and arousing interest than other media forms. On the other hand, other types of media provide a better support for precise actions (promotion of a new offer, technical or detailed argumentation, search for real contacts, etc.).

External and Internal Communication

It must be remembered that, more than any other group; company staff avidly read the company's advertising campaigns. If the communication is centred on the product, the staff – whatever the function – are interested in the advertising, adopt or criticise it, are either proud of it or find it fairly mediocre. But they are not really deeply concerned. In a way, company production is outside the firm, is no longer part of it. A good company can mess up a product without being completely turned upside down.

If, however, the communication concerns the company, the staff, its services (SKF's message is 'people of quality behind products of quality'), all the staff are concerned about the message transmitted by the communication. They are well placed to measure the appropriateness or the gap between the advertised promises and the internal reality. It is not surprising to hear people arguing that 'they would do better to give us the money [spent on the advertising] for better operating conditions or to increase our pay', etc. The use of 'they' reflects the gap between management (seen as responsible for the communications) and certain members of the staff. Thus, we must insist on the notion of *internal communication* – the company newsletter for example. Uncertain internal practices are a form of communication that can become unacceptable if the company intends to communicate to the outside world about the quality of these practices. The ISO 9001-2-3 guidelines are a good example, as they reflect good internal practices made available for the customers. Companies that use the granting of such certificates as a form of publicity use this approach. They promote their concrete and certified efforts that have been made both internally and externally. Staff motivation *and* customer benefits go hand in hand. In other words, the external promotion of company 'values' is directly related to the building and respect of these same values within the company. (For more information, see Chapter 11.)

Branding is the expression of this process. It attempts to guarantee perceived quality and to make it concrete and memorable for the stakeholders concerned. Obviously branding can take place either at the company level or at the product level. For example, SNR Roulements (Example 16 in Chapter 10) is selling current bearings under the company's brand name with just a distinction within the range of items based on an identification number. But they branded their innovative instrumented bearing under the ASB® brand name in order to add protection to the concept and make it recognised by customers and system builders. The value of the brand is increasingly referred to as 'brand equity', and is incorporated into evaluations of the company's goodwill (Aaker, 1995), even if it does not play the same role in the business-to-business environment as in consumer marketing.

Communication Management and the Role of External Service Providers

The main characteristic of business-to-business communication is the diversity and spread of sources, which explains the overlaps between internal and external communications. There are two solutions to this problem, the first is cultural, the second more technical.

The *cultural basis* of company communication is the senior management culture and personal sensitivity. The results of coherent and relevant communication are not known in the short term. It must be understood that a language (as stated by Françoise Dolto, 1987: 'everything is language') that is not very coherent is interpreted by those who receive it as a sign of the incoherence of its origins. This interpretation can only produce negative effects in the attitudes and behaviour of those who are interested, both internally and externally. To listen to the salespeople of certain companies is often enough to understand the difficulty and the necessity of their effort to correct customers' interpretation.

The *technical basis* of the management of communications includes aspects of organisation and work methods. The first point is the presence of a communications director who can advise the managers, transmit the culture of the communication inside the company and look after the technical aspects. It is more efficient to nominate one person as responsible for both internal and external communication and the training of staff members. This obviously depends on the size of the company. In a smallish company with, say, about 50 workers, the director usually does this. The second point involves the setting up of precise methods of operation:

- An *image development plan* managed by a committee
- A *visual identification system* and *corporate graphic norms*
- A *follow-up* and *control system* of the *transmitted image*
- An *information system* for the *registered image*.

All these concerns are also present when bringing in outside partners: a communications adviser, advertising agencies, design and graphics agencies, etc. External services companies (advertising agencies, communications advisory services, etc.) are professionals in the field of communications. They can help the company on three levels: advice concerning the process, the message creation and the media scheduling.

The role of the *communications consultant* gives the advertiser the possibility to talk about objectives, the content and the implementation of the communication. Their help concerns the technical aspects and the design of the communications strategy. Here, it is vital that the advertiser defines a *communications strategy* in their own words (stakes, objectives, etc.) that is then the basis of discussions between the consultant and management.

One of the aspects of these discussions is the *creativity* of the external consultant. The aim of communication is to attract the attention of those at whom it is targeted. This is difficult when using jargon or esoteric language. What the eye can see when skimming through a magazine is limited. These objectives and constraints mean the advertiser needs a style of communication that is called a *creative proposition*, and which, through the association of an image and text, can give life to the message. Business-to-business marketing still has a lot of progress to make in this field.

The *media scheduling* is probably the most technical aspect of the communications consultant's job. He or she becomes responsible for collecting information on the publications of the different media forms and allows for optimum budget use. It should be added that films are also a form of media at the same level as the others, and there management can only benefit from the intervention of an expert.

This brief description of the work of a communications consultant underlines the fact that communication is a co-production between the advertiser and the consultant. Thus, the choice of consultant is important (and difficult to make), but also the creation of a trusting relationship between the two, which reflects a kind of 'cultural' agreement concerning the values expressed by the company and their translation in communication terms.

References and Further Reading

Aaker, D. (1995) *Building Strong Brands*, New York, Free Press.

Arens, W. (1996) *Contemporary Advertising*, New York, Irwin.

Batra, R., Myers, J. and Aaker, D. (1996) *Advertising Management*, Englewood Cliffs, Prentice-Hall.

Dolto F. (1987) *Tout est langage*, Paris, Vertiges du Nord/Carrere.

Kotler, P. (2000) *Marketing Management, The Millennium Edition*, Englewood Cliffs, Prentice-Hall.

Loewy, R. (1953) *La laideur se vend mal*, Paris, Gallimard.

Lohtia, R., Johnston, W. and Rab, L. (1995) 'Business-to-Business Advertising: What Are the Dimensions of Effective Print Art?', *Industrial Marketing Management*, 24, 369–78.

Malaval, P. (1998) *Stratégie et gestion de la imarque industrielle: produits et services Business to Business*, Paris, PubliUnion.

Marion, G. (1989) *Les images de l'entreprise*, Paris, Ed. d'Organisation.

Ogilvy, D. (1983) *Ogilvy on Advertising*, London, Multimedia Publications.

Discussion Questions

1 How can you relate the respective roles of personal selling and advertising in business-to-business marketing?

2 What are the different definitions of the image of the firm? Why is it useful to distinguish between these definitions?

3 How can you differentiate between the role of advertising in business-to-business marketing and in consumer marketing?

Chapter 1
Competitiveness, Marketing and Business-to-Business Marketing
*What is marketing all about
Different marketing environments
B2B marketing*

Chapter 2
Business-to-Business Customers and Markets

B2B Generic Offers	Technological Innovation	Pure Services	Major Projects

PART I   STRATEGY FOUNDATIONS

Chapter 3	Chapter 4	Chapter 5	Chapter 6
Understanding Business-to-Business Purchasing	**Information and Information Systems**	**Markets and Suppliers' Strategy**	**Segmentation and Marketing Strategy**

PART II   STRATEGY IMPLEMENTATION

Chapter 7			
Generic Business-to-Business Offer Design and Management			

Chapter 8	Chapter 10	Chapter 11	Chapter 12
Market Access and Customer Management	**Marketing and Technological Innovation**	**The Marketing of Services**	**Major Project Marketing**

Chapter 9
Communication and Publicity/ Advertising

PART III   STRATEGY DESIGN

Chapter 13	The Role and Organisation of Marketing
Chapter 14	**Customer Position, Market Position, Marketing Strategies and Planning**
Chapter 15	**Issues and Specificities of International Marketing**
Annex	**The Internet and Marketing: Some Ideas**

10 Marketing and Technological Innovation

We pointed out in Chapter 1 that innovation is a major factor in the economic development of advanced economies and the competitiveness of their companies, and this has led to the publication of many works related to general company strategy. The concept of innovation can be studied from several points of view. We shall focus here on the relationship between innovation and the marketplace, and in particular the contribution of *marketing* to *innovation* and the ways in which it can be implemented. Having looked at the conditions affecting innovation in the company, we shall detail the differences between 'pull' and 'push' innovations, in particular 'push' innovations that require a very specific marketing approach.

The Company and Innovation

There are two points of view that can be examined here. The first is economic and focused towards the outside world, implying that the innovation is a major issue in company management in so much as companies are part of a world characterised by a continuous technical evolution. The second is more managerial and internally focused, and examines the conditions affecting innovation within companies.

A World Shaped by Technical Evolution

One aim of Chapter 1 was to show that innovation was the only path allowing a company operating in a country where labour costs are high to confront the competition with any assurance. The acceptance of this notion by the economic and industrial world and its use by both industries and governments has led to the present technical revolution. The search for competitiveness through cost strategies leads to *simultaneous innovation* concerning both the *offers* (what we make) and *industrial processes* (how we make it). Differentiation policies, on the other hand, promote innovation in the offer alone.

We do not wish to present an exhaustive survey of technological innovation and company strategy, which is more the field of technological management and innovation strategy management. However, we must take into consideration the notion

Figure 10.1   Life-cycle of a technology

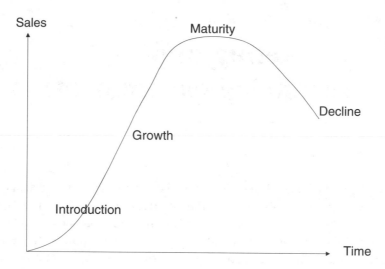

Note: Sales are the result of the relative performance of the technology compared to competitive technologies and also of the degree of coverage of the applications open to the technology.

of the evolution of problem-solving technologies. There are two elements to this. The first (Figure 10.1) shows that a technology evolves over time according to the life-cycle diagram. There is an initial exploratory phase we shall call 'introduction', then other phases, 'growth', 'maturity' and 'decline'. The second represented by the y-axis in Figure 10.1, represents sales that cover two dimensions. The first is technical performance (for example, vehicle speed on the ground has increased from 10 to 500 km/h in just 60 years) and the way in which a new technology can replace earlier ones. The second is the potential range of applications that the technology can be used for, and their successive approach in order to sustain growth. For example, the sequence of different Intel processors (Figure 5.5) is a good illustration of this. The degree of maturity of a technology, which reflects its evolution over time, results from the evolution of several factors (Foster, 1986):

■ The degree of *technical competence* of both the manufacturers and users
■ The *progression* in the nature of the technical work from fundamental research to applied research, development and then finally engineering
■ The level of *interest and activity engaged around the technology* (patents, etc.)
■ The *reduced costs* of the technology through the improved production process conditions
■ The *availability of*, and *easy access to*, the technology.

The replacement of one technology by another that is technically and/or economically superior is also a factor influencing the degree of maturity. The efforts made to maintain an ageing technology often take it to its best-ever level of perfection;

Figure 10.2   Diagram of technical substitutions: materials used for the construction of turbines

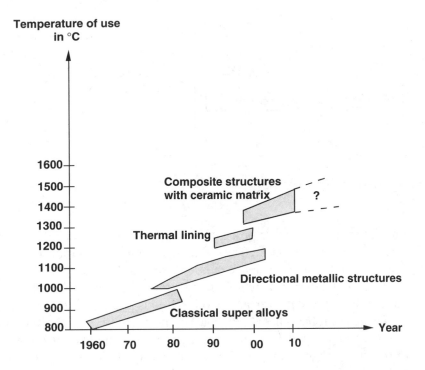

Source: Aït-el-Hadj (1989).

however, this is not always enough to protect it from emerging technologies. Thus, we could say that there is also a life-cycle for technologies that responds to the same application. In Figure 10.2 we present the different materials that support increasingly high temperatures (basic alloys, metallic structures, thermal coverings, ceramic composites), used in the construction of turbines. The evolution has not been spontaneous, but rather is the result of constant and complex research performed by the actors involved, and also the influence of unplanned events. The example of numerous failures (Corfam produced by Dupont, which was intended to replace leather) shows how difficult this evolution really is for the companies involved.

The innovating company is thus involved in an adventure that requires both a good understanding of the phenomena linked to innovation and a well-controlled process.

The Impact of Innovation on Company Management

One of the most tangible results of the innovation process can be seen in the launching of new products. Thus, it is possible to understand the 'efficiency' of certain

Figure 10.3   Sale of new products, market share and profitability

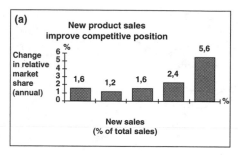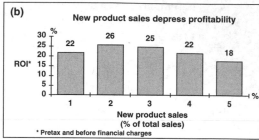

Source: Unpublished documents from SRI International.

companies in the innovation process by analysing their results: the extent to which they introduce new products. The PIMS programme has produced some interesting research into the role and conditions surrounding innovation. PIMS shows (Figure 10.3) that the introduction of new products, measured by the percentage of turnover they represent over any 4-year period, has a positive impact on market share. However, it has a negative impact on profitability over the same time period, which is expressed by the return on investment. Thus, innovation represents a *short-term risk* for the company, which confirms the evolution of numerous companies that have been created on the basis of technological innovations and cannot find the financial backing to support the growth of their activity, and are forced to look elsewhere for financing. On the other hand, the positive effect of the introduction of new products on market share has a positive affect on profitability, as shown in Chapter 5.

These results depend on the size of the innovating company. For leading companies with high market share, the results are practically reversed in relation to the average: the introduction of new products allows them to defend rather than improve their original market share. But it does not affect company short-term profitability. For small companies, the gain of market share is high, while short-term profitability can be greatly affected.

Two other factors, the *relative perceived quality* of the offer and the role of *marketing expenditure* give us interesting insights into the management of innovation. A higher relative perceived offer quality (calculated *before* the launch) permits the company to achieve both a better increase in market share and a better return on investment. On the other hand, an activity with a lower level of relative perceived quality would meet problems overcoming the expenses linked to the new product's introduction. Improving quality should therefore happen before the introduction of new products, for internal and external reasons. First, we can argue that the policy of quality used by the company will contribute to improving the internal innovation process. Second, the 'good' image of company quality, as recognised by the customers, will also have a positive impact on delays related to the acceptance of

Figure 10.4   Costs linked to the innovation

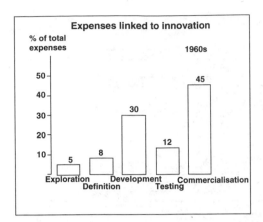 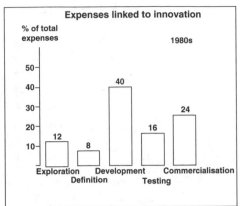

new products, which can make the situation for the initial tests easier for the company.

The PIMS research noted, however, that a high level of expenditure on marketing for new products (calculated as a percentage of sales) has no impact on market share gains, and moreover, has a negative impact on profitability.

These points reinforce the conclusions of Cooper's research (1982) concerning the success rate of new products in industrial companies. Cooper shows that if the level of company innovation is related to the level of research and development expenditure, the success rate is linked to the company's management and marketing qualities. This underlines the argument that the success of the innovation process in launching new products is the result of an *organised process*, including marketing, directed by management.

To make the innovation successful – in other words, to produce new products, services and processes – is a major issue for any company. Among many aspects linked to this objective, one of the major strengths in any company is the *intrinsic market value* of the innovation. To try and compensate for an offer that has been only partially adapted by increasing other supports (promotional or others) often simply increases costs and reduces profitability. Thus, the success of the operation is determined at the very beginning of the process. A survey (Figure 10.4) made by Booz-Allen and Hamilton (1982) confirms this: between the 1960s and the 1980s, costs linked to innovation moved upstream towards the exploration, definition and test phases of the process rather than towards commercialisation.

These results have been subsequently confirmed (Figure 10.5). There is a strong correlation between new product successes and an allocation of the innovation expenditures favouring the initial stages of development. The nature of these expenditures shows that they are related to successive technical studies and marketing surveys, which reinforces our recommendation of concerted development (Figure 1.4). The intrinsic market value of the new offer is a necessary but not sufficient condition for success. Thus, innovation develops inside a social system within

Figure 10.5   Impact of the initial phases of the development of innovation on success

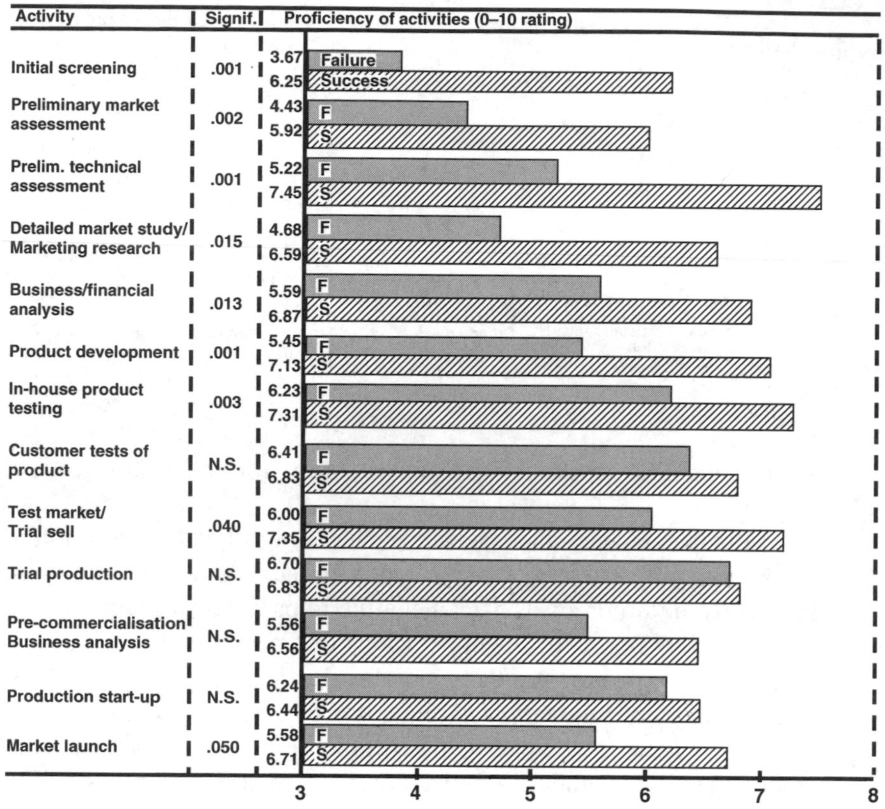

Activity	Signif.	Proficiency of activities (0–10 rating)
Initial screening	.001	3.67 Failure / 6.25 Success
Preliminary market assessment	.002	4.43 F / 5.92 S
Prelim. technical assessment	.001	5.22 F / 7.45 S
Detailed market study/ Marketing research	.015	4.68 F / 6.59 S
Business/financial analysis	.013	5.59 F / 6.87 S
Product development	.001	5.45 F / 7.13 S
In-house product testing	.003	6.23 F / 7.31 S
Customer tests of product	N.S.	6.41 F / 6.83 S
Test market/ Trial sell	.040	6.00 F / 7.35 S
Trial production	N.S.	6.70 F / 6.83 S
Pre-commercialisation Business analysis	N.S.	5.56 F / 6.56 S
Production start-up	N.S.	6.24 F / 6.44 S
Market launch	.050	5.58 F / 6.71 S

Source: Cooper (1988).

which players may present different behaviour towards the proposed offer. We shall come back on this aspect later in this chapter.

All the issues raised so far lead to the question of the role of marketing as a *function* and as a *methodology* upstream of the introduction and launching phases of the process, in other words within the research and development process. The idea suggested here is that marketing contributes to the innovation process in the initial phases of research and development, which are traditionally considered as the exclusive domain of the R&D function. Our intention is to show how this can be achieved. However, first we would like to give a definition to the concept of *technological innovation*.

The Technological Innovation

For any company, innovation can be defined as '*the successful implementation in an original and different way to satisfy a function of social and economic life*'.

Here, the innovation can affect the economic and social organisation as well as technical processes.

For Bruno Latour (1989) 'the idea of Diesel to design the ideal engine is called *invention*. However, since this meant developing this idea for it to materialise as a prototype that was able to work, this was the second phase called *development*, where the expression "research and development" comes from. We often use the term *innovation* to designate the next phase during which several prototypes are built and can subsequently be reproduced in thousands of copies and sold world-wide' (emphases in the original).

The 'Pull' and 'Push' Forms of R&D Projects

Innovation is most often performed within the framework of projects that are 'the smallest organisational part of company R&D [research and development] structures for an R&D activity to take place' (Courpasson and Gaillard, 1993). Thus, we can talk of a project if R&D activity includes a team, led by a team leader, with a budget, which operates within a space dedicated to such activity and recognised within the organisation as such. R&D activity typically evolves according to a six-phase sequence, the first two corresponding to the generation of the idea, the others to the development of the project:

- *Exploration* of the project
- *Launching* the project
- *Defining* applications
- *Choosing* the applications
- *Development*
- Preparing the *launch* of the innovation including *tests* and *marketing*.

This examination of the process has led to the forming of two different forms: 'pull' and 'push'. The difference comes from the nature of the problems to be solved and their links to the market reality.

In the *'pull' form*, the projects are based on a precise application or a defined problem to be solved, in relation to a known market with a specific customer. They originate as much from the marketing or sales divisions as the R&D divisions. Their main characteristic is that their objectives in terms of functions to do, performances to be reached and economic position in relation to an identified competition, are the object of a relatively precise description. Thus, it is possible to say that these projects are 'pulled from the market'. They are often based on the technical and scientific know-how within the company, which does not imply that they are of a lesser quality. They result from a specific and identified problem. We can speak here of the *development of new products* or *innovation*. The methods of industrial marketing previously mentioned (Chapter 7) are most often linked to the leading of 'pull' projects.

In the *'push' form*, things are different. They are 'pushed by the technology', that is, the driving force for their development. The company works to develop know-how on a new concept. The logic is scientific and technical. The project is initially developed without any commercial constraints with the aim of exploiting a technical possibility, which does not mean the development is performed uniquely within the company. Outside scientific and technical partners can be included: laboratories, universities, research contracts, etc. This leads to the expression *'technological innovation'* (Millier, 1989).

Between the two forms, 'pull' and 'push', there are a series of intermediary forms of R&D projects linked to the increasingly strong integration of market concerns and commercial issues. Indeed, the difference is not always so great. This can come from the speed with which a 'push' project goes through the initial phases, since the focusing on a particular application tends to give it a 'pull' form. Thus, a 'push' project can give birth to several 'pull' projects. Therefore, it is important to identify at which point it becomes relevant to make the switch, since development organisation and methods then differ. A comparison of the two forms is given in Table 10.1, based on the following characteristics: definition, development path, source of dynamics, technical principles, length, set of phases, rhythm of development, pressure, budget and composition of the project team.

So, we now have a model of the forms adopted by innovation projects in companies. Surveys on this theme usually do not make any difference as to the origin of the new products, which can have an effect on the contribution of marketing in the technical development. We would never suggest that there is any form of hierarchy between the two forms. 'Pull' projects represent the daily progress of a company and probably add more to turnover in the short term than 'push' projects, whose function is to create at a given time a positive break for the company, or to permit it to remain in the international technical and economic movement. Here, we shall concentrate on the contribution of marketing to 'push' projects. Indeed, we can say that under these circumstances the market – meaning simply the meeting of supply and demand – does not exist. If the market does not exist, how can we 'identify the needs' that have to be fulfilled? This requires an answer. To do so, we have to position the innovation is a new perspective before describing the marketing methods that are likely to position it in the market.

The Adoption and Development of Innovations

Many surveys have been made on the *adoption* and *diffusion* of the innovation processes. They concern both technical and social innovations, designed for organisations or individuals. We have grouped together some of the conclusions into two schools of thought: the school of diffusion and the school of 'innovation networks', the latter based on the existence and/or the creation of networks between actors who are concerned and 'recruited' by the innovation. We shall present both schools, even if the diffusion school has been the object of many criticisms owing to its

Table 10.1 Comparison of 'pull' and 'push' projects

Characteristics	'Push' projects	'Pull' projects
Definition	To explore possibilities of new scientific or technical principles	For a definite application, to find an answer based on scientific or technical innovations
Development path	These projects start vague and structure along with the progress of research; there is a large span of access to various applications; the development path is more of an end goal than an objective	The problem to be solved is quickly identified and made an objective; an agreement rapidly comes as the concept of an economic and commercial offer, based on specifications
Source of dynamics	Current or foreseen technical development 'pushes' the project	The identification of a market demand (customer, segments) 'pulls' the project
Technical principles	Not mastered at the beginning; very high mix of technologies	Evolution of known techniques; average mix of technologies
Length	Long, from 3–20 years	Average, from 1 to 3 years
Set of phases	Marked sequentiality; at the end of the first phases, a ('go') – ('no-go') decision is made	The first phase is separated from the others; at the end of phase 1, a decision leads to the follow-up of the project, the phases of which may be nearly simultaneous
Rhythm of development	Slow at the beginning, speeding up as applications become more defined	Steady
Pressure	Beginning to increase as applications become more defined	Steady and high in order to meet the time and economic constraints
Budget	The first estimate varies from hazardous to very hazardous; the return on investment of the project is not determined at start, it shows as a global budget without any item allocation, essentially made of researchers' time	Rather precise estimate at the beginning; a profit account is established to support the decision of launch, based on an appreciation of the foreseen investments; the allocation per item (development, prototypes, test, tooling, marketing, etc.) is good
Composition of project team	Most often only R&D people	Mixed from the beginning; very soon marketing takes the lead

mechanistic appearance. However, companies' behaviour surrounding their management of innovation shows that this diffusion model is still often applicable.

The *diffusion school* owes much to the research of the American ethnologist Rogers (1962) who proposed an outline of the adoption of innovation that has been widely used in subsequent research (Figure 10.6).

There are five categories that vary according to the speed of their adoption: innovators, early adopters, early majority, late majority and laggards. Several comments can be added to this presentation of one of Rogers' theories, based on the speed of adoption of an innovation or the characteristics of the different categories of adopters and the social process that allows for its diffusion.

The *speed of adoption* depends on several factors linked to the specificities of the innovation itself. Thus, some factors make the adoption faster: technical, social

Figure 10.6   Categories of people adopting the innovation

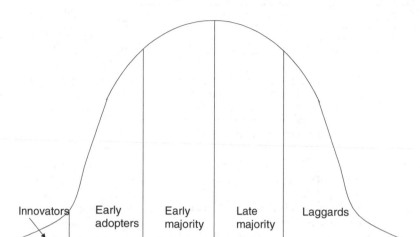

Source: Rogers (1962).

and economic advantages of the innovation in relation to existing problems; the compatibility with the social and technical systems into which it is introduced; the ease with which the innovation can be used; and finally, its degree of visibility at the time of the introduction. The level of complexity of the innovation is, on the other hand, a factor that slows down the speed of adoption.

The different *categories of adopters* have been characterised by common traits. These characteristics come in three groups: socio-economic, personality and behaviour. Table 10.2 identifies these characteristics. The world is fairly general, but does include personality factors that may be surprising in considering relationships between companies. However, it should be remembered that *individual behaviour within the organisation* conditions the innovation adoption process. The risk approach presented in Chapter 3 takes this element into consideration and permits us to analyse the adoption decision.

If personality can condition behaviour towards the innovation, then other elements linked to the degree of social participation can, too. Thus, we are entitled to integrate this phenomenon in order to describe and understand the adoption process of an innovation. Figure 10.7 gives a picture of the process for a collective decision, adapted from an individual decision plan.

The reader should look at Figure 10.7 from an innovating supplier's point of view, trying to explain the powers of influence that accompany the decision-making process (awareness → interest → desire → adoption) in a customer company. The former has access to information that is also available to other players in the communication network, among which there are competitors of the innovating supplier. The customer company will gain access to the awareness (that the innovation exists) through frequent contact with the sources and players, the extent of which depends

Table 10.2   Innovators' main characteristics

- **Social characteristics**
  - Higher degree of education
  - Good mastery of own language
  - Higher social status
  - Ascending social mobility
  - Strong economic and commercial orientation
  - Favourable attitude towards credit

- **Personality characteristics**
  - Empathy
  - No intellectual dogmatism
  - Ability to deal with abstractions
  - Rationality and intelligence
  - Favourable attitude towards change
  - Ability to accept uncertainty and risk
  - Favourable attitude towards education
  - Favourable attitude towards technical progress
  - Social ambition

- **Social behaviour**
  - Strong social participation
  - Participation in complex social networks
  - Other cultures' openness
  - Numerous contacts with change agents
  - Media proximity
  - Exposure to group communication situations
  - Active search for information
  - Awareness of innovations in general

Source: Rogers (1962).

Figure 10.7   Adoption process of an innovation diffusion school

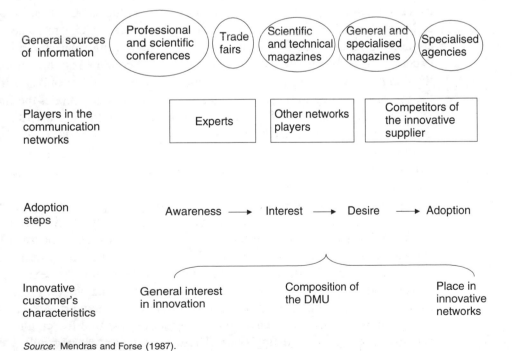

Source: Mendras and Forse (1987).

on the particular marketplace characteristics. The information the buying company collects, the pressure it is under and the way in which it will deal with all this, will all determine how rapidly it gains the knowledge, and move on to the other phases to finally arrive at the adoption phase of the innovation. One of the supplier's tasks is to identify these actors and powers to influence them in their favour.

All the above elements constitute a quick summary of the basics of the 'diffusion school'. This school of thought has been criticised for several reasons. It presents the hypothesis that innovation is preconceived in an autonomous way by the supplier, and then marketed, thereby beginning the adoption process. Thus, the supplier takes all the initiatives, not the customer who can only 'take it or leave it'. Inventors or geniuses are considered as supermen who alone can swing the market (Latour, 1989). The notion of swinging customer groups, who initially would be opposed to changes and slow down development, changing their mind and accepting innovation is difficult to understand. How can this happen? This diffusion vision of the innovation that stems from the neoclassical economic theory has greatly influenced company behaviour in relation to innovation. For example, the marketing mix approach in which the supplier autonomously preassembles an offer that is then launched on the market confirms the vision of a company that is part of a hostile environment looking to convince the users. Certain authors (Håkansson, 1987) advocate another view of innovation. We have grouped certain important elements of their approaches under the term the school of 'innovation networks'.

The *school of innovation networks* is based on the participation (Chapter 2) of companies into networks of *interacting actors* (companies and individuals). To fulfil their activities, they seek access to resources and develop others by using existing relationships or by creating new ones. It is the same for an innovation: it is inserted and built within these networks of actors which are linked by interconnecting relative positions, work processes, social, informational and technical exchanges that the innovation is likely to upset. To complete an innovation project, the company will 'recruit' or 'hire' a group of players whose only justification is the interest they find in it. They will take possession of and model the innovation; in the words of Latour (1989) they will 'translate' it into their own language (or preoccupations). Thus, according to Callon and Latour (1985), the innovation process is 'a collective activity that brings only at the end the qualities of profitability, efficiency and necessity and that continually reshapes the object as interests meet or diverge around it'.

The networks have pre-existing structures of varying density according to the degree of dependence between the players. Consequently, the innovation will be confronted, even if technical differences are great, with success factors of a different nature, linked to the interest of the players to adopt it or to reject it. Indeed, the innovation can require the creation of a new network that involves existing and new players and can drastically modify the structure of the networks. For example, in R&D pull projects, the innovation has little effect on the network and fits in without much trouble. On the other hand, push projects often entail the creation of a new network that replaces existing ones. These differences can partially explain the different length of the two forms of projects. Therefore, two conditions will define the path to success:

■ The first is the total understanding of the nature of the *obstacles* and *changes* provoked by the innovation and the search for ways to modify them to make the situation favourable

■ The second involves all the *work of adaptation* that leads to giving the innovation a configuration that will attract the interest of the actors concerned.

Example 16 illustrates our thoughts concerning the innovation process. It involves the development of the 'Active Sensor Bearing' (ASB) concept by the SNR Roulements company. This shows that the process of coming and going between the constraints modifies the relative positions of the players and their involvement in the innovative process. We can describe the people who receive the innovation by a series of functions:

Example 16 SNR Roulements*

Initial State

The expertise on the functioning of vehicle systems, in particular those dealing with contact with the road, is an essential factor of the technical development of car manufacturers. The present trend leads to manufacturers adding more and more devices able to supply data to the onboard electronic systems aimed to manage safety, traction and comfort. The rotational speed of each of the wheels is one of the most common among all parameters. The wheels, as a dynamic interface between the vehicle and the road, make up for a source of much data. These data concern speed, acceleration, deceleration, path, distance covered or other vehicle characteristics.

During the early 1980s the appearance of the first assisted braking systems (ABS) involved the development of a speed sensor device in wheels. To be schematic and to concentrate only on speed sensing, it is possible to say that two functions have to be provided. One is the encoding function that produces information. The other is the sensing function that 'reads' the available data, which are afterwards interpreted by an electronic calculating unit (ECU) that in turn makes decisions. In the case of the first ABS systems, the devices were based on the principle of a variable reluctance sensor activated by the rotation of a tone wheel. These devices are efficient and reliable in operation, although some disadvantages are now acknowledged:

■ The installation of sensors remains a difficult operation

■ The exposure of the sensor to the aggressive environment (temperature, vibrations, various sources of pollution) makes it a sensitive part of the system

■ The quality of the electrical signal at low speed is too weak to be used with certain systems

■ The technology is fully exploited, meaning that no significant progress can be achieved in managing the cost function.

In addition, while the ECU has evolved alongside other developments in electronics, the speed sensor has remained practically in its initial form, undergoing no significant innovation.

(continued)

Figure 10.8   SNR Roulements: pattern of the relationships between players

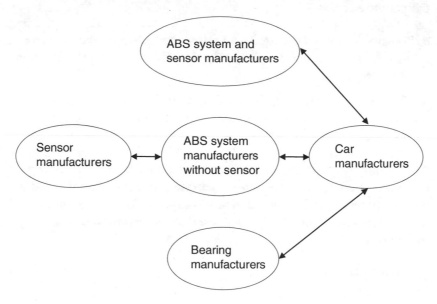

Example 16   SNR Roulements*

The relationships between players are presented in Figure 10.8. The bearing producer supplies the car manufacturer with wheel bearings. Equipment manufacturers who may or may not produce their own sensors design the ABS systems. The whole system is assembled at the car manufacturing plant.

The Development of the Sensor-Bearing Concept

In the middle of the 1980s SNR Roulements registered a patent on a 'data sensing bearing' allowing the sensing of the rotational speed of a vehicle wheel. At the end of the 1980s a study among the European car manufacturers provided the basis for the specifications of a wheel speed sensor bearing. They took into account the car design and its assembling techniques at the manufacturer, the after-sales conditions, its compatibility with other systems and its economical performance.

The Research and Development performed in parallel with the different types of technology available and those in an advanced enough state of development were used to select the sensing technology with which the actual components could be developed. The selected architecture is feasible only using active sensors (Hall effect or magneto resistor) combined with an activating element, based on a magnetic material. The speed sensor contains a Hall effect sensor or a magneto resistor with a single sensing element, which 'reads' a magnetic band incorporated into the bearing seal on which is 'printed' a regular succession of North and South poles. The magnetic encoder seal uses a material specifically developed for this application, an elastomer loaded with oriented magnetic particles. This new concept presents two major advantages in comparison to the previous technology: it is more effective and offers opportunities for further developments for the car manufacturers. Along with the progress of the project, SNR registered numerous patents concerning the concept and the technologies developed for the various elements. In particular, in conjunction with university laboratories and based on an intensive training of its engineers and technicians (basically mechanics), the firm developed a high level of competence on the technology of active sensors that were to be sourced from outside suppliers. At the beginning of the 1990s a

(continued)

Figure 10.9 SNR Roulements: modification of the distribution of functions among players as a consequence of the concept of sensor bearing

Case of a classical bearing:

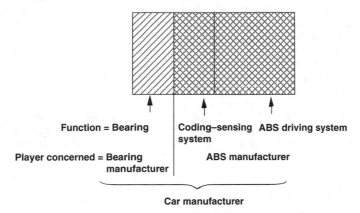

Function = Bearing | Coding–sensing system | ABS driving system

Player concerned = Bearing manufacturer | ABS manufacturer

Car manufacturer

Case of the sensor bearing:

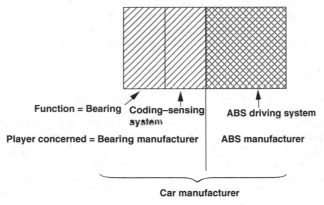

Function = Bearing | Coding–sensing system | ABS driving system

Player concerned = Bearing manufacturer | ABS manufacturer

Car manufacturer

Example 16 SNR Roulements*

project team gathered with the objective of obtaining the approval of the concept by the car manufacturers. The choice was made to offer a range of different offers based on a 'sensing–encoding–bearing' system and to present it to the various players concerned.

The car manufacturers showed great interest in the concept that eased further developments for future models. Nevertheless, the purchasing managers negatively evaluated the kind of monopolistic situation created by SNR as sole supplier of the solution. On top of that a bearing manufacturer is seen as a mechanics specialist and its competences in electronics are severely questioned. The new offer from SNR Roulements generated with the car manufacturers the perception of different risks at a high level. But they understood that this innovation provided them with the possibility of rocking the boat of the practices of some leading bearing manufacturers seen as 'arrogant'. On the other hand, there were few ABS systems manufacturers with a strong market position. This innovation, if turned to a general application standard, could allow them to modify these positions to their advantage (Figure 10.9).

(continued)

Example 16 SNR Roulements*

The ABS manufacturers at first showed some reluctance. These powerful firms act globally and are in a good position relative to the car manufacturers. As some of them also integrated the manufacturing of sensors, they would not consider abandoning this activity. Furthermore, there was no straightforward compatibility between the present ECUs and the new technology. The ABS manufacturers then strongly opposed the innovation. SNR understood that the new technology so deeply modified the relationships between players that it could not develop it with a traditional 'product' approach. It concentrated on the encoding–bearing part of the system and set another strategy based on the establishment of a professional standard. This strategy required the gathering of a core team of firms interested in the development and promotion of the sensor-bearing technology. It adopted the formula of an open standard that permitted offering the standard to any competitor to gain access to the core concepts under certain conditions. This coalition grouped three car manufacturers that elaborated the common specifications that made for a definition of the standard:

- Characteristics of the delivered electrical standard
- Architecture of the sensor bearing
- Electronic and mechanical interfaces.

These specifications were also open to other car manufacturers.

The first three car manufacturers showed an interest in the concept for two main reasons. The first was that the new technology could be introduced at a function cost equivalent to the present one, which was a basic condition for its acceptance. But the new technology would later benefit from the experience effect and the function cost was likely to significantly diminish over time. The second was the perspective to modify their position relative to their suppliers in their favour.

The core team was also made up of other players.

A world class ABS system manufacturer developed its interest in the new technology. Initially reticent, they brought in a sensor technology compatible with the SNR concept as soon as an open standard strategy was adopted. Their interest was the development of a higher-performing ECU and of other car electronics based on wheel speed sensing. As a counterpart they offered SNR a world impact on car manufacturers and eased the approach of new customers. Two other ABS system manufacturers quickly joined the team.

Three sensor manufacturers also embarked on the project.

Some other bearing manufacturers and magnetic encoder suppliers also joined with compatible devices. Initially SNR was a sole supplier of bearings. The car manufacturers requested that other bearing manufacturers had access to the standard under negotiated conditions. The ABS manufacturers then pushed the other bearing suppliers to join the standard.

Thus, the coalition reinforced itself to the satisfaction of the first actors that felt they had made the right choice at the beginning.

In order to stress the length of the innovation process, let us recall that the first patent was registered in 1984, the first marketing research took place in 1988 and the project team was built in 1992. The option of the open standard first appeared in 1993 and the first series of cars incorporating the Active Sensor Bearing® appeared in 1997. Since then several car manufacturers and bearing producers have adopted this technology that is likely to become a professional standard in the automotive industry.

* Company data SNR Roulements (now SNR Group) was founded in 1946 and has for long been a subsidiary of Renault SA. It is a bearing specialist, employing 4800 staff for a turnover of nearly 500 million Euros (2000). It produces 250 000 bearings a day in 6 plants (Europe and Brazil) and sells in more than 120 countries www.snr.fr/GB/GBPAGES/GRUPBASE.HTM.

- A function of *perception* of the novelty, the concept and its components

- A function of *legitimising the concept* in which they recognise its relevance in relation to the problems they have encountered, in Example 16, this concerns the Advanced Research Services of the car manufacturers

- A function of *integration* – that is, the acceptance of the innovation in their own activities

- A function of *production* of new concepts, uses or projects in which the user develops the innovation in ways which are far from the original intention of the innovator; this involves a 'translation' or even a 're-routing'.

In Example 16, the last two functions concern the car manufacturer's design office. We could say that the innovation does not really exist until the last stage has been completed. This favours an innovation project process that leaves technological alternatives open as late as possible, so as not to have to redesign or to remodel the innovation, which is both long and costly. Thus, the speed of development of an innovation depends on the understanding of these phenomena by the innovator and their position within the players' network in question. Now we can draw up a general outline of the innovation process that we shall develop later in more detail:

- To give the innovation a form that will be seen as an *offer hypothesis* designed for certain applications

- To identify the possible *uses*

- To analyse the *existing and future players* for each application in order to understand their power and the issues they represent

- To define the *uses* to which the innovation will be given priority

- To make the innovation *known* to the players concerned (perception)

- To work *with them* on the interest it represents *for them* and the form it should take to meet their requirements

- To listen to *new propositions* coming from those who receive the innovation, and to integrate them into the general development (production of new concepts)

- To show one's capacity to find solutions to all the problems raised, to continue the development and to begin the 'marketing' phase; obviously, this phase began much earlier, only here does it in its more classical form.

This shows the issues it is possible to include in the field of marketing; analysis and understanding of the markets, customers' and players' networks, the competitive position of the innovative offer, etc. However, two points must be added before entering into the details of the marketing of the innovation. The first is that the issues are mostly scientific and technical; consequently, part of the actions of marketing is to be found in the technical function. The second is that, despite all this, there are pure marketing tasks that have to be realised and which require a true marketing method and rigour to accompany and orient the development.

Technological Innovation Projects and Marketing

A technologically innovative project is characterised by its capacity to fulfil, in a new way, technical functions. For example, the substitution of an integrated unit for a series of separate functions, reorganisation of functions, addition of new functions in relation to a previous state of the art, or simply the replacement of one technique by another. Most commonly in these projects, the customers are difficult to identify and few in number, the competition is not yet in place, the technology is unsure and the customers are not aware of the offer and appear unlikely to evaluate it, as they cannot clearly define its problems and are wary of adopting new technology. Let us look at our example of Placoplâtre again (Chapter 2). It presented itself to the market as a substitute for bricks and plaster. This led to major changes in the building trade and the structure of the network in this sector. Indeed, several trades such as masons, plasterers and painters have either evolved or disappeared. This is an example of the changes and modifications that can happen with the introduction of an innovation.

Here, we shall look at the main points of the methodological process proposed by Millier (1989, 1995, 1999) by underlining the role of marketing in certain steps. The method applies to technological innovative projects, often called 'R&D projects'. Its principle is to work on the basis of two groups of data: the definition of the support of the new technology in R&D projects in industrial activities and customer behaviour in relation to this support, the two groups then being brought together to lead to a plan of action. A company dealing correctly with these two elements – one technical, the other economic and commercial – increases its chances of successful innovation. To help the understanding, there are five steps (Figure 10.10):

■ Technical analysis
■ Economic and commercial analysis
■ Marketing segmentation
■ Diagnosis of the marketing situation
■ Plan of action.

However, beware! The mechanical character and linearity of this method is simply to make the understanding easier. In fact, the process is not linear, there are reiterative steps, and backward movements, several iterations, and applying the method might even involve modifying the order in certain cases.

Figure 10.10 Marketing approach for technologically innovative projects

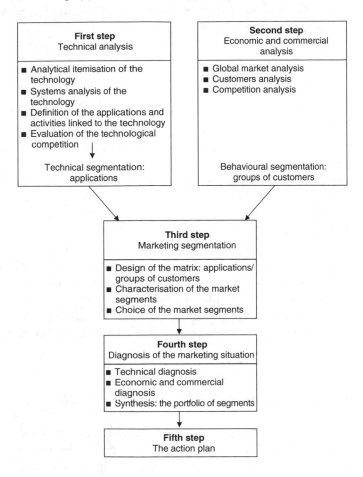

Step 1: Technical Analysis

The aim of this first step is to answer two questions: how can *we solve the customer's technical problem* using the technology (or technologies) involved in the R&D project, and how would *the competition* do so? The technology is here defined as the 'global technical package one has to master from the conception of the product through to the transfer of the solution to the customer'. The words 'transfer of the solution to the customer' are important here. This objective and concern will give a meaning to the process and orient the development: how will the innovation integrate customer activity in accordance with the position of the latter in the actor's network? For the supplier, this means mastering the technical parameters of the innovation and making them compatible with all the customers' demands. This means the innovator must integrate, as early as possible, as wide a vision as possible of the applications, therefore the markets that are accessible to the innovation on both the economic and technical levels, in order to be able to lead the development process. This involves five phases:

The Analytical Decomposition of the Technology

This permits qualifying the elements that make up the technology according to 4 main categories: theoretical, scientific and technical skills; components; capital goods; know-how. This first task identifies the level of *technological understanding and the competitive position* of the company for each element and the points that are to be developed or require the acquisition of supplementary technologies.

The Functional Analysis of the Technology

This involves identifying 'what the technology can do'. It means defining all the *functions* the actual technology can cover. For example, a metallic material presented as small fibre lengths can be incorporated into concrete. The functions it may cover include mechanical strength, thermal conductivity and resistance to corrosion. It is then possible to determine the *applications* to which this technology can be applied.

Determining the Applications and the Activity Linked to the Technology

This is one of the most important phases of technical analysis. An application can be defined as a technical problem that could be treated by the technology (or technologies) in question. It begins with a survey of the possible *uses* of the technology. For example, a new material can be used to make different parts for the automobile industry: piston, gearbox, disk brakes, etc. An initial survey showed that users seek to solve different generic problems: reduced dynamics, reduced static and/or improved physical characteristics. Grouping the uses around the one generic problem is an application. The major interest of this change of perspective is that a given application covers related technical requirements which itself gives a precise meaning to the job of the development to be made. Moreover, this allows us to define the products the company will then offer. All the identified applications will determine the contours of the activity to which the technology has access.

The Evaluation of the Technological Competition per Application

This is undertaken application-by-application according to the direct and indirect competition. Finally, we can examine the position of the technology and its durability while not losing sight of the fact that as the project advances the technical analysis should evolve. At the end of this iterative process it is necessary actively to collect information, (opinions, impressions, perceptions, etc.) concerning the technology, functions and applications that can be combined to identify the *initial paths for action*. Thus, the applications/functions combination allows us to identify the functions that are already inherent in the technology and those to add for a given application. In return, this reasoning has consequences for the technology itself that may need to be complemented with new elements. The technology–applications combination highlights the applications that add value to a greater number of determining components of the technology.

The 'Technical' Segmentation

This intervenes as the realisation of the first step of technical analysis. It involves creating a *segmentation tree*, as explained in Chapter 6, on the basis of only technological characteristics so as to determine the applications of the technologies involved in the project. Table 10.3 gives an example of segmentation for an ultra-fine, micro porous, opaque, white, soft and smooth mineral powder. It retains molecules and can be used in the composition of numerous products such as cosmetics, lubricants and various additives.

Technological analysis has allowed us to prove that 5 classified criteria have to be integrated in the following order to formulate technical segmentation and isolate the applications:

- *Criterion 1*: characteristics of the powder developed during use (2 classes)
- *Criterion 2*: role of the powder in the final product (2 classes)

Table 10.3   Example of 'technical' segmentation

Criterion 1						
Physical and/or physico-chemical properties of the powder		**Properties of the powder in relation with an active principle**				
Criterion 2		**Criterion 3**				
Structural constituent	Modulating constituent	Casting out support			Static support of reactions	Trapping support
	Criterion 4		**Criterion 5**			
	Lubrication or gliding properties	Aspect properties	Intergranular	Intragranular		
Powder used 'as powder'	Solid lubricating additive	Pigmentation agent	Intergranular reservoir of blend	Intragranular reservoir of blend	Support of micro-organism	Absorbing or adsorbing trap
A1	*A2*	*A3*	*A4*	*A5*	*A6*	*A7*

Source: Millier (1995).

- *Criterion 3*: action of the powder (3 classes)
- *Criterion 4*: property given by the powder to the final product (2 classes)
- *Criterion 5*: action of the powder (2 classes).

Thus, the segmentation technique presents 7 types of applications: A1, A2 . . . A7.

Step 2: Economic and Commercial Analysis

Here, the various applications to which the project technology permits access have to be clearly *structured*. In some way a customer has been defined and identified on the single basis of a 'generic technical need' that has been refined in accordance with possible applications. This construction has come about following numerous iterations between the supplier and the market actors. In Example 16 on SNR Roulements, this means all the pre-1988 phases. If the processes followed are marketing methods, no potential customer information is used as such; we cannot pretend to have built a marketing vision of the market. However, it is necessary to list and to select from among the potential applications those that seem most attractive and likely to succeed, taking the characteristics of the *market actors* into consideration.

In this step, the company pursues many objectives: to finalise the technical development of the project, to check its market value, to manage the expenses that remain to be made, to make past expenses profitable, and to determine if the new technology will make a major or minor contribution to the company's future. For reasons of cost and human resources within the company, it is rarely possible to realise all the identified applications at once. The example of the development of nylon shows that it took 20 years for a company as big as Dupont De Nemours to cover all the possible applications for their polymer. It would be wrong to make these choices on the basis of one technical segmentation and the assumption that one technical differentiation was enough to succeed.

Indeed, the technical segmentation was built on an organisation of data from the technical analysis, without worrying about two other essential dimensions. These are an appreciation of the degree of willingness of the customers and other actors of the networks to adopt the new technology, and an estimation of the consequences of its adoption on their activities (particularly their *cost structure*). The introduction of these dimensions leads to a behavioural segmentation process that takes into consideration the fact that, in the strictest sense of the term, the market does not exist. There is no customer as there is no exchange, no concrete definition of the offer. It is still at the sketch phase and requires a lot of adaptations and adjustments. In fact, even if we qualify this phase as 'segmentation' in the marketing sense of the word, it is in fact a process based on typology. It is based on the intuitive and iterative grouping of actor characteristics (customers), who may be interested in the innovation and who exhibit similar behaviour. Thus, the mechanical application of the general segmentation process (Chapter 6) is inadequate and a process directly related to technologically innovative projects must be followed. This is characterised by two points:

■ The construction of segments results from the comparison between the *buying behaviour* of various groups of customers and players concerned and the applications defined at the outcome of the technical analysis.

■ The segmentation cannot be built as a photograph of the market (as it does not exist), but on a 'cinematographic vision' of the movements of an *emerging market*. These results as much from the market's own evolution – in particular, buyer behaviour in relation to the innovation in question – as from the efforts made by the innovator to adapt it to certain applications. This being so, the innovators reinforce their capacity to interest the customer. See Example 16 on the SNR Roulements Company above.

The first part of the process thus involves the definition and search for information on all the customers and players concerned by the applications identified. This has three levels:

■ A *global level* of analysis that permits us to understand the functioning of the networks of players concerned with each application (market); an analysis of this kind is also presented in Chapter 12

■ A level of analysis relative to *decision mechanisms* within potential customer organisations

■ A level of analysis relative to the *competition*.

Similar to the technical analysis, this economic and commercial analysis leads to a behavioural segmentation, meaning groups of companies that are interested in the technological innovation.

The *global analysis* of the market begins with that of the channels or networks (the possible 'market'). It allows identification of the *interests* and *obstacles* of the players that make it up. It includes three stages: the first involves *delimiting the field* of the analysis to avoid too much wasted energy while remembering that, in this field, 'curiosity is a good quality'. The second is to identify the *powers of the players*, which means widening the perspective presented in Chapter 3, and the third is what may happen *between the players* participating in networks. This part of the analysis corresponds to the understanding of a potential 'market' which facilitates discovering the factors whereby a group of actors is more willing or less difficult to approach than another.

Customer analysis seeks to supply elements of judgement on the chances of success for the innovation. For this, it is necessary to acquire more precise information. This requires understanding the technical, organisational, commercial or

Table 10.4   Example of behavioural segmentation

Degree of manufacturing difficulty	Basic products or manufacturing	Sophisticated products or manufacturing		
Competence in terms of measure and control		In-competent	User competence	Expert competence
Segments	C1	C2	C3	C4

Source: Millier (1995).

competitive issues that the customers will be confronted with if they are interested in or can be interested in an innovative proposal, and under what conditions. This is possible only through direct interaction with certain customers or players who are historically closer to the innovator, or more innovative themselves, or more receptive than others to innovations. Everything we presented in Chapter 3 on the understanding of industrial purchasing applies to innovations. The notions of *perceived risk* and *behaviour of risk reduction* by the innovative supplier should be applied here. Thus, there is no need to propose new processes or tools to deal with the problems encountered in situations of innovation.

The *analysis of the competition* permits determination of the nature of the competitors already present or likely to enter the market, and to assess their strengths and weaknesses. The *behavioural analysis* allows for the interpretation of all of this information through a grouping of the customers in relation to the defined applications following the technical analysis. These characteristics concern the expectations, the motivation and the preoccupation of the customers in relation to the proposed innovation. The creation of the categories is therefore made case by case.

The matrix in Table 10.4 is a useful tool to show how the results of the second phase, or economic and commercial analysis, are applied. It concerns an innovation involving highly sophisticated measuring and control services based on ultra-modern equipment. Initial analysis identified 4 types of customer behaviour that could be explained by the following criteria:

- The level of the customer company *production quality*: basic or sophisticated
- Customer skill in *measuring and controlling*: incompetent, user competence, expert competence.

Table 10.4 groups the criteria used and the 4 types of customer behaviour that make up 4 segments: C1, C2, C3 and C4.

Step 3: Marketing Segmentation

Marketing segmentation sums up the main points of both the technological analysis that determines the applications of the project technology, and the economic and

Table 10.5   Determining market segments

Applications / Groups of customers	A1	A2	A3	A4	A5	A6
C1	S1					
C2			S2			
C3					S3	
C4	S4					
C5						

Source: Millier (1995).

commercial analysis that constitutes the homogeneous groups of companies concerning their behaviour when confronted by innovation. Thus, we can build a marketing segmentation matrix that maps out the battlefield (Table 10.5). It illustrates:

■ The applications that are accessible to the technology dimension (A1, A2, etc.) permit the supplier to define the *technical part* of the offer – the *product characteristics*

■ The customer categories dimension allows us to define both the *non-technical parts* of the offer (price, services, etc.) and *marketing tactics*.

In Table 10.5, an empty square means that a group of customers does not have the technical problem relevant to the application in question. Similarities between customer behaviour and applications permits grouping squares that are close and some segments can result from the joining of several squares of the matrix, for example, S1, S3 and S4.

This segmentation needs to be *validated* by looking at the key factors for success for the competitors (companies and technical solutions) that are relative to each segment. This will involve supplementary criteria that may alter, or even modify the segmentation. Moreover, modifications over time of customer behaviour towards the innovation and the project itself also influence the segmentation.

The use of successive segmentation by the innovator allows him or her to gradually direct their choices of technical development and marketing investment as the project advances. To round off this step and to prepare for the next, each segment must be characterised. This is not unique to technologically innovative products, so the reader is invited to study Chapter 6 that deals with segmentation.

Table 10.5 presents a matrix that is similar to the technology–applications matrix presented in Chapter 6 (Table 6.1). This is normal as it presents a detailed vision of the technology–applications line of the general matrix, which sums up all the applications accessible to the technologies that are available in the company. Table 10.5 is the analysis of a more complete process that can be slotted into the general matrix.

Step 4. Diagnosis of the Marketing Situation

Based on marketing segmentation, the innovator will make choices according to a process that is similar to that used in Chapter 6: the *determining of target segments*. According to the problems to be solved, this step involves two dimensions: the *technical* diagnosis and the *economic and commercial* diagnosis. A technical risk indicator expresses the technical diagnosis and an economic index expresses the economic and commercial diagnosis. The term 'risk' is used to define the risk for the *supplier* of such a project, not the risk for the customer, as explained in Chapter 3.

The *technical diagnosis* involves estimating *supplier capacity to finance the developments* that are required for each segment, the times and the corresponding costs and an estimation of the likely success rate. The success of an innovative technology depends on the modifications, improvements and additions to the initial offer for it to meet customer characteristics and requirements and also to be superior to the competition.

The criteria to use when estimating company technical risk include:

- The level at which the innovator *masters the essential technologies* and the developments to be made
- The *coherence* between the project and *company technological strategy*
- The *evolution potential* of the technology in terms of performance
- The performance of the technology in relation to *competitor solutions*, segment by segment
- The *image* of the technology in the *competent scientific community*
- *Supplier capacity* to accompany complementary evolutions
- The potential evolution of *competitor technologies*
- The problems of *integration* of the technology for the customers
- The problems of *operating*, particularly those related to the industrialisation of manufacturing processes.

The *economic and commercial diagnosis* is based on elements already examined in previous chapters. It takes place on two levels: the channels or networks of which the users of the technology are members, and the user's purchasing decision centre. The criteria to be taken into consideration to evaluate the economic risk are:

- The impact of the technology on the customer's *cost price*
- The possible *evolutions* of the economic performance of the technology (experience)
- The degree of *synergy* of the project with the commercial distribution of the company (investments to be made)
- The *financial weight of investments* to be made for the market segments

- Possible *market dynamics* (volume, growth rate, competition, possible profit margin, actor propensity to innovation, etc.)
- *Delays in decision* from the actions of the various actors
- Problems respecting the present and future *legal and regulatory constraints*.

Synthesis, the segment portfolio: the synthesis of the diagnosis is made on a technical risk/economic and commercial risk matrix within which the segments are grouped. According to the position of each segment on the matrix, precise orientations are given.

See Chapter 8 for the cases of problems related to the presence of *distributors* in the networks.

Step 5: The Plan of Action

There are a number of problems raised by the project and related to the methods of planning (see Chapter 14). These specificities are based on different points of view, including the need to co-ordinate the technical developments and sales approaches (particularly the use of company salespeople), the effects of technical or commercial synergy between the different segments, and the collecting of information for decision making.

The first principle is that a *team* (as seen in Chapter 13) manages the development project. The second concerns the *marketing information* required for decision making. One of the greatest weaknesses of industrial companies is to neglect the collection of information, to do it too late and to allocate ridiculous budgets to it. We know of a company that, for 8 years, had managed a research project amounting to some 7 million Euros, and decided to gather market information in the sixth year and was reluctant to give a survey budget of some 15 000 euros. It is in this light that some pseudo-market surveys come into existence, realised in good faith by the R&D team without any method or any concern for objectivity. Their results are very pernicious and may often lead to enormous costs for the innovator (for example in overestimating the size of the potential market). The worst situation is for a company to think it knows the market, only to find that this is not the case and that the players require things the technical development did not take into consideration. Also, to think one knows the market in advance when the success of the innovation results from a real construction process by a group of players (including the company) with more or less similar interests, is, we feel, thoughtless, pretentious and ignorant.

Some information must be available very early on in the process. The scope and the precision of the useful information progresses with the project. The first decisions can be made on relatively rough and ready information, then increasingly detailed and precise, to the point where the analysis of a major customer's purchasing decision centre is a key factor of success for a whole market segment.

Figure 10.11 Plan of action

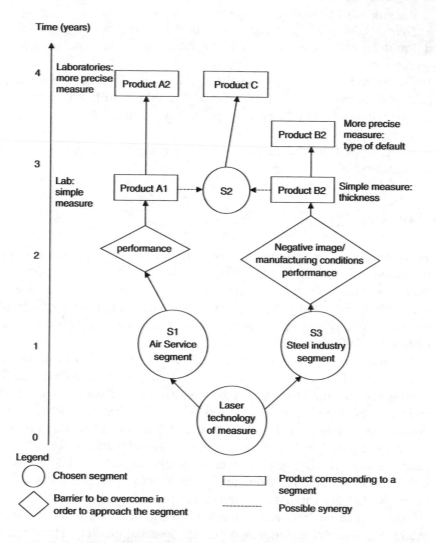

Information on various market segments is also necessary as early as possible after determining the applications. Not all market segments are equally commercially attractive to the company. Some coincide with the classical fields of action of the company and require only particular orientation of the marketing and commercial investments. Others are badly controlled and require large investments. Others can be completely outside the commercial bases of the company and require a lot of thought as to their approach: direct investment, with partners, as a licence or franchise, etc. Thinking about *key factors of success* can lead to considering certain segments as real areas of new strategic activity, which takes us back to the problem of company strategy, which can also be modified by the need to use an important innovation.

Table 10.6   Contribution of marketing to the development of an innovative project

Phases / Role	Description of the idea	Project launch	Definition of the applications	Choice of the application	Development	Test	Market launch
Information	■ Documentation ■ Creativity	■ Exploratory surveys ■ Concept tests ■ Understanding customers and their concerns	■ Evaluation of present solutions: satisfactions/dissatisfactions ■ Survey of value chains	■ Market and applications survey	■ Market segmentation ■ Structural analysis of value chain	■ Analysis of portfolio of customers	
Choice	■ Concerned businesses		■ Choice of point of entry into value chain and of types of customers	■ First design of offerings	■ Definition of basic offers	■ Choice of target customers (channels of distribution)	
Action						■ Choice of test customers ■ Tests implementation and follow-up	■ Budget ■ Sales estimates ■ Promotion ■ Selling ■ Promotion ■ Gathering of information

Among these modifications, although of minor importance, is that which concerns the action of the sales force and innovative projects. A transition period is reached the moment it becomes necessary to increase customer canvassing before the project is finalised. The salesmen must gather information from customers and potential customers and initiate the sale. This transition is delicate to negotiate. Specific training is compulsory to enable them to do their work well; sometimes a selection process may be necessary.

The final point to make concerning the management of market innovation concerns the *global approach plan*. Figure 10.11 represents the various issues related to the sequence in time and the effects of the synergy and differentiation that can affect the development of a project. Segments S1 and S3 should be considered first, they lead the way to the development of product plans A1, etc., B1 etc.). It is relevant to approach segment S2 only through the synergy resulting from work done during the development of products for the segments S1 and S3.

To conclude, Table 10.6 describes, phase by phase, the role and the nature of the (underestimated) contribution of marketing to the development of an innovative project.

One final conclusion is required, concerning the insertion of marketing as a process and function in such a project. The 'classical' marketing players, such as salespeople, find it difficult to follow the proposed process owing to conflicts between the short and long-term stakes. Efficiency would mean placing a marketing specialist in the research centre or even the project team, who knows all the tools and is able to accompany the development, as shown in Chapter 14 below.

References and Further Reading

Aït-el-Hadj, S. (1989) *L'entreprise face à la mutation technologique*, Paris, Ed. d'Organisation.

Akrich, M., Callon, M. and Latour, B. (1988) 'A quoi tient le succès des innovations?', *Annales de Mines*, Séries Gérer et Comprendre, 11, 4–17; 12, 14–29.

Booz-Allen and Hamilton (1982) *New Product Management for the 1980s*, New York, Booz-Allen and Hamilton.

Buzzel, R. and Gale, B. (1987) *The PIMS Principles*, The Free Press, New York.

Callon, M. (1989) *La science et ses réseaux: genèse et circulation des faits scientifiques*, Paris, La Découverte.

Callon, M. and Latour, B. (1985) 'Comment suivre les innovations? Clefs pour l'analyse socio-technique', *Prospective et santé publique*.

Cooper, R.G. (1982) 'New Product Success in Industrial Firms', *Industrial Marketing Management*, 11, 215–23.

Cooper, R.G. (1988) 'Predevelopment Activities Determine New Product Success', *Industrial Marketing Management*, 17, 237–47.

Courpasson, D. and Gaillard, J.M. (1991) 'La collaboration R et D/Marketing: un approche empirique de la notion de projet', *Gestion 2000*, 5, 67–91.

Courpasson, D. and Gaillard, J.M. (1993) 'Acteur du projet et acteur–project', *Compte rendue de recherche financée par le Ministère de la Recherche et de la Technologie*.

Foster, R. (1986) *L'innovation: avantage à l'attaquant*, Paris: Inter Editions.

Håkansson, H. (1987) *Industrial Technological Development: A Network Approach*, London, Croom Helm.

Håkansson, H. (1989) *Corporate Technological Behaviour: Cooperation and Network*, London, Routledge.

Latour, B. (1989) *La science en action*, Paris, La Découverte.

Mendras, H. and Forse, M. (1987) *Le changement social*, Paris, Armand Colin.

Millier, P. (1989) *Le marketing des produits 'high tech'*, Paris, Ed. d'Organisation.

Millier, P. (1995) *Développer les marchés industriels. Principes de segmentation*, Paris, Dunod.

Millier, P. (1997) *Stratégie et marketing de l'innovation technologique*, Paris, Dunod.

Millier, P. (1999) *Marketing the Unknown: Developing Market Strategies for Technical Innovations*, New York, Wiley.

Nantua, R., Michel, D. and Salle, R. (1999) 'Du solo à la cordée. Réussir le lancement d'une innovation par l'établissement d'un standard professionnel compatible: le cas de ASB chez SNR Roulements', *Décisions Marketing*, 17, 45–54.

Rogers, E.M. (1962) *Diffusion of Innovations*, New York, Free Press.

Discussion Questions

1 Why is innovation so important for the strategy of the firm? Can you relate Chapter 10 and Chapter 1 in this respect?
2 Why must the marketing of innovation be different from the marketing of offers based on existing technologies?
3 Why are firms and people reluctant to adopt innovations quickly?
4 Can you relate the content of Chapter 10 to the concept of risk (Chapter 3)?
5 Comment on the roles of networks in driving innovation.

Chapter 1

Competitiveness, Marketing and Business-to-Business Marketing

*What is marketing all about
Different marketing environments
B2B marketing*

Chapter 2

Business-to-Business Customers and Markets

| B2B Generic Offers | Technological Innovation | Pure Services | Major Projects |

PART I STRATEGY FOUNDATIONS

Chapter 3	**Chapter 4**	**Chapter 5**	**Chapter 6**
Understanding Business-to-Business Purchasing	Information and Information Systems	Markets and Suppliers' Strategy	Segmentation and Marketing Strategy

PART II STRATEGY IMPLEMENTATION

Chapter 7

Generic Business-to-Business Offer Design and Management

Chapter 8

Market Access and Customer Management

Chapter 9

Communication and Publicity/Advertising

Chapter 10

Marketing and Technological Innovation

Chapter 11

The Marketing of Services

Chapter 12

Major Project Marketing

PART III STRATEGY DESIGN

Chapter 13	The Role and Organisation of Marketing
Chapter 14	Customer Position, Market Position, Marketing Strategies and Planning
Chapter 15	Issues and Specificities of International Marketing
Annex	The Internet and Marketing: Some Ideas

11 The Marketing of Services

As indicated in Chapter 7, the industrial offer includes a number of associated services that can represent an important *source of differentiation* for the company. Moreover, one of the great changes in business since 1990 has been the extent to which companies make use of *external suppliers* (i.e. outsourcing), particularly of service companies. Completely new professions have appeared (suppliers of temporary staff, industrial cleaners, information technology, maintenance, security services, etc.) or have dramatically increased in numbers (staff recruitment, consulting, auditing, etc.), without mentioning more traditional professions that have also changed, such as transport, banking and financial analysts, market surveyors and so on. Thus, *service providers* surround any company. They themselves have also undergone changes. For example, an information technology company may use a communications agency, a temporary work agency, industrial cleaners, security services and many other service providers.

To look at this relatively new field of activity is interesting for many reasons. First, as explained above, understanding the reasons for a company deciding to use an external services supplier will clarify our understanding of what leads a company to sub-contract. However, the service provision covers specificities that need to be identified, as they influence the role of marketing in this specific field. These consequences are interesting as they concern the management of service companies, and also that of the offers of services that are linked to an industrial service centred on a physical or material supply (see Chapter 7). This notion allows us to combine the specificities of business-to-business marketing with the issues of the service provision to underline the originalities of such a mix.

Definition of the Notion of Service and Service Specificities

Paradoxically, whereas everybody recognises a service, the 'scientific' definition of the notion of service is still controversial, and constantly evolving in the world of management research. For example, a company salesman using his or her car to call on a customer does not make use of any service provider. But if the car breaks down, suddenly they do: a garage mechanic, a taxi service to get to the car hire firm, the hire firm to have a hire car for the day, the banking system to pay by credit card.

This suggests that during the service provision, the customer deals with individuals who operate inside a complete organisational system that nearly always involves a physical format (e.g. a room within a hotel system). The individuals and the organisation vary in importance according to the purchasing situation and the customers. However, when the salesman in question buys a car from the car dealer, they have not bought a service but rather a product, even if they were in contact with one or more people who helped them to define their choice. After the purchase, the buyer may feel that 'at the dealer, the service was fantastic', given that he or she requested delivery for a particular day and time and, not only was this done, but it was accompanied by a free full tank of petrol and free number plates. Thus, 'services' associated with the supply of the car are also the source of buyer satisfaction. This can reflect satisfaction in relation to the whole process from the first visit to the dealers through to taking delivery of the car, which does not offset the pleasure that the buyer gets from the characteristics of the car itself.

Definition of the Notion of Service

Let us remind ourselves of the following definition of a service activity (Grönroos, 1990): 'The service is an activity or series of activities which are more or less immaterial, which usually but not always, is created through interaction between the customer and the persons from the service provider who do or do not use resources or physical supports and/or systems which supply a solution to the customer's problem.'

This definition is interesting as it allows us to distinguish the field of business-to-business marketing from that of services to companies. In the first case the physical or material form is the object of the exchange, which is materialised through a transfer of ownership. In the second this is just the support of the exchange, the object of which is the realisation of the service. The combination of a group of definitions proposed by different authors, as indicated in the following paragraph, has led to the conclusion that *the service is an act that distinguishes it from a product*.

Service Specificities and Consequences on Marketing

This perspective of services has particular managerial implications and consequences. While each characteristic is insufficient to give the notion of service its full meaning, they do combine to contribute to defining what services are all about. These characteristics can be grouped into five categories (see, for example, Doyle, 1994):

■ The *intangibility of services*: the service is not an object, even if the provision of the service involves the use of material supports for its creation. This intangibility has several consequences. The service cannot be seen, touched or tried before purchase, all of which makes it difficult to represent mentally what a service is and often to define it in advance of the outcome. Thus, communication has a particular role to play in making the service more 'tangible' (or, as Kotler says, 'tangibilising the intangible'). This involves giving the customer a precise and as accurate as possible vision of the service. In this field, *word of mouth* is an important factor. There are also problems for the customer linked to the evaluation of the price. Even if the notion of specifications (usually referred to as a service level agreement) is a useful tool for the definition of an expected quality, it cannot always have the same degree of precision as for tangible objects. This intangibility explains the inherent difficulty of legally protecting service innovations, as the writing up of a patent becomes quite complicated.

■ The *simultaneity* between design, production and consumption of a service makes it impossible to keep it in stock (the obvious example being aeroplane seats). This raises problems for the management of the production of the service, as it means having to constantly ensure the appropriateness between the demand, which is often fluctuating, and the means of production, that are more rigid owing to the number and types of skills required by the production team. This notion also shows that the service provision requires a higher rate of interaction between the supplier and his customer, the latter being involved in its realisation and often its very design.

■ The *inseparability* reflects the fact that the service is made and consumed at the same time, with obvious implications for the level of customer care training for staff. The conducting of the process, the absence of any mistakes during its delivery and the constant attention to the customer are all elements of the success. This characteristic, which clearly distinguishes it from the production process of a product, led to the creation of the new word, *servuction* (Eiglier and Langeard, 1987).

■ The *service provider–customer interaction* during the provision of the service results directly from the above. Let us just add a few remarks concerning the concept of interaction used in the field of services and of business-to-business marketing (Chapter 3). Much research has been centred on the service provider–customer interaction system during the provision of the service. The accent is put on the *service meeting*, in other words the interaction between the individuals during the provision of a given service. From the IMP interaction model presented in Chapter 2, this is limited to the duration of the transaction. The IMP model is based on the interaction between two organisations (purchasing centre–selling group) in a short-term perspective (the *transaction*) and a long-term perspective (the *relationship*). This different choice of the unit of analysis in the two fields can probably be explained by the fact that there is more interaction in services. To explain this difference, some authors (Langeard and Eiglier, 1994) speak of *global relationships* in services and *commercial relationships* in industrial products. The reintegration of the two perspectives was proposed, taking the existence of three levels of possible interaction into consideration (Marion, 1996):

- The interactions linked to the *commercial management* of the relationship that involves the actors of the customer purchasing centre and the provider's selling group

- The interactions linked to the *co-production* of the service by the personnel involved

- The interactions of *operational co-piloting* to control the realisation of the service.

Thus, we can distinguish what is related to the commercial relationship and what is related to the realisation of the service. The individuals involved in the three levels of interaction may or may not be the same. The complexity can be greater when the provider for the same customer performs several services simultaneously. For the service provider, the co-ordination of the three levels is extremely important. Let us underline some consequences of the presence of these interactions. The members of the service provider company who are in contact with the customer are confronted with the position of having to defend the interests of the service provider *and* those of the customer. Hence the importance of knowing how to manage this interface and being trained accordingly. In particular, it is decisive for the provider to know how to manage this customer participation. Finally, the customer evaluates both the production process (how the co-production happened) and the outcome (what was produced). This double perspective (process and content) can be reintegrated into the risk approach method (Chapter 3) that is applied to the field of services to companies. This is realised through taking three dimensions of risks linked to the transaction into consideration: the technical risks that reflect the risks linked to the technical quality of the result, the risks linked to the realisation of the service and the financial risks (Table 3.8).

■ The *heterogeneity of the services* implies that the performance of the services can, and often does, vary from one customer to another because of the characteristics of the interaction between the provider and each customer, in accordance with the behaviour of the persons in charge of the service realisation and customer capacity to integrate the provider's service. The characteristics of the interaction could also evolve with time (for the same customer from one service to another, or even for the same service) and in space (for example, from one service provider agency to another). Because services are so dependent on the input of people, there is a far higher inherent variability than occurs in a machine-based factory. Again, there are clear implications for *staff training*.

These characteristics have a number of implications, which, if we think too closely about the notion of a 'product', can lead to miscalculations in the design, and implementation of a marketing policy. We shall deal with two issues. The notion of *quality* will allow us to define the objectives and the difficulties linked to customer satisfaction. The second concerns certain aspects of the *role of marketing in services*, such as the composition of the offer, customer portfolio management, and notion of 'internal marketing'. What follows completes what has already been mentioned in the book concerning the processes, tools and methods of business-to-business marketing (Multistrat model, segmentation, customer portfolio, offer, etc.) and looks at some particular points concerning services, whether associated with a material offer or not. First however, let us look at some explanations as to why companies call upon service providers.

Turning to a Service

There are two groups of factors that can explain the phenomenon of resorting to external service providers. The first comes from basic economic or sociological factors that we shall call the '*propensity for service*'. The second is related to the functioning and organisation of companies and can be summed up as the under-standing of '*the reasons for calling in a service provider*'. Both groups of factors are connected to the customer's point of view. This being so, one must not forget the impact of a phenomenon that the notion of interaction allows us to understand, which is the role of suppliers – and of a whole industrial sector – in the perfecting of offers to make even the most reluctant of customers interested. We shall come across this again when we look at the notion of the quality of the service.

The Propensity for Service

There are many reasons to explain why there is an increasing demand for services across almost all industries. According to De Bandt (1991b), companies that are confronted by an increasing level of complexity in their technical and economic systems tend to increase their *organisation and management costs* without significantly increasing output. Externalisation would be a way to reduce these costs and/or increase productivity. In particular, the problems of staff management linked to fluctuations in the level of economic activity – the costs and problems of hiring and firing – strengthen this argument: the company maintains a minimum staff for normal activity and contracts out the other tasks. This perspective is linked to the concern of limiting fixed costs and by replacing them with variable costs and thoughts about the notions of break-even and financing company activities. To move on from this perspective means radical changes in the very concept of a company, its boundaries, its culture and workforce that are more and more focused on what is usually called 'core competencies'. Thus, the more 'traditional' companies have fewer propensities to turn to services than the newer and expanding sectors.

To this behaviour, we can add the belief that the introduction of an outside supplier into company activity permits more than just the bringing in of a precise expertise, stimulation of internal behaviour through the introduction of competition to avoid routine and monotony and to make changes easier. Example 17 gives an example from the 1980s. The explanations given in Example 17 will become clearer after examining in more detail the reasons companies turn to service providers.

The Reasons for Turning to a Service Provider

There are five groups of reasons for which companies turn to service providers (this is based on the results of a non-published survey made by researchers at E.M. Lyon in 1987 covering 342 companies).

Release from Managing a Task that is not Vital to the Main Activity of the Company

This factor is related to what was mentioned above. The company must consider that a particular activity is a *subsidiary problem*, which is a notion that can vary according to the circumstances and the personality of the manager(s) involved. Some activities more naturally fall into this category: cleaning, security, transport, the company restaurant, etc. Others appear more solidly anchored in the company's activity and yet they are performed by external sources. In Example 5 in Chapter 5, Mory–Ancel finally understood that the transport company could take over the management of the shelving of the company products. It would appear that the development of a service offer by a given service provider of all a professional sector makes the turning to external sources easier (Hammer and Champy, 1995).

The Will to Call in a Specialist

This permits a company to bring in specialised skills that the company feels difficult to manage internally. This could include communications, translation services, engineering for very hi-tech fields that are closely controlled by legislation, etc.

The Service Provider's Capacity to Evolve and to Advise

This is particularly areas that are constantly changing and hard to master for a non-specialised company. The provision of computer services is a good example of this (see Example 17).

Example 17 The Relationships between CORTAL and CAP GEMINI SOGETI

The Marketing Manager of the software subsidiary of the CAP GEMINI SOGETI group was asked some questions: What does a partner-customer mean to you? How do you identify in your portfolio, customers that seriously ask for a partnership? What do these partners require from you as a service provider?

Here are his answers.

'I have a partner-customer. In fact I have several. But I shall refer to one case only, a company named CORTAL of which you most probably know. CORTAL is a subsidiary of the COMPAGNIE BANCAIRE Group that has a long track record of innovation. CORTAL was formed in 1946 from the ideas of the Group CEO on financing SMEs, which led to a number of innovations in the financial world (CETELEM for financing household expenses, LOCABAIL for financing company investments, CARDIF for insurance and capital investments and now CORTAL). What is the basic idea behind CORTAL? It aims to act as a long distance bank (mail, telephone, now Internet <see www.e-cortal.com>) and this goes with a strategic positioning as personal asset manager. CORTAL's service is a highly personalised, top-of-the-line service competing with major banks and financial institutions. But they do so at a very low cost in order to attract large numbers of customers. Then the question is: how to do it? CORTAL started with two ideas: "everyone keeps their job" and "the search for excellence". CORTAL focused on their business: recruiting and managing customers, and personal asset advice. They succeeded in employing high-level staff able to advise customers on the best terms. All the other competencies necessary to CORTAL's development have been sub-contracted. For example, CARDIF is in charge of the investments and CAP SOGETI holds all the business computing. The outcome is that CORTAL succeeded in recruiting 450 000 prospective customers between 1983 and 1987. A "prospective customer" is somebody having shown interest in CORTAL either through a phone call, or by sending back a send-in coupon. CORTAL turned 50 000 of the prospective customers into real ones and they are now recruiting 2000 new customers per month, which is the equivalent of a small bank agency.

What does it mean? This systematic partnership policy keeps fixed expenses down to a minimum. And it allows CORTAL to follow up the firm's development with flexibility and ease. Adaptation ability and size progression can be met with well-adjusted solutions.

How does the CORTAL–CAP SOGETI partnership work? CAP SOGETI is the only partner for computing questions and has an outcome objective. This objective covers planning, costs and quality. This functions through a joint authority, the "Projects Managing Committee", that is held once a fortnight with CORTAL's Managing Director and top managers, and the Account Manager and his Projects Engineers on CAP SOGETI's side. This committee allows the partners to realise an efficient management structure, characterised by a quick reaction to different eventualities. There is a regular planning check, good coordination between users and computer engineers, and a sound synergy that results in a good decision process.

The main conclusion is that this type of a partnership puts aside unnecessary preoccupations. CORTAL can focus on their business. They are a leader, they reach excellence and maintain this position. They work with CAP SOGETI on the basis of the expression of their strategic and operational requirements. CAP SOGETI, on their side, brings in its own added value and its professionalism, which means a highly secure approach, in complete compliance with their customer's objectives. I firmly believe such a partnership allows each partner to maximise his or her energies in a synergistic way.'

Figure 11.1 Diagram showing the reasons for turning to a service provider

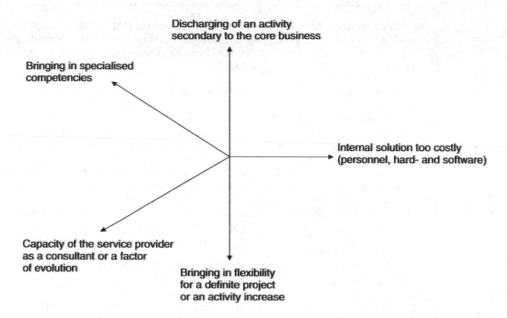

The Search for More Room for Manoeuvre During a One-Off Project or Busy Periods

These types of service offers have boomed (temporary work agencies, computer services, etc.).

The Wish to Replace a Costly Internal Solution in Terms of both Staff and Resources

This is related to the search for an improved output via a service provider, which will subsequently free staff and resources. Thus, the development of the long-term renting of industrial vehicles is related to an approach based on the intention to reduce company-operating costs.

It would appear that one or more of the above reasons can motivate the call for an external service provider. Figure 11.1 identifies those reasons that work to either inhibit or advance the level of adoption of external services. Thus, the contracting out of a subsidiary problem leads to the setting up of a stable and structured solution which cannot be dealt with in the same way as the search for flexibility or room to manoeuvre mentioned above. In the first case the choice of supplier, the appreciation of the consequences of this choice on the company organisation and the control systems that are set up, are different and more important. For example, using an outside catering service for the company restaurant is not the same as using a company for occasional one-off events. Also, the complete externalisation of the company computer organisation in the form of facilities management is not done in the same way as the use of a tailor-made service for specific projects.

It is also possible that several of these reasons can be combined. Therefore, it is important for any service provider to understand the different reasons as to why a customer calls them in, in order to adapt the service and how it is delivered. Motives such as a desire for release from managing a task lead to the search for increased output, the standardisation of the offer and the fixing of precise standards of quality. The case to bring in specialised skills, on the other hand, leads to a personalisation of the relationship and greater flexibility in the service. For example, a company's computer department may regularly call upon a service provider to use qualified staff under a sub-contracting agreement, while consulting other providers for specific computer projects. In the first case, the availability of individuals with the required skills at any given moment is vital and the service provider is considered as a kind of temporary work agency. In the second case, the technical and in project management expertise of the provider is essential. Finally, however, the same provider could be used, but this is not always the case.

Services Marketing

In service activities, the interaction between the *service provider* and the *customer* is crucial, as underlined above. The marketing of service activities, even if it promotes interaction more naturally than the marketing of industrial products, does not occupy a more important position in our minds in the continuum of marketing approaches. In services, it is equally possible to seek a market position through the standardisation of the service by reducing the level of interaction with the clientele during the delivery, as when operating the opposite policy of increasing interaction. The result of these choices is greater or lesser customer participation in the realisation of the service.

The processes, tools and methods presented above apply to the role of marketing of service activities to industry. However, we feel it is necessary to give some details concerning the particular cases dealt with in this chapter. The aim is not to define a complete conception of the marketing of services to companies, but rather to give additional insights that will allow us to make useful changes in the adaptation of certain elements concerning the offer, the adjustment between the demand and production capacity and internal marketing.

The Offer of Services

Services are a field in which the possibilities of evolution of the composition of the offer are high. To present a view of different possible combinations we shall use both the theoretical framework for service offers proposed by Eiglier and Langeard (1987) and Mory–Ancel (Example 5). The framework presents a description of a service offer as made of a 'basic principal service', a 'basic secondary service' and 'peripheral services'. Each class is detailed in 'elementary services'. Figure 11.2

Figure 11.2   Structuring a transport offer

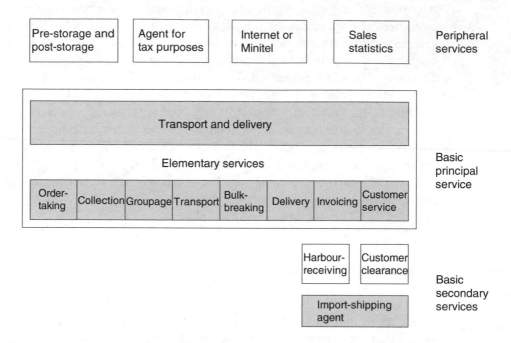

provides us with a view of the service exchanged at the beginning of the situation described. Figure 11.3 gives an account of the offer resulting from the significant changes that occurred between the two companies when developing their relationship.

A *'basic principal service'* means the response to the main reason for establishing the relationship, involving a series of *'elementary services'* whose totality is required for the fulfilment of the desired service by the customer. From the provider's point of view, the basic principal service is the *raison d'être* for the company and the profession as a whole. It is the principal service that the company develops, and which defines its position on the market. From the customer's point of view, the basic principal service is the reason why they enter into a relationship with the provider. If we use the terminology concerning the offer used in Chapter 7, it responds to the customer's *veto requirements*.

Secondly, the customer uses another series of elementary services for the receipt of imported goods at the ports, their customs clearance, and subsequent storage before being transported along with other products. These services form a group that can be called *'basic secondary services'* or 'subsidiary services', in other words 'maritime import transit'. The case described is not the only one, as many companies, to enrich their offer of services, include basic secondary services.

To support these principal activities, the transport company has developed *'peripheral services'* (pre-storage and post-storage, information processing through Minitel or the Internet, sales statistics, etc.) that the customer can use if they wish

Figure 11.3 Design of the principal basic service: 'shelf-space supply and management'

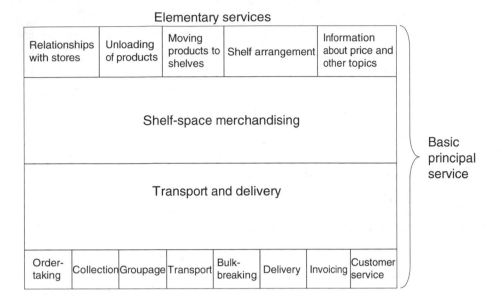

to, depending upon the characteristics of their own internal organisation. Figure 11.2 illustrates the structuring of the service provider's offer.

At this stage, Ancel, the customer, used three types of services (principal, secondary and peripheral – in grey in Figure 11.2) called 'global services', meaning what the customer actually bought. In the relations that followed between Mory and Ancel, this developed via an adaptation process of the provision, at Ancel's request, of the peripheral services (marking of the prices, additional packaging) which led to a new configuration of the 'shelf-space supply and management' as illustrated in Figure 11.3.

This new configuration of the service helps to define a *principal basic service* that is completely different from the previous one, involving the association of two service offers, one classical, the 'transport and delivery', the other new, the 'shelf-space merchandising'. The fact that the two are inseparable led to the defining of a new and more complex basic principal service and to the creation of a specialised Strategic Business Unit (SBU) by Mory. Indeed, it is impossible to deal with a customer's demand through the juxtaposition of a basic secondary service 'merchandising' with the basic principal service of 'transport and delivery'. The service required demanded changes to be made, resulting in the definition of a completely new basic service. Obviously, other basic secondary services and peripheral services remain at the customer's disposal in accordance with their needs.

This method of presentation and analysis has many advantages. It enables us to identify the nature of the services included in a service offer. This identification has two uses. First, it allows the customer to have an idea of the *service on offer*. Secondly, it can be used to find out the *cost* of each elementary service, thus serving the pricing policy and management control of the company. It is also very useful in the fight against a common trend in service companies, namely to broaden their service offering under the pressure of the competition, without having the customer pay the difference. Often the latter is not even aware of all the services being provided. The provider must, in all circumstances, enhance the value of the services in order to establish their reputation with the customer and to strengthen their competitive position, which does not automatically and systematically mean invoicing all the elements. But at least the customer needs to be made aware of them.

It is obvious that this type of reasoning feeds directly into our thinking on the notion of company marketing strategy: the search for competitive differentiation, market segmentation and the choice of target segments, offer flexibility and choice of target customers via customer portfolio management.

The Adjustment Between the Demand and Production Capacity

As indicated, the specificity of business-to-business marketing is the integration of both market and customer approaches and the fact that customer portfolio management is an important tool for company positioning (see Chapter 8). Everything we have said about industrial products is also applicable to industrial services. However, we also mentioned that services cannot be stored, which means that production capacity must be redefined to fit market demand. This adjustment is more difficult to perform than in manufacturing industries that seek to optimise the use of their production tools by playing with the level of their stocks if necessary.

For services, a distinction can be made between the *theoretically available* production capacity and *optimum* capacity, which corresponds to the workload of the employees above which service quality begins to fall. The adjustment between the demand (particularly if it is irregular or cyclical) and production capacity must take the following into consideration:

- Any demand in excess of theoretical production capacity leads to loss of business

- Any demand that is satisfied and is above the optimal production capacity risks having a negative impact on the quality, particularly if the situation continues

- Any demand below optimal production capacity weighs on the profitability of the company, reduces the staff motivation and can affect company image.

To respond to these challenges, the service company has three means at its disposal. One aims to regulate the demand through flexible pricing policies ('yield management'), as commonly used by transport services (the rail companies, airline companies, etc.). However, this type of approach is rather limited to the field of consumer services and more difficult to apply to business-to-business situations. A second is to manage the composition of the clientele through precise customer portfolio management and the identification of a mass of target customers such that their combined demand does not exceed the optimal production capacity. The required flexibility to make up for slack periods comes from the management of non-priority customers. Finally, the last method is to turn to external sources, sometimes 'friendly competitors', especially when the company is confronted by customer projects. This takes us back to our findings in Chapter 7 concerning the offer and in Chapter 12 on the marketing of major projects, but thus limited to a few areas such as computer services whose characteristics permit such practices.

Internal Marketing

This term implies a double phenomenon. The first is the prime importance of employee behaviour when in contact with the client, interacting in the delivery of a service. Secondly, and consequently, the heterogeneity in service quality comes first of all from the differences in skills and the capacity of those responsible for the realisation of the service to manage a relationship.

The issues, however, are more complex than this, as illustrated in Figure 11.4.

In fact, it is a game of three players. The management is responsible for the design of the service offer and the communication to the marketplace, while the staffs are involved in the interaction with the customer. The staffs play a decisive role in the quality of the service provision and customer satisfaction, while the remainder of the company acts as a group of support staff ready to intervene and assist the persons involved in the task. Hence the need to bring as much coherence as possible to the *promises* (reputation, references, communication, etc.) and the *service* made available. In this way, internal personnel in fact become the first customers of manage-

Figure 11.4 The issues of internal marketing

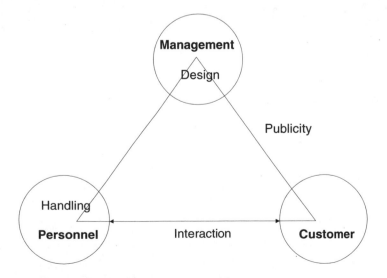

ment. They must be convinced, listened to and given the means and tools necessary to fulfil customer expectations. This explains the importance given to internal relationships, the search for coherence and staff solidarity in service industries.

Quality and Customer Satisfaction

In services, the problems of quality and customer satisfaction are difficult to deal with for several reasons. It is difficult for the supplier to define clearly the quality of a service offer and to guarantee this quality over time and space. Moreover, it is difficult for the customer to define and to give a precise idea of what exactly is expected from the service offer. Furthermore, there is the fact that the actors involved are numerous on both sides and have their own ideas of things. Figure 11.5 outlines these problems.

The creation of customer satisfaction, in other words the assessment of the service supplied by the service provider, comes from several different sources. ($D1$, $D2$, $D3$ in Figure 11.5).

$D1$ is the difference between the *desired quality* of the service by the provider according to their own analysis of the customer's needs, and the service that they provide *in reality*. This gap can come from internal staff problems concerning the identification of the customer's needs, a workload that means the most skilled people are not always available, or more simply, the inability to meet the requirements of the customer.

$D2$ relates to the difference between the customer's *implicit* and *explicit expectations* and his view of the *reality* of the situation. Not being able to test or try out the service in advance, the customer makes an assumption as to what the service should be like in relation to the problem to be solved. This representation is the result of a double mechanism. First of all there are the personal and cultural

Figure 11.5   Quality and customer satisfaction in services

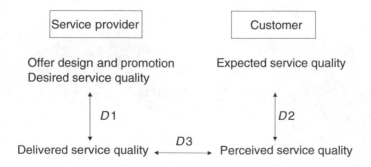

Reprinted with permission from the *Journal of Marketing*, published by the American Marketing Association: A. Parasuraman, Valerie A. Zeithaml and Leonard L. Berry, 'A Conceptual Model of Service Quality and Its Implications for Future Research', *Journal of Marketing*, vol. 49, no. 4, 1985, p. 48.

presuppositions (differences between Anglo-Saxons and the Latins on this point, for example) that will create a kind of substratum of what the customer expects from a particular service. Then, he or she will try to evaluate the providers' offer. This customer evaluation will be based on such information as documents supplied by the provider, the selling arguments, communications, advertising, references presented and what has been heard by word of mouth. If the service provider has previously acted as a supplier, this will also be part of the evaluation. This information contains objective elements, but also elements of appreciation, images and differences of opinion. A service provider can be highly appreciated by one customer yet not at all by another and will be able to explain this difference by problems encountered with the latter's behaviour. As the customer is represented by a purchasing centre and co-production centre, the differences in opinion between the various staff members involved can be significant.

Thus, the gap $D3$ is the result of two series of phenomena: the 'objective' difference between the promise and reality on the one hand, and the differences between customer expectations and reality. The level of customer satisfaction is directly linked to the *reduction* or the *increase of the gap*.

It is feasible to argue that the service providers are mainly responsible for the creation of expectations through their communication and interaction process, and therefore in a way for the gaps which may appear afterwards. The responsibility rests here with managing the ambiguities created by the arguments used to sell the service. These have to have a *trade off*, both stressing the positive aspects while also making the customers aware of what they can realistically expect from the service and the provider. Any effort made by the service provider to supply concrete descriptions on the dimensions of the offer, its characteristics (the outcome of the service/need) and the delivery process (the way the result is reached), all aim at making different elements of the offer more 'tangible' for the customer. This allows the seller to show the reality and simultaneously to contribute to bridging the gap between the two representations that the different actors have. This is essential. However, it must not be forgotten that, all in all, the realisation of the service also involves the *customer*, and from the provider's point of view, the desire and the quality of the customer participation as hoped for by the service provider is never guaranteed. For some authors (Chase, 1979, 1981) customer participation in the process is problematic, as the service provider cannot control the role, the behaviour and productivity. Finally, it is difficult to master the quality of the perceived service. According to this argument, the service provider must reduce customer participation. Others have shown that customer participation can help to improve the economic performance and be an element of the satisfaction (Lovelock and Young, 1979; Eiglier and Langeard, 1987). Thus, customer capacity and desire to participate are two important elements to take into consideration in each case, as they condition many dimensions such as perceived quality and satisfaction.

The following anecdote will help to clarify our ideas concerning the impact of customer participation on the technical quality of the service. Shell has, among its offers, a service named 'Engine Accuracy Audit' that allows users to check the state of their truck engines from analysis of the engine oil. This extremely highly sophisticated service offer requires the customer to collect a sample of the engine oil (during an oil change, for example) and to send it to Shell's laboratory. An analysis of one such sample indicated that, for reasons of hygiene, the person responsible for taking the oil sample had washed and rinsed his hands just before extracting the oil. Unfortunately, a little water then became mixed in with the oil. Water in the oil suggests there is a problem with the cylinder head, which could prove to be serious. This shows the type of diagnosis supplied by the laboratory to the customer for reasons of prevention and to anticipate problems in the future and the difficulties that may arise from customer's participation.

For more precision, we have grouped together in Figure 11.6 several dimensions of the service quality according to four headings: institutional, technical, relational and functional. The system formed by these four dimensions means they can reinforce one another, just as they can weaken one another through successive 'contamination'. The *institutional dimension* is both the result of the three others and yet also something more. All the elements linked to the communication and the image of the service provider include and go beyond the other dimensions. This insti-

Figure 11.6   The dimensions of service quality

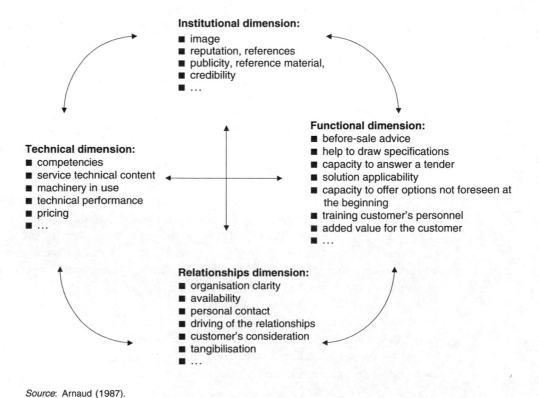

Source: Arnaud (1987).

tutional dimension contributes to the company being informed of bids for tender or being consulted spontaneously for its skills, which reduces overall commercial effort.

The *technical dimension* makes up the heart of the service offer, in other words the technical solution. Some elements of this are more visible than others. The means used and the competencies involved are less so. Thus, it is important to pay attention to the means involved to be able to support those that are less visible in the technical performance.

The *relational dimension* has more importance here than in other marketing environments. It is the maintenance of *credibility over time*. Arrogant experts, who are not very obliging and ill-suited to customer contact quickly become unbearable, whatever their training and competencies. The term *'functional dimension'* has been used to underline the idea that only the added value of the customer service has any real meaning as far as marketing is concerned. Thus, the following points are very important. The customer use of a provider's service depends on their internal organisation and ways of operating (availability of the people concerned, competencies, and so on). The concept of interaction takes on its whole meaning here. It is important that the suppliers adapt their service, in its design and realisation (as they gradually gets to know their customer) by integrating customer capacity to optimise their contribution.

Owing to the number and the variety of the quality dimensions of a service offer, the use of customer satisfaction surveys by management is even more essential where services are concerned (see Chapter 4). It is not surprising that a pioneer in this area, such as Rank Xerox, has initiated regular customer satisfaction surveys for its after-sales services and that it uses the results to motivate and manage the staff, which is logical in the quest for quality.

Conclusion

The specificities mentioned above for the marketing of service activities could, we feel, be useful for the directors of business-to-business companies. As underlined in Chapter 7, an industrial offer incorporates an increasingly large service element. In some industrial sectors, this element can represent an amount that is sometimes more important than the value of the material it is designed for (in computing, for example).

Such changes have led companies to increase their service offers, which has obviously not been without problems. A 'catalogue of services' cannot be established in the same way as a catalogue of products can, especially if the services are designed to be adapted to the clientele. The design of an offer of services, whether it is linked to a material offer or not, is different from that of a purely material offer.

Moreover, the sale of services to companies requires flexibility in the sales process, or even in the conditions and pay of the sales team. Functions such as 'sales engineer' or 'technical salesman', when they have a long sales record, cannot immediately change to becoming services oriented. The new issues linked to the design and realisation of the service (co-production between the supplier and the customer) demands much more of an effort to adapt the sales methods and behaviours that cannot be left to the resourcefulness of the supplier's staff.

References and Further Reading

Arnaud, J.M. (1987) 'Comment contrôler et gérer la qualité de service', Actes du Colloque 'Les synergies tertiares: qu'attendre d'un prestataire de servies', Paris, IRE.

Bandt, J. de (1991a) *Les services: productivité et service*, Paris, Economica.

Bandt, J. de (1991b) *Services et modèles de croissance*, Paris, Economica.

Chase, R.B. (1979) 'Entreprises de services: connectées ou déconnectées?', *Harvard l'Expansion*, 3, 87–93.

Chase, R.B. (1981) 'The Customer Contact Approach to Services: Theoretical Bases and Practical Extensions', *Operations Research*, 29:4, 686–706.

Doyle, P. (1994) *Marketing Management and Strategy*, Englewood Cliffs, Prentice-Hall.

Dumoulin, C. *et al.* (1991) *Entreprises de services: 7 facterus clés de réussite*, Paris, Ed. d'Organisation.

Eiglier, P. and Langeard, E. (1987) *Servuction: le marketing des services*, New York, McGraw-Hill.

Gadrey, J. 'Le service n'est pas un produit: quelques implications pour l'analyse économique et pour la gestion', *Politiques et Management Public*, 9:1, 22–33.

Grönroos, C. (1990) *Service Management and Marketing: Managing the Moments of Truth in Service Competition*, Lexington, Lexington Books.

Hammer, M. and Champy, J. (1995) *Re-Engineering the Corporation*, London, Nicholas Brearley.

Langeard, E. and Eiglier, P. (1994) 'Relation de service et marketing', *Décisions Marketing*, 2, 13–21.

Lovelock, C.H. and Wright, L. (1998) *Principles of Service Marketing and Management*, Englewood Cliffs, Prentice-Hall.

Lovelock, C.H. and Young, R.F. (1979) 'Look to Consumers to Increase Productivity', *Harvard Business Review*, May–June, 168–79.

Marion, F. (1996) 'La participation du client à la réalisation du service en milieu inter organisationnel', Thèse de Doctorat en Sciences de Gestion, Université Jean Moulin Lyon III.

Parasuraman, C.A., Zeithaml, V.A. and Berry, L.L. (1979) 'A Conceptual Model of Service Quality and its Implication for Future Research', *Journal of Marketing*, 49, 41–50.

Discussion Questions

1 What makes a difference between a product and a service?
2 Why is the definition of service quality different from that of product quality?
3 What are the components of the service delivered to a customer?
4 Why are customers increasingly calling in service providers?

Chapter 1

Competitiveness, Marketing and Business-to-Business Marketing

What is marketing all about
Different marketing environments
B2B marketing

Chapter 2

Business-to-Business Customers and Markets

B2B Generic Offers	Technological Innovation	Pure Services	Major Projects

PART I STRATEGY FOUNDATIONS

Chapter 3	Chapter 4	Chapter 5	Chapter 6
Understanding Business-to-Business Purchasing	Information and Information Systems	Markets and Suppliers' Strategy	Segmentation and Marketing Strategy

PART II STRATEGY IMPLEMENTATION

Chapter 7			
Generic Business-to-Business Offer Design and Management			

Chapter 8	Chapter 10	Chapter 11	Chapter 12
Market Access and Customer Management	Marketing and Technological Innovation	The Marketing of Services	Major Project Marketing

Chapter 9
Communication and Publicity/ Advertising

PART III STRATEGY DESIGN

Chapter 13	The Role and Organisation of Marketing
Chapter 14	Customer Position, Market Position, Marketing Strategies and Planning
Chapter 15	Issues and Specificities of International Marketing
Annex	The Internet and Marketing: Some Ideas

12 Major Project Marketing

'Major project' marketing encompasses the field of projects realised in many industrial sectors. A dam (civil engineering), an architectural development (construction), a container ship (shipping), a very high-speed train or a public network transport (transport), a national telecommunication system (telecommunication) or a turnkey factory (engineering) are all examples of major projects.

These operations are also often named 'deals' or 'business deals'. To clarify things, we conventionally adopt the term *deal* as seen from the supplier's point of view that will end with realising a customer's *project*. A major project can be defined as a 'complex transaction concerning a group of products, services and research, specifically designed, in a given period of time, to create specific assets for the buyer' (Cova, 1990). The project is different in scope and complexity from a system. The project is more typically a (simpler) combination of standard products and services, undertaken by the supplier (civil engineering, access roads, material, etc.). In this chapter, we shall use only the term 'project'.

Our aim is to identify the characteristics that are common to all these activities, first of all from the purchase point of view, and then to examine the consequences for the marketing process. In Chapter 2 we categorised the marketing of projects as having a higher degree of interaction between the supplier and the customer. We must now add a reflection on the discontinuous (one-off) nature of the transaction between the supplier and the customer. We shall see how the supplier–customer relation is modified in such a way that the tools required for a continuous relationship must be adapted to this particular situation.

Main Characteristics

As already indicated, the first characteristic is the *lack of continuity of the economic relationship* between the supplier and the customer. A customer in a developing country buying a hydroelectric dam or an oil refinery is highly unlikely to do so again for many years. Thus, it is difficult to speak of a 'relationship', as with industrial products or services handled on a more repetitive basis.

A second characteristic of project activities for the seller is the *uniqueness* of each transaction: each project requires the one-off mobilisation of company resources and network of partners for the creation and delivery of an ad hoc answer.

A third characteristic is the *complexity* of the transaction: the number of people involved is considerable on both sides, for the supplier and the customer. This adds an extra level of complexity, the main features of which may include multiculturalism, the price of the transaction that often requires elaborate financing, the length of the transaction that lasts several months, and the fact that the whole project can cover several years.

Because of these specificities, supplier–marketing strategy is based on trying to make up for this discontinuity in the relationship through *social and relational continuity*. The whole marketing approach is based upon the maintaining of relationships, either directly with the customer or indirectly via those who are somehow likely to be involved in a project with the customer. Relationships basically enable the supplier to hear about projects in advance and to prepare for them or to co-build or co-develop them with the customer, as it is the case with the creative offers we shall examine later.

The Characteristics of Project Purchasing

The examples mentioned in the opening part of this chapter show that, in many cases, the purchaser is a public organisation (the state, local council, semi-public company, etc.) This means that particular mechanisms and rules governing the public purchase (the invitation to bid) apply in a number of situations. There are many different forms for this (Cova, 1990):

1. The invitation to bid based on *price*, and the choice is made based on the lowest price

2. The invitation to bid based on the *best presentation*, choice is made based on criteria other than price

3. The invitation to bid is *limited to the best price*, there is an initial phase to short-list the candidates, then a second phase to allow the candidates to answer the invitation to bid, then the procedure is the same as 1 above

4. The invitation to bid limited to the *best presentation*; the candidates are short-listed, and then the process is the same as 2 above

5. The invitation to bid is *negotiated and competitive*, the most common form in business-to-business markets; the short-listed suppliers respond to the invitation, then various negotiations take place between supplier and customer.

The last form dominates business-to-business markets. For public- and government-sponsored markets, it would appear that things are moving this way, too, even if there remain doubts as to the openness of such a form of consultation. Given the similarity between the public and private markets, we shall not bother to make the distinction in the rest of this chapter. Instead, we shall look at the purchasing process and the kind of people involved.

The Purchasing Process

This is presented in Table 12.1. The process can be seen as being one of reducing the unknown factors that surround the project. The level of uncertainty at the start (as with innovations, see Chapter 10) can vary according to the projects and those involved. Better understanding of the issues involved progressively reduces uncertainty, which itself is the result of all the exchanges and dialogues with the various organisations that are involved. Little by little, the customers adjust their demand and short-list possible suppliers. Depending on the circumstances, the phases can change order. For some projects, such as architectural or town planning, phases 1 and 5 become the object of a special kind of procedure, a kind of *pilot study*, to give the planners time to reconsider various aspects. From the supplier point of view, any outline will show that consultation via an invitation to bid happens only in phase 5. Here, a number of mainly social and informative exchanges can take place with the potential suppliers, offering the suppliers an undeniable advantage.

For a supplier, the formalisation of the phases of the process is based on experience and any survey of the range of similar projects, which have either been won or lost, is rich in information. A reflection on the action led either directly (by the supplier himself) or indirectly (via other organisations concerned with the project) and on the phases of the process allows the company to identify some elements that can help to anticipate future projects.

Table 12.1   The purchase process

Phase	Events
1	Initiatory proceedings
2	Gathering purchasing partners
3	Definition of needs and requirements
4	Analysis of offer market
5	Short-listing or prior qualification of suppliers
6	Information exchange with short-listed suppliers – changes in requirements
7	Procedure of invitation to tender
8	Receipt, analysis and comparison of offers
9	Negotiations
10	Final selection
11	Final negotiation and clinching of deal contract
12	Fulfilment of the deal

Projects: A Broadening of the Notion of Purchasing Centre?

The high degree of interaction between the players involved can lead to the managing of the project by so many organisations that one can begin to wonder whether the notion of purchasing centre we gave in Chapter 3 is still valid. Let us look at the case of Eurotunnel. The decision by the public authorities not to finance the total project led associating consortiums of entrepreneurs to finance their work and to give them Eurotunnel shareholder status, paid later via the operating profits. The press (*The Economist*, 21–27 January 1995) expressed criticism concerning their behaviour in that they were suspected of promoting self-interest rather than that of the tunnel itself. Thus, an actor can have several roles. The initial supplier can integrate the purchasing centre to select a common sub-contractor and thus continue this dual role throughout the project.

This is why we prefer to maintain the broader notion of the system of participation in the purchasing process of projects (Figure 12.1), which goes beyond that of the basic purchasing centre.

Identifying the place, role and influence of each actor (both individuals and organisations) in the different phases of the process is the key to understanding the events that end in the selection of partners and in the evolution of the content and form of the project sentence. Therefore, a specific kind of analysis can act as a basis for project marketing. The high degree of uncertainty mentioned above has an effect on several levels. Who is the customer? When will the project be ready? What are

Figure 12.1   System of participants in the purchasing process of a project

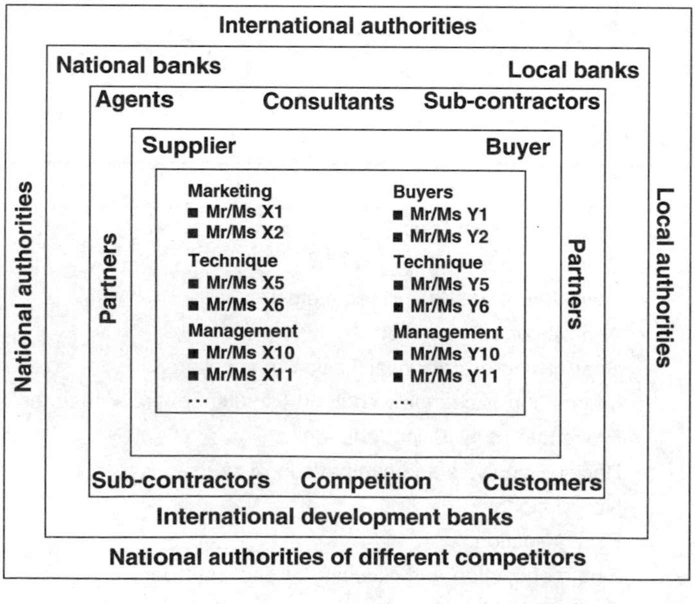

Source: Cova (1990).

the terms and conditions? Who are, or who will be, the partners? Which technologies and solutions have been accepted or rejected? Who makes the decisions? The interaction between the participants – and, in particular, the supplier's proposition capacity which is high upstream of the invitation to bid – are very important in the dynamics of the customer's project.

Thus, owing to the characteristics of purchasing process, the multiplicity of the participants and their involvement in each phase, the supplier has to anticipate what will result from the marketing phase as far upstream as possible.

The Marketing Phase in Project Industries

The formulation and elaboration of a project for a customer is a complex operation that can begin, as mentioned above, long before the consultation via the invitation to bid to the supplier market. This operation involves important customer resources in great uncertainty as far as the outcome is concerned. Thus, for the supplier at any given time, the 'market' is composed of a group of different marketing situations according to the degree of elaboration of the project for the customer and how much the supplier knows about this.

The supplier's marketing process involves mobilising resources on two interdependent and complementary levels:

■ On the one hand, there is an *external aspect* of the project. This means having the capacity to gain access to information to detect, far upstream, the existence of projects and developing and mobilising both internally and externally the skills (particularly financial and technical) that could then be brought together. This external project strategy allows the suppliers to present themselves in the best possible light. This process of anticipation is a key factor of success in as much as most professionals explain that a company is unlikely to get the deal if it finds out about it at the time of the invitation to bid.

■ On the other hand, there is also an *internal aspect* to a given project. For the supplier, this means adapting the offer and mobilising resources according to the project and the competition. This strategy requires company flexibility and reactivity, both of which are usually the result of off-project investments.

Figure 12.2 details this process by looking at the different phases of the two levels of the strategy: those external and internal to the project.

The External Project Process

The determination of *strategic priorities* is the result of a process we looked at in Chapter 5. As with any company, this means the allocating of resources between activities. These will allow for the purchase and development of skills (techno-

Figure 12.2   The project marketing process

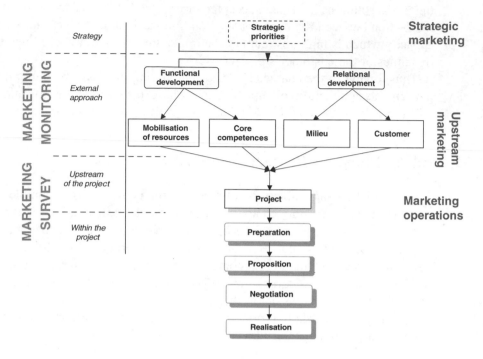

Source: Cova and Salle (1999).

logical and financial, etc.) to formulate offers for certain types of projects and to strengthen the company's market position. However, specificities do exist in project marketing, one of which concerns the nature of the skills to gather together to formulate the offers for the projects. Another is the characteristic of the markets themselves.

Many projects are *multidimensional and complex* and therefore require the availability of many different and complementary skills to put together a solution. Thus, a telecommunications project for the armed forces in a developing country requires, other than skills in telecommunications, the capacity to draw up a development plan, to complete the necessary civil engineering works (roads, buildings, etc.) for the relays and the necessary vehicles. Moreover, the capacity to propose a financial arrangement will be an essential element to the proposed solution. A telecommunications company is not a civil engineer, a vehicle manufacturer, or a bank. Consequently, it must mobilise in advance the skills (a consortium of companies) to enable it to have all the required competences for a given project, or it can become part of a consortium that is led by another company. Players in these environments must accept that the amalgamation of skills will change with each deal/project. It is obvious that this objective can be met only through the setting up of advanced co-ordination of the skills used and their evolution, the management of interests which are common and specific to each company and the spread of investments, thus the strategies of the companies concerned. All these strategic approaches may be grouped into two types: the *relational* development that aims to establish and enrich a relational position and a *functional* development whose objective is to build the supplier's functional position.

External relational and functional developments make up a second specificity of this business. With the purchasing centres being broken up into numerous organisational and individual participants, and the number of projects often being very few, it is difficult to make use of the notion of a 'market'. This concept refers to numerous customers and competitive suppliers, who are part of a more or less favourable environment. From the project perspective we have to go beyond the traditional business-to-business concepts. This implies also going beyond the Multistrat model (Chapter 6) in order to build an approach specific to project marketing.

The term 'milieu' is often used in reference to all the socio-economic actors involved in company activity (Cova, Mazet and Salle, 1998). The accent is put on the systems of influence and the informal or weak links between the different trading and non-trading players (implicit rules of the game). Generally, two dimensions limit a milieu: geographic and functional. For example, Electricité de France (the French Electricity Board) considers the distribution of electricity in Poland as a strategic unit: functional application = electrical distribution; location = Poland. A public buildings company may so consider that the network of the firms acting in a given geographical area represents a major issue. This company must then gather both the technical skills and the network of partner companies able to join it on a given project (i.e. functional perspective). It must also build a good position in relation to all the players taking part in any decision in the area in question (i.e. geographic perspective). This leads to make a distinction between the *offer milieu* that refers to all the players involved in building the offer. The *demand milieu* refers to the complexity of the customer's formation and decision making.

The external approach is implemented though a series of marketing actions with two objectives:

■ To build the capacity to formulate offers in accordance with the characteristics of each project. This translates (Table 12.2) into *investment in the networks*, particularly in the offer milieu, to mobilise the technical and financial skills and to ensure the development of the potential offer.

■ To gain the capacity to *detect customers' projects far upstream*. This means investing time and effort in the networks, particularly in the demand milieu, in a kind of 'project watch'.

We propose a 9-step method for the analysis of the company milieu, as shown in Table 12.2.

In relation to the process mentioned in Chapters 5–9, here we are more interested in a socio-economic perspective that applies to a heterogeneous network of actors.

Table 12.2   The milieu method of analysis

1. Identification of the approach to *defining and limiting a milieu* (functional/geographical)
2. Identification of the company's *activity milieu*
3. Identification and choice of *priority milieu*; these choices can be made with tools which are similar to those used for the SBU portfolio (see Chapter 5)
4. Identification of the *players*
5. *Characteristics of the players*: role, influence, evolution
6. Characterisation of *relationships between players* (conflicting, competition, co-existence, co-operation, collusion) and possible evolution
7. Identifying the *main players* and their evolution
8. Diagnosis of the *company position* in the milieu
9. Plan of action: *nature and target of investments* in the milieu

The investments to build the *relational and functional positions* correspond the strategic need to be well positioned within the players' networks that make up the milieu. The aim is to establish and develop a position within the network (milieu) giving the supplier the capacity, as far as possible, to control the developments and to gain access to resources. These are external networks in the supply milieu composed of potential partners that may come together to co-ordinate the elaboration of the offer for a given project; and in the demand milieu, made up of players who are likely to co-ordinate a range of activities with the customer. There are internal networks, too, in the case of subsidiaries of those industrial groups who have multiple skills to offer for a given project.

By investing in the networks of a particular demand milieu, the company 'knits together' this milieu through its social contacts with other central players who have relationships with many other players of the same milieu. For this, the company can use intermediaries (agents) or approach the players directly (this is an important task for senior engineers and company management). For example, an automatic road toll specialist who has developed skills in access to city centres will invest in a certain number of relationships in order to become someone who is consulted as soon as a project of this kind comes to light. This means knowing a number of traffic and road specialists in a number of different towns, going to congresses, trade fairs or colloquiums, keeping up relationships with other specialists (e.g. design offices) or public and financial organisations and institutions. These players have a central role in the milieu concerned which, depending on the nature of the relationships between them and the companies, permits them to be informed of projects far upstream. They add accuracy to the information and monitoring systems, which saves a supplier from having to overinvest haphazardly in order to be sure of getting the right information on potential projects. Figure 12.1 indicates that relational development can be driven through the combination of relationships with the milieu central players and with customers. In some environments, even if discontinuity is the law of project marketing, one may find some frequency of customers' projects, although each time the particular requirement will be somewhat different.

In these situations, the approach is similar to that of business-to-business marketing, but with a higher degree of complexity owing to the presence of many external players influencing the customer's decision process.

By investing in the supply milieu networks, the company also 'knits together' the central actors of a technical or financial or other resources network that it can approach and mobilise for a specific project (proposition in Figure 12.2). The central actors themselves do the same, thereby widening the information system and the possibilities of mobilising company resources. We can add that the structure of the major diversified industrial groups sometimes requires as much management effort within the supply milieu as when it involves independent partners. This proposition can be combined with the core offer. This core offer is made of the technical, financial and other competencies that the supplier develops internally and that make up for its position in their core market. This approach bears some similarities with the design of the offer in business-to-business marketing (Chapter 7).

In our hypothetical example of the toll system, the company could have contacts with the computer services companies, manufacturers of computer equipment, installers, civil engineers and other players to be able to create an offer for a given project whenever required. In these one-off projects, network investments, the links between individuals and between organisations are extremely important. Therefore, in certain industrial sectors, for example computer services or the building and civil engineering profession, individuals often change companies within the same sector, which enables them to know the supply and the demand milieu. Such practices make it easier to bring several computer service companies and a manufacturer together for major computer projects.

Marketing and technological monitoring is mainly based on the investments made in the networks, which allow the company to closely support the monitoring of critical elements in the marketing (socio-economic) and technical fields. Investment in the networks is one way of gathering information. But it is not the only one. Technological monitoring of patents, general documentation, permanent documentary surveys, market or Delphi surveys, trade fairs, congresses and databases are other such sources. Some players will be more closely monitored than others. For example, in civil engineering the major international engineering consultancies are precisely managed, with the maintenance of very precise files similar to customer files outlined in Chapter 7.

From our experience, we see that companies working in project marketing are gradually setting up more formalised systems of marketing and technological monitoring. Two types of monitoring process (particularly socio-economic) are used:

- The systems that are centred on *information* ('monitoring systems'). These are the collection, analysis and transmitting systems of information based on a documentary basis within a department that has formally been given this task.

- The systems that are centred on *individuals*. These systems work on the fact that certain individuals, owing to their function and role in the company, have access to important information concerning the market, the competition or the projects. The information comes from exchanges between individuals 'in the know' during events organised by the company: functions, meetings, etc.

In practice, companies combine the two systems with variations according to the type of information to be gathered. For example, a construction company will use an economically oriented system, which is organised to observe the markets and which treats statistical data (start-up date, geographical spread, evolutions, etc.). It may also utilise a system that concentrates on the people to treat the information that has been gathered from other individuals during contact with central actors from different milieu. The second system functions like a club, to allow exchanges and comparison of information between individuals.

The three steps of the external side of the project (determining strategic priorities) and developing both relational and functional capabilities, were identified in Figure 12.2. These are interdependent and can be combined. Indeed, determining strategic priorities is the result of information that has been gathered by the company. In particular, the division by milieu requires a sufficient level of information. However, determining strategic priorities conditions both the type of *investment* in the networks and also the evolution of the *information* sought via the marketing and technological monitoring.

The Upstream and Within the Project Approach

The investment in networks that are external to the project permits the company to detect the existence of several customers' projects. The company does not dispose of all the internal and external competencies to approach all the projects simultaneously. *Priority choices* have to be made; they will define the projects to embark on and the level of resources to be allocated to a given project.

The constitution of a *portfolio of projects* and the *definition of priorities* (projects or deals screening) is the basis of the approach. Potential projects can be identified and then prioritised through the utilisation of an 'external attractiveness/internal strengths' matrix, adapted from that used in analysing customer portfolios (Figure 12.3).

External attractiveness criteria can be adapted from those developed when we looked at portfolio management (Chapter 8). Internal criteria looking at strengths must take into account the relational and functional positions of the firm. The use of these methods requires being relatively cautious. They were designed to provide a kind of a photograph of rather progressive and slow-moving situations. They do not easily account for situations where the evolution over of a project or the modification of the behaviour of a player may have an important impact on the position of one project within the matrix. There again the analogy with technological innovation (Chapter 10) is enlightening. It is essential to spot the sensitive criteria that are likely to modify judgement substantially on each project. Therefore, it is

Figure 12.3 Portfolio of projects and entry modes in a project

Strengths of the firm

	Strong	Medium	Weak
Strong	General and sole contractor	General contractor or co-contractor within a pool	Sub-contractor of a batch
Medium	General contractor or co-contractor within a pool	Co-contractor within a pool / Sub-contractor	To be discussed or no-go
Weak	Sub-contractor of a batch / Sub-contractor	To be discussed or no-go	No-go

Project attractiveness

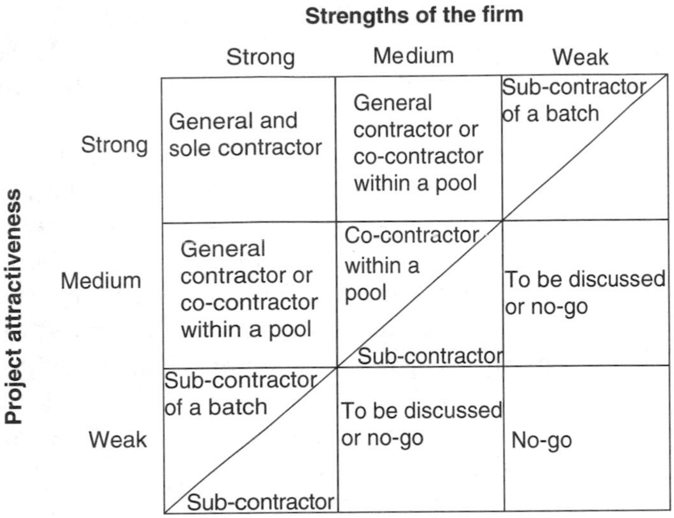

Source: Cova (1990).

necessary periodically to re-evaluate the portfolio according to how things have evolved. A project moving positively may well prove to be highly interesting at one point. Only the non-moving or those projects developing negatively have to be rejected. It is clear in our mind that some of these movements depend on the dynamics and initiatives of the supplier, acting to try and win the game (and trying to modify its setting accordingly).

The usefulness of this approach is not to limit oneself to the 'go/no-go' dilemma. Rather, it allows management to reflect upon and to develop their understanding as to the ways in which the company can or could invest in a given project, alone or with partners, with a constant reference to all the potential projects. Several entry modes in a project are possible according to its position in the matrix:

- general and sole contractor
- general co-contractor within a pool
- sub-contractor of a batch (alone or with partners)
- supplier of a contractor
- sub-contractor of a supplier.

Once this level of analysis is completed, the approach is centred on a given project. It is then compulsory to gather and consolidate all the data that can affect all the ongoing projects. Then, it is possible again to speak of a marketing (or projects) survey to stress this focus, rather than the term 'monitoring' that referred to a wider scope. The objective is to prepare the proposal, the actual offer as well as the ways of operating with the key decision makers.

This approach is largely dictated by the *relational investments* that were made with the central milieu players. However, some projects have to be dealt with under the form of calls for tender, since they will be discovered late in the process. In this case the supplier will begin a process of progressively adapting to the characteristics of each project. This ability is clearly enhanced by its external investments that made it more able to seize opportunities.

Defining the project approach is only slightly different from the general principles we looked at concerning the offer process in business-to-business marketing environments in Chapter 7. The keys to the success of the process are more classically the identification of significant adaptation for the customer and the handling of relationships with all the people involved from the purchasing centre. Here, the risk approach works very well, as we are dealing with a sufficiently defined and stable world, even if the purchasing centres are more complex and the offers more widespread and multidimensional. The particularity of project marketing is the wide range of options available for selecting the appropriate entry modes to create a suitable global offer: With which partners should we work? What role does our company play? Should we be leader or partner?

The choice depends on the position of the project in the matrix (Figure 12.3), and also on the availability of internal resources at the time of the response to the invitation to tender for the project in question. Thus, company responsibility can alter the mode of entry.

The *mobilisation of resources* is linked to the position adopted by the company and its position in the network of co-contractors. The flexibility surrounding how to enter the market compensates for the highly structured choices concerning the procedures of the invitation to tender, because the hierarchy between those giving the orders and the sub-contractors is not rigid. The company's capacity to anticipate developments is important here, as the mobilisation of the required resources provides the ability to be positioned in the programme that moves as the decision process evolves. The creation of project groups by the supplier makes this mobilisation easier, as it is otherwise quite difficult owing to the uncertainty which is linked to the notion of projects: When will this deal materialise? Will we get the contract?

Figure 12.4 reflects the range of possibilities that the company monitors permanently. In relation to a variety of possibilities that have been identified on the market, the company will choose to look to a certain *volume of business* (surveys to be made) which will lead to a *volume of offers made* and 'normally' to an *order book* (production). This succession of steps, which are all tainted with variable probabilities of success, helps to understand just how much anticipation and flexibility are crucial in such situations.

The *negotiation phase*. This involves continuous negotiations throughout the elaboration of the contract. Some negotiations are long, lasting several months or longer (for example, the negotiations led by Alcatel Alsthom for the Korean TGV, or in the telecommunications or weapons industries).

Figure 12.4 Projects and production capacity

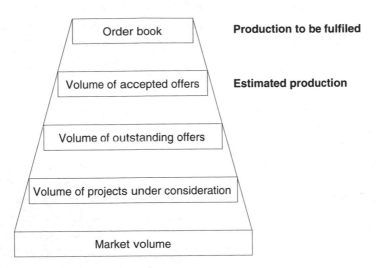

Order book — **Production to be fulfiled**

Volume of accepted offers — **Estimated production**

Volume of outstanding offers

Volume of projects under consideration

Market volume

Source: Stuart St. P. Slatter, 'Strategic Marketing Variables under Conditions of Competitive Bidding', *Strategic Management Journal*, vol. 11, 1990, p. 311. Copyright © 1990 John Wiley & Sons Ltd (with permission).

Large contract negotiations concerning the fixing of prices can be resolved relatively late, and – for international contracts in particular, concerning offers of economic compensation – the sub-contracting of parts of the project to local companies and the transfer of technologies.

The *realisation phase* corresponds to the production, albeit still managed by the project management team. However, the interaction with the customer does not end here, which gives the production phase a kind of marketing and commercial dimension. Two types of action require careful attention at the marketing level: the management of *modifications*, and the *maintenance* and *after-sales services*. On the one hand, these actions raise questions concerning the setting up of contracts and the continuity of customer satisfaction, on the other they represent opportunities to maintain relationships with all those involved in the initial phases of the process.

A particular case: *the creative offer*. The creative offer stems from previous strategic manoeuvres. If a project is spotted upstream in the decision process, the supplier has the possibility of orientating choices towards solutions that it handles particularly well. It may also create a project concept for which it can establish the technical, financial, legal, political and environmental feasibility. That is the way one of the managers of the Bechtel Group expressed their treatment of some strategic issues: 'If there is no project, we shall create one. If there is no customer, we shall assemble one. If there is no money, we shall find some.'

This strategic manoeuvre provides the supplier with the advantage of reducing the uncertainty linked to the call for tenders' procedures. It presents a particularly clear advantage with the anticipation of the economic aspects of the project. The customer is very often also a winner with this process as it may bring out new solutions that it could never imagine by itself. From the supplier point of view, creative offers can represent only a limited part (10 per cent according to several managers' estimation) of all the projects handled simultaneously within a company. The reason is that such a process often leads to divergence from the core competencies of the company in creating the specific offer. If the number of such projects grows in too uncontrolled a manner, the company's future might be endangered.

The organisation of a company working on the marketing of projects includes some unusual aspects, particularly the role of the project engineers who are responsible for the project file. However, many companies that use more classical marketing methods have also had to set up a project organisation, often for the running of innovative projects. This is why we shall examine the questions related to the definition of the organisation of the marketing function (Chapter 13).

In this chapter we have not looked at the financial aspect that is vital for winning deals. Financial arrangements are extremely complex, and therefore we recommend our readers to consult the specialist works that are devoted to this particular subject.

References and Further Reading

Cova, B. (1990) 'Marketing international de projects: un panorama des concepts et des techniques', *Revue Française de Marketing*, 9–38, 127–8.

Cova, B., Mazet, F. and Salle, R. (1998) 'From Districts to Milieus: In Search of Network Boundaries', in P. Naudé and P. Turnbull (eds), *Network Dynamics in International Marketing*, New York, Pergamon Press, 195–210.

Cova, B. and Salle, R. (1999) *Le marketing d'affaires*, Paris, Dunod.

Slatter, S. (1990) 'Strategic Marketing Variables Under Conditions of Competitive Bidding', *Strategic Management Journal*, 11, 309–17.

Discussion Questions

1 Why is major project marketing distinct from other business-to-business environments?
2 What are the features of major project marketing that are often adopted by marketers placed in different environments (economic, social, environmental, etc.)?
3 In what way is the project marketing process similar to, and dissimilar from, the Multistrat model in Chapter 6?

Part III Strategy Design

Chapter 1
Competitiveness, Marketing and Business-to-Business Marketing
*What is marketing all about
Different marketing environments
B2B marketing*

Chapter 2
Business-to-Business Customers and Markets

B2B Generic Offers	Technological Innovation	Pure Services	Major Projects

PART I   STRATEGY FOUNDATIONS

Chapter 3	Chapter 4	Chapter 5	Chapter 6
Understanding Business-to-Business Purchasing	**Information and Information Systems**	**Markets and Suppliers' Strategy**	**Segmentation and Marketing Strategy**

PART II   STRATEGY IMPLEMENTATION

Chapter 7
Generic Business-to-Business Offer Design and Management

Chapter 8
Market Access and Customer Management

Chapter 9
Communication and Publicity/ Advertising

Chapter 10	Chapter 11	Chapter 12
Marketing and Technological Innovation	**The Marketing of Services**	**Major Project Marketing**

PART III   STRATEGY DESIGN

Chapter 13	The Role and Organisation of Marketing
Chapter 14	Customer Position, Market Position, Marketing Strategies and Planning
Chapter 15	Issues and Specificities of International Marketing
Annex	The Internet and Marketing: Some Ideas

13 The Role and Organisation of Marketing

The large variety of business-to-business marketing environments, characterised in particular by the different types of interaction between suppliers and customers (Table 2.3), has led to some confusion surrounding the role and organisation of the marketing function. From one company to another – and often, indeed within the same company – the marketing situations that are encountered can differ widely, and this leads to practices (organisation, methods, tools) that need to be adapted to each situation. A company that has even moderate technical diversification, having a product range that is limited in its uses, can be organised into several different marketing units (see Example 14 on Roulements SA). This can mistakenly lead us to think that no rules can be formulated, with each company being an individual case, rather than searching for models surrounding the role and organisation of the marketing function. In this chapter, we have decided to sit on the fence somewhat: we propose some organisational typologies or structures, while at the same time recognising the *uniqueness* of organisations and rejecting the very idea of having 'rules' to dictate optimal structures.

Many ways of approaching this subject have been proposed (particularly concerning the structure of the organisation including the marketing department). Let us remember that the structure of the organisation (and that of the marketing organisation) is the result of the combination of several internal and external factors. These include the complexity and dynamism of the environment; the type of customer relationships; the degree of dependence of the organisation (for example, if it belongs to an industrial group or cluster); the characteristics of the products; the technology used; the organisational characteristics (directors, culture, strategy, etc.); and the degree of interdependence with other departments (Marticotte and Perrien, 1995). For the approach that we have adopted, we stress the degree or extent of customer–supplier interaction as being the principal factor in defining the organisation of the marketing function in business-to-business environments. Indeed, several of our examples used throughout this book show that the choices made concerning the marketing organisation have an influence on the mode of interaction with the customers. On the other hand, however, developments within a customer relationship (innovations, for example) can also modify the degree of interaction and create new skills and resources that the company will subsequently make available to other customers. Thus, the evolution in strategy dealt with in Chapters 5–9 can in return lead to an evolution in the marketing function and improve the efficiency of this interaction with the customers. Here, we are entering the logic of coherence between the dimensions of marketing strategy (the choices) and the means to put this strategy into operation, which obviously means returning to the Multistrat model (see Chapter 6).

After presenting the framework within which marketing operates within the business-to-business environments and underlining the main issues, we shall look at the questions that are raised by examining two typical situations that are sufficiently different concerning supplier–customer interaction. They will serve as our reference points when answering questions concerning the issues of a particular marketing situation. It will then be possible to identify some general principles and to examine some more particular situations.

Remarks and Issues

As already mentioned, in business-to-business marketing, one has to remember that some of the tools and methods of analysis used in consumer marketing are not necessarily relevant. In consumer marketing, a well-defined 'marketing department' typically handles a large number of the tasks of the marketing function. This is not the case in business-to-business environments. For example, the technical issues, clearly in the hands of research and development (R&D) that make up the heart of the offer design, are also a key element in the ongoing relationship with the clients. The choice of target customers, one of the key points in marketing strategy, is usually left to salespeople. Thus, marketing is partly handled by technical experts and not only by a 'marketing department' that has been pinned down and clearly identified. One of the possible solutions could be not to create a marketing department at all and to leave it in the hands of those who naturally have some power. This idea should not be rejected automatically, the marketing and sales director of a subsidiary of a large industrial group has said that marketing had found its real position in his company as there was no more marketing department as such. It would be wrong to accept this position unquestioningly, as it probably represents a special case in business-to-business marketing. But the example forces us to the necessity of giving a more precise description of the tasks to be assigned to the marketing function, before examining the questions linked to its organisation in a firm involved in a particular environment.

The issues influencing the position and structure of the marketing function in business-to-business environments depend on our understanding of eight successive issues: marketing information and the understanding of the markets, the expertise in understanding the customers' business, monitoring the value chain, offer design, promotion and publicity, business-to-business marketing models, the management of profitability, and strategic marketing.

Marketing information and market understanding come first. It is difficult to design a marketing strategy without a minimum of marketing data concerning markets and customers' dynamics and an evaluation of the company's competitive position. Too many companies believe that they can introduce a marketing approach without dedicating the necessary budget and time to gathering, storing and using marketing information. Chapter 4 covers this subject from a technical perspective. Some years ago companies used to employ the service of a 'market studies bureau' that dealt with general and professional statistics, sales reports and figures or some kind of market surveys. Unhappily, few companies have been able to turn this embryonic system into a true marketing information system (MIS) adapted to today's more complex and competitive environments. Often they tried to develop a marketing department without providing it with a satisfactory information base. Marketing requires accurate, fluid, and up-to-date information, interpreted and available to decision makers.

But the understanding of markets is not dependent upon mere data availability. It results from the organisation, the interpretation and the explanation of data held by a large number of individuals within the company (design office, maintenance, after-sales service, salespeople, formalised market surveys, various statistics, etc.). This amount of data can be used with different levels of precision and accuracy. This depends on the quality of the implemented information system (Chapter 4) and on the managers' understanding of their markets and customer dynamics. The implementation of segmentation and customer portfolio methods lies at the heart of successful strategy implementation. They are the basis of a truly professional approach to the marketing function within business-to-business companies that must think in terms of both *markets and customers* in order efficiently to contribute to strategic thinking.

But more than just information, good marketing requires the company to develop its expertise in *understanding the customers' business*. An example will illustrate what we mean. A manufacturer of glass bottles operating in the alimentary liquids market (beer, wine, soft drinks, fruit juice, etc.) must be an expert in its customers' trade in two ways. The first is linked to understanding the customers' *manufacturing process*. The supplier has to direct efforts at improving the productivity and quality (even sanitary levels) of its customers' process. It has to be an expert in bottling techniques. The other is the understanding of the requirements of the food channels *towards their customers*. The supplier has to anticipate the channels' preoccupations: presentation for self-service, product shelving, merchandising and logistics (costs and stock reduction). So, the bottle manufacturer must employ staff with a detailed knowledge of the food channels, their issues, their requirements and their relationships with their own suppliers (i.e. understanding the network). These staff must maintain contacts with key players within the food channels, be known by these people and constantly update their expertise. This expertise is defined by technical parameters as well as by the economic, social and managerial characteristics of a particular industrial sector.

The monitoring of the *value chain* is an issue that has to be marketing-led. It involves constantly identifying the ways that the company has to follow in order to deliver value to its customers (Figures 1.5, 2.6 and 2.7). And customers do not find value for themselves only in their supplier's offer. They also find it in non-offer competitive benefits useful for the customers. These benefits stem from three sources. The first is the efficiency of the supplier's own value chain (for example, what is the firm's ability to transfer R&D findings into manufacturing?). The second is the efficiency of the links between the supplier's and the customer's value chains (for example, if the customer is asking for a heavily adapted product that affects manufacturing, how can we deliver it under satisfactory conditions of quality and time?). The third involves implementing actions from various players in the surrounding networks (for example, if we are not equipped to ensure the clearing, transfer and treatment of our customer's used oils, what is the most reliable partner we can call in to achieve these tasks?). The idea here is not that marketing should take direct responsibility for all these issues, but that it should be in a position to make sure that choices are made to ensure customers' satisfaction, and not only be focused on internal efficiency. It is important to note here that marketing has to be transparent in its process of translating the external market requirements to the other players within the firm. They have to present market and customers' issues and constraints and not their own vision of achieving it, which would mean merely sustaining an internal battle for resources.

The *elaboration of the offer* is probably the dimension that includes the greatest number of functions and individuals within a company: the design office, production, quality, logistics, the salespeople, management; all spend time, energy and know-how. The role of marketing is obviously to participate in a collective effort, but within a perspective of mobilisation and co-ordination of internal resources. Marketing represents the market and customer point of view; it continually gives a representation of the market (segmentation, networks, environment) that allows the company to define the characteristics of the offer and a market position and to fix objectives. The position integrates the originality and the suitability of the offer for its uses: performance, appreciation of the perceived quality (the notion of 'quality in use'), competitive differentiation (products, services, prices), conditions of invoicing (services, quantities, adaptations), distribution and delivery. It is necessary to introduce again the role of innovation in offer renewal.

Offer dynamics aim at creating the conditions of success at the customer. This involves monitoring and participating in the *promotion* and *publicity* surrounding the advantages and the differences of the offer (sales presentations, communication, promotion), supporting the sales force at major accounts and acting towards the various players of the value chain.

Defining and understanding help in using business-to-business *marketing models*. The analysis of any new deal, the running of a new project, customer portfolio management, the development of new services for a given customer, all require a definition and understanding of the technology (i.e. the internal process and tools) that have to be adapted to the company situation. In such cases, marketing has a role of methodological and pedagogical support for other functions, particularly the sales force (operational marketing). Moreover, it can contribute to the internal transfer of winning ways (particularly for the salespeople). It may largely contribute to the understanding of the markets and of company's choices through an explicit presentation of these issues to many internal individuals not directly involved in marketing (manufacturing, personnel, finance, etc.). We feel this dimension is, today, a major challenge for the marketing function.

Profitability management of the firm's position in particular markets and for individual customers is, curiously, the sign of progress in marketing and its maturity within the company. How many companies go as far as establishing a survey of the profitability of the management of their customers and seek to optimise their investments in winning new customers and keeping existing ones? Looking at what happens in practice has shown that a lot remains to be done in this field. The tools presented here are all aimed at contributing to this and to 'teaching marketing staff to count'.

Last but not least is the contribution of marketing to *strategy design*. This function of synthesis has two faces. The first is the design and implementation of the firm's marketing strategy (Chapter 14). The second is the contribution of marketing to the elaboration of the firm's strategic planning. Marketing has to bring its understanding of the present and future trends of the market and all the market-related data that are necessary for designing the firm's strategy.

Despite this brief look at the marketing function, it must not be forgotten that marketing has an essentially *dynamic* role: to ensure the definition and the winning of profitable markets of the company and to be one of the motors of change. Marketing ensures this direct and sensitive relation with the environment that works in both ways: How can we benefit more from this environment (for example, win an order)? How should we change to increase our impact on the environment? This involves the people who make it happen, and thus we have to look at the relationships they create with the other company functions via its organisational structure.

The Responsibilities of Marketing

Before examining the definition and the organisation of the marketing function in two typical marketing environments, let us first look further at the responsibilities generally attributed to the marketing function. This is based on three points of view: what marketing does, what it has in common with other functions and the direction that it gives to senior management.

Marketing is involved in two kinds of activities: *reflection* and *action*. Reflection activities cover the collecting and transmitting of information, the feasibility studies for the elaboration of an offer, participation in the design of the offer, the choice and definition of work methods and the management of the competitive position and profitability. Operational (action) activities exist owing to the fact that this function is responsible for establishing, maintaining and developing the interaction with the customers, prospects and the members of the overall network.

Marketing, along with other functions (the board, R&D, production, quality, etc.), manages the position of the company in the industry (the markets covered),

Table 13.1 The two positions of marketing

Thoughtful marketing	Active marketing
■ Market surveys, marketing information system	■ Knowledge of customers and prospects
■ Expertise in the identified customers' businesses, networks and environment	■ Management of the competitive position at customer level (portfolio of customers and prospects, customer by customer)
■ Offer design	■ Customer adaptation
■ Management of the competitive position and of the profitability of markets, segments and customers	■ Direct promotion
■ Use of marketing models	■ Sales pitch and sales
■ Presales action and participation in selling	■ Distribution management
	■ Logistics, sales administration

the competitive position (per market), the offer portfolio, customer portfolio and marketing budgets. It reports to the board the marketing strategies, the plans and their implementation, volumes sold, market shares, offer and customer profitability and return on investment.

These rather generic responsibilities of the marketing function vary little from one situation to another. In fact, it is their precise characteristics and their allocation among the individuals concerned and the organisational structures chosen by the company that vary. Before examining these points in more detail, let us look at the distinction between marketing and sales. Until now, this has remained ambiguous; at times we have said they are one and the same, at others that they are two different things. In fact, both are true and the ambivalence of our position results from the superimposition of the two points of view that can be qualified schematically as more reflexive and anticipatory ('tomorrow's offer') for marketing and more active and immediate ('the present offer') for sales. The question is difficult and the choice of examining different marketing environments further in this chapter will allow us to clarify things because, according to these different cases, the degree of superimposition is not the same. Table 13.1 gives a very schematic view of the differences between the two.

A major consequence of the above viewpoint concerns the way of dividing the hierarchical responsibilities linked to these two facets. Should they be concentrated on one person or split between two people in charge on the same step of the hierarchy? Consumer marketing has generally known disassociation: the marketing director (end customer, surveys, offers, communication) and the sales director (intermediary customer, sales, promotions, logistics) are traditional and well-defined functions. Both directors are on the same level, and are members of the board. This dichotomous division relates to the environments where the two facets are clearly separate, as often in such a profession, although the rise in power of business concerns (intermediary customer) with its 'trade marketing' has tended to upset the classical set-up in many companies. If the intermediary customer becomes an influential actor in the definition of the offer of the manufacturer who, from the producer's side, will make the synthesis of the diverging points of view?

The marketing director, who represents the end customer, or the sales director who represents the intermediary customer? Or maybe a marketing and sales director?

In industry, things are much more difficult. We shall base our argument on the degree of interaction between the supplier and their customers (Table 2.3). As argued there, direct interaction can vary between weak and strong, helping us to define two extreme situations and to examine the consequences for the organisation of the marketing function for each one. Between these two extreme cases, there are many other possible situations that correspond to intermediary levels of interaction.

The Organisation of the Marketing Function

One of the objectives of this section is to establish that the 'classical' patterns of the organisation of the marketing function – typically based on consumer marketing practices – do not usually answer the requirements of the marketing function in business-to-business environments. Table 13.2 illustrates very clearly what we mean here.

The left-hand side of Table 13.2 shows the features of consumer marketing practices and the organisation modes (market manager, product manager) created in the late 1920s by Procter and Gamble. The idea of the 'marketing department' has been developed over more than 60 years' experience. The course to be followed to become a marketing expert has become classical: training in management, starting as an 'assistant product manager', then 'product manager', then 'senior product manager', then ' brand or group manager' and finally 'marketing director' on the way to 'marketing vice-president'. The course takes 5 to 15 years depending upon the firm and individual involved. But, on the whole, well managed by companies, it ensures a remarkable professionalisation of 'full-time marketers'.

Table 13.2 The marketing function and the degree of interaction with customers

... There is no one best way
... But various possibilities exist based on the degree of the interaction with customers

According to the degree of interaction	
The marketing function is	
Centralised	Diffused
Localised	Dispersed
Well-defined	Split among marketing, sales, R&D, project managers, etc.
'Market manager'	'Marketing and sales director'
'Product manager'	'Development director'
Widely used quantitative methods	Uncertain qualitative methods
Highly professionalised	Weakly professionalised
'Full-time marketers'	'Part-time marketers'

But very few circumstances in business-to-business marketing allow management to apply such a concept. Most of them belong to the right-hand side of Table 13.2, which is dominated by the spreading of the marketing function between other typical functions of the firm and the consecutive notion of 'part-time marketers'.

Cases of Weak Interaction

Examining this situation shows that its characteristics are hybrid. They are in the direct interaction zone, while having some of the traits of simulated interaction: low flexibility of the offer, a predetermined range of offers, weakness of the social exchanges, much attention paid to market share. In such situations, marketing must accept the predetermination of the offer, which leads it to using techniques that are close to those used in simulated interaction (sampling), while being able to give a certain form of personalisation to the relationship with the clientele.

The characteristics of this kind of situation lead to *localising* and *centralising* the marketing function, this means creating a 'marketing department' whose structure and role are close to those that have been used for years by companies in situations of simulated interaction. Most organisations of marketing and sales services can be grouped into three categories: the commercial department, the operational marketing department and the functional marketing department.

The *commercial department* (Figure 13.1) leaves the marketing element of the design of the offer to the sales manager (in consultation with the board, the technical development department and, often, a customer technical assistance service which is usually part of the technical department).

To all appearances, this kind of structure would suit small and medium-sized companies (SMEs) marketing a range of products of average complexity. It is con-

Figure 13.1 Organisation of a commercial department

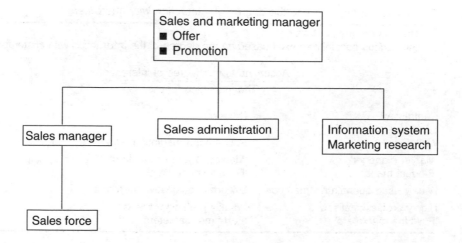

cerned with the efficiency of the sales action and transfers the elaboration of the offer to the technical department, in collaboration with the sales manager. When the number of people working here grows and the tasks require increased anticipation, it is moving towards a more operational marketing type of structure.

The *operational marketing department* (Figure 13.2) gives the marketing and sales director all the levers, of reflection and action, of marketing and the responsibility of the results.

This structure is present in a number of medium- to large-sized companies. It is necessary for a number of reasons: having people in the company able to set up and use previously developed approaches to elaborate offers in complex conditions of diverse customers and markets, and to provide an important capacity to reflect on the elaboration of efficient marketing strategies (Chapter 14). The responsibility is in the hands of the person in charge of both the vision of the strategy and that of the operational aspects.

We shall see later how to define the functions of product manager and market manager. Some services (represented by the dotted box) may or may not be under the control of the marketing and sales department. They often belong to the technical department, usually because the technologies concerned evolve quickly and this is the best way to keep the technical training programme up to date.

The *functional marketing department* (Figure 13.3) is justifiable when product ranges are extremely standardised and unlikely to change suddenly (for example, office equipment and stationary) and the company tends to use direct marketing and distribution channels rather than direct sales visits to keep up customer contacts. The offer is specific to markets or market segments, and not open to adaptation. The company chooses to respond to the variety of the *demand* via the variety of its *offers*. In many other cases, we see the misapplication of consumer marketing

Figure 13.2 Organisation of an operational marketing department

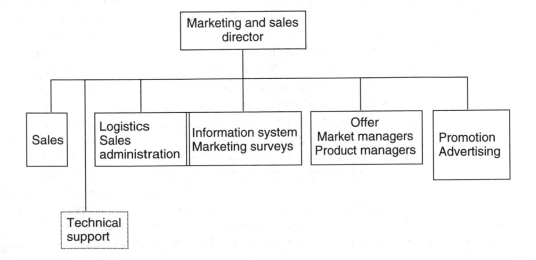

Figure 13.3 Organisation of a functional marketing department

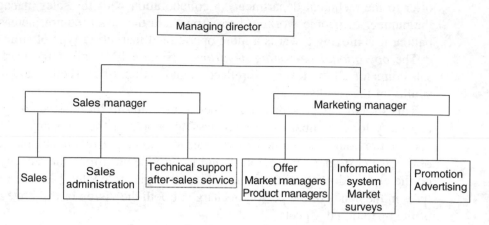

perspectives and models (simulated interaction) to business-to-business environments (direct interaction). The adoption of a structure that has been transferred from the mass-consumption model, because it is the only one commonly used in publications, is too easy and often leads to inadequacies and to delay in the introduction of marketing in the company.

On the other hand, it is difficult to find people who meet all the required standards to hold down the function of marketing and sales manager. This takes an unusual mixture of intellectual qualities and a sense of reality (customers, intuition, taste for action, etc.).

For two of the three types of organisation presented, we have mentioned the existence of the product or market manager functions in charge of the offer elaboration. We shall now look at the two functions in more detail.

Product (or market) manager functions first saw the light in Proctor and Gamble in 1927, in other words, before even the discipline of marketing had begun to really exist. They are usually grouped within a marketing department responsible for managing the company's offer. They correspond to a functional position whose responsibilities include the knowledge and understanding of the markets (information system, segmentation, competitive position), to monitor the development and evolution of the offer, to follow the offer (performance, quality, profitability), the sales dynamics, strategy elaboration, timetabling and budget. These responsibilities correspond to a function of recommendation to the board (to ensure the right decisions are taken for the product) and of monitoring that the strategy is being followed correctly. Thus, it is a function of *strategist* or *planner*. It is not that of the *decider*, an actor in charge of operational responsibilities, as discussed in Chapter 14.

A system of *product managers* is adopted to exploit the position of an offer on one or more market segments. Such an organisation structure allows the company simultaneously to manage several offers on the same market within the same 'unit' (company, division, department, etc.). It corresponds to the desire to create an *offer expertise* such that the utmost coherence is ensured between all the elements that are aligned to build market position and profitability. The product manager is the company 'specialist' concerning his or her product, and their support is essential in many sales negotiations.

Organisations with *market managers* aim at ensuring the best possible market coverage. This structure is often used when the offer includes major elements coming from both the company itself and from other peripheral elements (services, additional offers proposed by other companies). This type of organisation corresponds to the desire to create real market expertise that allows management at any time to *optimise market knowledge*, the *corresponding offer* and the *means* used for this. In complex industrial groups, they co-ordinate offers coming from several units for the same market.

Large international companies, such as those in the crop protection industry, have generally adopted a double structure of product and market managers. The reason is that these companies produce specialities that often are effective on many different crops, for example a product against vine, tomato or rose mildew. Writing off the R&D costs (20M Euros and 10 years' work) for such a product means using all the applications in the best possible conditions while relying on a perfect knowledge of the conditions of its application on each crop, alone or in association with other specialties. An international product manager is responsible for this optimisation. But each geographical subsidiary of this company can justify a sales presence on a market, for example in France that of the vineyards, only if it can group together several treatments at the same time (mildew, black rot, oidium, green fly, etc.). Since it is not possible for each company to have a complete and effective product portfolio, a vine market manager will typically gather the best possible offer on the French vine market by using combinations of specialities or local sales agreements and by ensuring their promotion (relationships with local authorities, the relevant administrative authorities, distributors, etc.) and the dynamism of the sales force. Other market managers can be responsible for the cereals markets, arboriculture, etc.

It is easy to see why the required qualities for the two types of jobs (product and market manager) are different: more scientific and technical, more varied and profit oriented for the first; more specialised in the professional milieu, more of a negotiator and sales promoter for the second. Also, we can see that these structures correspond to marketing environments in which the offer shows little flexibility. Strategy is typically based on markets and market segments; the variety of the offer responds to that in the demand, as previously mentioned several times. Thus, we can see that situations of strong interaction require different organisations.

Cases of Strong Interaction

These marketing situations are characterised by the company possessing a *core technology* that it has chosen to develop to give it the capacity to adapt to specific customer requirements. The capacity of flexibility, the negotiation of the content of the offer, the mobilisation of internal or external resources at any given moment are key factors for success. It is obvious that the company's marketing structure must make their implementation simple. There are two cases here, if the customer is a stable structure with regular and ongoing relationships (a car manufacturer, for example) or a temporary structure linked to a particular project (even if it lasts for several years, as with Eurotunnel concerning construction, but not including operation).

In both cases, there is a movement in the centre of gravity of the marketing of the offer design towards the *relationship with the customers*. It is the people who are directly in contact with the clientele who have the information and the necessary sales and marketing levers to elaborate and operate the marketing strategy. This does not mean that the role of the marketing function is limited to establishing and maintaining customer relationships, even if this is important. Three different organisational structures are typically possible here, corresponding to variations in company size, issues related to the customers and the kind of problems that need to be solved. They all direct the sales and marketing responsibilities to one decision maker according to a system similar to that of the operational marketing manager (Figure 13.2). These three types of organisation are the operational market managers' structure, the key account structure and the major project structure.

The *operational market managers' structure* involves widening the mission of the markets managers by including, other than the tasks mentioned above, the responsibility of sales action either directly (Figure 13.4, model 1) or indirectly (model 2). This means a complete mission on a market, which can be the world market. The market manager may act alone or be assisted by a few salespeople. The manager is responsible for the sales results, but acts in collaboration with local sales entities that follow the market manager's instructions and contact him or her for important negotiations.

In this type of structure, the market manager is responsible for the *strategy* (and information system), the *offer* (which is usually defined in collaboration with the technical staff), *sales objectives* and *profitability*. The support services are varied: documentation, management control, after-sales services, etc. The skills of those working with the manager can evolve over time according to the issues and the need, if necessary, to bring in new resources. The market manager co-ordinates all the functions that use the technological core of the company to define and perform the adaptations required by the customers of a given market, while remaining in touch with the market and the company's competitive position. Obviously, this structure corresponds to a weak-to-medium level of complexity in the relationships between the supplier and customers. Above a certain level of complexity and commitment to certain customers, the accumulation of tasks is so great that it is necessary to move on to the key customer structure.

The *key accounts structure* appears when the market is composed of major customers (in size) who each demand specific treatment (Chapter 8). The complexity of the purchasing centres and the technical nature of the problems require a double

Figure 13.4   Marketing structure for operational markets managers

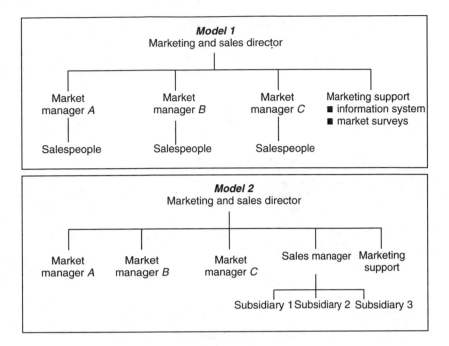

approach: *commercial* and *technical*. The car manufacturing market is a good example. Based on a defined technology, each manufacturer sets precise constraints and requirements related to their technical and marketing strategies and the variations involved in each car model. Each deal is therefore the result of a different definition. The organisational response that is generally given (Figure 13.5) is a *two-tier commercial structure*: sales engineers who are responsible for leading the relationship and following all the deals that are taking place, and technical application engineers who design answers and control the quality for the customer.

The essential elements of the strategy are conceived and executed by the unit that is responsible for each customer. The overall market synthesis is the role of the marketing and sales director and assistants, often aided by a marketing support service. This service would be in charge of managing a marketing information system (MIS), surveys concerning the industry as a whole and the competition, elaborating adapted marketing models, managing the communication and public relations and contributing to the development of the long-term strategy. Naturally, the way in which key accounts are structured organisationally will depend upon both the company's strategy and how the market develops. Naudé and McLean (1999) provide an illustration of how the structure varied over time within British Telecom.

The *major projects structure* is different. As seen in Chapter 12, this situation is based on the need to manage actions which are both external to projects and in defined projects. It is often difficult for the same people to perform both at the same

Figure 13.5 Key accounts marketing structure

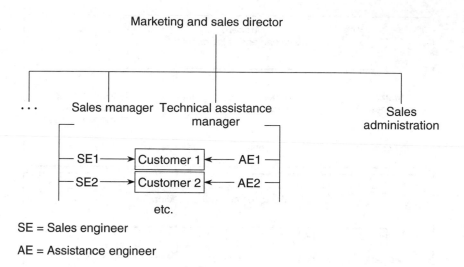

SE = Sales engineer

AE = Assistance engineer

Figure 13.6 Major projects marketing structure

time, even if a lot of the information and actions are of a similar nature. However, we feel it is better to separate the two, as in Figure 13.6.

The external-to-project strategy is based on the departments (information system, market monitoring, strategy and scheduling) that undertake the more classical marketing tasks as described in Chapters 12 and 14, and long-term missions in the wider network. On the other hand, two departments that are generally rarely present in marketing structures are present here. One is the *technical support department*, whose role is to intervene in the pre-invitation to tender phases and during negotiations that happen afterwards. It responds to the need to present to the decision makers a well-prepared argument on these highly complex operations or on technologies that are often innovative and require specific or original operating skills. It is often difficult for researchers, who create these new technologies, to be good company representatives. The most salesperson-like of them could therefore be given this role. The other is a department that is responsible for the *co-contracting* and *sub-contracting* agreements. It can be part of the purchasing department or the marketing department, or spread over the two since it covers aspects that are linked to both.

In a project, strategy is defined per market, according to the customers and networks or milieu that correspond to a particular demand. For example, a company specialising in the supply of different lines of packaging can be organised according to the markets: the food industry, chemicals, fertilisers, electrical equipment, hardware, etc. Knowing the market and the characteristics of the products to be packed is considered a major advantage around which all marketing responsibilities must operate. The commercial responsibility of the project operations can be performed in several different ways. It can be given to a project manager (or business engineer) who, for the duration of the project, unites a team of specialists, or a project manager who gets the same specialists to work in a matrix structure. It can also be given to an independent operational section of the marketing department.

It is also possible to build an organisation that will follow the main steps of a project. Thus, a large Group distinguishes:

■ the *business developer*, who is in charge of the position within the milieu, the monitoring and the evolution of the milieu, of the project design and of an eventual counter-project

■ the *business engineer*, who is in charge of the upstream screening of the deals, of participating in the design of the specifications and in putting the proposal together

■ the *business manager*, who is in charge of the operations linked to the tender to the project and the management of the deal.

Most companies that deal with major projects are present in several geographical markets. A local commercial presence is therefore vital and it participates locally both in the project and in the wider network. The wide variety of possible methods of organisation reflects that of the marketing environments covered by the term 'business-to-business marketing'. Thus, it would be of little use to present an organisation that will be valid in all cases. However, we can present a few general principles often associated with the problems encountered in business-to-business marketing organisations.

A Few General Principles to Remember When Organising the Marketing Function

Our aim here is to offer suggestions for improving the marketing function in business-to-business environments. This raises the question of the *appropriate marketing structure* in the company. Positioning a marketing department in the organisation of a company, with its own staff and nominating a head of marketing, is not in itself a guarantee for success. If the above questions concerning the organisation are important, it is necessary to create the conditions to give the function a real meaning in any business-to-business company. Currently, this seems to be far from the situation. Today, there are only a few companies in which the function has taken on its real importance. There are two types of situations. The first happens at the beginning, when the structure is first created. Who should be asked to join the structure? How to give them objectives and evaluate the results? How to allow them to become efficient in their work and gain internal recognition? It is not always easy to answer these questions. Indeed, does the question need to be asked at all? All too often, young engineers, with no training in marketing, struggle to understand what the company expects from them in this function and look to make themselves useful in the organisation.

The second corresponds to the situations where the marketing structure has a certain history, but has not yet proved its worth and therefore has yet to gain internal recognition. There can be two reasons for this. There are some companies where, after just a few months, all the marketing staff are asked to change department and are replaced by new staff members who have no knowledge of marketing and to whom any transfer of know-how is not without its problems. This represents a return to the beginning. In others, marketing has not been formalised, there are no methods, no tools, particularly no information system. It has become simply a link in the chain where people use their intuition and intellectual capacity for a few years before moving on.

In both types of company, irrespective of size, the marketing function has no *professional reality*, unlike R&D, production, accounts, etc. What are the reasons for this? We shall look at two such reasons: the relationship between marketing and sales, and that between marketing and the technical function. Then, we shall conclude by looking at the conditions required for professionalism of the marketing personnel and the case of innovative technologies. The common jargon used here is sometimes ambiguous; the term 'function' refers both to the tasks to be done and the persons who execute them. To solve this problem, we shall use the term 'marketing structure' to refer to the fact that, in a company, people are clearly nominated to be responsible for the function.

The relationships between the *marketing structure* and *the sales team* are often difficult, even if the purely commercial tasks are part of the marketing function. These conflicts are frequent during the creation of a marketing structure in the company, but they can last longer, everybody recognising the problems, but nobody having the time – courage? – reasons? – to find a solution.

The first area of conflict concerns *customer and market information*. We saw (Chapter 4) that the salespeople quite naturally withhold a lot of the marketing information. They may feel in danger, or robbed, if they have to hand the information over to marketing, who in turn may feel deprived of an essential working tool if they don't have it. The second concerns the fact of setting up in the company a strategy that accounts for both *customers and markets*, in other words from the moment the marketing function begins to act its real role. The natural tendency, in a purely sales-oriented way, would be to pull the company towards increasing the variety of the offer, either through greater flexibility, or by increasing the number of references. The role of marketing is to limit this tendency via the creation of an explicit strategy. On the other hand, a functional vision can become bureaucratic and generate offers that are ill-adapted to the real situation. In such cases, it is not uncommon to see the salespeople trying to get round the official company strategy by creating unofficial relationships with the company design office and production services.

Depending on the required level of interaction, the stakes for the marketing function are not the same in different companies. The organisational outline of the marketing function presented above will allow managing these differences, the rest depends on the working procedures, methods and marketing tools held by the company.

The relationships between the *marketing structure* and *the technical function* have been the object of many studies that have reached some astonishingly negative conclusions. Table 13.3 outlines one such study.

To avoid such problems, there is no miracle solution, just a wide range of converging efforts to be made. The causes are numerous. First, differing opinions: the technicians are concentrated on their work and often have a distorted view of market demands. Second, a difference of language: technical language is complex, and the more complex it becomes, the more difficult it is to understand it. Another is a conflict of power: Who decides – the technical department? the marketing department? And behind the choices lie those waiting for the power. In addition, there may be incoherence between the choices: company managers have often underestimated marketing's capacity to partake in technical choices and this has often led to

Table 13.3   Relations between R&D and marketing

R&D/Marketing interface states	Number of projects with each outcome within each interface state			
	Complete commercial success	Partial commercial success	Commercial failure	Total
Harmony	27	16	10	53
Mild disharmony	8	13	4	25
Severe disharmony	4	8	26	38
Total	**39**	**37**	**40**	**116**

Source: Souder (1981).

incoherence between the choices of technology and market positions (Chapter 7). Curiously, the move to quality management has managed to change ideas concerning the need to take customer expectations into consideration more than marketing was typically able to do, so now it does benefit from this quality move. However, a lot remains to be done.

This could include bringing the people of the two functions closer. Team solidarity is unbeatable. This would involve giving relevance to this newly created team via the physical proximity of the two structures, the regularity of meetings and the use of tools that have been created together, such as the defining of quality functions (QFD or House of Quality). Also, a carefully oriented policy of *human resource management* helps improve mutual understanding: training for all on technical and marketing themes, transfer of individuals from one function to the other and the dissemination of positive results. However, it is often necessary to go further than these few points, as we shall see. The *professionalisation* of the marketing function must be carefully examined and the move made towards a *project management* approach.

The paths towards a *professionalisation of the marketing 'function-structure'* are a challenge for managers of business-to-business companies. They have to realise that marketing becomes efficient only if it is managed like a normal and complete company function. This does not mean simply adapting the structures and working methods used for consumer marketing. What is important is to identify the *marketing environment(s)* that the company operates in, and to find appropriate structures for the people concerned. It is true that the low proportion of industrial company directors who clearly understand the process and methods of industrial marketing also makes this difficult. Nonetheless, and whatever the marketing situation in question, we feel it is possible to draw up certain principles to help identify the stakes involved in the creation of a marketing structure, and its relationships with the sales team and the technical department.

The first is to adapt the structure of the function to the marketing situations of which the company is part. From this point of view, two criteria help in the analysis: the degree of *customer concentration*, and the choice between the *standardisation* and *adaptation* of the offers. The overlap between a concentrated clientele and an adapted offer leads to a decentralisation of the marketing function towards a sales structure with technical support, whereas a dispersed clientele and the standardisation of the offers leads to a centralisation around a marketing structure of the markets and products manager type. Companies that develop offers on markets whose characteristics are different according to these two criteria are consequently forced to create several approaches to their marketing and sales organisation. Roulements SA (Example 14) is a good example of this.

The second is to ensure that sufficient *transfer of knowledge* of the business-to-business marketing process, the models and tools takes place across the company. If the responsibilities are spread among several functions in the company, each person with responsibilities must have access to the relevant information and systems. This transfer of knowledge begins with the board of management that is responsible for defining the work methods and their use. It must include several functions (marketing, production, quality, purchasing, etc.) at a certain level of responsibility.

The third is to consider the marketing function as a *separate function within the company*. This means that, on the one hand, the persons who move into the marketing structure are prepared for this mission that becomes part of their professional career, and that, on the other hand, it is seen as an important move and finally that the transfer of information of the methods and know-how is done in a satisfactory manner. If these conditions are not respected, the marketing structure cannot reach its true dimension.

The fourth, which is in fact obvious from the above, is that the company *builds its own marketing methods and tools*. First of all there is the information system. This means that a marketing function has a budget to enable it to develop the required methods and tools.

The fifth involves paying attention to the choice of those *people brought into the marketing function*. Some qualities are vital: a sense of communication, the capacity for analysis and synthesis, and a capability to argue about quantitative and qualitative elements. However, these qualities are not enough in themselves to run the function. Knowledge of the markets and the customers, acquired during sales or technical experience, allows people to understand the issues involved, and to gain the recognition that is so important in a marketing function.

So far, we have described the main traits of the professionalisation of the marketing function in industrial companies. It is important for many companies, but does not automatically solve all their problems. Therefore, we propose to look at the *organisation per project* that is becoming increasingly important in company management.

The *organisation per project* was introduced when we mentioned the development of innovation, and where we argued that the usual model of sequential development was often not appropriate. A project is essentially all about managing the *joint skills* required for the completion of a complex task. This type of organisation applies to the management of a number of kinds of tasks to be done in a company, the construction of a new production unit, a physical move, the management of an innovation, approaching a major prospect, etc. It involves the collaboration of people who belong to different internal structures, without having them leave their usual department. This means, as is shown in Figure 13.7, the implementation of *a matrix organisation* that must be thought out and managed with suitable management methods (involvement of the hierarchy, management control and budgetary control, etc.).

This type of organisation leads to a matrix structure that raises specific problems of management linked to the existence of different project forms. Four types have been proposed (Hayes, Wheelwright and Clark, 1988): projects with a functional structure, co-ordinated projects, projects with a project director, and issued projects. It does not seem suitable to approach such a level of specialisation within this book. For more details, the reader is invited to consult the works mentioned in the

Figure 13.7 Matrix organisation per project

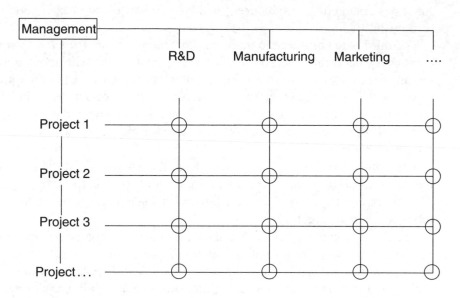

Source: Giard (1991).

References and Further Reading for this chapter. However, let us briefly look at the question of technologically innovative projects which, from a marketing point of view, needs to be examined.

The marketing of *technological innovations* brings in original questions that we have examined before. It also involves consequences at the organisational level of the contribution that marketing has to a technological innovation project (Table 10.6). The specific marketing process of the initial phases of the project (such as explaining the project, launching it, defining the applications, choosing the applications), and the fact the project is far from its marketable form, makes handing over the marketing aspects of the project to more classical marketing structure very difficult. During these early phases, it is better to introduce one or more *marketing managers* into the project team that continues to belong to the R&D department. Their entrance into the later stages of the project would mean moving all or part of the team towards the marketing department where the project could be managed just like a market offer (or several offers, depending on the versatility of the technology used). In other words, more like the more classical methods.

Conclusion

Having chosen to look at the role and the organisation of the marketing function by taking the level of interaction between the company and the customers into consideration, we have proposed answers based on our observations of practices in industrial companies. These practices are identical to those identified by many other authors. Their research has distinguished the mechanistic structures characterised by a high level of specialisation, differentiation, formalisation and centralisation from the less specialised organic structures, less differentiated, less formalised and less centralised. The most efficient companies choose organic structures in a turbulent and dynamic environment, and mechanistic structures in a stable and predictable environment.

References and Further Reading

George, M., Freeling, A. and Court, D. (1994) 'Reinventing the Marketing Organisation', *The McKinsey Quarterly*, 4, 43–62.

Giard, V. (1991) *Gestion des projets*, Paris, Economica.

Hayes, R.H., Wheelwright, S.G. and Clark, K.B. (1988) *Dynamic Manufacturing: Creating the Learning Organisation*, New York, Free Press.

March, J.G. and Simon, H. (1993) *Organisation*, Oxford, Blackwell.

Marticotte, F. and Perrien, J. (1995) 'Les déterminants de la structure du département de marketing', *Recherche et Applications en Marketing*, 10:1, 3–22.

Morgan, G. (1996) *Images of Organisation*, New York, Sage.

Naudé, P. and McLean, D. (1999) 'Watching the Concert: How Global Account Management Developed within the Concert Alliance', *Journal of Selling and Major Account Management*, 2:1, 13–30.

Souder, W.E. (1981) 'Disharmony between R&D and Marketing', *Industrial Marketing Management*, 10, 67–73.

Discussion Questions

1 In what ways is the marketing function different as between consumer marketing and business-to-business marketing?

2 Why is the project organisation pattern a good way of resolving the difficulties that arise between different functions of the firm?

3 Discuss the importance of having some expertise in your customer's business. Within a firm, who are the experts in the customers' businesses?

4 Why is information the basis for the installation of the marketing function?

Chapter 1
Competitiveness, Marketing and Business-to-Business Marketing

*What is marketing all about
Different marketing environments
B2B marketing*

Chapter 2
Business-to-Business Customers and Markets

B2B Generic Offers	Technological Innovation	Pure Services	Major Projects

PART I   STRATEGY FOUNDATIONS

Chapter 3	Chapter 4	Chapter 5	Chapter 6
Understanding Business-to-Business Purchasing	Information and Information Systems	Markets and Suppliers' Strategy	Segmentation and Marketing Strategy

PART II   STRATEGY IMPLEMENTATION

Chapter 7			
Generic Business-to-Business Offer Design and Management			

Chapter 8	Chapter 10	Chapter 11	Chapter 12
Market Access and Customer Management	Marketing and Technological Innovation	The Marketing of Services	Major Project Marketing

Chapter 9
Communication and Publicity/ Advertising

PART III   STRATEGY DESIGN

Chapter 13	The Role and Organisation of Marketing
Chapter 14	Customer Position, Market Position, Marketing Strategies and Planning
Chapter 15	Issues and Specificities of International Marketing
Annex	The Internet and Marketing: Some Ideas

14 Customer Position, Market Position, Marketing Strategies and Planning

In Chapters 1 and 2 we systematically analysed some of the different areas of the application of marketing, showed how business-to-business marketing justifies the use of additional concepts and methods, and indicated how the marketing function could become even more efficient. These elements were then examined more closely in subsequent chapters. We particularly stressed the need to establish a link of strategic co-ordination between a company's global strategy and its marketing strategy, via the introduction of the *resources and technology variables* as the keystone to company strategy. We also showed how and why business-to-business marketing must consider *customer relationships* as vital when considering strategy, by introducing the *resources–technology–markets–customers relationship* as the backbone to marketing strategy.

These two new approaches were developed in Chapter 6, and led to the presentation of the Multistrat model, an analytical and decision making support tool for the design and implementation of marketing strategy in a business-to-business environment.

In Chapter 5, we outlined our notion of company strategy in the field of interorganisational marketing by stressing that, owing to the complexity of the sources of performance, the strategic process has to be an *iterative and systematic process* involving all the decision makers in the organisation. We also argued that it is impossible to integrate the real complexity of the interorganisational milieu into the global strategy, which means giving this role to marketing strategy itself so that it may ensure the coherence between all the levels of decision making.

The need to propose conceptual frameworks and methods to deal with the natural complexity of the interorganisational milieu could be seen as our being a little too 'rational' compared to everyday reality. But this is not the case. We recognise the somewhat empirical character of the decision-making process in this field, the flexibility required to seize opportunities, the practical impossibility of foreseeing all possible situations. In this chapter, we are again up against a fundamental reality of management: how to implement 'rational' methods of behaviour and systems, while not disturbing the entrepreneurship, the creativity, the intuition, or even the genius of others, whatever their position in the organisation.

As in Chapters 5 and 6, we shall propose a methodology of marketing planning with its limitations, and the ways to ensure that it does not result in a meaningless exercise or else in inhibiting personal initiative. This requires looking lucidly at reality, while trying to guide reflection and action. In the first part of the chapter we define our notion of the planning process and what this involves. In the second part we look again at the outline of the design of marketing strategy and of the underlying rationale, and end by proposing a way of drawing up a marketing strategy.

A Conception of Strategy Design and Implementation

For many years, the *strategic planning school* of thought dominated the strategy design process. They advocated (1) a greater formalisation of the process, (2) the sophisticated treatment of quantitative data based on trend extrapolation and (3) the delegation of the strategic planning process to a specialist in the area. Their influence is fading, but rather too slowly, as Mintzberg (2000) has argued.

The Limits of a Formalised Strategic Planning Process

Strategy development is an intellectual process, an abstract activity that aims to provide a picture of the future state of a market, and the competitive position that a company can hope to occupy. In the same way that market segmentation is a useful representation, shared by the decision makers, of the present position of a market, so the strategic planning process produces a *shared view of the future* to guide managerial decision and action. The task is not easy, however. All the more so because organisational acceptance of this view is supposed to lead to definitive decisions concerning the investments to make and the company organisation. Thus, the paradox of strategic management is clear: that while the future is uncertain, we have to have a view of it in order to operate at all.

Therefore, the aim is to ensure the quality and the validity of this view. Figure 14.1 shows, a little ironically, how a large company can create an erroneous vision of the future, and we can imagine also how it has constantly taken a series of wrong decisions.

So the future can play tricks on us. How many examples exist of politicians or economists who have said that the 'experts' misled them? Is this inevitable? It all depends on the role given to the view of the future (belief or probability) and the method used to produce it. Figure 14.1 illustrates the limits of the extrapolation techniques to foresee the future, and indeed their total inadequacy for the turbulent technological and economical environment since 1980.

Naturally, not all companies are so blind, and many companies have adopted more suitable approaches, more flexible, more related to reality of the the likely future. The balance between the will to achieve goals and the flexibility of adaptation to reality is often obtained by bringing together several forms of strategy design in the company. If there is nearly always a general guide as to what the future may be like produced by a formalised procedure, it is very often complemented by other

Figure 14.1 Years of wrong forecasting in an American multinational

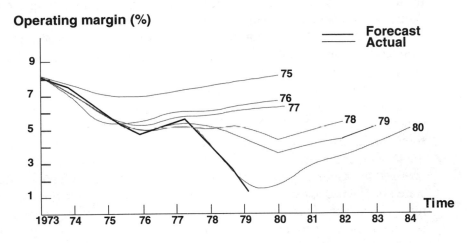

Source: Mintzberg (2000).

Figure 14.2 Forms of strategy

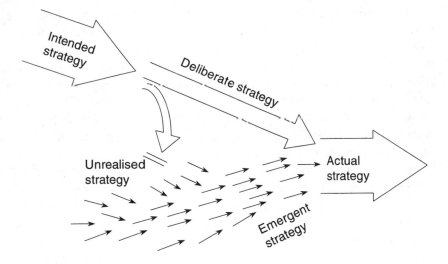

Source: Mintzberg (2000).

competing internal initiatives that, although unofficial, may well become more generally accepted in the future as they represent evolutions of reality. By carefully analysing the description of the real strategic process in Figure 14.2, it is possible to relate the strategic planning process to an *internal policy process* that is influenced before, during and after its formalisation, and therefore subject to many successive adjustments. Managers need to understand that the best approach is probably to accept that nothing is certain, that they have collectively to be constantly ready to make changes, while also refusing the complete absence of any formalisation. This may seem ambiguous at first, but it is probably the only realistic way to approach strategic analysis, while avoiding unnecessary risks for the future of the company. Obviously, this way of conceiving of the strategy process excludes delegating its design to a group of specialised decision makers, as the strategic planning school of thought proposed. We feel it is in the interest of the company to have as many internal decision makers as possible participating in a dual 'top-down' and 'bottom-up' process (Figure 5.15).

Figure 14.2 illustrates this, showing the gap between projected strategies and strategies that in fact were implemented. This gap exists for two main reasons: some strategies were abandoned because they were proven to be impossible to implement, or were replaced by others that were thought to be better, while others emerged over time and were seized upon and used by the company, although they were not planned at the beginning. Figure 14.2 underlines the possibility of recognising a mistake in the management of a formalised strategic process, and in fact is a good argument for lucidity and pragmatism.

Many examples exist to illustrate this. Example 5 on the relationships between Mory TNTE and Ancel shows how company flexibility, coupled with a constant desire to improve efficiency and to work closely with customers, can lead to strategies emerging from the relationship. The *iterative nature* of the design of these emerging strategies often gives the company the chance to reflect on new directions proposed by relationship partners, and gives it the time to think about decisions that have to be taken and what they may mean when a one-off opportunity becomes generalised. This all comes down to being open-minded, but can also be made easier if strategic views are shared and everybody is mindful of opportunities and possible acceptance. This may of course be done by using other means (market surveys, etc.), which usually cost more and most probably involve higher risks. Business-to-business environments are full of such opportunities waiting to be identified, analysed and seized upon.

To sum up, there are two conditions that must be combined in order to make the choices of mid-term direction for the company more efficient. First, the 'strategic spirit' must be spread throughout the company (particularly in the sales function). Secondly, the formal strategic planning process itself must be drawn up in accordance with its natural limits, remaining flexible and open, and therefore adjustable whenever it is felt necessary. This does not necessarily mean that the formal strategic planning process cannot itself also progress. To clarify certain important aspects of this question, we shall examine the problems linked to forecasting, the involvement of decision makers in the process, and the issues related to the formalisation of the plans.

The Capacity to Foresee the Future

Let us begin with the hypothesis that our ability to foresee the future is naturally weak. The year 1973 – the year of the first oil crisis – dealt a blow to the notion of forecasting the future through the extrapolation of past trends, which until then had been generally accepted and satisfactory. The appearance of discontinuity, of frequent turbulent periods and of the increasing number of new technologies, all combined to make the traditional methods of foreseeing the future more complex and more uncertain.

The nature of the data upon which forecasts are based has changed. Qualitative data and the identification and systematic interpretation of 'weak signals', supposed indicators of new trends, have become as essential as quantitative data. We have already looked at this in Chapter 4. The encoded information is often too 'dry' or sanitised to allow for a real understanding of the phenomenon, too aggregated to be of any real use, too late to be used efficiently and not always as reliable as it was made out to be.

Consequently, strategic planners have placed greater importance on developing a more profound understanding of the mechanisms of market evolution, the technologies – or, more generally, of the *context of the company's activity* – in order to give a meaning to the information. Therefore, the forecasting of the future is often based on a combination of qualitative and quantitative data whose treatment is as much a judgement as it is a calculation. Our own view of interorganisational marketing is this. We feel that it is better to understand how a supplier–customer relationship can operate positively than to know how many products a customer will consume in the following year, seeing that they can very often get their supplies elsewhere. Sorting out the probable trends from the uncertain ones, identifying what is likely to happen and what is less likely to happen is the key to understanding the future. By combining the estimated probabilities, one has no longer just one possible trend but *several likely trends*, from which a choice can be made. Therefore, the scenarios and Delphi methods (Chapter 4) become better adapted than extrapolations and traditional quantitative methods to formulating views of the future. It is all a question of identifying those events that will influence the evolutions of the business' future environment, and to be ready to act accordingly.

The general method of *scenario development*, of which the Delphi method is one possible approach, is, in reality, the best way to overcome the limitations mentioned above. More complex than the traditional high, mid and low hypothesis, this approach suggests that, among all the possible identified futures, one is selected for a number of given reasons. *Substitution scenarios* also emerge from such a method. Their role is to prepare the decision maker for other alternatives. One must, however, remember that the scenario chosen by this approach corresponds to an imaginary situation (a combination of probabilities), and that they never happen exactly as envisaged. Rather, it is taken as a sort of psychological preparation for possible strategic surprises. Accepting reality and its systematic interpretation (see above) enables managers to remain vigilant and ready to seize any unexpected opportunities. This particular combination of methods and openness is a good solution to the problems raised by the general uncertainty that is generated by increasing environmental complexity and technological change.

The Involvement of the Decision Makers

It is almost impossible to base the identification of realistic views of the future on the *a priori* collecting and analysis of information. In reality, the identification of the 'subversive' and potentially rich facts that really define the future is never clearly signposted. Involvement in the field, based upon more or less formal information networks, and the attention given to the tangible and significant details, are as important as the organised systems. And we believe that only an operational manager, at a certain minimum level in the organisational hierarchy, can consolidate this information. Therefore, it is essential that this person play a role in the strategy development process based upon the information that they hold or uncover. It is also essential that the company managers remain involved in the action to avoid any bureaucratic procrastination and to remain in touch with what is going on.

As an example, it should be remembered that in the strategic planning process the assessment of the strengths and weaknesses of a company is not just an intellectual exercise. It can also result from *organisational learning* following the successes and failures found in everyday life. For decision makers, this process is based on intuition, experience and close attention to detail, which allows them to identify the key points and to anticipate their development. Patrick Massardy, when President of the Maco Meudon company, spoke of his trip to the United States following the first delivery of concrete-breakers for his American customers. Having visited the sites where the machines were supposed to be used, he noticed that they were stored away and that a competitor's machines were being used. He was told that his products, although better, vibrated too much for the workmen who therefore preferred not to use them. This allowed him to launch an emergency programme to modify the equipment, and to strengthen his company's position in the American market. With a classical information system, the facts would have taken months to emerge and would have only given reasons for the loss of the American market.

The elaboration of a strategy can therefore depend on both a structured reflection based on the methods and tools presented in Chapters 5 and 6, and upon the emerging intuition and experiences that often include useful precepts. However, to argue that the operational management must pilot the process and that a strategic spirit needs to be present throughout the company does not rule out the need for a special strategic unit. This is for many reasons. One is to carry out basic studies making use of time and expertise in this specific domain. Another is to force the operational management to take the time out for strategic reflection, which is sometimes difficult owing to the personalities of certain managers. The role of the strategic unit, however it is organised, is to push reluctant managers into thinking again about their vision of the world that might have become outdated and in need to re-evaluation. Pierre Wack (1985a), the former planning director for Shell, gave the term 'microcosm' to this vision created in the minds of the decision makers, and often shared by others in the company. This microcosm can differ from the 'reality of the world' (Wack's 'macrocosm'). As long as the two 'cosms' are not too far apart, the decision maker can continue to control the situation. But when events, although uncertain in detail and time, modify the company's environment, then the risk of inappropriateness of the manager's vision becomes a reality. The main role of the strategic unit is to present an alternative vision of the future that may progressively modify that of the decision maker. This early warning system is largely fulfilled by the company's marketing information system (MIS), which needs to determine both the phenomenon to be watched over and the best way in which to do it.

The Formalisation of the Strategic Planning Process

Formalising the planning process does not guarantee the delivery of the strategic vision, just as formalising the strategic choices does not automatically guarantee their relevance. However, formalisation is necessary to make the strategy operational, and to allow a true comparison with the observed reality. It is important also to explain the consequences of the strategic choices in a number of areas. One of the major benefits of formalisation is the possibility of setting objectives for the company's players, for which they will be granted resources and for which they are then responsible. Motivating teams and individuals is partly based on this process.

The extent of useful formalisation varies with the complexity of the company and the planning horizon. Complexity is linked to the size and the operational set-up of the company (divisions, departments, production sites, etc.) and the range of the offer within an operational unit. The planning horizon is something different. To confront the problems of forecasting, some recommend pushing the horizon back further: 'if the three year vision is foggy, take it to ten and the fog will lift'. This view is not very popular as it simply means putting off the problem until a later date. The question is not so much the horizon chosen, but rather the identification of events likely to affect the *evolution of the environment* concerned. For some companies an annual plan is enough, or maybe even a six-month plan, as the phenomena that affect their strategy happen within this time perspective. Others must plan 3, 5 or even 15 years in advance so that their strategic vision coincides with the duration of the paying off of their major investments. This is not linked to the fact that the markets are or are not affected by upheavals. A strong level of turbulence does not necessarily indicate that short-term planning is required. The drop in price of electronic components, for example, heavily affects the computer industry. However, it can prepare for this by paying particular attention to the factors behind this drop in price, such as the effect of experience curves for component manufacturers or the technological progress made by research laboratories.

The question of the principle of formalisation is therefore easily solved. There are many convincing arguments to justify systematic formalisation, and few against;

from the moment the company protects itself against perverse effects such as bureaucratic attitudes (when the planning becomes an almost routine job in itself and its initial aims and purposes are forgotten). From our experience of implementing the Multistrat method, another question can be asked. Is one plan enough (a marketing plan, to simplify matters)? Or are several planning levels required (marketing plan, sales plan, etc.)? Other than the question of the burden of such a complex procedure, which can in fact be dealt with via the choice of planning method, the question is worth raising but does not necessarily require answering. In some cases, depending on company issues and success factors in its markets, we have had to set up several distinct plans to ensure the implementation of difficult but strategically important actions, particularly when they involve the participation of members of other company functions. For example, in a computer services company, the reorientation of the marketing strategy towards greater flexibility meant creating a major modification of the sales division, with greater involvement from the technicians. This minor internal cultural revolution in a company that was used to the clear distinctions of 'back-office' and 'front office' personnel and in favour of separating the two, led to the setting up of a temporary formalisation plan of the sales division for the different types of prospects. After a while, this plan became unnecessary, as the message had got through.

Once again, being *open-minded* and *flexible* is of utmost importance.

The determination of plans and the management of the strategic process as described above, highlight the 'philosophy' of the methods to come. Before proposing a framework for the creation of marketing plans, let us first mention a few points concerning the elaboration of marketing strategies.

Marketing Strategies and Planning

In Chapter 6 we presented Multistrat, a basic model of marketing strategy in an interactive context, in order to integrate the results of our research and as an alternative to the 'marketing mix' model that is not at all well suited to an inter-organisational environment.

For dispersed customer bases, the Multistrat process involves the definition of *homogeneous market segments* for which a basic offer can be designed according to customers' requirements, the company's strengths and the competitive situation in each segment. The building of homogeneous customer groups allows management to clarify such questions as the possibilities of adaptation of the basic offer and customer strategies (customers and prospects). Targeting segments and customers then facilitates the setting of priorities that help in orientating the organisation of human resources and the company's commercial investments.

The above steps in the decision process are made while systematically taking the competitive situation into consideration in order to define, whenever possible, partial superiorities (differentiations) over the competition. A similar approach can be established for concentrated customer bases.

Table 14.1 Some typical business-to-business marketing strategies

– *Standard offer and price competitiveness*	■ Offer design ■ Manufacturing process ■ Commercial coverage of the market
– *Technical leadership through innovation*	■ R&D ■ Technical co-operation with customers
– *Logistical reliability*	■ Manufacturing process ■ Quality control ■ Internal and external logistics
– *Global superiority of offer*	■ Competitive analysis ■ Attention to customers' requirements ■ Design and manufacturing of the offer
– *Total adaptation*	■ Supplier–customer relationship ■ Selling group organisation ■ Flexibility of the manufacturing process

Source: Valla (1991).

Examples of Interorganisational Marketing Strategies

The coherence of this set of complex decisions must be ensured even if it is not a simple process. Managers may find examples of coherence in typical business-to-business marketing strategies. We shall not examine here some of the usual strategic alternatives (leader, follower, offensive, defensive, etc.). Our objective is rather to identify the possible positions of strength in a business-to-business market and how they may be applied (Table 14.1).

The key company investments are different for each of the choices and they also apply to different levels of strategic involvement and decision in the company (global market, market segment, or customer). It is important to remember that the five strategies described in Table 14.1 are all *strategies to gain a stronger position* in a market, market segment or for a specific customer. They are basically *generic positioning* strategies. The *entry strategies* in a market, a market segment or with a customer are different, even if there are parallels between one strategy and another (see Chapter 8). For example, a low-price strategy can be adopted temporarily to penetrate a new market. This involves the less sophisticated part of the product range and therefore in no way implies a strategy based upon the standardisation of the offer.

In the Multistrat approach, planning is one of the elements of the company's marketing system. It is one of the ways to make sure that the marketing strategy chosen and the targeted positioning are indeed made operational. One of the problems of this implementation is integrating the *customer dimension* into the strategic process. This requires further more detailed examination.

Customer-Based Strategies and Customer Position

The notion of *positioning* was raised in Chapters 5 and 6. It was defined on a global level as including two dimensions: the importance of the *supply market* (quantitative: market share performance) and a positioning on the *demand side* (qualitative: company image). In the marketing strategy of a business-to-business supplier of products or services, the notion of positioning can in reality be divided into three different fields of decision: the global market, the systems of influence and the individual customers. Once the position on the *global market* has been defined, the choice of a position within the *systems of influence* involves three aspects. These are (1) a complete analysis of the *networks of relationships* in a given market or in the environment of supplier–customer relationships (structure and dynamics of the network, relationships between the actors, the role and importance of each actor, identification of each actor, etc.). This is followed (2) by the identification of the *influential actors* in relation to the supplier's targeted objectives. And finally (3) comes the *exploitation* of a temporary or permanent position with some of them (alliances, contracts, etc.), and/or the development of a *relationship strategy* with some or all the members of the network (creation of links with the key actors within the systems of influence). Major project marketing (Chapter 12) systematically uses these approaches.

Similarly, to be more efficient and to mobilise internal resources better, the supplier should formally define a targeted position for each of the target customers or prospects. *Customer strategy*, whose principle basis is the management of the customer portfolio (Chapter 8) thus includes:

- An *analysis phase* customer by customer, prospect by prospect ('customer' database)
- A *targeting phase* (determining customers and prospects)
- The choice of a *targeted position* phase (supplier intentions and objectives)
- *Mobilising internal resources* phase, according to the objectives and the marketing situation (sales centre, sales investments, etc).

A good example of these steps can be found in the work of Turnbull and Zolkiewski (1997).

Marketing planning, which could mean a sales-based plan of action, will allow the company to formulate these choices and to supervise their implementation while preparing interaction with the targeted customers or prospects. In some cases the intentions may correspond to the supplier's present position with the customer, and therefore simply confirm or reinforce the status quo. In other cases, supplier objectives may correspond to a change in position for the customer and require heavy investments (to change the image, change role in the customer's purchasing strategy, restore customer confidence, etc.).

These choices have to be considered as strategic in business-to-business environments. Observation has shown that this is where the company's global strategy is decided, in the customer interaction process, or in the development of contract and negotiations with prospects. Either the sales centre acts on the basis of precise strategic choices per key customer, or else it simply 'does its best' according to the particular situation. Then the actual supplier strategy is essentially the result of the

Figure 14.3   General method for choosing a position with a prospect

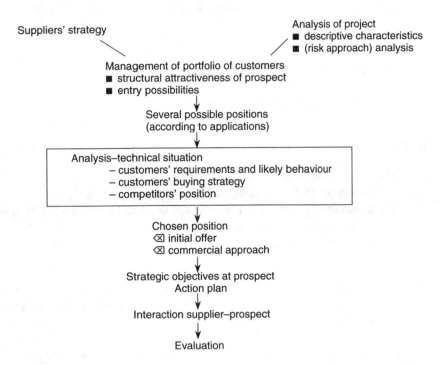

negotiations and depends on the existing customer–supplier balance of power. To keep control of the interaction and not to deviate from the predefined strategy is not an easy task. We decided to focus on strategies to acquire a new customer in order to develop this point. The same approach, although in a simplified version, can be used to develop or defend a position with a customer.

The choice of a *targeted position with a prospect* (Figure 14.3) corresponds to the situation where the supplier has drawn up a marketing strategy for the market segment in question and where the salespeople contribute to its implementation via their prospecting. The prospects present several possible applications for the supplier's offer. As they do all not represent the same potential benefit for the supplier, a *choice* – or at least a hierarchy – must be made between them in order to produce an efficient sales action plan.

The convergence between supplier strategy on the one hand and the information obtained about the prospect on the other, allows the salesperson to position the potential customer in the customer portfolio (Figure 8.2). Careful analysis of the prospect then allows the salesperson to identify several possible applications that must be evaluated according to four criteria (the technical situation, the requirements and probable behaviour of the prospect, the purchasing strategy and the position of the competition) in order to determine which position to aim at. This position will help to define a *strategy* for the customer and an *action plan*.

The *technical* situation can be analysed from three points:

- The advantages for the prospect from the use of the *supplier's technology* in relation to the competition's technologies, for example:

  - cost advantages
  - ease of use
  - the respect of regulations (norms, etc.)
  - advantages in quality
  - advantages for the customers of the prospect
  - etc.

- The relative attraction of the applications for the *supplier*, for example:

  - the volume represented by the application
  - the dynamics of the application (according to life-cycle)
  - the position of the prospect for this application (making a profit or not, investment or non-investment, etc.)
  - the possible profit margin
  - etc.

- Determining the applications for which the prospect *would gain most in the medium term*, in other words, those applications in which the prospect stands to gain most by changing supplier.

The *requirements* and *probable behaviour* of the prospect are determined by the *risk approach* analysis. What is the potential downside of the offer (technical risks, financial risks, risks linked to the use of the products and services by the customer, risks linked to the availability of the products and services)? What does the buyer expect from the supplier (expectancies in relation to the supplier–customer interaction)? How will the customer react to each of the different variants of the offer that are possible, as predicted by the application of the risk approach analysis?

The description of the prospect's *purchasing policy* concerns general policy information whether it exists formally or implicitly. Its analysis involves finding answers to the following questions:

- Does the prospect tend to develop partnership policies or proceed via regular invitations to tender?
- Is the prospect looking for long-term agreements or not?
- How many suppliers do they select in general for a given application?
- Do they develop a unique source or multisource policy for an application?
- Does the response to these questions vary according to the importance for the prospect of the application (strategic, important, ordinary)?

The position of the *competitors* with this prospect are analysed according to the general information concerning them and what it is possible to know about their particular position, application by application. This means establishing a compara-

Table 14.2   Comparative analysis of competitive positions per application

Criteria	Competitors' performance*			
	A	**B**	**C**	**Us**
■ Price competitiveness	4	1	2	–
■ Delivery time	3	3	2	–
■ Delivery reliability	3	1	2	–
■ Technical quality	2	2	1	–
■ Quality constancy	1	2	1	–
■ Innovation capacity	1	3	2	–
■ Quality of the relationship with the customer	1	2	3	–
■ etc.				

* Grading scale =
1 Very good   3 Average
2 Good   4 Insufficient

Conclusion:
■ Application held by competitors
■ Application winnable if we invest accordingly
■ Application easily winnable
■ Other (to be determined)

tive analysis of the competition in relation to oneself, in other words an analysis of differentiation based on the model presented in Table 14.2.

These analyses will allow the salesperson to choose a *targeted position* with the prospect that will be characterised by the application (or applications) on which the supplier will look to position itself, via a particular offer or sales approach. The desired objectives or outcomes (date of the decision, date of the first delivery, expected turnover and profit margin, etc.) will at the same time be clearly defined and compared to planned investments.

The final touch of this analysis involves a *plan of action* as outlined in Table 14.3. In the resulting *supplier–prospect interaction*, both actors will look to reach their fixed objectives. At the relevant moments, the interaction process will allow for an *evaluation* of the situation and its evolution.

This methodological approach and its different components could be applied, with one or two adjustments, to the *development of a position with a customer*. The creation of new opportunities with an existing customer often comes from (1) a favourable development within the purchasing centre, (2) new customer investments (factory, technology, etc.), (3) weak competition, or (4) new supplier propositions (reduced costs, improvement of value for the customer, advantages for the customer's customers, etc.).

Defending a position with a customer is a similar process, bearing in mind that the reasons for a supplier to look for other possibilities in the supply market are symmetrical to those in the previous paragraph. Changes and innovations with the customer often contain the beginnings of difficulties for the established supplier, as

Table 14.3   Plan of action for the acquisition of a prospect

Description of the application:

....

....

....

....

Probability of success (degree of technical difficulty)	Weak ☐	Average ☐	High ☐	Very High ☐

Investments required to succeed

                      for the supplier   for the customer

- time for the customer (man/day)
- development time (man/day)
- equipment (cost)
- other expenses

Total ( )

Necessary team (competences):

                Names   Foreseen time

Mr/Ms .... days

Mr/Ms .... days

Mr/Ms .... days

Mr/Ms .... days

Foreseen time: _____ weeks

Objectives:
- market share of the application: _ %
- market share of customer's potential: _ %
- turnover   _
- expected margin/turnover   _ %
- expected margin (value)   _

Time of return on investment:
- for the supplier   _ (number of months of turnover)
- for the customer   _ (number of months of purchase)

they add to the desire to assess new alternatives. Moreover, this new investigation into other alternatives may be provoked by supplier incompetence (lack of services, supplier arrogance leading to neglect, technical or sales conflicts, higher prices compared to the competition, etc.).

The Notion of Market Position

At the beginning of this chapter we mentioned a specific aspect of business-to-business marketing, namely the potential *versatility* of the technology involved. The case of emerging technologies clearly shows the importance of this aspect, as it may change the classically admitted boundaries of a market. We have a strong example with the evolutions of the computer and telecommunication markets. They are now so interdependent that it is no longer possible to separate them into two

Figure 14.4 Technology and markets – applications

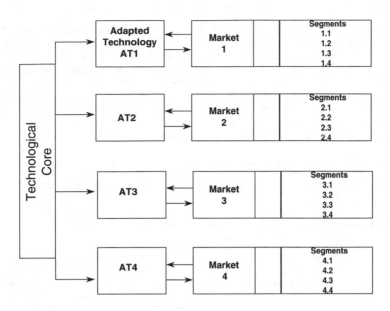

different market definitions. As mentioned in Chapter 13, the expertise of an industrial supplier is based on two elements: the mastering of one's own technology (for example, electronic instrumentation) and the understanding of the applications in which it is used (for example, the running of the ABS systems for car brakes). Thus, the supplier must couple *technical skills* with *market expertise*. Yet the character istic of a technology is to create access to distinct 'markets', in which the key factors for success differ greatly. This means that the supplier's technological capabilities must be such that the company can adapt to the characteristics of these different markets–applications. The process indicated for innovative technologies (shown in Figure 10.11) clearly shows this problem. Consequently, the notion of market position must allow for greater clarity in all these ambiguities. Figure 14.4 presents an outline of this question.

The core technology gives access to adaptations that permit the supplier to enter markets where the willingness to adopt the company's technology is not homogenous, which in turn leads the company to define market segments. The basis for segmentation can be the degree of customers' willingness to adopt the new technology. An initial definition of market position is given by the supplier's choice to concentrate on a market or to cover several markets, according to the typology presented in Chapter 5.

We can give a second definition to the notion of market position. We saw in Chapter 6 that it was most often preferable to substitute a sector-based segmentation with one based upon explanatory segmentation. Figure 14.5 illustrates the significance of such a change.

Example 18 Laboratoires Chauvin

Laboratoires Chauvin chose to concentrate on one of the markets accessible to the SODA technologies, (superoxydes dimustases analogues used as a means of withstanding the 'free radicals' that develop with age). They identified ophthalmology for applications concerning the treatment of glaucoma, and chose to co-develop the technological core with a partner who has undertaken the other applications–markets. Chauvin chose to remain a laboratory specialising in ophthalmology, which corresponds to a definition of position. It is possible that a larger laboratory would have sought to continue the development of the SODA on all the potential applications–markets, thereby establishing a position of a generalist project manager for the medicinal applications of the SODA.

Note: Based on real data, company name confidential.

Figure 14.5 Technology and segmented markets – applications

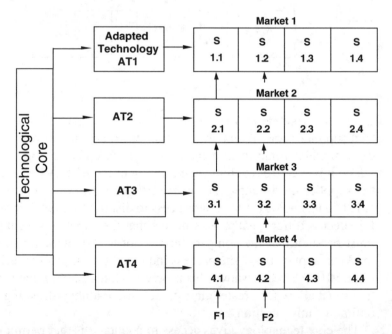

F1 = supplier positioned on segment 1, with an identical definition on several applications–markets
F2 = supplier positioned on segment 2, with an identical definition on several applications–markets

Figure 14.5 can be read in the following way. Suppliers *F*1 and *F*2 have identified the existence of customers with similar behaviour on several applications-markets, on which they have established their positions, one, *F*1, as being the specialist of segment 1 (*S*1.1, *S*2.1, *S*3.1, *S*4.1), the other, *F*2, of segment 2 (*S*1.2, *S*2.2, *S*3.2, *S*4.2). If we look at the example of Table 3.6, we may consider that the positions occupied by the three suppliers with a customer correspond to clear strategies. These strategies are based on their strategic choices and the corresponding

Figure 14.6   Development of the business-to-business company

Degree of
mastering of
the technology

	Identical	Close	Different
New	Market penetration through innovation	Market extension through innovation	Market diversification through innovation
Close	Market penetration through technological evolution	Market extension through technological evolution	Market diversification through technological evolution
Mastered	Technological exploitation and market penetration	Market extension through technological exploitation	Market diversification through technological exploitation

Degree of
proximity to the
customers

Source: Ansoff (1988).

technological investments (performance level, prices, delays, degree of innovation and flexibility, services policy, etc.). We are entitled to think that these choices lead a company to develop positions with different customers similar to the one described in Table 3.6 for each of these suppliers. It means that customers recognise and exploit the differential capacities created by each supplier. Indeed, it is difficult, even unthinkable, that a company simultaneously develops such different strategies, for reasons of cost and efficiency. The company has then to seek customers that allow it to optimise its strategic choices on all the markets accessible to its technology definition.

As a synthesis, it is possible to say that the business-to-business company has to develop a strategy that takes its technical development possibilities and the market developments into consideration, as illustrated in Figure 14.6.

Without going into a detailed description of each of the possible strategies shown in Figure 14.7, it is important to note that the company must identify the underlying format of its development and be aware of the requirements of each form. The approach of different customer types can contain important financial implications, and risks of failure that are as high as those linked to technological innovation. If the innovation has extensive development potentials, these often come to light with customers who are not part of the traditional customer base of the company, whether this distance is founded on their nature ('psychic distance') or the geographical

Figure 14.7 Company strategy and marketing strategy

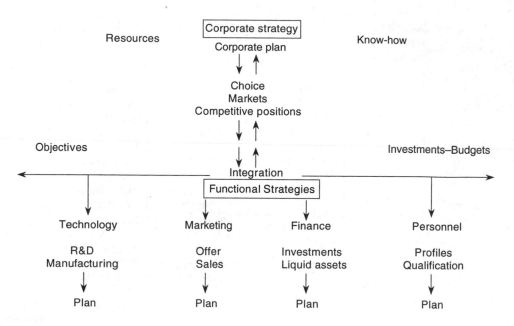

location. Therefore, it is necessary to plan efforts according to both the possibilities of the technical evolution and also the time required to approach the markets and the customers.

So far, we have only looked at the question of planning from the *qualitative position* (or *strategic posture*) of a supplier in their markets. This leads to the *quantitative position (market share)* that the supplier can attain. The fact that the company specialises (per market or customer segment) automatically means that there is a limit to the accessible market. Appreciation of the market share, however, remains a useful measuring device to assess the results of company effort, and to provide management with an indicator of the competitive situation (see Chapter 5). The question is how to calculate market share. The definition of the appropriate reference market is a problem raised by opposition to the 'served market' concept (PIMS) – which is close to that of market segment – and a broad determination (BCG) of the notion of market itself. The question is important as it determines the *set of competitors* to which the company is to be compared. To make it simple: has Mercedes a small market share of the world car market? Or a large market share of the world luxury car market? Does Mercedes compete with Fiat, Ford, Toyota and Renault or with BMW, Saab, Infinity, Lexus and Alfa Romeo? For us it is important to follow the two levels of market definition, the *segment* and the *global market*. This is a good approach to evaluate simultaneously several important elements: the size and evolution of the global market, the market segment and company position.

Thinking about qualitative market segmentation, in Chapter 4, we outlined the difficulties inherent in identifying the volumes of the market segments and the construction of a suitable information system. (We recommended a customer basis for this.) We also remind the reader that what we call a 'customer' relates to the marketing definition of the customer (establishment, department, factory, work-shop, etc.) and not the legal definition. For a supplier of car equipment, VW represents maybe a dozen or so different 'marketing customers' to a particular supplier.

The Elaboration of Marketing Strategy

Obviously, the marketing strategy is part of a company's global strategy. It supplies information on the competitive position and its perspectives, and contributes to the elaboration of the general strategy. Figure 14.7 illustrates the *decision phases* involved. Two aspects are important here. The first is the search for *vertical coherence* between the overall company strategy and each of the functional strategies. As far as marketing is concerned, reference to the Multistrat model allows us to understand that this search is fundamental to our strategic analysis. The second challenge is the *horizontal coherence* of the functional strategies, particularly within the technical department–marketing department relationships, which often create problems for companies.

Definition of the Unit Within Which the Marketing Strategy is Designed

Marketing, other than its contribution to the overall company strategy, is also responsible for its own functional strategy. This is difficult. The first problem is to determine the appropriate level at which the marketing plan has meaning within the company. Let us return to Roulements SA (Example 14 in Chapter 8). If there is a need to consolidate the technical, financial and human investments required by the car and industrial divisions, then the presentation of a global marketing plan will have little significance. In this example, the customers, the external issues, the competitive environment, the distribution and the product ranges all differ from one division to another. As indicated in Chapter 13, the two divisions are in very different marketing situations. They are not at all in the same business-to-business environment. Therefore, it is normal that each division (or SBU – see Chapter 5) determines its own marketing strategy, even if some co-ordination is unavoidable (see Chapter 5 on the basis for strategic analysis) between the two units on certain points (company image, communication, manufacturing and R&D investments, etc.).

We recommend drawing up the marketing strategy within a 'unit' that has enough internal homogeneity, an autonomous marketing and sales structure and for which is it reasonable to create an *operational plan*. This definition is valid for an SME or the department or division of a large company. One of the possible rules of thumb is to define it so that the same person handles the marketing and sales re-sponsibility. This is important as it defines the decision maker, described earlier as being the person in charge of the design and implementation of the strategy. It is therefore within this 'unit' that we shall examine the determination of marketing strategy and the construction of the operational plan.

The Process of Determining the Marketing Strategy

The unit can continue to present a high level of heterogeneity in terms of markets and customer segments, distribution circuits, offers and product ranges. Subsequently, it can be divided into several elementary units, each relatively homogeneous and with one person in charge of functional marketing.

As outlined above, the design process must respect the somewhat contradictory constraints. It must be time-determined so as to be able to use the information that can be collected only at certain periods, but with enough flexibility to allow for any new elements. While the decision maker is responsible for defining the strategy, he or she typically has little time for this and the functional manager often finds it difficult to get the required output. The decision maker believes that he or she has a clear implicit strategy, but their collaborators are often confused. It is necessary to have a global vision, but some points require detailed attention. Analytical methods must be used (Chapters 5 and 6), but these should not, however, stifle intuition.

One of the best ways to solve these contradictions is to elaborate a marketing strategy on two interdependent levels, the *unit* and the *elementary units*. The process is outlined in Figure 14.8.

The objective of this process is to ease the transition between a detailed perspective and a more global vision, between the analysis of functional staff and

Figure 14.8 Design process of a unit marketing strategy

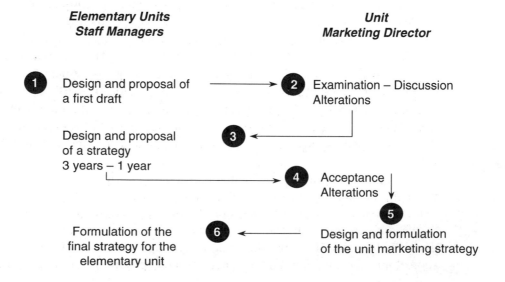

intuition based on the decision maker's knowledge of the sector. It also enables the phases to be drawn up over time, which gives time for thought, and for the exploration of new ideas. For situations of average complexity, about 3 months between steps 1 and 6 in Figure 14.8 is considered as normal. A similar process is relevant for the elaboration of elementary unit strategies, the movement happening between the functional manager and the sales managers, as shown in Figure 14.9.

The starting point of this process is the comparison between the *synthesis phase* (S – the general view of the competitive position of the company and its environment), and the *analytical phase* (A – which takes the visions of the same issues, based on points of view that are part of the everyday sales life). This comparison has many advantages. It avoids an overly bureaucratic construction of the strategy. In due time the commercial reality can be formally incorporated in the whole process. It deals with emerging strategies, new experiences and weak signals that may herald changes in the future and requiring additional surveys to assess their relevance and importance. This, of course, does not mean that the planning process must constitute the only time when this can happen; but it presents a regular and formal occasion for it. Although this approach is difficult to implement, it is an excellent *internal learning opportunity*, and a process that facilitates the interaction of different opinions and experiences. The main conditions for its success – and its usefulness – are honesty and the respect of others. The danger is to spend too much time on the process. It is just a support for the real task, which is to analyse and to devise a strategy. The conclusion of the whole process is then the creation of a marketing plan.

Figure 14.9 Elaboration process of an elementary unit strategy

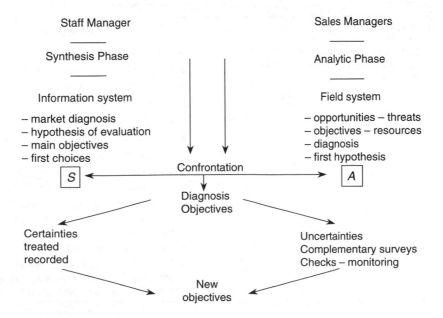

The Formalisation of the Marketing Plan

Formalising the Plans

We have already mentioned some principles that guide our thoughts on the degree to which the plans and their generation is part of a formalised process. We have only alluded to the fact that this level can be linked to the personality of the decision makers and how they see their role and, consequently, the documents that bear their name. Our experience of managers and the examination of their plans has enabled us to come up with the typology presented in Table 14.4.

It would be wrong to reject the relevance of differences in character completely, and each planning system will always partially reflect the personality of the decision maker. This does not mean that we are suggesting giving the decision maker total freedom. The formalisation of an operational plan has numerous advantages and only a few inconveniences that we have summed up in Table 14.4.

Table 14.5 requires further comment. Although formalisation does not answer all the problems, it can deliver a lot when it is based on good strategic analysis.

Table 14.4 Typology of managerial temperament and the formalisation of plans

The straights	The anxious	The visionaries	The sharers	The energetics
One plan for all All for the plan	Without plans I can't find my way	I am the plan	Bring your plan to me	The plan? Yes, tomorrow
50 pages	100 pages	1 page		

Table 14.5 Advantages and disadvantages of the formalisation of plans

Drawbacks	Advantages
■ Decrease of capability to respond to turbulence, surprise and change ■ Decrease in flexibility ■ Bureaucracy leads to demotivation ■ Every eventuality cannot be examined	■ A perspective to guideline functions ■ An agreement on objective/objectives ■ Motivation through sequence: objectives–means–results ■ A useful tool to relate causes and effects ■ To allow re-examination of decisions ■ To minimise risks of error ■ To introduce idea of testing: design of hypothesis, checking, conclusion ■ To increase capacity to estimate in order to reduce risks taken on the profitability of investments ■ To reduce uncertainty ■ Bankers, suppliers, stock holders, financial analysts and potential employees are given a formalised, forward-looking perspective

Companies that have managed honestly to combine the objectives–means–results sequence, and to use this as an instrument of motivation and team management, will constantly benefit from it. This point of view reinforces the need for decision maker involvement in the creation of the strategy and the formalisation of the plan. Thousands of plans that have been thought up by functional managers are lying in cupboards, their only function being to supply the occasional data and to be used in training sessions. That is why we recommended that the plans be established on two levels: that of the *unit* and that of the *elementary unit*.

The Marketing Plan of the Unit

This should clarify the main directions of the company, and the choices concerning the allocation of all the resources (investments, budgetary expenditures, etc.) between the various sub-units. It explicitly states objectives of volume, turnover, and profitability that are included in the general plan, and makes up the basis of other functional plans (human resources, production, R&D, etc.). It is the link between the general plan and the plans of the elementary units that contains the required details. Its horizon coincides with that of the general plan, with intermediary steps that are generally between 5 and 3 years and a 1-year plan. Table 14.6 illustrates the process.

The broad-brush character of this plan is intentional. It must not be substituted by the plans of the elementary units that deal with market realities, customers, competitors and company marketing action. Its role is to provide a clear vision of the objectives, the risks and resources in the different markets, to identify the elements to be monitored and to draw up contingency plans. Its originality comes from the information system, whose structure, organisation and content are related to the objectives of the sales and marketing manager. Only he or she has the authority to create and maintain these plans.

Table 14.6   Marketing plan for a strategic unit

I	Reminder: corporate plan – strategy – objectives – consequences on market positions and strategies
II	Objectives – global – per market
III	Resources – global – per market
IV	Information systems Elements to be specifically monitored
V	Budget
VI	Performance control (criteria)
VII	Replacement scenarios
VIII	Synthesis (1 page)

Table 14.7   Structure of a marketing plan for an elementary unit

1 Market
   1.1 Historical data – evolutions
     – Economical environment: general–specific
     – Perspectives at 1–3 years–5 years (or more)
     – Major facts passed/expected, certain and uncertain
   1.2 Segmentation
     – Segments dynamics
   1.3 Main customers
     – Evolutions and strategies
   1.4 Major players
     – Strategies of the players

2 Competition
   2.1 Main competitors per segment
   2.2 Main competitors' strategy
   2.3 Position of competitors at main customers

3 Competitive position
   3.1 Global
     – Qualitative
     – Quantitative
   3.2 Per segment
     – Qualitative
     – Quantitative

4 Diagnosis and evolution perspective 1–3 years (or more)
   4.1 Diagnosis of past and future
   4.2 Different possible scenarios
   4.3 Choice of one scenario – reasons why

5 Action plan
   5.1 Global objectives
     – Objectives per segment/customer's portfolio
   5.2 Description of the means
   5.3 Provisional income statement
   5.4 Detailed plan of actions (start–end – responsible – means – cost – result)
     – Information
     – R&D
     – Manufacturing
     – Offer
     – Pricing and margins
     – Customers
     – Distribution channels
     – Sales forces
     – Communication
     – Promotion
   5.5 General planning

6 Control–contingency scenarios

7 Synthesis (1 page)

Marketing Plans of the Elementary Units

These plans give details at the level of the global markets, the market segments, the customers, the competitors, company offers and actions to be undertaken. Therefore, they are detailed and must help company management to understand the 'functioning' of the different markets that company serves. Their role as the *memory of the market* is also vital, as anybody from the company can consult the documents for any required information (Table 14.7).

The structure of this document reflects the functions that it has to fulfil. The first (parts 1–3) is that of memory and anticipation, which are closely linked. It is important to remind oneself what brought the market, the competitors and the company to the present position to be able to predict the future. The second is that of the analysis, to give a meaning to the facts, to the evolution of the market and to the future. If several futures are possible, it is important to draw them into a *scenario* and to give reasons why one of the possible scenarios has been selected. The *action plan* comes from this scenario, which is a precious guide for operational implementation, with each detailed action plan possibly being the object of a separate document presented by those responsible for the actions.

Conclusion

The elaboration of the company's strategy and the planning that supports it, like the marketing function, are themes that are very dependent on the characteristics of a company. Its size, internal complexity, concentrated or dispersed customer base, the continuous or discontinuous nature of the relationships with the customers and the degree of interaction and the time needed to pay back investments, all lead to considerable differences in the procedure, the structure of documents and the main points of attention. What we have proposed here aims to be a synthesis, an overall view, to provide a tangible format and to represent a really concrete tool for a user. For others, the approach hopefully highlights future paths for reflection, and for further change and adaptations. We apologise for the work that they still have to undertake.

References and Further Reading

Ansoff, I. (1988) *Corporate Strategy*, London, Penguin.

Day, G.S. (1980) 'Strategic Market Analysis: Top Down and Bottom Up Approaches', *Working Paper*, Marketing Science Institute, Cambridge, MA.

Day, G.S. (1990) *Market Driven Strategy: Processes for Creating Value*, New York, Free Press.

Hamel, G. and Prahalad, C.K. (1996) *Competing for the Future*, Boston, Harvard Business School Press.

Luck, D.J., Ferrel, O.C. and Lucas, Jr, G.H. (1989) *Marketing Strategy and Places*, Englewood Cliffs, Prentice-Hall.

Makidrakis, S. and Wheelwright, S. (1978) *Forecasting: Methods and Applications*, New York, Wiley.

Mintzberg. H. (2000) *The Rise and Fall of Strategic Planning*, Englewood Cliffs, Financial Times/Prentice-Hall.

Turnbull, P.W. and Zolkiewski, J. (1997) 'Profitability in Customer Portfolio Planning', in D. Ford (ed.), *Understanding Business Markets*, New York, Dryden Press.

Valla, J.-P. (1991) 'Options stratégiques en marketing inter organisationnel: un nouveau modèle à partir d'une nouvelle compréhension de l'environnement', *1ère Conférence Internationale de Gestion Stratégique*, 'Les options stratégiques', HEC Montreal.

Wack, P. (1985a) 'Scenarios: Shooting the Rapids', *Harvard Business Review*, November–December, 139–50.

Wack, P. (1985b) 'Scenarios: Uncharted Waters Ahead', *Harvard Business Review*, September–October, 139–50.

Discussion Questions

1 How are the concepts of market position and market share linked?
2 Why must any planning process include some flexibility?
3 How are the concepts of customer position and market position linked?
4 Are the concepts of customer and market position linked to the organisation of the firm's resources?

Chapter 1
Competitiveness, Marketing and Business-to-Business Marketing
What is marketing all about
Different marketing environments
B2B marketing

Chapter 2
Business-to-Business Customers and Markets

B2B Generic Offers	Technological Innovation	Pure Services	Major Projects

PART I   STRATEGY FOUNDATIONS

Chapter 3	Chapter 4	Chapter 5	Chapter 6
Understanding Business-to-Business Purchasing	Information and Information Systems	Markets and Suppliers' Strategy	Segmentation and Marketing Strategy

PART II   STRATEGY IMPLEMENTATION

Chapter 7
Generic Business-to-Business Offer Design and Management

Chapter 8
Market Access and Customer Management

Chapter 9
Communication and Publicity/ Advertising

Chapter 10	Chapter 11	Chapter 12
Marketing and Technological Innovation	The Marketing of Services	Major Project Marketing

PART III   STRATEGY DESIGN

Chapter 13	The Role and Organisation of Marketing
Chapter 14	Customer Position, Market Position, Marketing Strategies and Planning
Chapter 15	Issues and Specificities of International Marketing
Annex	The Internet and Marketing: Some Ideas

15 Issues and Specificities of International Marketing

We started this book with a perspective that placed marketing as a central player in the formation of any firm's international competitiveness. The subsequent chapters presented a more technical perspective aimed at describing implementable methods and tools within a general context. In this chapter we once again look at the international dimension, in order to see if marketing practices over several different countries highlight any specific issues for company management.

As we have argued, the marketing approach is based on *understanding* and *reacting to demand diversity*. Any company seeking to build a long-lasting competitive position uses marketing to organise and manage this diversity in order to understand it and to adapt accordingly. Thus, the firm is bound to make numerous choices: target segments, target customers, prioritised deals, offer design and so on. Our initial perspective and the numerous examples we have introduced naturally placed our views within an international scope. Doing so makes the point that acting in an international context places the firm in an environment of a *higher degree of complexity*. This is the result of the view of the marketplace: differences on technological levels and cultural habits between geographical areas and countries, diversity of customers and their organisational structures, the variety of networks and value chains or clusters. The marketing approach and methods that we have discussed are well adapted to deal with market diversity and heterogeneity. We could well stick to a technical point of view and not examine the international field at all. However, this increased complexity challenges any firm in organising its marketing activities, and it is necessary to identify and attempt to solve the questions that it raises. Understanding this complexity is not an easy task, as it does not present itself uniformly when dealing with different industrial sectors, customer portfolios, competitors' position or types of offer.

A first difficulty appears when trying to separate international marketing from the firm's international strategy. Consequently, we chose to limit our discussion to the design of an *international customer* and offer policy, and to the questions linked to the organisation of the marketing function in an international arena. We shall not treat such themes as how to take a foothold in foreign markets, the localisation of the manufacturing units, the specificities of local tax or legal systems, the international financial operations and other important issues.

Two realities actually affect international marketing. First, what is the *kind of firm* that we are looking at? Is it possible to analyse the international marketing strategy of large concerns such as BP or Dow Chemical and that of a small European company such as Elcometer <www.elcometer.com>, that nevertheless exports a significant amount of its output, in the same way? Secondly, the degree of *concentration* of the customer base has to be taken into account. We indicated as early as Chapter 2, that it is not possible to use the same approaches and methods for 15 car manufacturers as for 5 million garages. We shall try to define clearly all the time the situation that we have in mind.

We start with a definition of what we mean by the *diversity of international markets*. This foundation will allow us to deal with the international segmentation and the management of international customer portfolios, once the initial situation of the firm has been understood. We shall then be able to address the issues linked to the coverage of international markets and those of the international marketing organisation of the firm.

On the Diversity of International Markets

If the world were uniform and homogeneous, this chapter would not exist. Common sense brings forward evident differences: languages, social habits, lifestyles, foods and so on. However, some innovations – the mobile phone and Internet, for example – appear simultaneously in all countries and develop in spite of these true differences. Marketing textbooks typically deal with international issues only from the point of view of consumer goods or services. Differences between countries are typified through such criteria as standard of living (Gross National Product), the structure of consumption patterns (the respective claims on disposable income of food, clothing, furniture, leisure and so on), a national preference for certain type of consumption, and local regulations. These criteria are not particularly relevant to business-to-business environments. A new technology – such as an innovative sensor bearing for the car industry – is likely to offer solutions acceptable to any customer in any country, whatever the nationality or language. But the bearing manufacturer may not meet the same degree of success in all the countries concerned, even if it expended the same effort throughout. This chapter seeks to explore why this might be so.

The Reasons Behind Diversity

The most obvious international dimension is *geography*. Remoteness creates a kind of mental or psychic distance between a decision centre and a large number of operational fields. One spontaneous and historical trend is to simplify this variety through *clustering countries* within geographical areas. So, for example, IBM's world is divided into EMEA (Europe, Middle East and Africa), the Americas, and the Pacific Rim. From a purely marketing point of view this is based on the assumption that these areas present a high degree of homogeneity on numerous criteria (and in IBM's case, the time differences in between units in one area are minimised). But this homogeneity is not universally true.

Differences in *required performances* come for any country from its degree of technical sophistication: the general level of education, technical training of engineers and technicians, standards of the research centres, level of the industrial equipment both in general and for a particular sector, and so on. This degree of sophistication is closely correlated with a more general indicator, the Gross National Product per head. The behaviour of a firm in a country is closely connected to the 'local' resources that it may call for. This is a direct application of the cluster theory (Figure 2.11). The performance and development of a firm are partly determined by the conditions of its environment.

Example 19 Imaje

> At the end of the 1980s Imaje, a French firm specialising in very high-speed ink-jet marking for production and packing units, naturally positioned their operation centre for the Asian area in Japan. The major objective of the Japanese centre was to gain customers and market share in Japan, the highest potential market in the area. Imaje's offers were upgraded on a number of dimensions in order to meet Japanese customers' expectancies. This represented significant and costly improvements on the initial European standards. These 'Japanese' offers were marketed to other customers in other countries in the area, with a very low degree of success. These new customers did not have the same level of requirements as those of the Japanese customers, and could not afford the same price level. In fact, the gap was larger between Japan and these countries than between them and Western Europe standards. In this case geographical proximity, as seen from a European centre, masked important differences between customers. And this delayed for years the design of an adapted strategy for the rest of the area.
>
> We may group these differences in two clusters (Figure 15.1): required performances and professional practices.

Figure 15.1 A view of the diversity of international markets

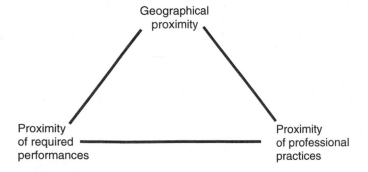

The *proximity of professional practices* combines several points that may have led national firms to adopt similar practices:

- *Norms and regulations* intervene in all domains. They still play a protectionist role in many countries. Most often they are the result of joint work between public authorities and the profession. It suffices here to note how Electricité de France has been able to establish French norms in terms of transport and distribution of electricity. In has succeeded in influencing the performance of the firms acting in the sector. A firm that is used to meeting high performances is not adapted to produce simpler products at low cost. Conversely, firms used to lower performance norms do not easily comply with higher norms. Norms may slow down the entry of foreign firms as much as the export capacity of national firms does. It may be the inability to adapt to other norms or the refusal to support the related costs. Nevertheless, the trend is towards an increased influence of international norms (ISO, EC standards, and so on.).

- *National networks and value chains* also establish particular practices: different division or allocation of the tasks from one value chain to another, different roles from the supporting industries, the impact of various public authorities and so on. All these dimensions shape different market structures from one country or area to another. We have already mentioned the particular nature of the links established by the Japanese car manufacturers with their upstream suppliers (Example 19). In order to sell small electrical motors to a car manufacturer, a foreign supplier had no choice other than to approach the usual supplier of this manufacturer. Trying to force an entry, typical practice in Europe or North America, is not a possibility in Japan; this is a general comment concerning the Japanese car industry. Let us note that each car manufacturer has built its own network that should be examined specifically (Chapter 2).

These dimensions take on precise forms within a given environment. In their concrete form, they make for a basis for international segmentation.

The Forms of Diversity

The forms of diversity vary according to the industrial sector concerned and the nature of the customers' problems to be solved. An example to illustrate our point concerns the purchasing of office furniture. This decision is linked to several criteria:

- The *size* and *location* of the office: enclosed offices for 1 or 2 staff or open-plan spaces for 3–50 staff
- The size of the *firm*
- The *firm status*: public or private.

Figure 15.2 Example of the office furniture market

(a) Space typologies, by country (per cent)
(b) Market potential breakdown, by company size and public versus private

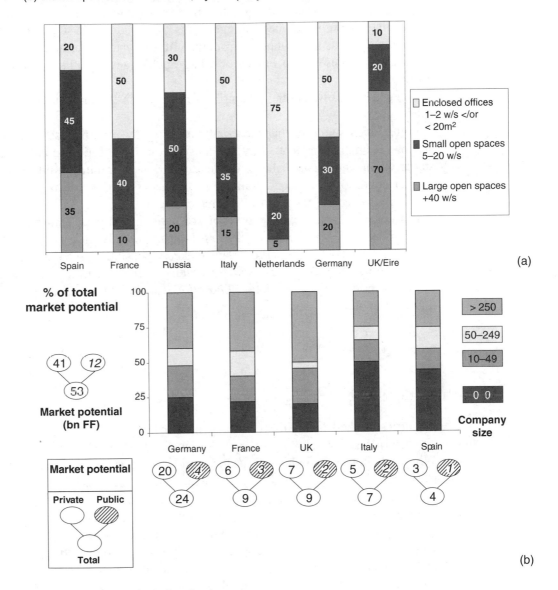

Source: Private survey; w/s:-number of workers per space.

Figure 15.2 reports on the variations of these criteria between some European countries.

In spite of its simplicity, this example does show how compromises have to be made in order to design 'European office furniture'. The same furniture does not fit an enclosed office for one person and an open space for 20. The habit of large open spaces, as in the UK or Spain, creates a demand for furniture adapted to this particular type of environment. A large group requiring refurbishment may present requirements for adaptations that a smaller firm would not. Because of the relatively large number of bigger firms, a pan-European supplier could expect more requirements for adaptation from the UK, Germany or France than from other countries, the presence in France of a large public sector is likely to drive prices down.

Figure 15.3 shows another example of diversity in the market for human vaccination products.

Figure 15.3 suggests that the combination of the willingness of a country to accept vaccination (measured by the consumption per head), the public or private status of the market and the price determination procedure build very different market conditions from one country to another. Is it possible to place the same 'offer' in the face of these 'local' characteristics?

Both examples describe the diversity of national markets. But they also tell us that it is possible *to understand diversity* through applying a systematic analysis to the different countries/markets. This makes it possible to recognise the elements common to several countries as well as their differences. In the case of dispersed customer bases, it is the basis for *international segmentation* (Figures 15.6, p. 419, and 15.7, p. 420).

Competitive Positions

Countries/markets have different competitive positions as well as different market characteristics. The *cluster theory* helps our understanding of these phenomena. When looking at an industrial sector worldwide, one realises that several competitors have arisen from different clusters. All these clusters did not have the same characteristics, and they gave birth to competitors with different strengths and weaknesses. Firms' strategy and the features of the clusters combine to shape different competitors. With the process of globalisation being relatively recent (15 years or so), each competitor typically still holds a relatively strong position ('the historical leader') in its own country (but not necessarily so – look at the very great changes that took place in the global automotive industry in the late 1990s). Each one developed internationally along a process of successive development that resulted in the fact that some competitors were active in some countries or areas before others. In this way, a foreign competitor meets new competition structured differently to that in its own country. And the same competitor does not hold the same positions in different countries: being relatively weak in one, it may be the leader in another. And this should affect the managers' reflection on the ability of their firm to approach new countries and customers.

Figure 15.3 Example of the European market for human vaccination products

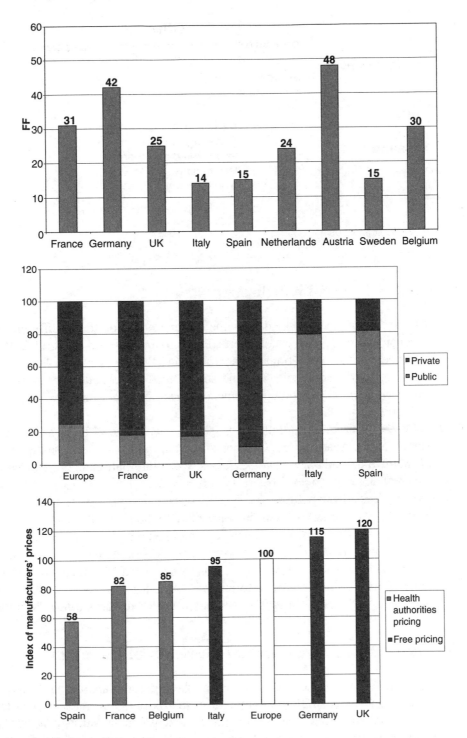

Source: Private survey.

Figure 15.4 Analysis of markets globalisation

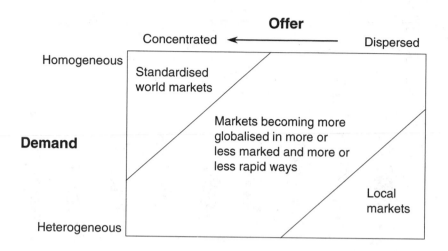

Some Degrees of Market Globalisation

We have attempted above to draw the reader's attention to the differences existing between national markets. Nevertheless, some powerful factors (scale and experience effects, international standardisation of norms, criteria of return on investment, demand homogenisation and so on) lead more and more markets towards *world unification*. But this phenomenon does not affect markets in a similar way, as Figure 15.4 shows.

On the basis of the arguments just used, the debate is open as to the extent of variety and standardisation. One has to be cautious not to confuse the *globalisation of competition* and *offer standardisation*. Truly international competitors may bring different answers to the necessary compromises between forces to standardise, and degrees of adaptation to different market requirements. If a standard offer causes losses in market share in some markets because of insufficient adaptation, what does the firm win? Our idea here is that demand variety is still the major theme of thought. It is not possible to force standardisation further than customers are willing to accept. But the first step in analysing what this means for a firm's international marketing strategy is to analyse what in many cases hinders the choices open to it, and that is the firm's own initial stance towards *internationalisation*.

On Differences Owing to the Initial Situation of the Firm

It is difficult to argue that international marketing issues are similar for, say, General Electric and for a small, innovative firm that is planning international expansion. We can identify four cases that, with the exception of 'start-up' firms, represent three steps in a kind of historical progression of development of any firm at an international level:

- Going international from a national position
- International marketing for a firm with positions in several countries
- The case of innovative 'start-ups' that must build an international position from scratch
- International marketing of a largely international firm.

Going International

This concerns the type of company located nationally but growing fast. For one of many possible reasons, it decides to embark upon international expansion. The first step is often a simple *export activity*, which typically involves the following tasks:

- *Export diagnosis*: an appreciation of the firm's capacity to approach foreign markets and the ways in which to do it
- The design of an *international offer*
- Development of *establishments abroad* and choice of the corresponding forms (agents? local sales force?)
- Building *confidence* and starting *international negotiations*.

This step very often is an opportunity for any company to discover differences between the conditions that formed the firm's strategy in its own home base and those of foreign countries. The main difference is that of locally required performances, that may well be higher or lower than in the country (or area) of origin, as Example 19 on Imaje shows. Figure 15.5 provides the reader with a simple representation of this decisive phenomenon.

Figure 15.5   Variety of required performances in different countries

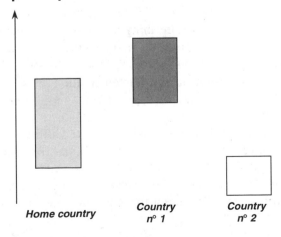

Scale of required performances

The International Development of the Firm

Having successfully completed the first phase, a firm then typically continues exporting to the stage at which it has to *manage establishments in several countries*. It will pursue its development and meet new challenges:

- A closer appreciation of the *markets and segments* on which to be active
- Building *international coverage*
- Design of *international offers*
- First formalised ideas on possible alternatives as to how the firm should be *organised*.

The Case of Immediately International 'Start-Ups'

In this case, the firm will very soon make use of some of the elements presented above. Particularly, it has to design an *offer* that will integrate the particularities of foreign markets.

The Marketing of a Largely International Firm

The core issues here are the design and implementation of an appropriate *international marketing plan* for a firm that is already operating at an international level, covering a large number of major countries or geographical areas. It has to manage a truly international organisation, which requires the allocation of its resources between countries and areas. The rest of this chapter is based on having this framework in mind, whether the firm has a dispersed or a concentrated customer base.

International Market Segmentation

We examined this subject in Chapter 6 and concluded that segmentation, in its strictest sense, was most meaningful when considering a *dispersed customer base*. We then studied principles and methods that are every bit as valid when considering the international scene. What is to be studied here is the impact of the geographical dimension on the implementation of segmentation, since the geographical location can play a major or minor role, depending upon the environments concerned.

It is of major importance when there are differences in *customer behaviour* (mainly the level of technical development), *networks* and *norms* in one area that make the segmentation used in the original country (or area) inapplicable. In such cases it becomes necessary to reconsider the whole basis of the market segmentation. The objective is to search for what, in spite of their differences, constitutes

Figure 15.6   A scheme for international segmentation

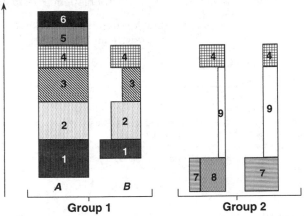

common features shared among the different territories, thereby making it easier to treat the absolute differences.

It is minor if 'another market' is so similar to those already covered that it may fit into an existing group of countries in which a common segmentation exists (Figure 15.6).

In Figure 15.6, each rectangle, marked with hatching and a number, represents a segment. The segmentation produced 9 different possible segments, all present in each country, but with highly variable volumes. Segment 9, for example, is peculiar, being present in two countries only. It corresponds grossly with the same levels of performance as segments 2 and 3, but with such local variation that it has to be considered as a segment by itself. Only segment 4 is present in all countries in sufficient volume to be treated equally throughout. On the basis of this segmentation, countries *A* and *B* show very common features and may be combined into one group (Group 1). This is similar for *C* and *D* (Group 2). Thus, marketing managers can recognise similarities (segment 4, groups 1 and 2) and differences (other segments, each country has an original structure). This view facilitates the dialogue between headquarters and subsidiaries. It avoids the trap of 'my country is different' that may lead to *too many and too diverse local strategies*. It also avoids the other trap of the whole standard that would lead to work only on segment 4, as it is the only really common element. Table 15.1 and Figure 15.7 provides the reader with an example of the results of such an approach.

The results of such a segmentation exercise would give rise to obvious problems. It shows that geographically dispersed countries are in fact similar, requiring similar offers and area management strategies. France and Brazil should receive similar offers, in the same way as the UK and Mexico. The South American and European management units show very weak homogeneity in marketing terms. Thus, several dimensions of the international strategy have to be reconsidered: organisation and

Table 15.1   Segmentation of the international chicken vaccination market

Criteria	Segments			
Nature of breeding	Farming[1]	Standard industrial breeders[2]	Sophisticated industrial breeders	
			Slaughterhouses' ownership (downstream integration)[3]	Rearers' ownership (upstream integration)[4]
Number of segments	1	2	3	4

Notes:
1. Farming does not use vaccines.
2. Standard industrial breeders suffer from few diseases and present a low use of vaccines.
3. Sophisticated industrial breeders, when owned by slaughterhouses, vaccinate a low percentage of the population (<10 per cent).
4. Sophisticated industrial breeders, when owned by rearers, vaccinate a high percentage of the population (>60 per cent).

Figure 15.7   Vaccination intensity

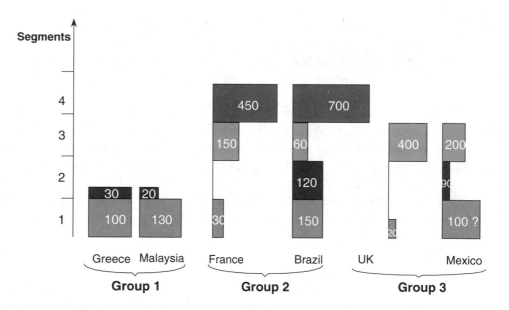

allocation of management responsibilities, offer design, allocation of manufacturing and marketing investments and the localisation of technical support staff or promotional policies. Such a vision of the markets allows management to approach the questions of the international coverage of the markets and the investment priorities in new ways. However, we already mentioned that segmentation, as it is presented here, is valid for the case of dispersed customer bases. As for concentrated customer bases, the importance of the single customer is such that useful methods are to be found in what we call the *international management of customers* and *international customer portfolio management*.

The International Management of Customers

This aspect of the marketing approach can be useful in all marketing environments, but is clearly applicable in the case of concentrated customer bases. There are two different situations. The first one corresponds to the existence of purely national customers. A 'multilocal' management system, a very classical approach, can be applied. However, this system loses its impact when any company focuses on customers with international operations. The issue is then to go from a multilocal perspective over to an integrated international one, which is explained later in this section.

The International Management of National Customers

This situation, often found among firms given levels of globalisation, corresponds to the approach taken in this book. We find two different situations. The first one covers the existence of a customer base whose *decision centre and operational field are essentially national*. Each country gathers customers, sometimes very similar and of limited size, and has real decision autonomy and acts at a national or local level. We previously mentioned the example of garages. A supplier of garage equipment has some 5 million customers worldwide, and national subsidiary deals directly with its customers. At an international level it gives way to a rather simple organisation (Figure 15.8). The international management of the subsidiary is in the hands of headquarters, which is also in charge of international marketing, and hence the offers. This situation is not always easy to manage, as the subsidiaries have the autonomy necessary for customer management. They then tend to exert a centrifugal force on decision making, especially on the offers.

Figure 15.8 Management of a national customers base

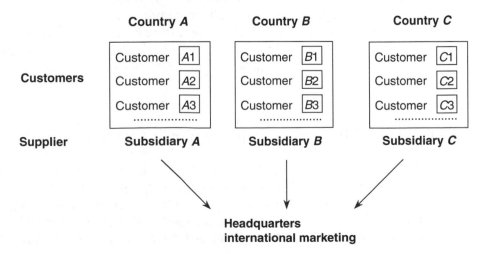

A different case is that of *powerful national customers*. We find that this is often the case in industrial sectors that are monopolies or quasi-monopolies. That was typically the case of the European telecommunications industry prior to deregulation. In a given country, one customer could represent 90 or 95 per cent of the potential national market. These situations have changed with the progressive suppression of monopolies and these customers now represent only 50 or 60 per cent of their national market. However, such a reduction does not really change the issues facing a supplier:

- To ensure a very strong social and *cultural presence* close to the different purchasing centres of the customer, at all levels

- To be able to offer the customer the *exact nature and level of competence* they expect

- To introduce *innovation* as required

- To be organised to offer *information and technical studies* with little delay

- To offer the *required adaptations* while still ensuring appropriate levels of quality, reliability, delay and cost.

This means that the local subsidiary must be granted *sufficient and adequate resources* to meet these issues. It is not possible to tell a Taiwanese customer that competent engineers will come from Frankfurt within 15 days to examine the issue raised. The international organisation of the firm must ensure adequate answers to these questions. It is easy to understand that this type of customer exerts a force much more powerful than in the previous case. The power of these major customers is considerable. If these customers, typically both the originator and user of new ideas, reinforce this power, then any supplier is compelled to strongly reinforce and support its local resources. But the problem is that this can be done only at the prejudice of central resources (research and development, manufacturing, marketing). The consequences are a difficulty in co-ordinating research policies, a proliferation of adaptation work and a resultant increase in costs. This is a case where the debate surrounding the centralisation of adaptation is endless, and we find that many companies continually change between positions of localisation and centralisation.

The International Management of International Customers

Truly international customers are not a novelty for many companies. What is certainly true is the reinforcement of the international characteristics of customers, and furthermore the modifications in their organisation suggested by the current levels of globalisation. The questions that we raised for suppliers evidently affect customers as well, in a similar manner and for the same reasons. Consequently, a

Figure 15.9 An international customers' base

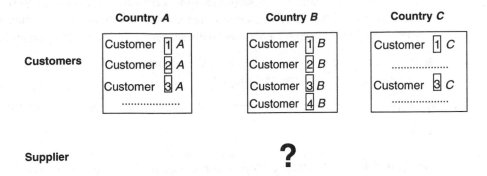

similar perspective has to be taken to analyse international customers. Figure 15.9 provides the reader with a brief account of current issues.

Figure 15.9 can be read as follows. Looking at a set of countries where the supplier is established, one can see that customers are irregularly present throughout them. Each country has a particular customer base. Each customer presents a particular set of establishments. It is easy to see what this means for a supplier in terms of *conflicts of interests and issues*. Should the country or the customer axis be prioritised? Should the investments be made on a country or a customer basis? If we remember that success is partly linked to the proximity and availability of specific resources and expertise, the debate is well balanced. A traditional type of company organisation is on a geographical basis. We find here again the question of *key account management* that we examined Chapter 8. We shall just complement what we said there on two points.

Approach of an International Customer

The point of view to be adopted is the following: to what extent, and on what basis is any customer *international*? To answer these questions a supplier can use a method of analysis derived from the risk approach method. But it has to complement and orientate the analysis towards an understanding of the issues raised above. This corresponds to examining the following topics:

- Is the customer's *general organisation* centralised or decentralised?

- What is the degree of *autonomy* of the subsidiaries?

- For each *key function* (purchasing, research and development, manufacturing, marketing), is the decision making process centralised or decentralised?

- How does the customer *evolve*? Does it modify its organisation towards centralisation or decentralisation? Who are the key persons in the process and what role do they play?

- Are the subsidiaries *specialised* in different ways? Are resources spread evenly among them? If not, is it possible to spot a division of resources that is significant for the customer? For example, are there subsidiaries more innovative than others and consequently endowed with research facilities in a particular field?

- If it exists, what is the make-up and organisation of the *international buying centre*, and who are the key players?

- Is there a major unit that is *directing decisions* in general or on particular points?

- And so on.

One possibility is to draw a *map of the geographical siting of resources*, coupled with an *index of power and competence* for each subsidiary. For a supplier, it is dangerous to overestimate or underestimate the degree of customer centralisation. It is as erroneous to address a decentralised customer with a global proposal as not to design one for a truly centralised customer.

This whole analysis must not forget that customers are also *multisegments* from the supplier point of view. An analysis of a portfolio of customers has consequently to be made at two levels. The first is the global issues linked to a global customer. The second concerns the customers acting in a given segment. That is the point of view we examine in the following section.

Management of a Portfolio of International Customers

The general approach developed in Chapter 8 (Figure 8.2) applies directly here. We want to stress the specificities that an international perspective brings to this topic. The question can be examined at two levels. The first is the management of *global customer accounts*, and there is little to be added to what has been previously said. The second one is the approach of a *particular market segment*. If a global customer represents an issue to be dealt with, its various national subsidiaries are very often heterogeneous when viewed from the angle of a given segment. For historical reasons linked to the building of the company (mergers, acquisitions) or to the development of national subsidiaries (local opportunities in terms of a national cluster, presence of a major and innovative customer, and so on), the whole picture of the company towards a segment may be a very heterogeneous one. Consequently the subsidiaries of a largely international company may present very different issues for a supplier. If it dedicates resources to the subsidiary in country *A*, this might result in a loss of time and money, while dedicating efforts in the direction of the subsidiary in country *B* could prove highly rewarding.

Such an analysis helps in designing an action plan: the commercial approach, a common testing plan, pricing policy, sales and manufacturing forecast, etc. The design of the plan inevitably guides allocation of the necessary resources. Which

Example 20 Paint Additive

An example can make this point dearly. A chemical manufacturer developed a new additive for the manufacturing of powder paints. Its customers are paint producers. The additive has properties that help the hardening of the paint when applied on a surface, and also provides other qualities (a flattening agent). The chosen segment is that of the 'European market of hardeners and flattening agents for the manufacturing of powder paints'. When conducting market surveys to guide technical developments, the supplier noticed the heterogeneous characteristics of the national subsidiaries of the potential customers. It tried to sort out this heterogeneity through the application of an *analytical grid* (Table 15.2).

Two axes define this grid. The horizontal axis typically represents the attractiveness of the customers (here, the various subsidiaries) for the supplier. The vertical axis is an attempt to evaluate the interest and capacity of each subsidiary to utilise the new additive. A broad definition of the different types of subsidiaries is shown in Figure 15.10.

This definition is complemented by the designation in each box of the actual subsidiaries and their location, which indicates the national subsidiary in a company that has to be approached first (upper right-hand box in Figure 15.11).

Table 15.2 Example of a grid for the analysis of international customers

Segmentation criteria

Technical orientation of prospect		Attractiveness for supplier	
– Propensity to innovate		– Level of present technical performances	
■ Low	1	■ Ability to flatten up to 30 per cent	1
■ Medium	2	■ Ability to flatten 30–50 per cent	2
■ High	3	■ Ability to flatten >50 per cent	3
– Interest in undertaking common tests		– Freedom to buy outside parent company	
■ Low	1	■ Low (buy >80 per cent)	1
■ Medium	2	■ Medium (buy 50–80 per cent)	2
■ High	3	■ High (buy <50 per cent)	3
– 'Price oriented' versus 'Solution oriented'		– Manufacturing capacity	
■ Price concerned	1	■ 0–2000 tons	1
■ Halfway	2	■ 2000–7000 tons	2
■ Solution oriented	3	■ >7000 tons	3
		– Image	
		■ Follower	1
		■ European leader	2
		■ World leader	3

resources and how much are necessary to succeed with a given customer? What are the nature and amount of central resources to be mobilised? What are the nature and amount of the required resources in each country? Are the present supplier's subsidiary resources sufficient? If not, do we have to increase some of them temporarily or permanently? How to plan all these allocations within budgetary constraints? Who will be responsible for the operation (the project) at the supplier? Somebody at headquarters? Or somebody within a subsidiary? All these questions

Figure 15.10 Example of a general definition of a portfolio of international customers

Technical orientation

	Weak	Medium	High
High	'Too demanding'	'Demanding'	'Heart of the target'
Medium	'Ignore'	'Medium'	'Followers'
Weak	'Ignore'	'Ignore'	'Guinea-pigs'

Attractiveness for supplier

Figure 15.11 A portfolio of international customers (national subsidiaries)

Technical orientation

	Evode GB	Courtaulds RFA Herberts I Akzo F Ferro S
	Ferro G.B./R.F.A. Herberts S Arson Sisi I CWS RFA	La Celliose F Casco Nobel F Courtaulds F Oxyplast B
Nater E ICI (Ferro) F	Croda GB Vérilux F Blancomme F Carrs GB	Bellaria I Synthésia Sa

Attractiveness for supplier

relate to topics to be examined after one has dealt with the international coverage of national markets.

The International Coverage of National Markets

When a firm has international ambitions, one of the first questions raised is the *nature* and *number of countries* to be covered. For a firm that already has international operations, the question becomes one of how to optimise the international position. These two questions are somewhat different. However, the same approaches may be used. The issue here is to identify investment priorities and resource allocation between geographical areas in order to implement the company's objectives. Several methods are possible. We shall present two classical ones, that of the *portfolio of countries* and that of the *global market share*. We shall moreover define two original methods, the *similarity of countries* approach and the route of *following customers*.

The Method of the Portfolio of Countries

This method follows the McKinsey matrix principles (Figure 5.13). However, in this case, the axes are defined somewhat differently as the attractiveness of the countries involved and the competitive strengths in each country (Harrel and Kieffer, 1963). Here again, the efficacy of the grid relies on the *selection of the criteria used*. Managers' consent on this point is an important step on the way to building a successful global strategy. The criteria have to be precisely selected in each case. The example presented at Figure 15.12 therefore has no universal application, being merely an example.

This method provides interesting results. But there is an important limitation. It assumes that the company would deal with all the countries involved in a similar way. And the international segmentation of markets tells us that national markets present both similarities and differences in structures, at least as far as a market

Figure 15.12 The portfolio of countries method

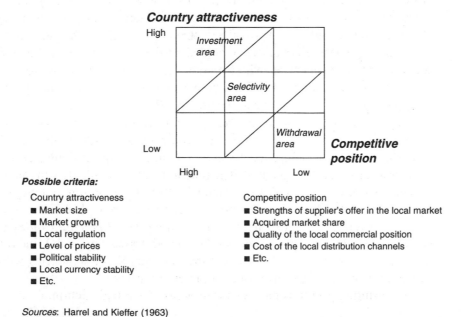

Possible criteria:

Country attractiveness
- Market size
- Market growth
- Local regulation
- Level of prices
- Political stability
- Local currency stability
- Etc.

Competitive position
- Strengths of supplier's offer in the local market
- Acquired market share
- Quality of the local commercial position
- Cost of the local distribution channels
- Etc.

Sources: Harrel and Kieffer (1963)

Figure 15.13 The method of the world market share

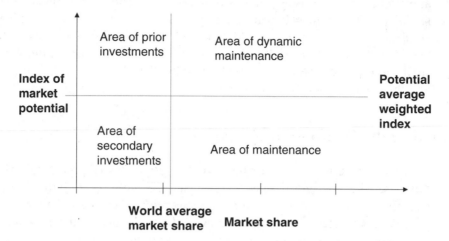

segment is concerned. If this is true for a particular segment, it is not possible to consider these countries–markets as *autonomous and independent units*. Another approach is then necessary.

The Method of the Global Market Share

This method is based on the idea that *global market share* is a major issue for a firm, that gaining or improving share is the major strategic objective, dictating the firm's investments. The method again uses a two axes matrix (Figure 15.13). *The horizontal axis* shows the values of the present market share for each country. It is divided into two parts by a vertical axis that corresponds to the value of the present world market share, all countries included, of the firm. On the left-hand side of this axis we find all the countries with a market share lower than the world market share, on the right-hand side those with a higher one. This provides management with a first clue on where efforts have to be directed. But this is incomplete, since all countries do not present the same *market potential*. It must therefore be complemented with a reference to a classification of the countries according to their market potential. The *vertical axis* consequently shows a hierarchy of the countries according to their respective market potential. The potential can be marked as the present value. It seems wiser to use an index of potential – that is, the present potential multiplied by a growth index. Such an index provides management with a better view of future issues. It even possible to calculate a *weighted world potential index* (the world market divided by the number of countries) and draw a horizontal line dividing the vertical axis into two. The upper part then clusters all the countries with a higher potential index, and the lower one the other countries.

The resulting grid thus proposes four areas of strategic action:

- The *primary investment areas* identify those countries where the firm's market share is inferior to the global one. These are the countries where a gain in market share will have the highest impact on the global market share.

- The *secondary investment areas* group the countries where investments will moderately influence the ratio.

- The *dynamic investment areas* correspond to those countries where the firm's market share is already well established. If this has been achieved in the past, the necessity to sustain customer satisfaction or resist competitive pressure requires constant investment anyway. Overinvesting in these countries might prove less profitable than in the two previous areas, unless some important customer opportunities arise.

- The *maintenance areas* indicate that those countries with a lower potential index should not receive overinvestment.

This method is well adapted to companies for which the objective of *world leadership* is a major one. It is usable if the definition of the market is sufficiently homogeneous. In the case of heterogeneous markets, it can be used for strategic business units (SBUs) (Chapter 5). It can also be used for more restricted areas than the world market, such as Western Europe or South America. It is, in fact, very similar to the BCG method (Chapter 5), and possesses the same quality of simplicity. Its limits are that it does not consider many criteria, such as the *entry barriers* that may be very strong in some countries that are of primary interest. These barriers may represent unreasonable costs for a firm, which would therefore first consider alternative investments in other countries.

The Method of the Similarity of Market Structures

If we think back to Porter's cluster theory (Porter, 1990), we may think that a cluster of countries might grant to a firm that developed in it some form of *competitiveness*. This is based on the argument that it would be organisationally more efficient for a company to expand first into those countries whose structure is similar to that of the original cluster. So, a more efficient path for the international development of a firm or of an offer would be to start with the most similar countries and then expand into countries with similar structures. This path is illustrated in Figure 15.14.

Figure 15.14 shows the development of a firm starting in country *A*. This country is positioned at the mean in terms of market requirements. It is also, by construction, at the origin of the geographical distance axis. A segmentation of the world markets shows groups of countries (group *A* very similar to country *A*, etc.) classified by order of progressive distance on the two axes. Each group presents some degree of internal homogeneity and differences with the other ones, and so

Figure 15.14 A development through progressive distance from the original cluster

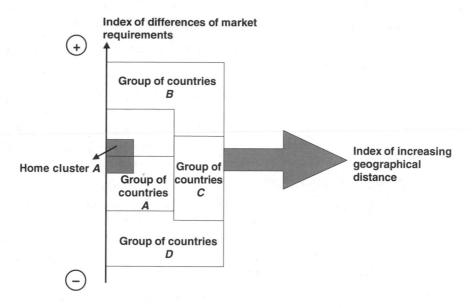

could be thought of as *market segments*. The international development of this firm will start with group *A*, the countries most similar to *A*, then successively to the other groups, *C* (whose distance is mainly geographical), then *B* (with an enriched offer) or *D* (with a downsized offer). This concept of groups of countries, if we come back again to the theory of clusters, makes us think that one country in each cluster is a kind of a *leader*. If this is true, then all the countries in one group do not represent the same issue for the internationalising firm. The method suggested by Harrel and Kieffer (1963) is then adapted to make choices of priority of investment between countries *inside a group*. But we understand now that it is more difficult to use it in an environment where the global market is too heterogeneous. We shall return to this debate when dealing with the role of the subsidiaries in an international company.

We next have to think about defining the best strategy to *enter a group*. We can describe two typical strategies. The first is commonly called a *frontal attack*, for example investing the home country of the world leader (e.g. IBM in the USA), and attacking its main segments. Experience tells us that success is linked to a *power balance* between the leader and its challenger, and the theory suggests that the challenger needs to employ about three times the resources of the defendant. The second strategy is based on gathering experience of the group with *secondary countries and/or segments*, experience that is not too costly and allows the firm to invest later on in major countries with the benefit of better experience. For example, Belgium has very often been the European test market for American or Japanese firms, in the same way as Quebec plays this role for French firms aiming at the North American market. Japanese car manufacturers subsequently learned the ropes of operating in the European market through their footholds in Finland, Norway and Sweden, countries with extreme climatic conditions that tended to be over-looked by the major European manufacturers.

The Method of Following Customers

We said earlier that suppliers may base part of their development on the relation-ships that they have with particular, typically large and/or important customers. When such customers develop their own international operations, they tend to call in their *known and trusted suppliers* to follow them abroad. One could say that they export the *most competitive part* of their cluster. Preparing to follow a customer in its international development is a good way to invest a country and also in other countries of the same group. This movement is particularly clear in the car indus-try. For example, in this way the Volkswagen Group attracted their (predominantly German) suppliers to their establishments in Spain, Brazil and India. We then see that part of the original networks migrates towards other geographical areas, cus-tomers calling in their first-tier suppliers that, in their turn, tend to gather second-tier suppliers. This movement creates *local poles of activity and development* that facilitate the supply chain of a major manufacturer in its new setting, but it also makes it easier to export to other countries of the same group or to other groups.

The International Marketing Organisation

The particular issues linked to an international setting stem, as we said at the begin ning of this chapter, from the increased complexity of the problems to be solved. Management meets questions to which, if they are not careful, they may well give contradictory answers. It is possible to sum up issues as follows.

International marketing manages the firm's *world market share*. It is clearly pos-sible to give a more limited scope to this objective: for example, a more restricted geographical area or a more strictly defined market segment. In this latter case ques-tions, although less complex, remain the same. The level of market share is the result of numerous factors, the technical aspects of which have been examined pre-viously. What is now necessary is the identification of the combinations between factors and their interrelationships. The first is the design and the evolution of the *international offer*, which is closely linked to that of the *geographical coverage*, the number and the nature of the countries covered. Some geographical extensions result in transformations of the offer in an almost quasi-automatic way. This imme-diately raises the question of the *speed of diffusion of the innovative parts* of the offer. This is clearly linked to issues surrounding the management of innovation in the firm, and also the ways in which it is able to simultaneously cope with the requirements of geographically dispersed markets. As we have often said through-out this book, success is linked to the physical proximity to the customer of the supplier's resources. The question then raised is the *organisation and localisation of the firm's resources*. And this question calls for the examination of the decision process in the firm and the respective role of headquarters, still very often located in the original cluster, and also of the subsidiaries.

We can throw some light on this by looking at the issue as being the opposition between the *centripetal market forces* and the *centrifugal economic forces*. Market centripetal forces stem from the intensity of differences between local demands, different from industrial sector to industrial sector. They are well summarised by *adaptation* requirements coming from local settings. Centrifugal economic forces are based on the competitive capacity of the firm to produce offers marketed under the *required conditions of profitability*. The issues here are the capacity of *standardisation* (experience effect, scales economies) and of *sharing operating costs* between countries and market segments.

Market Complexity and Consequences for International Marketing

We have already raised these questions many times, as they are central for management. It seems useful to sum them up in a manner that will place them in an international context. Figure 15.15 illustrates the 'scissors effect' that will threaten a firm not able to sustain its competitiveness while increasing its international settings.

The consequence of this 'scissors effect' is to *increase the firm's break-even point*. The CEO of an international company with an American origin once questioned the reasons why the increased level of their international operations had not brought

Figure 15.15 When complexity affects competitiveness

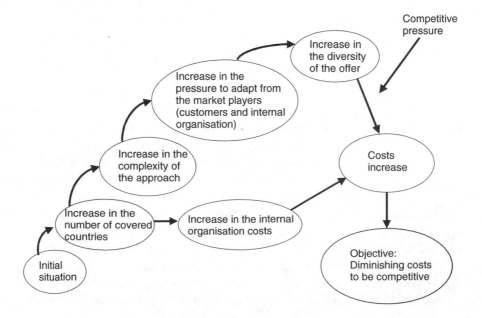

Figure 15.16 Comparison between the operating results of the American and European operations in an international company

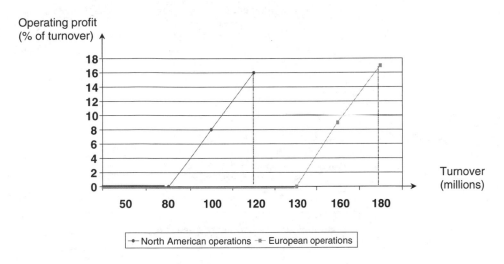

Figure 15.17 Diversity, efficiency and competitiveness of any international company

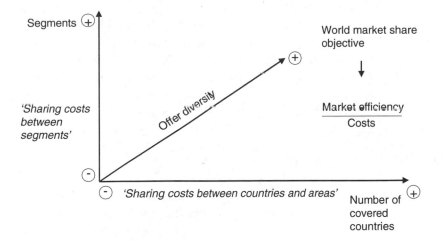

the company the expected increase in profitability. In fact, he noticed a decrease of their return on investment. He requested a comparison between the break-even points of their American and European operations. The result, clear and simple, showed that they needed $50 million turnover more in Europe than in the USA to reach the break-even point. To obtain the same level of profitability in both areas, Europe needed $60 million more (Figure 15.16). The reasons were exactly those we considered: too diversified an offer and a much higher level of European operating costs.

It is possible to draw a simple picture of the operations issues (Figure 15.17). An increase in the number of countries covered allows the firm to reach its *objectives*

Figure 15.18 Different perceptions between 'centrals' and 'locals'

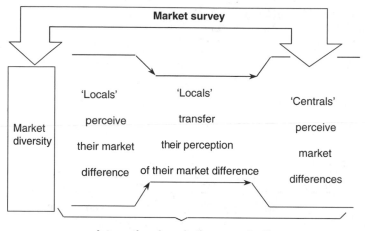

of world market share. This movement 'naturally' involves an increase of the number of market segments, which in its turn leads to a *more diversified offer.* This is considered as compulsory to reach the objectives of market share country by country, thus answering an imperative of *market efficiency.* The increase of diversity-related costs stems from these evolutions. This is represented in Figure 15.17 by the 'market efficiency/costs' ratio. The way to limit costs, *without losing market efficiency*, is that of *sharing costs as much as possible between segments and countries.* The first objective is more linked to offer design and commercial costs, the second to the international organisation of the firm.

The Behavioural Issues of the Organisation

The history of the international development of the firm is studded with ongoing conflicts between headquarters and subsidiaries. These are always disguised as being because of the 'technical' aspects we studied above ('my market is different'). But the true nature of conflicts often comes from other roots (Figure 15.18). These lie in the differences in both the *power* and the *objectives* between headquarters (the 'centrals') and subsidiaries (the 'locals'). Such oppositions can largely be explained by the way in which market reports are used and interpreted.

When headquarters' understanding of the local markets is interpreted incorrectly, this often leads to decisions that penalise local customers and markets. This may be due to two factors. The first one is *too close an assimilation* between international headquarters and the country in which they are located (most often the original cluster). In this way the world is perceived through local glasses only ('what is good for our customers must be all right for yours'). The other is tied to too much attention being paid to *standardisation* ('we have a good offer at a very competitive price; if customers do not buy it, the reason lies in your lack of sales-manship'). Conversely, if market intelligence is left in the hands of the locals only, and if its transfer to headquarters is 'biased', then the centrals have no possibility of being efficient and managing competitiveness. If the centrals make attempts to obtain market intelligence over the heads of the local organisations, sources of conflict multiply, based on the criticism of the 'quality and accuracy of Headquarters' market surveys'. These are sterile and endless debates, all the more of a waste of time when we see the role that marketing tools such as segmentation can play in creating an agreement between the stakeholders.

Any company needs qualified and competent staff both centrally and locally. Any unjustified imbalance between the allocation of tasks and decisions in favour of either pole leads to the impoverishment of the other. How to retain a competent person if he or she finds the tasks he or she has to accomplish are inadequate? The answer clearly lies in careful thinking about this division and the implications for human resources management.

Resource Allocation and the Decision Process

It is obviously difficult to establish principles and rules that can apply uniformly to all these various environments. Firms never face exactly the same decisions during their international expansion, given how markets differ in terms of overall structure. Nevertheless, two things will always preoccupy managerial thinking for the globalising firm: the *allocation of resources* between headquarters and subsidiaries, and *decision responsibility*.

Subsidiaries' Roles and Resources

We have often noted in this book the fact that customers require quick and easy access to a specific supplier's resources. This requirement can range from answering requests for information, wanting a maintenance technician available within 2 hours, or the practicalities of building a new factory near to that of the customer. Answering these requirements is compulsory for a supplier. But as the geographical scope covered increases, so there must be an associated allocation of the supplier's competencies and resources. This is as important as the question we examined under offer diversity above. Companies need to find a balance between overcentralisation and a poorly implemented division of resources. The size and nature of the resources should be determined by the *relative importance* of the various national markets covered by the supplier. Figure 15.19 provides the reader with some ideas on how to approach this.

The objective is to allocate resources to subsidiaries that are important to the firm in achieving its objective of global coverage. It then becomes a process with two aims: choice of the *countries* in which to invest, and the *allocation of resources*.

Figure 15.19 The role of subsidiaries

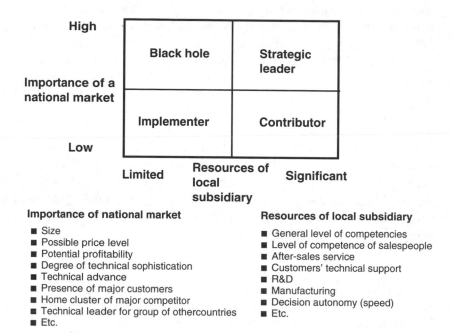

Reprinted by permission of Harvard Business School Press. From Christopher A. Bartlett and Sumantra Ghoshal, *Managing Across Borders: The Transnational Solution*, 1989, p. 106. Copyright © 1989 by the Harvard Business School Publishing Corporation: all rights reserved.

The Question of the Decision Process

One of the criteria stated in the analysis of the subsidiaries' resources (Figure 15.19) is related to the autonomy of the decision-making process. This criterion may have other aims than the satisfaction of a local manager's ego. It is potentially decisive when related to decision speed, and then becomes a major organisational issue. Facing a question, a requirement or a claim from a local customer, any subsidiary must be able to answer, to mobilise resources and to respond quickly. *Speed is a competitive tool* that might be seen by the customer as an expression of competence. Obviously, this raises the question of centralisation versus decentralisation. An inadequate allocation of resources leads to dispersion, confusion and to an increase in costs. Overcentralisation of resources that should rather be close to customers leads to dissatisfaction on the part of customers and, ultimately, to losses. It is worthwhile for managers to pay a lot of attention to the ways in which decisions are informed and made. This is illustrated by Figure 15.20, in which a firm determines its decision-making process subject by subject:

■ Total centralisation means decisions are formulated by headquarters and *imposed* on all subsidiaries; local managers may or may not be formally consulted in order to inform the decision process

Figure 15.20 Decision profile in two international companies

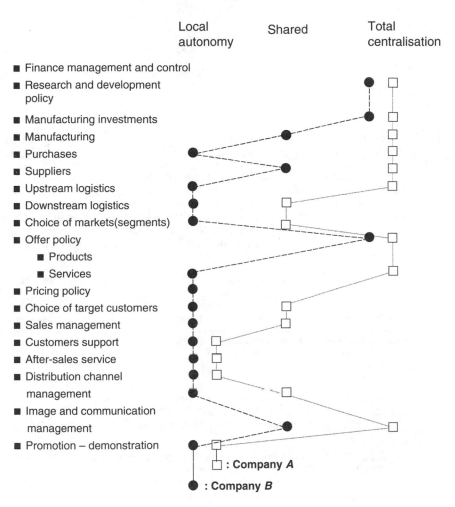

Decision process

Source: Day (1990).

- A *shared decision* is formulated through a formal process that includes local managers in both the decision-making process and its implementation

- *Local autonomy* means local management has great freedom of choice within the company's general objectives.

The example of Figure 15.20 shows two companies, belonging to different industrial sectors, which have different decision-making profiles. Local managers may perceive a centrally made decision as 'a stupid one made by the head-quarters' technocrats' or as 'a good decision that is the best compromise between divergent interests among the players concerned'. Being at either of these poles depends on the *nature of the decision*, as well as on the ways it has been *made* and *implemented*.

Conclusion

We find it appropriate to conclude this chapter and this book with an example that illustrates our objectives.

Example 21 The Japanese Pharmaceutical Industry

In the year 2000 the Japanese pharmaceutical industry was not a major world player. It nevertheless implemented a strategy in the early 1960s (outlined in Table 15.3), aiming to be an important player between 2010 and 2020. A semi-perfect illustration of Porter's (1990) theories, this approach shows that the issues of international competition are made up of challenges on both the understanding of general economic conditions and on the management of the firms. A company can build an international position only if it masters all these dimensions.

Table 15.3   The process of internationalisation of the Japanese pharmaceutical industry

■ **Structure of the world pharmaceutical market in the 1990s:** (%)
   USA + Europe   62
   Japan   22
   Rest of world   16

■ The Japanese **home market** is becoming a major one:
   – Population is ageing and increasing its medicine consumption
   – Per head annual consumption of medicines is one of the highest in the world: US$385

■ In **1990**
   – Japanese pharmaceutical firms have obtained a 0.5 per cent market share of the combined USA + European market
   – European and American firms have obtained a 24 per cent market share of the Japanese home market

■ In **1960**
   – The market was very small with little pharmaceutical research undertaken in Japan

■ **1960–80**
   – Japanese pharmaceutical firms built research units in Japan and in Asia
   – They established numerous agreements with European and American partners

■ **Since 1980**
   – The Japanese home market has grown quickly
   – Foreign firms have established direct subsidiaries in the Japanese market
   – Japanese firms led their research in new directions, often based on biotechnology
   – Japanese pharmaceutical firms now hold some promising new drugs for the world market, but remain average exporters (10 per cent of their turnover)

Table 15.4   Japanese pharmaceutical firms implement a strategy for internationalisation

Improvement of international managerial ability	Increasing foreign presence
■ All staff are trained in languages	■ Extensive presence in international professional events
■ Young Japanese personnel are sent to the USA for MBA training	■ Opening of offices in major foreign countries
■ Selection of young executives to be assigned to foreign establishments	■ Licence agreements with foreign firms for development of promising new drugs
■ Selection of foreign personnel to be integrated within Japanese units	■ Mergers with foreign firms (or acquisitions)
■ Training of senior managers on the issues of innovation and market globalisation	■ Creation of their own foreign subsidiaries

Source: Kummerle (1992).

References and Further Reading

Bartlett, C. and Ghoshal, S. (1992) *Managing Across Borders: The Transnational Solution*, Boston, Harvard Business School Press.

Das, D. (1993) *International Finance: Contemporary Issues*, London, Routledge & Kegan Paul.

Day, G.S. (1990) *Market Driven Strategy: Processes for Creating Value*, New York, Free Press.

Dunning, J.H. (1993) *Multinational Enterprise and the Global Economy*, Reading, MA, Addison-Wesley.

Harrel, G.D. and Kieffer, R.O. (1963) 'Multinational Market Portfolios in Global Strategy Development', *International Marketing Review*, 10:1, 60–72.

Keegan, W.J. (1989) *Global Marketing Management*, Englewood Cliffs, Prentice-Hall.

Kummerle, W. (1992) 'The Global Strategy of Leading Japanese Pharmaceutical Enterprises', *ZFB-Ergänzungsheft*, 2, 101–17.

Porter, M.E. (1990) *The Competitive Advantage of Nations*, London, Palgrave Macmillan.

Usunier, J.-C. (1999) *Managing Across Cultures*, London, Pearson Education.

Van Zandt, H.R. (1970) 'How to Negotiate With the Japanese', *Harvard Business Review*, November–December, 47–55.

Discussion Questions

1 What marketing tools are important when considering an international development or diversification?

2 What is the meaning of the concept of 'groups of countries'?

3 What are the differences between the management of a 'local' customer and of an 'international' customer'?

4 How is the idea of an international portfolio of customers linked to that of the 'marketing customer'?

Chapter 1
Competitiveness, Marketing and Business-to-Business Marketing
What is marketing all about
Different marketing environments
B2B marketing

Chapter 2
Business-to-Business Customers and Markets

B2B Generic Offers	*Technological Innovation*	*Pure Services*	*Major Projects*

PART I   STRATEGY FOUNDATIONS

Chapter 3	Chapter 4	Chapter 5	Chapter 6
Understanding Business-to-Business Purchasing	Information and Information Systems	Markets and Suppliers' Strategy	Segmentation and Marketing Strategy

PART II   STRATEGY IMPLEMENTATION

Chapter 7			
Generic Business-to-Business Offer Design and Management			

Chapter 8	Chapter 10	Chapter 11	Chapter 12
Market Access and Customer Management	Marketing and Technological Innovation	The Marketing of Services	Major Project Marketing

Chapter 9
Communication and Publicity/ Advertising

PART III   STRATEGY DESIGN

Chapter 13	The Role and Organisation of Marketing
Chapter 14	Customer Position, Market Position, Marketing Strategies and Planning
Chapter 15	Issues and Specificities of International Marketing
Annex	The Internet and Marketing: Some Ideas

Annex: The Internet and Marketing – Some Ideas

In previous chapters we have mentioned the use and the impact of new information technologies whenever it seemed to be interesting and relevant. Let us now ponder upon the impact that one particular technological development – information technology (IT) – will have upon our own task, i.e. marketing management. We see these developments having an impact simultaneously at two different levels:

– On the one hand, they are likely rapidly to influence just how companies *get things done*. For example, electronic mail facilitates exchanges between suppliers and customers. Of course, prior to recent developments such data already flowed between them in other forms, but not at the same speed and not with the same potential cohesiveness.

– On the other hand, we see *new patterns of behaviour* appearing in markets and companies. It is too simplistic to think that these technologies would only reduce problem-solving time, improve synchronisation of procedures and co-ordination of activities between companies, and reduce costs, without also deeply affecting the way in which companies and markets operate. For example, the implementation of *electronic marketplaces* between competitors in the same industrial sector will, in all likelihood, modify the balance of power between players of the sector. It can also prompt suppliers of these companies to create their own *upstream e-marketplaces* to modify this new balance of power. As a consequence, the whole structure and dynamics of the value chain could be modified.

This Appendix tries to take a snapshot of this fast-moving environment, and looks at the impact of information technologies on marketing practices in companies. Given that these technologies are new and fast-developing, it is difficult to predict what their effect will be in few months (recall the dangers of forecasting discussed in Chapter 14. In addition, although we mainly focus on business-to-business exchanges, we will sometimes consider business-to-consumer environments in order to develop ideas on how they might influence the former.

New Information and Communication Systems

The recent enthusiastic adoption of developments in information technology is due to companies' need to *co-ordinate and integrate information* that is flowing between and within them. The whole movement is accelerated by the incredible changes in the telecommunication and computer sectors. Based on recent technological developments, three types of network have emerged, which we can examine according to the information linkages between the company, the network and the whole market. Obviously, these correspond to the use of Intranets, Extranets and the Internet.

Intranet

An *Intranet* is simply an internal electronic communication system of a company. Computers within the company are linked via a network, allowing information to be exchanged between different people and services. Through the Intranet, diffusing data within the company is easier, faster and wider.

As the Intranet increases internal communication, so it fights against the compartmentalisation of services and against the duplication of databases. It facilitates co-ordination and improves value chain efficiency.

When we dealt with information and information systems in Chapter 4, we mentioned how abundant information is, located in different places, sometimes duplicated and redundant, not always well-integrated and available. However, the adoption of ERP (enterprise resources planning) systems and the development of the Intranet do improve information systems in companies even if their implementation is not easy. We are thinking here of companies such as SAP, BAAN, Oracle, J.D. Edwards, People Soft and others who have been at the forefront of developing these ERP systems. Initially based on one functional area – for example, accounting, operations management, human resources management – they have evolved towards *global packages* integrating software able to manage the whole information required for the running of the company.

Extranet

An *Extranet* is a network that integrates a company and its main suppliers or its main customers (the extended network) or other stakeholders. Through the Extranet, exchange of data between companies, suppliers and customers is facilitated. The different players who constitute the whole value chain or network are hence likely to co-operate in order to optimise overall performance. However, there are some limits.

An Extranet allows companies to optimise their operations bilaterally with their customers and/or theirs suppliers, but it does not provide access to other potential customers or suppliers. It does not facilitate companies finding new partners, or comparing them with competing suppliers/buyers. And it does not always permit optimisation of the value chain through selecting the best performing partners (For more ideas on this theme, see Naudé, Holland and Sudbury, 2000.)

Internet

The *Internet* is the public network to which (just about!) every computer can be connected. It provides free access to the network for all suppliers and customers (subject to the telephone costs involved, which vary from country to country). The Internet thus creates a huge potential market where a company can easily and quickly get in contact with partners that are likely to answer their needs.

While the Internet is unquestionably a powerful tool, using it to develop supplier–customer relationship shows some limits such as security and performance guarantee, for example. The IT vendors have developed software packages facilitating the management of relationships between any company and its customers (CRM: customer relationship management) or its suppliers (SCM: supply chain management). Supported by the appropriate communication systems (Intranet, Extranet, Internet) they present an *integrated information chain* that avoids using several different, heterogeneous and sometimes inconsistent databases. Figure A.1 draws up a schema of these various communication systems.

The benefit of these information technologies is ambiguous or questionable. On the one hand there is no doubt of their ability to increase network interdependence, with companies increasingly reliant on their information-linked partners for information. But the systems also facilitate access to information, and thus result in increased autonomy. The models of how markets function that we have presented in this book are still valid in this new system. We have nevertheless chosen to

Figure A.1   The company and its different information and communication networks

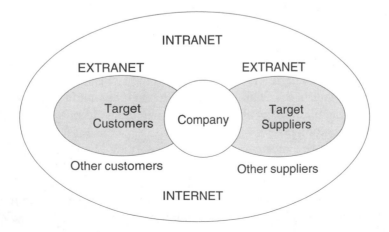

describe some aspects that we feel are likely to consolidate or to change some of what we have said before in the short–medium term future.

The Modifications to Supplier–Customer Relationships

The Factors of Change Coming from the New Communication Tools

Some economists think that the Internet will see the realisation of a *pure and perfectly competitive market*. Companies will easily, quickly and at a low cost gain access to information on the relevant players. Any company then benefits by having a larger choice of suppliers, and has the opportunity to select those that best fit its requirements. And the levels of competition between suppliers will increase in the same way.

The Internet simplifies and quickens communication between customers and suppliers. As a consequence, the *quantity of data* exchanged also increases. This development favours communication between firms. Their management becomes more transparent, and each of the partners has a better view of the others' activities. The value chain can consequently be designed as a whole and no longer as a set of successive 'black boxes'. The activities of firms are better co-ordinated and the value chain is included in a quasi-integrated information system. Consequently, frontiers between firms become less clear. The management of the firm's activities is so much more dependent on the behaviour of others that it is difficult to delineate each partner's outline. This has been called the *extended company*. (For an example in the UK car retail industry, see Naudé and Holland, 1996).

This quasi-integration and the better mastering of the supply chain allows companies to optimise the whole process of value creation, to reduce costs, to improve quality and the design of the offer, to reduce time-to-market and thus to be more competitive.

E-Marketplaces: More Fluidity or More Pressure?

E-marketplaces have emerged from the development of the Internet. They constitute virtual meeting places between customers and suppliers. Potential customers issue their calls for tenders, and suppliers put in their bids, as in a true marketplace. Their advantage lies in their ability to connect efficiently and rapidly with multiple customers and suppliers. This allows all the participants to optimise their purchasing and supplying processes.

E-marketplaces are a recent and constantly evolving phenomenon. They emerge like mushrooms in numerous industrial sectors and stimulate the creation of more complex services, whose mission is to better transaction efficiency and smooth the running of the whole value chain. These services will be used to help transactions, manage catalogues and facilitate the selection of the right partner. *Trade hubs* (an example of double trade) offer dynamic supplier selection services for a buyer or the detection of deal possibilities. For example, a manager with a car rental company reported on the results of a reverse auction: they had wanted to buy just 25 cars (far smaller than their usual purchases), and had involved just three leading car manufacturers in the auction. The end result of this mini-auction was that they saved some 30 per cent off the price that they would normally expect to pay (which in itself is already heavily discounted from the high-street price).

Some e-marketplaces are completely open, they are merely Internet sites where any company can come and call for a tender or make a bid (see <www.MRO.com>, for example). Others present more limited access; companies have to apply for membership before being authorised to enter the site and to execute transactions. E-marketplaces may belong to a group of firms (for example, three or four car manufacturers) or have been created by IT specialists that make use of their expertise to serve as intermediaries in business-to-business trades. These specialists may play several roles on the e-marketplace:

- Sometimes they originate the e-marketplace, design it, and ensure its management
- They may design, host and manage the site and also offer a technical product/service to the owner
- But they may also provide a minimum service such as original design or hosting.

Huge turnovers are at stake with these marketplaces. In the car industry, the world-wide marketplace created by the main car manufacturers handles some $1000 billion. The manager of an e-marketplace dedicated to buying and selling spare parts for the aircraft industry has stated the reasons for its creation at the beginning of the year 2000. The airship industry is a very fragmented one, with 700 companies and 15000 parts manufacturers. Thus, it was very difficult to get data information in time and to ensure rapid delivery to realise maintenance. The site provides the players with significant improvements in all these tasks (See <www.exostar.com> for an example of a site in this industry.)

Modification of the Purchasing Processes

It seems to us that the Internet is bringing important modifications in purchasing. It both facilitates spot transactions and also allows companies to rationalise those purchasing processes that are more mundane and repetitious.

Facilitated Spot Exchanges

The Internet, as we have mentioned, can be seen as a huge world marketplace that facilitates the intersection of offers and demands. It rapidly multiplies dealing opportunities and it makes it easier for companies to find an offer matching their requirements. This access to an enlarged offer eases spot transactions for standard products with no associated servicing. Thus, much of the initial products and services on offer over the Internet concern what are usually known as MRO – maintenance, repair, and overhaul – goods and services. As Renault's purchasing manager said (*Libération*, 17 April 2000) 'Purchases that we buy through the e-marketplace processes concern fountain pens and travelling, which are not part of our core business.'

The Internet also allows companies virtually instantly exchange of large databases. This helps to reduce uncertainty and risk about the exchange product. Any buyer can very quickly obtain all the specifications of the offered product in order to check its conformity to requirements and obtain rapid answers to complementary questions. Risks of misunderstanding are reduced, even with a supplier that the firm has never used before. In this way comparison between different offers become easier, as is the possibility of placing suppliers in a competitive environment that facilitates making the best choice.

But more than just increasing competition between suppliers and accentuating pressure on prices, the *interactive characteristics* of the Internet facilitates the setting up of bidding procedures. Through bidding, customers have the say and the market sets prices. The purchaser is sure to obtain the right price for the real value of the purchased product. This movement will probably lead to a greater effort towards standardisation for non-strategic purchases. Both suppliers and customers will find a common interest in more standard definitions. Suppliers will find more selling possibilities, and customers gain access to a larger range of suppliers.

What About Strategic Purchases?

There is the obvious downside to the Internet as far as sellers are concerned: it encourages comparison and forces down prices, hence decreasing margins. And the more standardised the product, the more margins will be forced down, and relationship become far more transaction-driven. But the case of strategic purchasing is rather different. Buyers would hope that with less time and attention being dedicated to standardised products purchasing, they would have more time to concentrate on strategic issues. Not all purchases will be dealt with transactionally. As Renault's Purchasing Manager argued, 'We will not throw away our partnership policy. First-rank suppliers will not be placed in an increasingly competitive position. The Internet will not replace thousands of hours spent working out problems together.' So, do not throw away this book and what it has to say about interaction and relationships just yet!

Rationalising Supply Procedures

Example 22   Spie Batignolles

> Spie Batignolles, a large multinational French company active in the construction of large civil works and buildings, has presented a 'Cybercatalogue' that is a good illustration of the supplying of standard products (see <www.spie.fr>).
>
> Spie Batignolles' many local sites used to purchase numerous standard products. Each site manager had to find local suppliers, start negotiations and make the final decisions. This process was time-consuming and not very effective (various prices for the same items from one site to another, quality problems and so on). Thus, the question was examined centrally and led to the creation of a catalogue for the traditional site purchases. A central purchasing unit was created to examine the whole process, to select suppliers and to negotiate global contracts on specifications, prices and delivery times. Site managers have access to this 'Cybercatalogue' and may place their orders directly. All sites orders are gathered centrally and transferred to the suppliers that deliver directly to the different sites. The site managers found this process a great improvement on previous ways: less work, less paperwork and better results.
>
> Spie Batignolles estimate that they have gained some 20 per cent reduction on the purchase budget, not counting the large time-saving for all the people involved and a better control on all suppliers. The whole process is not yet optimal, owing to the fact that not all suppliers are yet Internet connected, and this slows down the automatisation process.

A New Design Process

The new information technologies also lead to a wider sharing of data, circulated in real time to a large number of players. We increasingly find that *project information systems* (using e-mail, Intranet, and/or Extranet), and making use of groupware, linked CAD/CAM (computer aided design/manufacture) systems, and electronic document management systems are radically modifying design activities. (See <www.southco.com> for an example of a company offering this kind of services to their customers).

Information technologies are affecting the way we think, behave and work. They increase visibility, at any moment and for all concerned, which leads to the emergence of a will or a necessity to co-operate that induces new practices. For example, in car design we would previously have had different offices working on sub-elements independently. This implied difficult transfers from one office to another that would take time and generate infinite debates from the moment of conception through to the final agreement. Now these offices can work upon the basis of *shared documents* that are *constantly updated* and made available to all concerned. Consequently, decisions are better informed as viewpoints from different players are better co-ordinated and integrated during the design process. A real follow-up of each office is possible in real time.

Such technologies also make it possible to include the *final customer* in the process. The purchaser of a lorry for specific uses may send its requirements via the Internet to a manufacturer that will assemble the necessary elements and make a proposal to its customer. The latter can then give its advice and receive final specifications with a much shorter delay than previously. One may say that these new processes replace former less effective ones. But the alternative view is that they are likely to stimulate partners in a deal to invent completely new, and previously unthinkable, ways of doing things. As an example, Renault and its partner Matra developed an extranet system for their Avantime project. They were aiming at three objectives:

- To improve relationships for both partners through a common tool
- To ensure unique information for both parties
- To ensure data circulation in real time and to all concerned.

The results were a much wider exchange of data, reduction of time-to-market, and better quality standards.

A Strategic Reorganisation of the Firm's Activities

We can here bring in again the *transaction cost theory* (which we first discussed in Chapter 1). Information technologies allow us to organise a more open marketplace, as the liberal economics theory sees it. Customers can address the whole world of suppliers without any restriction, and at a much lower cost. They then may think of sub-contracting activities that they were previously forced to undertake by themselves.

This also implies that new and closer forms of co-operation will emerge between customers and suppliers. A less integrated organisation efficiently replaces more rigid internal systems. We may find that some parts or sub-assemblies are co-developed and manufactured by suppliers within their own premises. So, information technologies accelerate the movement that we described earlier in this book, when stating that a customer may call upon a supplier to run specialised activities within their own premises, activities that do not belong to their definition of their own core business (for example, a paint shop within a car manufacturing plant). Low value activities will lead to spot transactions, as partnerships will compensate for the lack of competencies in other activities. Only the core business activities will remain within the company.

New Means for Market Monitoring

The Internet provides completely new ways of monitoring market information:

- Easy access to competitors' web sites
- Frequently updated information on some competitors' sites

■ Exhaustive information on regulations (e.g. government sites)
■ Numerous useful sites (the press, magazines, public institutions, databases, etc.).

E-Commerce: Access to the Market

The Outburst of Sales Through the Internet

The Internet is a *media revolution*. Lots of talks and tons of ink have already been spent on the theme. The saying that 'everything is going to change' brings in a profusion of statistics and prognostics.

But let's be calm. Present statistics have varying validity. It is difficult to count the actual number of web users or the number of individuals having completed a Net transaction. Forecasting is hazardous, too. As is the case with all real breakthrough technologies (television, computers, video systems, etc.), forecasts have constantly been largely underestimating what ultimately happens in reality.

An estimate from Jeff Bezos, chairman of Amazon.com, concludes that e-commerce will ultimately, when mature, account for about 15 per cent of total distribution output. While this is a lot, it is not that radical a shift away from today's reality.

Some Facts and Figures about E-Commerce

■ Number of web users: 320 million in 2002
■ E-commerce growth: +150/200 per cent per year in the next 5 years
■ World turnover: $400 million in 2002
■ 40 per cent of web users are likely to purchase through the Internet in 2002
■ E-commerce growth in Europe: 40 times the world economy growth (5 per cent per year up to 2010)
■ Share of business-to-business transactions in e-commerce: 80 per cent
■ US online auctions in 2001 (*La Tribune*): $15.5 billion
■ Ibazar: 110 000 calls per day, 5–6000 transactions a day <www.ibabzar.com>
■ Auto-by-tel: 1 million cars sold through this means in the USA within 3 years <www.autobytel.com>
■ Allocine.Fr: 1.5 million calls per month, turnover 1999: $9 million <www.allocine.fr>.

Source: Popular press reports, 2000.

What Slows E-Commerce Down

While the growth has been phenomenal, there certainly are some factors that inhibit the growth or uptake of e-commerce:

- Lack of specialised personnel

- The number of web users is still limited; in France, they represent only 10 per cent of the population

- Technology is complex and becoming more so every day, which puts off the general public

- Necessary computers are still expensive

- In some countries (France) connection costs are high

- In France, the presence of the Minitel system makes the access to the Internet less attractive, as many services already exist on Minitel

- Some national cultures (France, Spain) are less adapted than others to the Internet way (speed, rapid testing, dispersed and flat organisations, etc.)

- Europe has a rigorous legal environment that limits companies from exploiting all the Internet possibilities

- There are still some differences between countries that force companies to adapt to local conditions at some cost

- Telecom infrastructures do not always support the traffic, or else fail (e.g. rupture of the line between Singapore and Australia in November 2000).

Some Factors for E-Commerce Development

If that is the downside, what about the upside? There are definitely many factors combining to ensure that Internet use continues to grow:

- The lowering of connection costs, especially notable in the UK
- The general diffusion of and education about the system
- Newer, easier, more comfortable and cheaper means of access (mobile phones, television sets, etc.)
- Better security for payment (to provide purchasers with a higher level of confidence, electronic signature)
- The building of a more adapted legal background.

Placing the Customer at the Centre of the Firm

The Internet facilitates the interaction between companies and their customers. Any company can more easily communicate with its customers, send them more information and treat them in a more personal way, even on a mass market. But above all the Internet *makes it easier for the customers to speak up*. Consequently, company and management practices have to be modified even more to looking after the customer. A CRM (customer relationship management) tool, for example, allows any company to implement such modifications, particularly for dispersed customer bases.

The Internet helps customers to express their requirements and stimulate suppliers to answer in order to remain competitive. This drives companies from a product to more of service logic. More and more, we see them being forced to propose associated services and to personalise their offer on the ground of what they know about the customer, or else they will be forced to play a lowest-cost strategy. As we argued in Chapter 7, adopting a service-led approach is a very different strategy, and requires the supplier to make important changes in order to adapt their organisation.

Information technologies also facilitate the integration of the customer in the *design* of the offer, as the Dell example at the beginning of Chapter 3 shows. In the near future other firms will follow the same approach. Winners in the game will be those able to sell prior to manufacturing, and it is easy to imagine the consequences of this on manufacturing processes.

Pricing is affected, too. Auction procedures are likely to develop quickly. We have identified some 600 online auction sites worldwide; The US online auction turnover grew from $1.5 billion (1998) to $15.5 billion (2001). A number of companies already auction some of their products (Nouvelles Frontières for travelling, Ibazarpro.com for professional materials). As mentioned above, *reverse auctions* are also possible, whereby customers set the price that they are prepared to pay, and get what they want according to inventories or other offers. Priceline.com uses this way to sell discount flights fares, as does Degriftour in France.

A question that remains is that of interaction. The Internet permits both customer and supplier to interact in some ways, but this interaction remains at a low intensity, far lower than in face-to-face situations. So, there are two aspects of relevance here. Some exchanges that do not require face-to-face interactions are appropriately dealt with through the Internet, and that may prove to be a much better way than the present use of phone, fax, telex, etc. But some major face-to-face meetings and working sessions will remain unchanged and made still more efficient through Internet data exchanges.

E-Commerce Key Success Factors

The use of e-commerce requires new competencies linked to people, and hence to training. But it also carries a burden surrounding the usual management issues. There are some key success factors that need to be recognised, and the question is: What are the firms best disposed to gain from e-commerce?

Mastering a Virtual Environment

The Internet is a new medium with its own characteristics. The first step towards e-commerce is acquiring the appropriate technical skills. The use of new technology always upsets and/or inconveniences many people by radically traditional ways of doing things. Established firms and managers find it difficult to adapt to new ideas and, as we know, there were many people predicting the end of those companies that could not adapt, owing to the benefit that the dot.com companies would bring. The following attitudes are crucial:

- To be *first in the marketplace*. Pioneers have a strong advantage. Established firms have tended to invest in the new medium with their traditional views, taking time to discover new opportunities in their areas, and planning their entry with care. Only then to find that some new kid on the block has got there first and already launched a site doing something similar.

- To be an *enthusiastic early adopter*. One does it before it is formulated. Start-up companies do not waste time planning in advance, they try and implement and modify and start again until they get it right. Waiting is taking the risk that somebody would occupy the spot.

- To be *Internet minded*. The Internet carries a specific culture (Internet values, sense of the community, sharing and facilitating, etc.) that impregnates all the 'technical' solutions. People in the company must be immersed in the Internet culture in order to build up satisfactory solutions. A disappointed web user is a lost one.

- *Mastering of the technology*. So as to not have disappointed users, any company's site must be technically good enough. Web users will not come back to a technically weak site, they are volatile and find their way elsewhere.

Passing from Virtual to Real

Mastering the 'e' is not enough for e-commerce. All of traditional management remains as well. Numerous dot.com companies find difficulties in meeting the challenges of the real world. Technical sufficiency is not enough, as companies like last-minute.com have discovered. They still have to achieve customers' confidence, and have to possess the infrastructures necessary to embody their promises. The strength of brands and logistical efficacy are still necessary parts of the whole process, and there established companies have a decisive advantage.

- *Branding*
  Success in e-commerce comes through being well-known and well-liked. The Internet is a wide universe and any web user can get to a site only if he or she knows that it exists. Therefore dot.com companies spend huge amounts of money in order to build *potential customer awareness*. It is also difficult for the potential buyer to appreciate or to know in advance much about the real service that will be rendered. It is often the brand that is the only guarantee that the customer

will be provided with. As in the traditional world, an established brand and a powerful image constitute major advantages.

■ *Logistics*

The Internet facilitates selling, and eventually huge sales may well materialise. But that is only the tip of the iceberg. Companies must ensure that the back-office jobs, the unglamorous side, gets done. Products have to be designed, manufactured, stored and delivered on time. The rapidity of the information flows makes web users much more demanding in terms of delivery expectations. Working at 'click speed', they expect the whole channel to react at the same speed. Not meeting these requirements can lead to difficulties for suppliers. The main problems are:

- a lack of real-time information between back office and front office
- available inventories to ensure timely delivery for the core of the range of products
- available inventories to ensure timely delivery for the whole range of complementary products
- ability to manage pending orders
- chain reaction to cope with any customer modifications
- management of the final delivery
- design and implementation of a value-added final delivery
- the management of returns.

Here again traditional firms possess distinct advantages owing to their existing infrastructures, and they have to organise their logistics in order to meet the e-commerce demands. Companies starting e commerce activities usually follow a four-step development process (AFUU, 2000):

- *Strategic mimicry*. Companies are aware that the Internet might turn distribution channels upside down and recognise the medium or long-term potential. They then imitate what has already been achieved in other industrial sectors and develop an onsite selling process.

- *Front-office deployment*. Such a company must immediately develop an up and running front office that provides web users with an adequate, satisfying and reliable site where they will find what they expect.

- *Back-office deployment*. Then the company has to set up the organisation to fulfil its promise to the customer. That requires the design and implementation of a back-office support system that executes the online orders.

- *Back-office global design*. Traditional back offices are often outpaced by the activity generated by the front office, and typically have to be rethought and redesigned. This must be done quickly, and the disruption between the new and old modes of operation minimised.

The Ability to Build Alliances

Dot.com companies and more traditional 'bricks and mortar' ones both have their respective advantages and disadvantages. Dot.coms master the technical side, but experience difficulties in ensuring service quality. Inventories are held to an absolute minimum, and the geographic area covered is vast. Early trading results do not always immediately bring in a sufficient turnover to cover the investments of the basic infrastructures or the network. If these investments are not realised, then the company meets difficulties in managing logistics.

As we said before, established companies have an advantage in this respect. They have built a logistical capacity to ensure good service. They have inventories in their warehouses and stores. They have offices up and running in those territories that they cover, which means that they are geographically closer to Internet customers. This enables them to deliver on time and manage any eventual returns. They also benefit from a general brand image, which is a basic reference point for the web users. And they of course have the essential advantage that they develop additional success by developing their own Internet site.

Internet businesses are part of a wider network. We find that media, traditional distribution channels, as well as logistics and delivery companies are all potentially important players in this game, since they can easily develop their own web-based capabilities.

Their great advantage is their ability to generate traffic and to build their customer base. However, they have to develop their ability to design offers compatible with web delivery.

Traditional distribution channels have some power over their suppliers, based on their local presence, being known locally, inventory levels and so on. They have many potential strategic advantages. But they have to add web-based capabilities to their existing structures, which is not always easy to implement. In addition to site design, they may have to cope with home delivery, which has implications for costs and pricing.

Logistics and delivery companies usually have transport and delivery expertise and local know-how. They have to expand their ideas of just what good service really means in order to meet the web users requirements (rushed jobs; night, weekend or exact time delivery; delivery payment; efficient returns management). These players must develop new services or new ways of providing services in order to get into this market. If they do not, some other players may come in, such as specialised mail-order companies.

Given these potential advantages and disadvantages, we see many alliances being developed between Internet start-up companies and more traditional players in many areas.

The Internet Site as the Supplier–Customer Interface

We indicate here some basic ideas on site design and operation.

The Objective: Attracting Customers

A Simple Name

Many web users access web sites by typing the address directly into the navigation bar, with the implication that companies must have a simple address that the web users can find intuitively. For an established company, this means its name (for example, we think that Danone.com, IBM.com, or SouthCo.com are good examples where existing customers will guess correctly. <www.-4ibm.com> is not exactly intuitively obvious!). For a start-up company, the trick is to find and register a simple name that mentally suggests the nature of the offered services and which is easy to memorise (lastminute.com? rugby365.com?).

To be Referenced in Other Sites

Web users surf and visit sites that overlap with their interests. Web users that share the same kind of interests form a new kind of community or network. Target customers may well belong to the same community, as they are interested in the same products or services. A way to address these customers is to be referenced in a site addressing the same community. The company then must determine its target customers precisely, discover the corresponding sites and develop alliances in order to establish *cross-references*. This technique is likely to stimulate efficient traffic, but can be costly – such as the expense occurred in having your banner on Yahoo!'s site.

This situation exists in business-to-business environments as well. Some industrial supplies wholesalers (for example, grainger.com in the USA) offer a large range of components. A manufacturer may find it efficient to create links between its site and those of partner wholesalers.

Banner Ads

Links with other sites can be established with banner ads. The company pays the owner of a particular site to place a banner ad directing traffic back to the company's site. In this case, it is wise to select a heavy-traffic site so that many people may see the banner, as with the example of Yahoo! above.

Again, it is preferable to select a site visited by the same community. The efficiency of advertising panels is still not well understood, but it seems obvious that they are a waste of money if seen by persons not belonging to the company's target customer base. And the banner must be attractive in order to stimulate the potential user's interest (Xe.com usually has some good ones).

Get to be Known: Advertising in Other Media

Many web users go directly to sites by typing the address in the navigation bar rather than via search engines. In such cases the address must obviously be known in advance. Other than the ways listed above, advertising campaigns in traditional media (television, panels, magazines, press) help build awareness and image (see Chapter 9). Start-up companies spend huge amounts of money in doing this.

Retaining Customers

It is not enough to get web users onto your site. They have to be *retained*. It is an important issue as web users are notoriously fickle – if the site does not capture their attention within 7–10 seconds, they click out, whether the page has been downloaded or not. They will not usually come back to a disappointing site: a disappointed web user is a lost one.

Design

Site design is crucial. It must attract potential customers with contrasting colours, animation and original drawings. It must also be clear and readable. Too much data makes reading difficult. A better choice is to select relevant information and present it on a clear screen, with readable signs.

Contents

Site contents are equally important. It must contain the information that the web users would expect to find there, which requires a clear identification of the target population, knowing what data these people want to see and in what order. This requires no more than basic market survey procedures, as discussed in earlier chapters. Moreover, data must be reliable and updated. If data do not present these qualities, the web users will be disappointed and likely not to come back again.

Ease of Navigation

The typical web user is impatient and in a hurry. He or she does not accept having to wait more than a few seconds for your homepage to download. Avoid using large files taking too long to download, and divert attention to quick navigation between pages.

Multiple Links to Other Sites Have to be Avoided

Keeping a web user in one's site means avoiding too many links and banners. If he or she is given too many opportunities to leave the site, chances to see him or her again are low. (Check out NHS.org as a site that we feel has too many links.)

Collecting Data on Customers

To Stimulate Any Web User to Provide Data

An Internet site is an efficient way to gather information on customers. The site design must invite the customer to give his or her address and other data. The web user has to find some interest in doing this, which can be a free service on a theme that is meaningful to him or her. They can be informed on new products or services, be offered a free gift or a privileged access to some data (see Naudé *et al.*, 1998, for an example of how Xenon <xe.com> collected data via the web in order to design their next offer).

Don't Infringe Upon Private Life

Private life is one of the Internet's taboos. Web users are very sensitive and do not appreciate the feeling of being hunted down – the Web equivalent of too much direct mail! Therefore, do not ask for too much personal information unless the user can see that it is core for the future generation of product or service offerings (as at January 2001 we feel that mylife.com is guilty of this).

The Use of 'Cookies'

Cookies are small computer files that track how a user navigates around different sites, and are recorded by many sites. They are very useful as they allow the site engineer to know when any web user is connecting and what are their favourite sites. This allows the site engineer to establish the user's precise profile.

To Personalise the Relationship with Customers

All the collected data can be stored in a database that will be used to personalise the offer and to help future selling. Information coming from cookies can be used to improve site design and use. It may thus be upgraded better to match the web users' interests and to propose new services that they are likely to purchase.

To Transform the Surfer into a Customer

To Comfort Customers

Internet users are still rather cautious about their private life and means of payment. It is therefore difficult to transform a web user into a customer. They have to be *comforted* and *informed*: personal data are not to be passed onto third parties, payment security must be explained, phone assistance must be available in case of difficulty, and so on.

To Facilitate Transacting

Again, any web user is impatient and in a hurry. Most Internet purchasing is spontaneous. Therefore, transaction time must be quick (less than 10 minutes) to avoid stopping the order process. That is not the right time to ask for the filling of forms or other data collection system.

To Personalise the Offer

As we stated before, offer personalisation is facilitated through data collection. Databases are a powerful tool to understand customers better and to act accordingly.

Prospection

Data collected by the site can also be very useful for the sales force. Salespersons can use them to initiate prospects in the real world, constituting an efficient introduction. Similarly CRM software is useful to store market data and to form the basis of segmentation and targeting.

References and Further Reading

AFUU (2000) 'Actes des conférences net 2000', Net 2000 (AFUU, Cité des Sciences et de l'Industrie de Paris, 27–29 March).
Financial Times (2000) 'Understanding CRM, Special Report' (see <www.ft.comm/crm>).
Ford, D., Berthon, P., Brown, S., Gadde, L.-E., Håkansson, H., Naudé, P., Ritter, T. and Snehota, I. (2002) *The Business Marketing Course: Managing in Complex Networks* (see especially Chapter 9), Chichester, John Wiley.

Kaplan, S. and Sawhney, M. (2000) 'E-Hubs: the New B2B Marketplaces', *Harvard Business Review*, May–June, 97–103.

Naudé, P., Blackman, I. and Dengler, S. (1998) 'The Managerial Implications of Real-Time New Product Development in Financial Services', *Creativity and Innovation Management*, 7:2, 54–61.

Naudé, P. and Holland, C.P. (1996) 'Business-to-Business Relationships', in F. Buttle (ed.), *Relationship Marketing*, London, Paul Chapman Publishing.

Naudé, P., Holland, C.P. and Sudbury, M. (2000) 'The Benefits of IT-Based Supply Chains – Strategic or Operational', *Journal of Business-to-Business Marketing*, 7:1, 455–67.

Roberti, M. (2000) 'The Industry Standard, 16 October' (see *www.e-gateway.net/infoarea/news/news.cfm?nid=1092*)'.

Wise, R. and Morrison, D. (2000) 'Beyond the Exchange: The Future of B2B', *Harvard Business Review*, November–December, 86–96.

Index